The Essential
Bible Guide

Bible Background with Maps, Charts, and Lists

MENASHE HAR-EL, PAUL WRIGHT, & BARUCH SAREL

Abingdon Press
Nashville

THE ESSENTIAL BIBLE GUIDE
BIBLE BACKGROUND WITH MAPS, CHARTS, AND LISTS

ISBN 978-1-4267-0757-5

Originally published in separate volumes as:
Understanding the Geography of the Bible: An Introductory Atlas
Menashe Har-El/Paul H Wright © 2005 Carta, Jerusalem

Understanding the Old Testament: An Introductory Atlas to the Hebrew Bible
Baruch Sarel © 1997 Carta, Jerusalem

Understanding the New Testament: An Introductory Atlas
Paul H. Wright © 2004, 2007 Carta, Jerusalem

Scripture quotations in Section I are from *TANAKH: The New JPS Translation According to the Traditional Hebrew Text*. Copyright 1985 by the Jewish Publication Society. Used by permission.

Scripture quotations in Section II are from the King James or Authorized Version of the Bible.

10 11 12 13 14 15 16 17 18 19—10 9 8 7 6 5 4 3 2 1

MANUFACTURED IN MEXICO

Contents

Section I: Understanding the Geography of the Bible

List of Maps in Section I

Section II: Understanding the Old Testament

List of Maps in Section II

Section III: Understanding the New Testament

List of Maps in Section III

Understanding
The Geography of the Bible

Introduction

The marl caves of Qumran where the Dead Sea Scrolls were discovered, near the northwestern shore of the Dead Sea.

The majority of the biblical story took place in a very small yet interesting land nestled along the southeastern shore of the Mediterranean Sea, the land of Israel. To provide the proper geographical context of the biblical story, however, it is necessary to cast a wider net, one that encompasses Israel's neighbors near and far. While at its maximum the world of the Bible stretched from Susa in Persia (Esther 1:2) to possibly Spain (Romans 15:28), for practical purposes our sweep can be limited to two regions that intersect in Israel: to the south and east, the lands surrounding the Fertile Crescent (often called the ancient Near East) and to the north and west,

the Mediterranean Basin as far as southern Italy. In a sense, a line dividing east from west is artificial, and the lands where the two meet (including Anatolia, Egypt's Nile Delta and the entire eastern seaboard of the Mediterranean) properly have characteristics of both. Yet it is sometimes helpful to make certain important generalizations up front, such as that the hill country of Israel tended to be oriented to the east, while the coastal plain more often than not faced the sea. This state of being in between the geographical and cultural forces of the ancient world has given variety, richness and depth to the biblical story.

CLIMATE

Introduction

It is often wondered if the climate of the Middle East today is the same as it was during the biblical period. While local fluctuations in climate—i.e., in temperature and aridity—can be traced over a period of years, decades or even centuries, a fair analysis of the data (including rock weathering, the presence of plant and animal species over time and historic patterns of human settlement) suggests that the overall climate of the Middle East has been essentially stable for at least the last five thousand years. In addition, biblical statements about climate (e.g. Deut 32:2; Job 38:22–30, 34–38; Ps 65:12–13; Prov 25:14; Jer 4:11; Mk 4:37) ring as real today as they did when they were first written. For this reason, it should be assumed that the following look at climate, although based on data of the modern Middle East, is applicable to that of the biblical world as well.

Several elements affect climate in the Middle East. Of these, the most important is *location*. Most of the countries of the Middle East lie between 15° and 40° north latitude, near the Tropic of Cancer (23.5° north of the equator). As a result, the climate throughout the region is largely subtropical. Within this subtropical zone lie some of the warmest and driest regions in the world, where long summers, subject to a sustained high barometric pressure, are characterized by high temperatures and no precipitation. The heat of the summer is intensified by the strong rays of the sun that enter the earth's atmosphere at an angle perpendicular to the Tropic of Cancer.

In winter, the sun moves southward to the Tropic of Capricorn (23.5° S), and westerly winds blow toward the Middle East over the Mediterranean Sea. For most of the winter the northern part of the Mediterranean is subject to a low barometric pressure characterized by high precipitation and cool temperatures. The winter's often heavy rains are born in the buoyant, humid air of the Atlantic Ocean and the Mediterranean Sea, air that rises, cools, condenses, and releases precipitation. The season's cool temperatures are a result of the horizontal angle of the sun's rays in and around the Tropic of Cancer.

Topography is the second element that affects climate. Plains and valleys are generally warmer and dryer in all seasons than are hilly or mountainous regions, which are generally cooler and wetter. For instance, the amount of precipitation that falls in coastal regions, in interior cold mountain recesses or in the warm heartlands will vary greatly. As a specific example, extreme temperature differences exist between the valleys and basins of the central Persian Plateau, which suffer from unbearable heat reaching 130° F (54° C) in the summer, and the peaks of the snow-covered mountains on its perimeter.

The third factor that affects climate is *proximity to large bodies of water*. Regions situated near oceans or seas will

The high, sandy desert of the central Sinai Peninsula offers harsh living conditions dictating the lifestyle of the Bedouin.

MEAN ANNUAL PRECIPITATION OF THE MIDDLE EAST

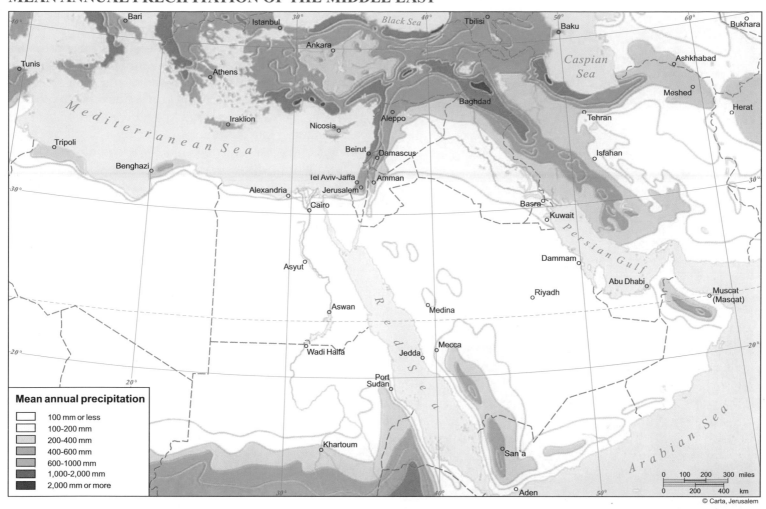

Mean annual precipitation

- 100 mm or less
- 100-200 mm
- 200-400 mm
- 400-600 mm
- 600-1000 mm
- 1,000-2,000 mm
- 2,000 mm or more

© Carta, Jerusalem

MEAN TEMPERATURES OF JANUARY

(Degree centigrade)

© Carta, Jerusalem

MEAN TEMPERATURES OF JULY

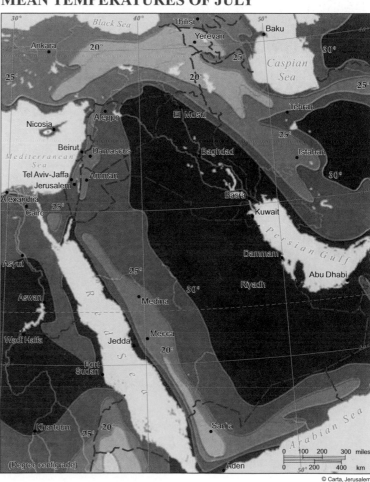

(Degree centigrade)

© Carta, Jerusalem

The interplay of sun and rain in Israel's fertile Huleh Basin forms a fitting backdrop for the remains of an Iron Age storehouse at Hazor.

As for the eastern Mediterranean Basin, the climate is influenced by European rather than Middle Eastern forces, and is moderated by the influence of the sea itself. Throughout the Mediterranean world the sea is the overwhelming natural phenomenon and tends to hold temperatures within each season relatively stable. The differences between the summer and winter, however, can be dramatic. Hot, dry summers are usually offset by wet winter storms that are powered by a combination of hot air from North Africa, moist air from the Atlantic and cold air from the European interior. The eastern seaboard of the Mediterranean, including the land of Israel, is a climatic transitional zone between the wetness of the sea and the dryness of the desert, and where wild fluctuations between "feast and famine" are to be expected.

Because of these climatic extremes, the regions of the biblical world are home to a great variety of flora and fauna, as well as patterns of human settlement. For instance, the foothills and river valleys of northern Persia and Anatolia, covered with primeval forests, have dense human and animal populations, while desert regions such as Rub' al-Khali and Nafud in Arabia are among the most sparsely populated in the world. The region's various climatic boundaries, then, demarcate the parameters of the fertile areas and wasteland regions of the biblical world.

Climatic Regions

The geographic extent of the Middle East, its varied physical structure and the interplay of desert, mountain and sea create six distinct regions of climate, agriculture and possibilities for human settlement:

1. The Pontic climate of Anatolia. The cold and wet Pontus region enjoys more than 40 inches (100 cm) of rain throughout most of the year. This area has the richest forests in the Middle East and supports both irrigated and non-irrigated crops.

2. The interior mountain climate of Armenia. This region, which receives about 20 to 40 inches (50–100 cm) of precipitation annually, is very cold and snowy in the winter and cool in summer. In winter the land completely freezes over, while in summer flocks graze on the mountains and fruit and grain are cultivated in the river valleys.

3. The subtropical climate of the Anatolian and Persian plateaus. This region is very hot and dry in summer and cold and somewhat humid in winter, with 16 inches (40 cm) or less of precipitation annually. Barley and wheat are cultivated and flocks of sheep and goats are raised in the mountains and valleys, while the central salt deserts are completely barren.

4. The Mediterranean climate throughout the eastern Mediterranean Basin. This region has an average of 20 to 40 inches (50–100 cm) of rain in the winter and no rain in the summer. A wide variety of fruit and grain is grown solely on natural rainfall, and cattle, sheep and goats thrive in the valleys and on the hillsides.

5. The desert climate. The deserts of Arabia, Egypt

have a more temperate climate both in the summer and winter, for the sea can absorb the sun's rays to a depth of up to 656 feet (200 m) below sea level, thereby moderating temperatures and retaining warmth the year around. The landmasses that are more distant from the sea have a more extreme climate because the soil retains the warmth of the sun's rays only to a depth of 3 to 6 feet (1–2 m) from the surface.

Overall, the climate of the Middle East is quite varied. The central part—Egypt and Arabia, Israel, Syria, and southern Mesopotamia—has a subtropical climate with dry summers and rainy winters, as described above. The southern extremities, however—Ethiopia, Sudan, and Yemen—are characterized by a monsoon climate in which the seasons are reversed: the summers are rainy and the winters dry. As most of the Middle East is covered by or in close proximity to deserts and surrounded by lofty mountains, climatic variations throughout are extreme. However, areas that touch the sea, in particular the Mediterranean, are temperate, wet and warm, and it is here in particular that

CLIMATIC REGIONS OF THE MIDDLE EAST

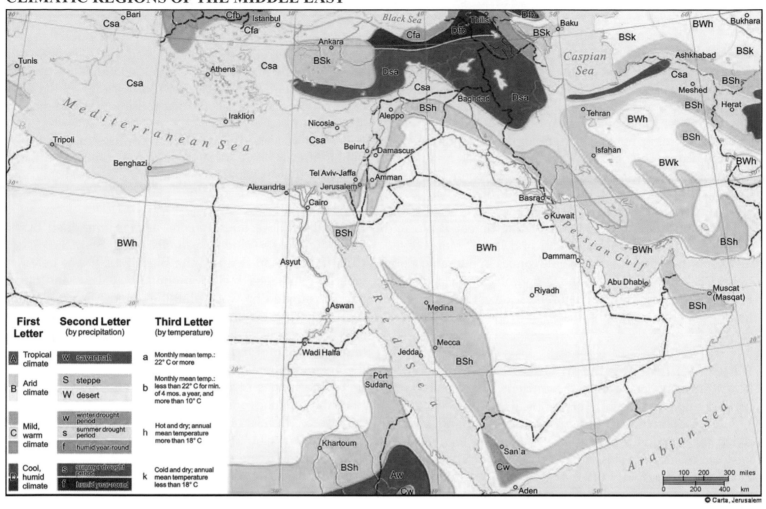

First Letter

A	Tropical climate	
B	Arid climate	
C	Mild, warm climate	
D	Cool, humid climate	

Second Letter (by precipitation)

W savannah
S steppe
W desert
w winter drought period
s summer drought period
f humid year-round
s summer drought period
f humid year-round

Third Letter (by temperature)

a Monthly mean temp.: 22° C or more

b Monthly mean temp.: less than 22° C for min. of 4 mos. a year, and more than 10° C

h Hot and dry; annual mean temperature more than 18° C

k Cold and dry; annual mean temperature less than 18° C

© Carta, Jerusalem

Clouds bearing a hint of winter moisture envelop Jebel Haroun, Petra, one of the most prominent sandstone mountains overlooking the Rift Valley in southern Jordan.

and the southern part of Mesopotamia are dry for most of the year, receiving less than 8 inches (20 cm) of rainfall annually. Crops are irrigated in the river valleys, and desert oases provide homes to sheep, goats and camels.

6. The monsoon climate of Sudan and Yemen. This region receives some 20 to 40 inches (50–100 cm) of rain annually. Here, in antiquity, plants for incense and perfumes were grown under irrigation, and cattle were bred.

PHYSICAL GEOGRAPHY AND HUMAN SETTLEMENT IN THE ANCIENT NEAR EAST

The lands of the ancient Near East included the large river valleys of Egypt and Mesopotamia as well as the rainy hills and valleys of the eastern Mediterranean seaboard. In the history of the ancient world, the countries that filled this Fertile Crescent had outstanding opportunities to establish profitable trading networks, complex social organizations, mature urban centers, sophisticated political institutions, lofty religious ideas, and refined skills in communication, manufacturing and the arts and sciences. Advances in culture spread from the Fertile Crescent to the east by way of Persia (Iran), westward into the Mediterranean Basin, and to the southeast through Canaan and Israel. Many of the factors that spurred these initial advances in human cultural development are rooted in the geographical realities of the ancient Near East: climate, natural resources, routes and the region's overall geographical setting in the known world of the time.

Major Centers of Human Culture

In the most general sense, the ancient Near East can be divided into three distinct geographical regions:

1. A mountainous northern region extending laterally along the boundary of the temperate zone in a generally east-west direction. This fertile region includes the lands of Persia, Anatolia, and, to their south, Mesopotamia.

2. A southern region, located along the boundary of the monsoon zone and extending in a longitudinal north-south direction toward the Red Sea and Nile River. This is a desert region that includes Egypt, Cush (Ethiopia), Arabia, and Yemen.

3. A third, and smaller, zone consists of the lengthy Syrian-African Rift, a long, longitudinal rip in the surface of the earth that in some ways joins the larger northern and southern regions to each other, and in other ways separates them.

Together, these three regions are circumscribed by five seas: the Mediterranean Sea, the Red Sea, the Persian Gulf, the Caspian Sea and the Black Sea. It was here, in a great amphitheater built of mountains, valleys and deserts and surrounded by water, that the world's first civilizations arose. The specific histories of the many peoples who lived in the ancient Near East—the rise and fall of empires, the tenacious cling of individual city-states to their homelands, the migratory patterns of semi-nomadic herders up and down the fringes of the desert—in large measure can be read through the prism of the geographical realities that each faced. Details of climate and fertility may be found in rainfall and available water resources, but these in turn have their roots in larger geological forces that laid the structural foundations of the earth.

PHYSICAL MAP OF THE ANCIENT NEAR EAST

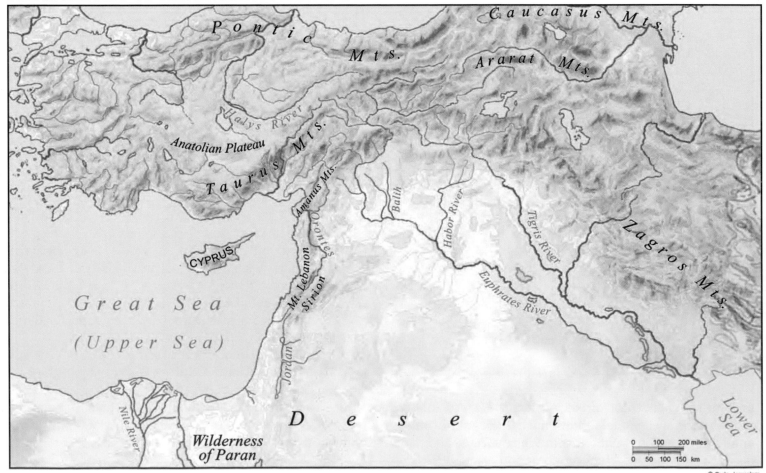

© Carta, Jerusalem

GEOLOGY OF THE MIDDLE EAST

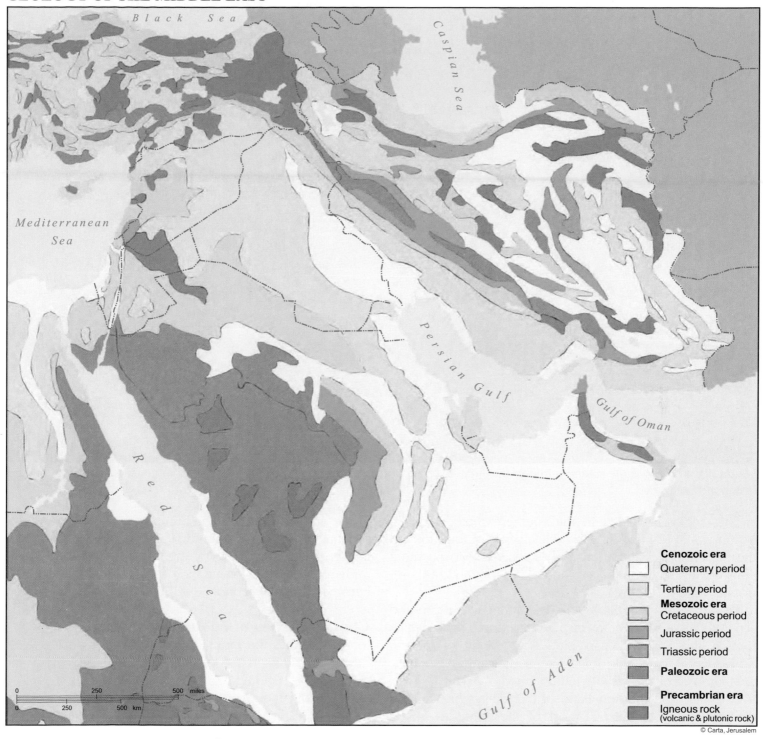

Black Sea

Caspian Sea

Mediterranean Sea

Persian Gulf

Gulf of Oman

R e d   S e a

Gulf of Aden

Cenozoic era	
☐	Quaternary period
☐	Tertiary period
Mesozoic era	
☐	Cretaceous period
☐	Jurassic period
☐	Triassic period
Paleozoic era	
☐	Precambrian era
☐	Igneous rock (volcanic & plutonic rock)

© Carta, Jerusalem

Geological and Tectonic Structure

The Near East can also be divided into three major geological and tectonic structures: (1) ancient massifs (i.e., principal mountain masses); (2) young Alpine folds and faults which were responsible for individual mountains, mountain ranges and valleys; and (3) sandstone and salt plateaus, primarily deserts.

1. Three ancient massifs define the region: the Arabo-Nubian Massif, the Anatolian Massif and the Midian Massif in Persia. Here, in small, protected and well-watered valleys and on rocky yet fertile hillsides, the earliest known villages in the ancient Near East arose. Here, too, ancient man quarried for copper, silver, gold, iron, and semi-precious

stones. These metals and gems provided raw materials to make tools, weapons, implements of agriculture and jewelry. Such raw materials not only provided a stimulus for manufacturing but were a catalyst for competition in trade, and at times led to all-out war among the peoples and great nations who sought control of their access.

2. The young Alpine folds raised mountains to heights of 13,100 to 16,400 feet (4,000–5,000 m) above sea level. These include the Pontic and Taurus mountains in Anatolia together with the basalt "seam" in Armenia to their east, the Elburz and Zagros ranges along the border of Mesopotamia and in Persia, the mountains of Yemen and Ethiopia near the Red Sea, and those of Oman in the Persian Gulf.

Mount Hermon forms the southern end of the Anti-Lebanon mountains, a prominent range of folded mountains separating modern Lebanon from Syria.

This folding subsided in the southern margins of the region where a simple, relatively low series of folds formed the backbones of Lebanon and Israel, rising to no more than 9,900 feet (3,000 m) and 3,300 feet (1,000 m), respectively.

Throughout the entire region, mountains were torn and separated by a series of faults, the most prominent of which formed the Syrian-African Rift. The activity of faulting turned areas of simple folds into complex topographies, with jumbled highlands and hidden interior valleys.

3. Other than the homeland of the Hittites high on the central Anatolian plateau, most of the countries in the ancient Near East were surrounded by desolate deserts of sand, gravel or salt. Typical desert plateaus of sandstone are found in Arabia (Rub' al-Khali and Nafud) and, to a lesser degree, Egypt and Sudan. The basalt and flinty desert plateaus in Syria, Arabia, and northern Sinai provide harsh living conditions that lack adequate water resources for permanent human settlement and generally inhibit plant growth. The principal salt plateaus of the Near East, Dasht-e Kavir and Dasht-e Lut in Persia (Iran), and other, smaller ones in areas near Lake Tuz in Anatolia, served as obstacles to both man and beast and were always the most desolate and infertile lands in the entire region.

It can be argued that the best natural border is a desert, for a desert acts as a frontier or barrier between nations and can prevent or deter wars. At the same time, because the deserts of the ancient Near East held important natural resources such as iron, copper, turquoise and high-quality stone for construction or works of art, once the skills of forging trade routes and traversing the desert were harnessed, they became centers of economic or political development.

Characteristics of Folded Mountains

In several ways the mountain ranges of the ancient Near East contributed to the growth of human settlement and culture in the region:

1. The lofty mountains of the northern region in particular receive and store a great amount of precipitation, including snow-cover, in winter and spring. Here crops are watered by rainfall, while natural thickets of oak, pine, beech, fir, cypress, cedar, and other trees flourish, providing lumber for construction and making implements, tools and weapons of war. Throughout antiquity farmers cultivated the slopes and valleys of both the higher mountains in Anatolia and Persia and the lower ranges adjacent to the Mediterranean Sea.

2. From the heights and slopes of the folded mountains flowed the headwaters of the great rivers of the ancient Near East, the Nile and its sources in Cush (Ethiopia) and East Central Africa, and the Tigris and Euphrates with their sources in eastern Anatolia. To a lesser extent we can add to this list the smaller rivers of the Levant: the Orontes and Litani in Aram-zobah (Aleppo) and in the kingdom of Hamath in the Valley of Lebanon; the Abana and Pharpar in

Aram-damascus; and the River Jordan in Israel. In addition, important oases can be found in the desert regions at the foot of these high mountains. Thus, irrigated agriculture became possible in the flat arid lands below the mountains. Egypt and the Mesopotamian countries developed river transportation in papyrus boats, and the rivers formed the principal artery of communication and life within those lands.

3. The folded mountain ranges served as defensive rings, protecting for instance Persia, Anatolia, and Arabia from enemies beyond their frontiers. The ancient capitals of these lands—Susa, Hattusa, Mecca and Medina—were established in interior regions that were surrounded or bordered by high mountains.

4. In the high mountain meadows, ancient man raised flocks of sheep and goats and cultivated grain, products that provided basic food and clothing.

But these mountains held disadvantages for human settlement as well. Perhaps most importantly, the high mountains constitute a barrier against the rain-bearing winds that blow inland from the seas. As a result, the leeward sides of the mountains were arid and tended to lack fertility. In addition, the rugged mountain slopes led to destructive soil erosion, making cultivation here difficult but depositing heavy alluvial soils in the river valleys below. The great height and ruggedness of these mountains also made it difficult to build and maintain good roads, with the result that the heights of the mountains resisted population growth and commercial development.

In the mountains above Mesopotamia, these geographical conditions were adequate for small village farming and herding, but it was only when people moved down to the open Tigris and Euphrates river valleys below, to areas that received the blessing of run-off water and eroded alluvial soil from the mountains above, that the age of true urbanization and empire-building could begin. At the same time, the geographical divisions within the ancient Near East encouraged the establishment of many small, independent city-states and kingdoms in isolated and remote desert and mountainous areas. These smaller nations grew under the shadow of the cultural and religious influences cast by the mighty nations of the day—Babylonia, Assyria, Persia, Egypt, the Hittites, Greece and Rome—rising in their wake and sinking together with them.

The Fertile Crescent

The most important centers of urbanization and culture in the ancient Near East, then, were located along the great river valleys of Mesopotamia and Egypt, while a region of secondary importance lay between them, adjacent to the eastern seaboard of the Mediterranean Sea. This entire area has been called the Fertile Crescent because of its crescent-like shape and the inherent possibilities of the land to support permanent settlement. The soil lying in the

The towering sandstone mountains of Wadi Rum in southern Jordan are typical of the desert landscape of the northern Arabian Peninsula.

© Carta, Jerusalem

Tigris and Euphrates river valleys in Mesopotamia and the Nile river valley in Egypt was very fertile due to the annual heavy deposit of silt brought down from their mountainous headwaters at flood time (autumn in Egypt; spring in Mesopotamia). As the result of irrigation, these arable flood plains could be quite productive. Conversely, the lands of the eastern seaboard of the Mediterranean, including Syria and Israel, owed their agricultural productivity to the winter rainfall carried by the prevailing Mediterranean winds. Here agriculture was less certain than in Egypt or Mesopotamia, but the variety of crops grown nicely complemented those of the great river valleys. The writer of Deuteronomy accurately described this aspect of the Fertile Crescent:

> For the land that you are about to enter and possess is not like the land of Egypt from which you have come. There the grain you sowed had to be watered by your own labors, like a vegetable garden; but the land you are about to cross into and possess, a land of hills and valleys, soaks up its water from the rains of heaven. (Deut 11:10–11)

What conditions were needed for human settlement to take root and grow in the lands of the Fertile Crescent? Four geographic factors contributed to the rise of settlement and subsequent cultural development there:

1. Fertile alluvial soil, warm sunshine during most of the year and a consistent supply of water were of utmost importance. Such conditions exist in the river lands and in the coastal regions of the eastern Mediterranean Sea, but also in the monsoon regions of the Horn of Africa and south Yemen, both lying outside of the Fertile Crescent.

2. The river valleys were afforded natural protection by deserts and mountain ranges.

3. The Euphrates and Nile rivers, and to a lesser extent the faster-flowing Tigris, served as internal avenues of transport linking together the cities and power centers that sprang up among the fertile fields along their banks. From these, land routes connected Egypt to Mesopotamia through the plains and mountain passes of the eastern Mediterranean Coast.

4. Perhaps most significantly for the long run, the political, economic, and commercial importance of the Fertile Crescent lay in the fact that it served as a land bridge between three continents: Africa, Europe and Asia, including the Arabian Peninsula. From many points along its length, land and sea routes radiated into the world beyond. Although the Fertile Crescent was the birthplace of urbanization and true cultural advance, its position between larger world powers east and west eventually caused it to be overrun and its heritage transported to other lands, where it spurred and enriched further cultural development.

Agriculture

Several factors combined to limit large-scale agriculture in the ancient Near East to the river valleys, coastal plains and adjacent intermountain valleys, the plateaus and hills of the Mediterranean region and the mountainous areas of the monsoon lands. All had to do with the adequate retention of arable soil. First, in the mountainous, steep-sloped regions, heavy rainfall and annual flooding scoured soil from the fertile mountainsides and deposited it in valleys, depressions, lakes and seas. Second, desert regions see an intensive negative movement of soil in which dry winds

The Nile River valley receives virtually no rainfall, so fields in rural Egypt must be irrigated, in this case by a water wheel.

move enormous quantities of sand, constantly threatening to cover oases and water sources. Third, the parching effect of the desert climate itself wreaks havoc on the fertility of the soil. As a result, the cultivated areas in the Near East have always been confined to no more than 15 percent of its total land area.

Due to the large number and variety of productive ecosystems in the ancient Near East, the availability of indigenous products, both plant and animal, was extensive. These offered sufficient food for a varied, healthy diet, and material for both durable and elaborate clothing.

For millennia, people inhabiting the lands of the Near East have engaged in three major types of food production:

GEOBOTANICAL REGIONS

© Carta, Jerusalem

1. *Irrigated agriculture.* The large river valleys (Tigris, Euphrates and Nile) and their deltas were extensively irrigated as early as the third millennium B.C., bringing life-giving water to otherwise unproductive, arid soil. The main crops grown in these areas were grain, legumes, vegetables, dates and flax.

2. *Rainfall agriculture and horticulture.* A variety of crops has always been grown in the hilly and mountainous areas throughout the ancient Near East, areas that cannot be irrigated. The principal rainfall crops are orchard crops: grapes, olives, pomegranates, figs and almonds. Grain is also cultivated on plateaus and in valleys throughout the region; the grain fields of Anatolia, Persia, al-Jazirah in Mesopotamia and the Hauran in the east central Levant are particularly productive.

3. *Livestock.* Goats, sheep and donkeys have always been raised along the edges of the desert and along the border between the cultivated areas and the wastelands, in regions that receive between 4 and 8 inches (10 and 20 cm) of rainfall per year, less than the minimum needed for agriculture. Suitable grazing land for cattle can be found throughout the region, in the river valleys and plains where moisture and fresh grass are found throughout the year. In biblical times horses were bred in the steppe regions with natural pasturage, such as Asia Minor. Domesticated camels habit the edge of deserts, where the annual average rainfall is less than 4 inches (10 cm).

A perennial threat facing these lands, wedged as they are between desert, mountain and sea and always tottering

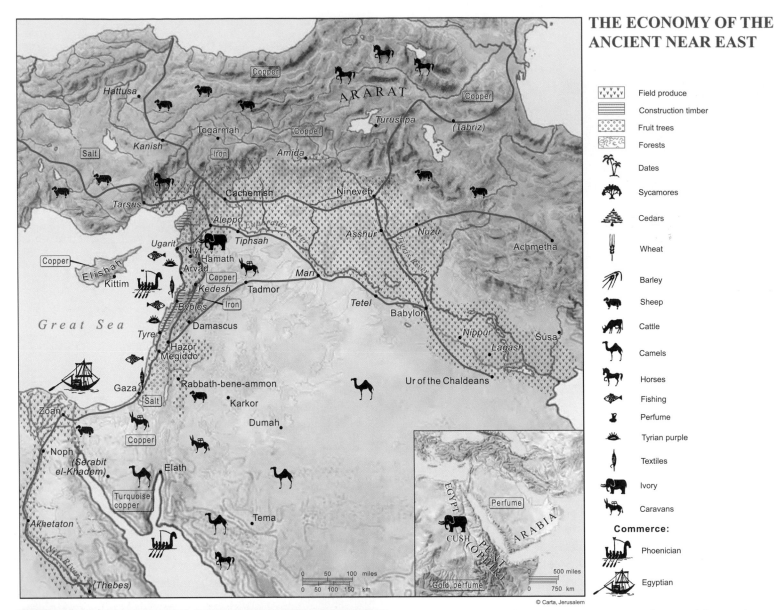

Field produce	
Construction timber	
Fruit trees	
Forests	
Dates	
Sycamores	
Cedars	
Wheat	
Barley	
Sheep	
Cattle	
Camels	
Horses	
Fishing	
Perfume	
Tyrian purple	
Textiles	
Ivory	
Caravans	

Commerce:

Phoenician

Egyptian

© Carta, Jerusalem

(clockwise, top left) Barley, acacia blossoms, olive trees, wheat.

between feast and famine, was invasion by neighbors whose own crops, flocks or herds had failed. From the point of view of farmers who had plenty, such invaders seemed "like locust for number . . . coming into the land to devastate it" (Judg 6:5). For the one who had to flee lands in the grip of famine, however, the intent was just to survive, to "sojourn" somewhere productive like Egypt until conditions back home improved (Gen 12:10). Clearly, the yearly effects of climate and fertility—the base-line of economic independence and success in the ancient Near East—proved to be points of contention for both individual farmers and herders, and for nations.

Transportation

A line of high, rugged mountain ranges running from the western Himalayas through Persia and Anatolia into the Balkans formed a rugged northern "backbone" for the lands of the ancient world. The overwhelming geographical reality of these mountains largely determined the basic pattern and east-west direction of the road system in the ancient Near East.

Other geographic features affecting the location of routes in the ancient Near East are longitudinal in direction. These

14

Rainfall is adequate for agriculture in the region of Iznik (ancient Nicea), in northwestern Anatolia.

mountains; the Cilician Gates through the Bulgar Daglari range in the eastern Taurus Mountains; the Menderes and Gadid passes in western Turkey; the Zonguldak and Trabzon passes on the Black Sea; the Tiflis (Tbilisi) Pass in Armenia between the areas of the Black and Caspian seas; the Rasht and Demavend passes in the Elburz Mountains in Persia; the Zagros Pass between Hamadan in Persia and Baghdad; the Bulan Pass between Persia and Pakistan; the Strait of Hormuz and Büshehr leading from the Persian Gulf to the Makran and eastern Zagros mountains, respectively; the Bir Ali Pass in southern Yemen;

were created by longitudinal folds and the sinking of the Syrian-African Rift. Mountain ranges in the vicinity of the Syrian-African Rift, namely those of Arabia, Midian, Transjordan, Canaan, Cush and Egypt, tend to run in the same north-south direction as the Rift. The main line of east-west routes met the main line of north-south routes in the northern Levant.

Roads in the ancient Near East gradually developed as a result of international trade, wars between nations, the migration of nomads from region to region, and, eventually, the journeys of pilgrimages to holy sites and shrines. The recurrent challenge faced by nations or individuals bent on journeying into the outside world was how to navigate through the mountains and wastelands in a way that most efficiently and effectively connected one point to the next, and allowed the traveler to return home safely. Natural routes, then, connected main population centers by following areas of least resistance, through mountain passes and over river fords, from water source to water source. Springs found in the foothills of the mountains or in the desert wastelands became oases and meeting places for travelers of all sorts, and those who knew the whereabouts of these water sources or determined who might have access to them *de facto* controlled the entire route.

A number of natural passes threaded the ridges and clefts of the lofty and lower mountain ranges. Among them are the following, each indicated by its modern name: the Tripoli Pass between the Lebanon and Ansariyeh mountains; the Syrian Gates between the Ansariyeh and Amanus

and the Jedda Pass on the Red Sea between the Asir and Hejaz provinces in Saudi Arabia. Additional points of access through mountain ranges were natural lowlands or basins that extended inland from the coast, such as the Jezreel Valley and the Beer-sheba Basin of the biblical Negeb. To these we can add four sea passes: the Straits of Bosporus and the Dardanelles connecting the Black Sea with the Mediterranean through the Sea of Marmara; the Strait of Bab el-Mandeb between the Red Sea and the Indian Ocean; and the Strait of Hormuz between the Persian Gulf and the Gulf of Oman.

One of the most significant routes connecting east and central Asia with Mesopotamia and the Mediterranean Sea was the Horse and Silk Road. By the dawn of recorded history in the late fourth millennium B.C., travelers had already discovered metals, primarily tin, along this route, transporting it to Mesopotamia and Egypt. Similarly, the horse was introduced to the West from the steppes of Kirghiz and Turkistan via this route as early as the eighteenth

This Bedouin shepherdess heading home at sundown preserves remnants of an ancient lifestyle that has always been found along the desert fringe of the Fertile Crescent.

Camels have been the preferred mode of long-distance transportation on land routes in the ancient Near East for millennia.

century B.C. The Horse and Silk Route also carried the silk trade from China to the Mediterranean lands from the Roman period onward.

Equally viable to the land routes of the ancient Near East were water routes on its five seas or that followed the course of the Nile or Euphrates rivers. For instance, trade through the Persian Gulf to the fabled lands of Magan and Meluhha, perhaps located somewhere in India or eastern Arabia, brought exotic goods into Mesopotamia, as did Red Sea travelers from Sheba (perhaps Yemen or Ethiopia; 1 Kgs 9: 26–10:13) and other points south.

Five Seas Amid Three Continents

The Near East is unique among regions of the world as a meeting point of continents and seas. Not only does it serve as a hub between Europe, Africa, Asia and the Arabian Peninsula, the region is circled by five great seas, each of which is a doorway to the world beyond. The Near East in fact has been called "the region of the five seas," a reference to the role that the Mediterranean, Black, Caspian and Red seas, together with the Persian Gulf, play on the larger world's geopolitical and economic stage.

Of these five seas, the Caspian Sea is the only one fully enclosed, without a natural outlet to the ocean. In modern times its usefulness has been increased by a series of canals connecting it to the Black Sea by way of the Volga and Don rivers. In the world of the ancient Near East, however, the commercial value of the Caspian Sea as a vehicle of transportation was largely nil, and the east-west configuration of the mountain ranges of Persia directed travel westward, to the Black and Mediterranean seas instead.

While the southern part of the Black Sea has a comfortable climate, its shoreline largely lacks suitable inlets and anchorages, and its storms further hinder shipping. In the past only a few seaports were built along this coast, and even today they are small in number. The Black Sea has a single outlet to the west, through the Sea of Marmara and the Dardanelles; this saltwater passage flows into the Mediterranean Sea and facilitates shipping in that direction.

Ships have plied the Persian Gulf since at least the late fourth millennium B.C. These ships carried trade that originated in India and the southern Arabian Peninsula into Mesopotamia, or, via the Euphrates, to markets in lands bordering the Mediterranean Sea.

On the Red Sea, where the shore is for the most part harsh and desolate, fleets of the kingdoms of Yemen, Cush, and Egypt brought goods destined primarily for the inhabited shores of the Mediterranean. These commercial fleets sailed the Red Sea throughout the biblical period, as evidenced by Egyptian texts from the second millennium B.C., the account of King Solomon and the Queen of Sheba in 1 Kings 10, and the role of Tyre as a trade middleman for the ancient world in the mid-first millennium B.C. (Ezek 27:22–25).

For many reasons the Mediterranean Sea was and remains the heart of the Near Eastern economy, and warrants special consideration below.

THE SYRIAN-AFRICAN RIFT

Introduction

The great similarity between the western coastlines and rock formations of Africa and the eastern coastlines and rock formations of South America led to the discovery of enormous geological rifts parallel to the continents in the bed of the Atlantic Ocean. These coasts and rifts provide evidence that sometime during the geological past, what are now the continents of Africa and South America formed a single landmass. These continents drifted apart when an enormous rift developed in the crust of the earth, creating the Atlantic Ocean. Similarly, within the Syrian-African Rift the continuity in the landscape and ancient rock strata on both sides of the Red Sea and Gulf of Aden suggest that in the early geological eras, Africa and Arabia were one landmass.

It appears that the formation of all of the world's great geological faults and rifts were formed by a combination of various tectonic activities exerted on the surface of the earth. These in turn were a result of vertical pressures emanating from tremendous heat below, which reaches 9,000° F (5,000° C) in the earth's liquid and gaseous core. The main tectonic processes responsible for the shape of the earth's surface are defined below:

1. *Expansion*: a geological process in which, as a result of strain, one landmass drifts away from an adjacent landmass causing it to divide along a lengthwise axis.

2. *Pressure*: a geological process in which one landmass presses upon an adjacent landmass, creating folds in the earth's crust, sinking or elevating portions of it so that it breaks along a lengthwise axis. For instance, the pressure of what is now North Africa upon southern Europe caused a massive fold in the earth's crust, forming the Alps in southern Europe and Atlas Mountains in North Africa, with the enormous depression of the Mediterranean Sea collapsing between the two.

3. *Sinking*: a geological process in which the edges of two landmasses, when drifting from each other, collapse and sink to a great depth. This creates a rift.

Formation and Shifting of the Rift Valley

The Syrian-African Rift is a display case for the many geological activities that occurred along its length. This enormously long and narrow cleft extends, almost continuously but with some breaks, for some 3,730 miles (6,000 km), from southern Turkey to the Zambezi River in Mozambique. The Rift was formed by a series of complex processes over the course of several geological eras. In general terms, opposing pressures from the north-northwest and south-southeast created a series of roughly parallel fault lines, and eventually the surface of the earth lying between them collapsed to great depths. There is evidence from the rock strata that at roughly the same time, parts of the landmass east of the Rift slid north. For instance, in the southern Levant strata of chalky limestone that are found in the area of the Timnah mines in the western Arabah do not

appear in the mountains of Edom opposite, but rather in the mountains of Moab northeast of the Dead Sea. Also in the Levant, four geological depressions were formed at right angles to the Syrian-African Rift; these are the Negev Basin, the region of Lower Galilee and Bashan, the Homs-Palmyra Gap and the Antioch Saddle in the far north.

In the geological present, high mountains or cliffs edge much of the Rift, in places rising to a height of 6,560 feet (2,000 m) or more. Many of these contain remnants of an ancient volcanic landscape of basalt and lava, or igneous rocks such as granite. In the Rift's tropical regions in the south (east central Africa) and in areas of ample rainfall in the northern Levant, the soft lava and hard basalt rocks have dissolved and blended with other materials, including limestone, to create fertile soil. In the arid and semi-arid portions of the subtropical regions (northeast Africa, the Arabian Peninsula and the southern Levant), these rocks have largely resisted disintegration into soil, and the windswept landscape, composed of stony, barren ground, is typically inhabited by semi-nomads. Portions of the Rift

PRINCIPAL GEOLOGICAL FEATURES

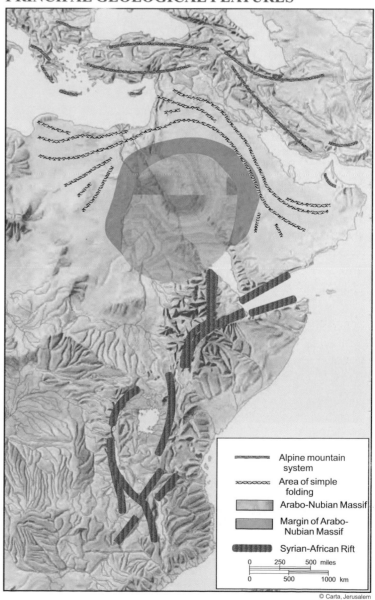

⌒⌒⌒	Alpine mountain system
⤬⤬⤬	Area of simple folding
▓▓	Arabo-Nubian Massif
▓▓	Margin of Arabo-Nubian Massif
▦▦	Syrian-African Rift

0   250   500 miles

0   500   1000 km

The northern, higher portions of the Rift Valley in the Levant, such as this area just north of Metulla, Israel, are quite fertile.

(below) The southern, lower portions of the Rift Valley in the Levant are among the driest and most inhospitable areas on earth, such as the wilderness rising from the southern end of the Dead Sea.

itself form dry valleys, such as the Arabah in the southern Levant, while other places in the Rift have become riverbeds (e.g. the Jordan, Litani and Orontes rivers). The lowest spots of the Rift have filled with runoff rainwater and the output of rivers (the Sea of Galilee, the Dead Sea and the Great Lakes of east central Africa), or, in the case of the Red Sea, by an elongated arm of the Indian Ocean. The Rift remains geologically active, and places along its vast length are still centers of volcanic or earthquake activity.

In terms of human activity, the Syrian-African Rift has served as an important transportation and migratory route between Africa, Asia and Europe. The four geological depressions that cross the Rift at right angles are conveniently spaced at equal distances along the length of the Levant; together, they provide passes through the cleft of the Rift and its high parallel mountain ranges enabling the routes from Mesopotamia to connect with those of the Mediterranean Sea.

THE LEVANT

Introduction

Largely because of its highly dissected topography, the eastern Mediterranean seaboard has always been home to a number of independent-minded people groups who tend to resist politically unification. It is therefore difficult to assign a single name to this entire region; rather, in the historic period each area has typically taken its local name from the people who lived there. For much of its biblical history, the names "Canaan" and then "Israel" were dominant in the southern, drier half of the land, while in the more fertile north the west was called "Lebanon" or "Phoenicia" and the east "Aram" or "Syria." The Roman term "Palestina," in various forms, designated the entire land during the early centuries A.D. For convenience, it is perhaps easiest to call the entire region the Levant, a modern term which solves the problem of ancient nomenclature.

In spite of its many subregional differences, the Levant constitutes a single geographical unit of mountains and local deserts that run parallel to, and are squeezed between, the Mediterranean Sea and the upper reaches of the Arabian Desert. From south to north, the extent of the region is described by the biblical phrase "from the River of Egypt [probably the Wadi el-Arish in the mid-Sinai] to the Euphrates" (2 Kgs 24:7; cf. 1 Kgs 4:21). The northern part of the region is rainy and the soil is fertile, while deserts such as the Negeb (Gen 20:1), Shur (Ex 15:22), Sin (Ex 16:1), Sinai (Ex 19:2), Paran (Num 12:16) and Zin (Num 21:1) predominate in the far south. The width of the land is defined by two natural boundaries: the "Great Sea" (i.e., the Mediterranean; Num 34:6) to the west and the desolate deserts of Transjordan and Arabia to the east; in the Bible these deserts are called "Kedem" or the "land of the Kedemites" (i.e., the Easterners [Gen 25:6, 29:1]). With the effects of Mediterranean rainfall dominating the north and west and arid deserts lining the east and south, landscape and fertility, as well as options for human sustenance, change dramatically as one travels from the fertile agricultural lands of the northwest to the dry shepherd lands of the southeast.

The defining physical feature of the Levant is the Rift Valley and its two parallel mountain ranges, one lying to the west (the "backbone" of Lebanon and Israel) and the other to the east (the highlands of Syria and Transjordan). The western (Lebanon and Cisjordanian) range begins in the high Amanus Mountains in north Syria and gradually diminishes in elevation along the mountains of Lebanon and Israel until it reaches the Red Sea, then rises dramatically again in the southern Sinai. The eastern (Anti-Lebanon and Transjordanian) range is also generally higher in the north and maintains a height significantly above that of the mountains of Israel in the south before joining the soaring range that lines the western shore of the Arabian Peninsula.

The Mediterranean coastal plain near the ancient Philistine city of Ekron remains one of the most fertile regions of the Levant.

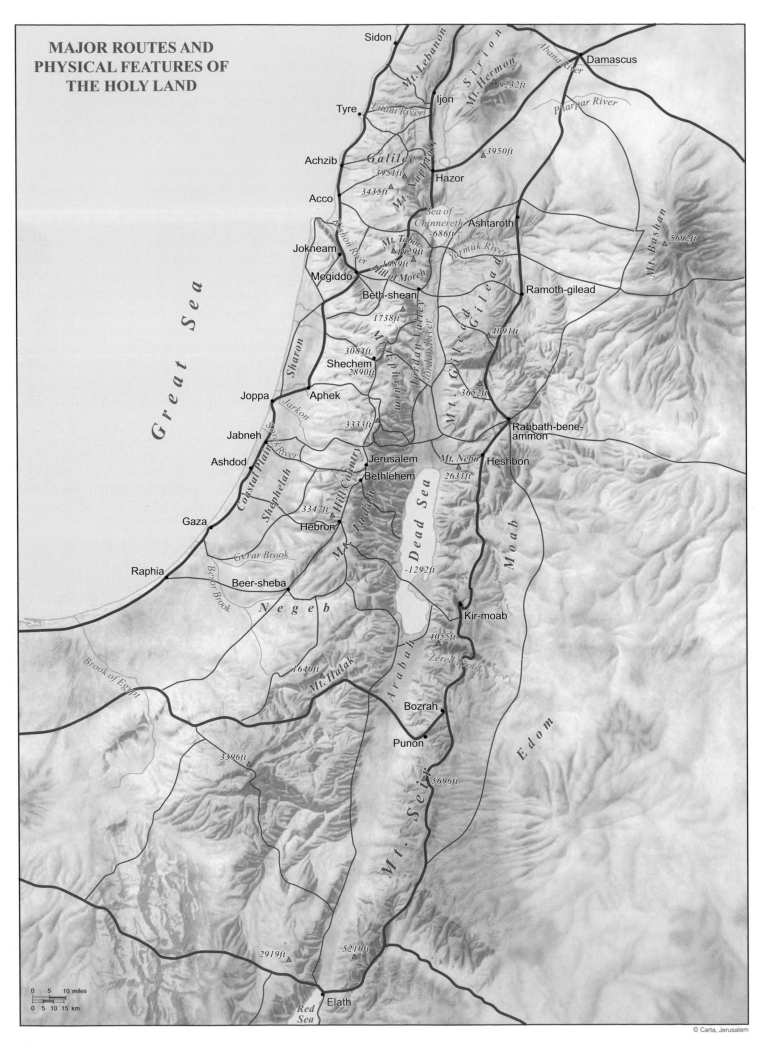

MAJOR ROUTES AND
PHYSICAL FEATURES OF
THE HOLY LAND

Sidon

Damascus

Mt. Lebanon

Sirion

Mt. Hermon
9232ft

Abana River

Tyre

Litani River

Ijon

Pharpar River

Achzib

Galilee

3950ft

Hazor

3951ft

Acco

3435ft

Mt. Naphtali

Sea of
Chinnereth
-686ft

Ashtaroth

Mt. Bashan
5692ft

Jokneam

Kishon River

Mt. Tabor
1929ft

1689ft
Hill of Moreh

Yarmuk River

Megiddo

Beth-shean

1738ft

Ramoth-gilead

Great Sea

Sharon

3084ft

Mt. Ephraim

Shechem
2890ft

Jordan Valley
Jordan River

Mt. Gilead
Gilead

4091ft

3652ft

Joppa

Aphek

Jarkon

3333ft

Jabneh

Sorek River

Rabbath-bene-
ammon

Ashdod

Coastal Plain

Jerusalem

Mt. Nebo
2631ft

Heshbon

Shephelah

Bethlehem

Hill Country

Dead Sea

Gaza

3347ft

Mt. Judah

-1292ft

Moab

Hebron

Gerar Brook

Raphia

Besor Brook

Beer-sheba

Kir-moab

Negeb

4055ft

Zered Brook

Brook of Egypt

1640ft

Mt. Halak

Arabah

Bozrah

Edom

3396ft

Punon

Mt. Seir

5696ft

2919ft

5210ft

0 5 10 miles
0 5 10 15 km

Elath

Red
Sea

© Carta, Jerusalem

20

The low, rolling foothills and broad agricultural valleys of the Shephelah provide ample resources for settled life.

The western slopes of each of these ranges are wet and fertile, while the leeward slopes lie in a dry rain shadow. The international routes that bisect the region and join Mesopotamia and Europe with Egypt parallel these lines of mountains. This route tracks along the eastern base of the Anti-Lebanon range, then splits into two branches south of Mount Hermon: the "Way of the Sea" (Isa 8:23) following the Mediterranean coast and the "King's Highway" (Num 20:17) along the crest of the Transjordanian mountains in the east. For millennia these routes have tied the lands

of the Levant to larger powers in the north and south, carrying opportunities for economic growth but also the threat of invasion. The four east-west geological depressions mentioned above, the Negeb Basin, the lowlands of Galilee, the Homs-Palmyra Gap and the Antioch Saddle, have served as historical corridors binding west to east. Through these passes the peoples of the Levant have benefited from trade flowing between the lands of the Mediterranean and those of Mesopotamia and Arabia, but by them they also faced invasion from the eastern desert (e.g. Judg 6:1–3).

The Natural Division of the Southern Levant

In biblical writings, the southern part of the Levant is divided into two major regions separated by the Syria-African Rift (here called the Jordan Valley and the Arabah): "the west side of the Jordan" (Josh 12:7), and "the east side of the Jordan" (Josh 13:27), or, "beyond the Jordan" (Deut 1:1; Judg 5:17; Mk 3:8). This division can be further subdivided into five secondary regions, each differing in its rock strata, climate, soil, economy and inhabitants. From west to east, these secondary regions are:

1. *The coastal plain.* Known in the Bible as "the coast of the Great Sea" (Josh 9:1), the coastal plain was inhabited in biblical times by Canaanites (Num 13:29) and Philistines, as well as larger powers such as Egypt, Assyria, Babylon, Persia, Greece and Rome, all who sought to control its port cities and the international route that ran its length. Here

The hill country of biblical Judah and Israel supports a village life dependent on agricultural products that are most suited to rocky mountain terraces: grapes, figs, pomegranates, olives, and almonds (see Deuteronomy 8:8).

The rock-cut tombs of Petra in southern Transjordan bear silent witness to the prosperity of the region during the first century A.D., *when the city was an important terminal on the Nabatean Spice Route.*

the coastline is straight and relatively free of inlets that might be suitable for heavy Mediterranean vessels, other than at Dor in the Sharon area and Acco/Ptolemais in Galilee. The coastal plain broadens in the south toward the Negeb and Judah, and narrows as one proceeds northward through Sharon and Galilee. Two or three low ridges of soft sandstone (*kurkar*) rising from 100 to 200 feet (30–60 m) in height run the length of the coastal plain, but are more prominent in the Sharon area than in the south. When cut into blocks, this sandstone is fairly durable as a building material and was used to construct houses and public buildings in cities along the coast such as Dor, Caesarea and Ashkelon. In terms of agriculture, the coastal plain was cultivated for grain and flax in biblical times.

2. *The Shephelah*, or lowland (Josh 11:16). This region of soft limestone and chalky hills rising between 500 and 1,500 feet (150 and 450 m) above sea level is located between the coastal plain and the higher hill country of Judah to the east. The rocky hills of the Shephelah are good for grazing, and the valleys are well suited for grain (Judg 15:5). The limestone of the Shephelah is too soft to be used as durable building material, but the hills are covered by a hard, limey crust of *nari* that was used to build fortified cities such Lachish and Gezer. The Shephelah receives runoff rainwater from the higher Judean hills to the east, and the broad valleys through which this water flows to the coast became the focal point of a rich agricultural village life in the region. These valleys also served as local routes carrying traffic between the Judean hill country and the coast. The Shephelah was coveted by the kings in Jerusalem who needed access to its agricultural land and routes, but also by the inhabitants of the coast as they sought to expand eastward. The Samson narrative (Judg 13–16) and the story of David and Goliath (1 Sam 17) best illustrate this geopolitical dynamic. Small areas of the Shephelah are also found in the Mount Carmel range and the foothills east of the coastal plain in Galilee.

3. *The hill country*, also called "the hill country of Israel" (Josh 11:16, 11:21), and, locally, "the hill country of Ephraim" (Josh 24:33) or "the hill country of Judah" (Josh 11:21). Initially populated by Amorites (Num 13:29), this range of hard limestone hills constitutes the central "backbone" of the land. Its elevation varies: the highest points are 3,963 feet (1,208 m) at Meron in Galilee, 3,333 feet (1,016 m) at Baal-hazor in Samaria, 3,369 feet (1,027 m) at Hebron in Judah and 3,379 feet (1,030 m) at Rosh Ramon in the Negeb. The rainfall at such heights is plentiful, and the water-holding capacity of the hard limestone hills provides many useful springs. The fertile soil of the terraced hillsides in the hill country is excellent for grape vines (Isa 5:1) and orchard crops (olives, figs, pomegranates and almonds). This is also an area that enjoys natural defenses: rugged hills and deep valleys face the west, while the desolate Judean Wilderness, the land of the shepherd, drops off to the east. These defenses protect the best agricultural

land and the major cities of the hill country, all of which are balanced along the top of the watershed ridge (Hebron, Bethlehem, Jerusalem, Gibeon and Bethel) or nestled in valleys protected by the hills (Shechem, Shiloh, Tirzah and Samaria).

The hard limestone and basalt hills of Lower Galilee, the region of Galilee that lies between Acco and the Sea of Galilee (the Kinneret), are relatively low (generally less than 1,700 ft./520 m) and open, with wonderful fertile valleys and easy highway access. To the north, Upper Galilee merges with the high hills of Lebanon, areas that are well-watered but favor small, isolated villages due to the ruggedness of the terrain.

4. *The Jordan Valley*. The section of the Syrian-African Rift through which the Jordan River flows is the lowest surface depression in the Levant, dropping to 1,312 feet (400 m) below sea level at the river's entrance to the Dead Sea. What is called the Jordan Valley today was called the Arabah (lit. "desert plain") in the Bible (Josh 18:18; 2 Kgs 25:4); similarly, the Dead Sea was called the Sea of the Arabah (Deut 3:17; Josh 3:16). The southern extension of the Rift between the Dead Sea and the Red Sea is referred to as the Arava today, and apparently that region also bore the same name during the biblical period (Deut 2:8).

The plains of the Jordan provide areas for crop cultivation (Gen 13:10). Because rainfall throughout the Jordan Valley is sparse, most crops need some form of irrigation and so in biblical times were grown at the outlet of springs (especially around Jericho, the "city of palm trees"; Deut 34:3; Judg 3: 13) or streams that flowed out of the hills on either side of the valley. The most extensively irrigated of the plains were in the northern half of the Jordan Valley: the plain at the southern end of the Sea of Galilee, the plain around Beth-shean west of the river, and that at the mouth of the Yarmuk and Jabbok rivers in the east. During the biblical period, flax, balm and dates were grown successfully in these regions.

5. *The Transjordanian highlands*. The mountains in the southern Levant east of the Syrian-African Rift became home to a number of peoples who established kingdoms at the same time that Israel and Judah formed viable states in the west. These were the kingdoms of Assyria (which encroached into Bashan), Ammon (with eyes toward the rain-rich hills of Gilead), Moab and Edom, people who were as suspicious of those living west of the Jordan as Israel and Judah were of them. All-in-all, the elevations east of the Rift were higher than those to the west: these include Mount Hermon at 9,232 feet (2,814 m), Mount Bashan (of the Druse) at 5,692 feet (1,735 m), Mizpeh of Gilead (Jebel Um ed-Daraj) at 4,091 feet (1,247 m), Jebel Dabab in southern Moab at 4,265 feet (1,300 m), and Jebel Mubarakh in Edom at 5,666 feet (1,727 m). These peaks, even in southern Edom, can be snow-covered in winter. From them four perennial rivers flow into the Rift: the Yarmuk in Bashan, the Jabbok in Gilead, and the Arnon and Zered in Moab.

Variations in climate, soil and landforms throughout Transjordan play a large role in shaping the particular subsistence base of each region. In Bashan in the rainy north, a broad

By the time of the New Testament, Greco-Roman culture had taken deep root in the Levant. Cities such as Pella in Transjordan helped to hold Rome's eastern frontier, both militarily and culturally.

band of arable black basaltic soil provides excellent fields for grain, and during the Roman period much of the grain from this region was shipped to other lands in the Mediterranean. Bashan is also known for its cattle-grazing land (Ps 22: 12; Amos 4:1). The high, hard limestone Dome of Gilead supports vines and fruit trees typical of the hill country of Israel lying immediately across the Jordan to the west. Balm from Gilead was prized for its medicinal properties (Jer 8: 22); its modern identification remains uncertain. The high, flat and chalky plateau of Moab, east of the Dead Sea, was known in biblical times as prime grazing land for sheep and goats (2 Kgs 3:4), and although its climate borders on being arid, this land can produce large crops of grain. Farther south, in Edom, the extent of arable land narrows considerably. Although this region's high altitude (Obad 3) usually attracts enough rain for a minimum grain harvest, its economic base is grounded in shepherding (Isa 34:5–7) and control of the northern end of the Arabian Spice Route.

EGYPT

Introduction

Egypt was the outstanding oasis of the ancient Near East and the natural bridge into Africa from Asia and the lands of the Mediterranean. In addition, Egypt was the only great power of the Fertile Crescent that was almost entirely surrounded by desert. Its entire existence and economy depended solely on the lengthy Nile River; "Egypt is an acquired country, the gift of the Nile," the historian Herodotus would say in the fifth century B.C. Today, Egypt is 95 percent desert land; in ancient times, the remaining 5 percent, the Nile valley and delta, *was* Egypt. The ancient Egyptians called their land Kemet, "the black land," after the rich color of its soil, and the surrounding wasteland Deshret, "the red land."

The Nile River historically has given Egypt two distinct advantages for agriculture: an abundance of water and a ready supply of soil. The Nile discharges on average 21 billion gallons of water per year. This is fed by perennial rain in the equatorial zone, most of which originates in the monsoon rains of Ethiopia and by rainfall formed by evaporation from Sudan's marshes. Before the construction of the Aswan dams in the last century, the Nile would typically flood its banks during the summer months to a height of over 20

Like the Tigris and Euphrates rivers in Mesopotamia, the Nile brings fertility and life to an otherwise arid land.

feet (6 m). Not only would this distribute water throughout the canals and backwashes of the Nile Valley, it would also annually fructify the soil by leaving a fresh deposit of rich organic material and leaching out unwanted salts. Thus, Egypt was the cradle of the ancient Near East for cultivation of grain and flax and, in the modern period, also cotton.

The Nile, which crosses the entire width of the eastern Sahara Desert, flows alternatively through regions of hard limestone, granite and dolomite. In places, these rocks create a series of rapids, or cataracts, that provide a natural defense against attacks by ship from the south. In fact, the Nile's six cataracts tended to separate peoples and lands along the length of the river: in the deep south lay the wet, fertile highlands of Ethiopia, with natural resources of gold, incense and perfume; to the near south was Nubia, fabled in the ancient world for its supplies of gold; and above the first cataract at modern Aswan lay Egypt itself.

Vast stretches of hostile and inhospitable land crowd both sides side of the Nile Valley. In the Western Desert a series of small, scattered oases led to the Libyans, Egypt's ancient enemy to the west. Eastward, a relatively narrow band of rocky desert fronted the high band of mountains bordering the Red Sea, with the Sinai and Arabian deserts beyond. Canaan, across the Sinai to the northeast, offered Egypt the best land and sea link to the world beyond via shipping routes along the Mediterranean coast and land routes running parallel to the shore. In all, access into Egypt was quite difficult from the west, south and east, with the northeastern corridor through Canaan the only viable connection to the greater world. In fact, most invasions into Egypt came from the north, both over land and by sea, and it was through Sinai and Canaan that the New Kingdom pharaohs launched Egyptian imperialism upon the world.

THE NILE DELTA

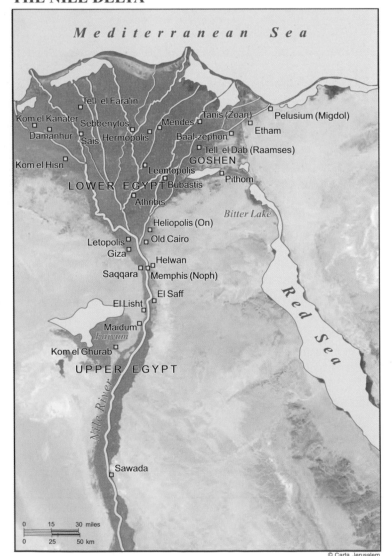

Mediterranean Sea

Tell el Fara'in
Kom el Kanater
Sebbenytos
Damanhur
Sais
Hermopolis
Mendes
Tanis (Zoan)
Pelusium (Migdol)
Baal-zephon
Etham
Tell el Dab (Raamses)
Kom el Hisn
GOSHEN
Leontopolis
Pithom
LOWER EGYPT
Bubastis
Athribis
Bitter Lake
Heliopolis (On)
Letopolis
Old Cairo
Giza
Helwan
Saqqara
Memphis (Noph)
El Saff
El Lisht
Maidum
Fayum
Kom el Ghurab
UPPER EGYPT
Nile River
Sawada
Red Sea

0   15   30 miles
0   25   50 km

© Carta, Jerusalem

Settlement

Internally, Egypt is divided into two natural regions:

1. *Lower Egypt*, from the Mediterranean to the southern tip of the delta. Because of its large, contiguous size, this was the cradle of Egyptian agriculture. In ancient times the

24

Nile split into multiple branches below Memphis (modern Cairo), with numerous canals and lines of communication. Perhaps because all areas of the delta are so self-sufficient, this region has tended to fracture into competing centers of power. Important towns include Memphis (Hos 9:6) and On or Heliopolis (Jer 43:13) in the south; Bubastis (Ezek 30:17), Raamses (Ex 1:11) and Zoan (= Tanis; Num 13:22) in Goshen, the eastern delta; and Sais in the western delta. These population centers were concentrated along the branches of the Nile at some distance from the Mediterranean, partly because of the difficulty of exercising control over the marshes that were fed by the Nile but also out of fear of invasion and piracy from the sea. Indeed, the only important city on the coast until Alexander the Great founded Alexandria was Sin-Pelusium, the "stronghold of Egypt" on the northeastern corner of the delta. During Pharaonic times, Lower Egypt was symbolically identified with the cobra and the papyrus.

2. *Upper Egypt*, the narrow length of the Nile Valley from Memphis to Syene (Ezek 29:10, 30:6; today's Aswan at the first cataract). It was this part of Egypt that was most isolated from the rest of the world. Despite the length of their land, the people of Upper Egypt tended to remain unified. Important towns were No-amon or Thebes (modern Luxor; Jer 46:25; Nah 3:8) and Akhetaten (the site of Tell el-Amarna in the central Nile Valley). Ancient Egyptians symbolically identified Upper Egypt with the vulture and the lotus.

Three times in its long history—during the Old, Middle and New Kingdoms—forces within ancient Egypt forged political unity in the entire land, each time by a pharaoh from Upper Egypt. While the perennial religious capital was at Thebes in Upper Egypt, the political capital tended to

The assured fertility of the Nile River valley provided an economic basis for ancient Egypt that spurred monumental building projects such as the Pyramids, and fueled an army that in the late second millennium B.C. was the most powerful on earth.

move with expediency. Memphis, the first capital of united Egypt, was perhaps the most logical choice for a political capital since it sat at the juncture between north and south. The pharaohs of the New Kingdom built their royal cities in the eastern delta in and around the land of Goshen (Ex 1:11), from which they launched massive campaigns of conquest into Asia. The biblical account of Israel in Egypt finds its setting in this context of Egyptian imperialism.

Economic Conditions

Ancient Egypt was rich in irrigated grain crops such as wheat and rye, from which the two staples of the Egyptian diet, bread and beer, were made. To grain we can add a variety of vegetables, including beans, lentils, onions, leeks,

Natural geographical barriers protected ancient Egypt on all sides: Nile cataracts to the south, the Mediterranean to the north, high mountains and the Red Sea to the east and the sandy Sahara, shown here, to the west.

cucumbers and garlic (Num 11: 5), and fruit such as dates, figs, pomegranates and mandrakes, which were also irrigated. Grapevines were cultivated in the delta, although not extensively, and provided wine only for the rich. The Egyptian diet was protein-rich in fish caught from the Nile, its canals and backwater lakes, from brackish marshes along the seacoast and from the salt waters of the Mediterranean and Red seas. In addition, geese and ducks were raised in the Nile and its canals, while cattle, pigs, sheep and goats grazed on lush Nile grass. Non-consumptive crops included flax for linen, and papyrus. Farmers used oxen for plowing and threshing, and donkeys as beasts of burden. The horse arrived in Egypt only at the beginning of the eighteenth century B.C. with the coming of the Hyksos; within a short time it became an indispensable tool of war. The Bible notes Egypt's role in international horse-trading in the time of King Solomon (1 Kgs 10:28–29).

Alabaster, granite and dolomite were quarried from the Eastern Desert, and some limestone and sandstone were cut from cliffs along the Nile. The harder stones were reserved for statues, artwork and religious objects, while limestone and sandstone were used to construct temples and tombs. For reasons rooted in the Egyptian religious world view, it was important for structures related to eternity to be built to last; by contrast, palaces, governmental administrative buildings, public storehouses and common houses were all made of mudbrick. Lumber for shipbuilding and as construction material for elaborate buildings was imported from the northern Levantine coast. Egyptians tapped mines of copper and turquoise in the Sinai, but had to import gold from Nubia and semi-precious stones such as carnelian and lapis-lazuli from the mountains north of Persia.

By far the easiest means of transport in ancient Egypt was along the Nile and its branches in the delta. Boats moving northward were carried along by the currents; southward travel was aided by the northern winds that blow steadily from the Mediterranean. Skill in river navigation encouraged the use of sailboats on the open sea as well. Egyptian mariners sailed to Phoenicia, Crete and Cyprus to bring back lumber, metals, and agricultural products. They sailed the Red Sea for perfumes, incense, gold, frankincense, and ivory. The prophet Isaiah heard of Egyptian ships "which send envoys by the sea, even in papyrus vessels on the surface of the waters" (Isa 18:2).

From the earliest days of recorded history the farmers of Egypt have been able to grow a surplus of food. This encouraged urbanization, which in turn prompted unification of the country and the development of formal trading networks within Egypt itself, then with neighboring lands in Africa, Asia and the Mediterranean Basin. At the same time, the lack of some basic resources served as both an excuse and an impetus to invade these same neighbors. Throughout its history Egypt looked covetously at its adjacent and more distant neighbors—and they at it—and long periods of peaceful trade were invariably broken by campaigns of conquest.

Egyptian merchant ship from the days of Hatshepsut, c. 1500 B.C.

MESOPOTAMIA

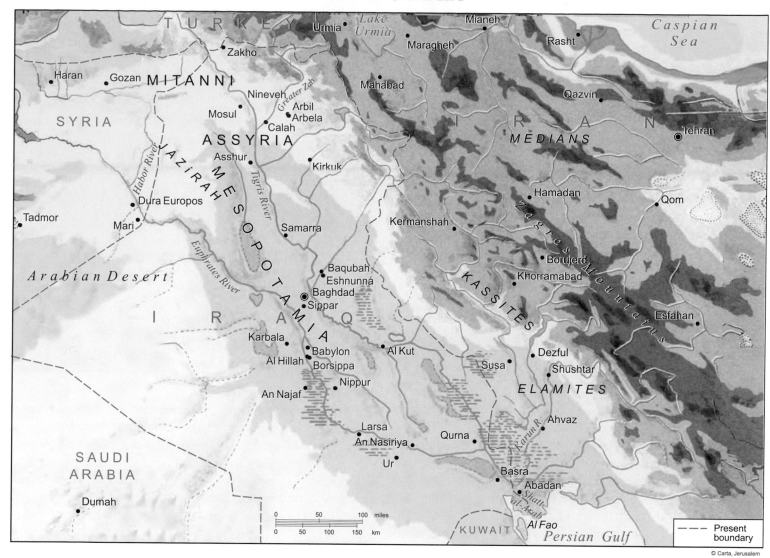

© Carta, Jerusalem

Introduction

The word "Mesopotamia" refers, literally, to land lying "between the rivers." This term was first coined by the Greek writers Polybius (second century B.C.) and Strabo (first century A.D.) to refer to the land lying between the Euphrates and Tigris, in particular where their courses draw together above the Persian Gulf. Some modern historians suggest that perhaps "Mesopotamia" is better understood to reflect the Hebrew term "Aram-Naharaim," the land lying between the upper reaches of the Euphrates and its important northern tributary, the Habor River, which includes the region of Haran and Nahor of the patriarchal narratives (Gen 11:27, 11:31–32, 24:10). Be that as it may, most scholars are comfortable to speak in more general terms and label as Mesopotamia that land which lies between the Mediterranean Sea and the Persian Gulf, and between the rugged Zagros Mountains to the north and northeast and the vast reaches of the Arabian Desert to the south and southwest. In spite of these geographical boundaries, most of which might at first appear to provide natural defenses, the lands of Mesopotamia were invaded and ruled by various ethnic peoples intermittently throughout their long history. In fact, due to its location as a corridor connecting east and west and combined with an intrinsic economic advantage that derives from the water and fertility of the Tigris and Euphrates river systems, Mesopotamia became both the cradle of civilization and a major crossroads of the ancient Near East.

The Tigris and Euphrates rivers, yielding on average 19 billion gallons of water per year, flow through the Mesopotamian plain. Of this the Bible says: "O you who dwell by many waters, rich in treasures..." (Jer 51:13). Thus the lands of Mesopotamia produce a variety of agricultural crops watered both by natural rainfall and irrigation, and support animal husbandry. The area's economic wealth, based on the fertility of its land, led to the development of important cities at the dawn of history.

The landforms of Mesopotamia, much more varied than those of Egypt, can be divided into five natural regions:

1. The delta. This is the lower, southeastern corner of Mesopotamia, just above the Persian Gulf. Here the kingdom of Sumer arose. The delta marshes adjacent to the Gulf appear to have been the ancestral home of the Chaldeans.

2. The plain where the Tigris and Euphrates rivers converge. This was the seat of the kingdoms of Accad (Gen 10:10) and Babylon (Jer 51:13–14), and the region to which the Jews were taken into exile (Ps 137:1).

27

The remains of Nimrud (Calah), lower left, with the Tigris River in the background.

3. The Jazirah. This is the heights above the convergence of the Tigris and Euphrates and the seat of the kingdom of Mitanni.

4. The foothills of the Zagros Mountains. From here streams feed into the Tigris River. The ancient kingdoms of Elam (Gen 14:1, 14:9) and the Kassites were centered on the southern Zagros foothills and the plain below, while Asshur (Gen 10:22), or Assyria, arose in the foothills of the northern Zagros Mountains.

5. The southern Syrian and Arabian deserts, from which various Semitic tribes entered Mesopotamia.

It is important to note that the two best known Mesopotamian kingdoms, Assyria and Babylonia, found their respective homelands at opposite ends of the confluence of the Tigris and the Euphrates rivers. These rivers, which together form the natural transportation artery of Mesopotamia, differ in their characteristics and somewhat in their direction of flow. The Euphrates originates in the mountains of Ararat and Pontus in Anatolia. It flows first in a south-southwesterly direction to a point within 100 miles (160 km) of the Mediterranean where it connects with an important land route through the Antioch Saddle to that sea, then bends southeast for its long, somewhat sluggish run to the Persian Gulf. In this the Euphrates plays a unique role in the ancient Near East, joining the main bodies of water west and east. The Euphrates has two primary tributaries, the Balik River on whose banks sat Haran, from where the Patriarchs set out for the land of promise (Gen 12:5), and the Habor River, to which the king of Assyria exiled the inhabitants of Samaria (2 Kgs 17:6).

The Tigris River (Gen 2:14) descends from the Zagros Mountains near the cities of Nineveh (Gen 10:11), Calah (Gen 10:11) and Asshur in several fast-moving tributaries. It runs roughly parallel to the lower half of the Euphrates before discharging into it just above the Persian Gulf. The Tigris flows faster and more erratically than does the Euphrates, and the lands along its banks have always been more susceptible to flooding. Much of the flat alluvial plain lying between the two rivers, from the point where they first come to within 25 miles (40 km) of each other (modern Baghdad) until the point that they enter the Persian Gulf 250 miles (400 km) downstream, has for millennia been laced with manmade canals (e.g. the Chebar; Ezek 1:3), providing one of the greatest agricultural breadbaskets of the ancient world.

History and Settlement

Ancient agriculture did not originate in the river valleys of Mesopotamia, where superior administrative skills and technological organization was needed in order to control the Tigris and Euphrates so that the plain between them could be irrigated, but in the high Zagros Mountains to the north and east. These mountains rise 2,625 to 5,250 feet (800–1,600 m) above sea level and receive from 10

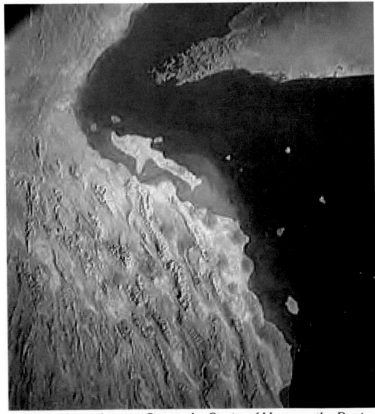

Satellite photo showing Oman, the Straits of Hormuz, the Persian Gulf, and part of the Zagros Mountains of Iran.

to 24 inches (25–60 cm) of rainfall each winter, conditions sufficient for rainfall agriculture. The early inhabitants of these mountains lived a peaceful life and over time learned how to domesticate livestock and cultivate wild grain. The population slowly changed from food-gatherers to food-producers. Farming villages dating from the Neolithic period (the New Stone Age, beginning around 7000 B.C.) have been found at Jarmo, in the Zagros Mountains of Kurdistan. In the fifth millennium B.C., these early farmers descended from the mountains to the valleys of Mesopotamia and began to cultivate irrigated crops. Only in the fourth millennium, during the Chalcolithic period (Copper Age), were cities first built in Mesopotamia and nations and kingdoms first established in the river valleys.

The impetus for urban development in Mesopotamia was the cultivation of crops under irrigation from the waters of the rivers that flowed throughout the year. In the winter the tributaries of the Euphrates and Tigris are fed by rainfall, and by the beginning of the summer the snow on the mountains melts and provides abundant runoff. Once the technology was developed for channeling the water as irrigation water, it became possible to grow surplus crops and support an increasingly large population. Success at farming and animal husbandry, and a ready accessibility to trade routes along the river valleys, provided a source of wealth for the inhabitants of Mesopotamia, spurring the rise of towns, then cities and urban life.

As a result of various social factors, including a division of labor and a re-channeling of human endeavors from basic subsistence activities to other pursuits, these early civilizations witnessed a flowering of creative activities in literature, religion and the arts, as well as rudimentary attempts to understand and control the natural world through technology and what is called today "science." For instance, the farmer's observation of the growth patterns of the flora and fauna planted seeds that would lead to the development of biology. Ease of transportation along the flat river valleys and the need to harness the benefits of the water prompted the development of the wheel, cart, pulley and, eventually, the water wheel, all based on principles of physics. Control of the rivers' water flow through dams and canals led to advances in engineering and architecture. Observation of the heavenly bodies, the rise and fall of waters in the rivers and Persian Gulf, and the seasons of the agricultural year spurred the development of astrology and then astronomy. All this led to an early understanding of sophisticated mathematics and to the creation of a calendar to accurately mark and predict the passage of time. At the same time, the inhabitants of ancient Mesopotamia felt a close connection to the world of the divine as it was seen to manifest itself in natural phenomena: the sun, moon and stars, wind and rain, mountains and rivers. The combination of religious and rudimentary scientific understandings of the world around them helped to make the Sumerians, and eventually the Assyrians and Babylonians, carriers of a great religious tradition that influenced the entire ancient Near East and beyond. By the late fourth and early third millennia

Flock of sheep along the Tigris-Euphrates river valley.

B.C., the invention of pictographs and then cuneiform writing facilitated international links and trade between countries, spurring and spreading further developments in art, literature, science and religion across the known world.

Political Status

The nations and empires of Mesopotamia enjoyed considerable political status in the ancient world, a reality that was directly dependent on their location as a hub of land and sea routes from Europe and Africa into Asia and back again. Through the easily navigable Persian Gulf to the Indian Ocean and Far East; across the Zagros Mountains into Persia, Afghanistan and on to the Horse and Silk Road of China; up the Euphrates Valley then across to Anatolia and the Mediterranean and Aegean seas; or down the Levant to the Red Sea, the Arabian Peninsula, Egypt, East Africa and beyond—Mesopotamia was truly a hub between east and west.

Since Mesopotamia was located at one of the most important crossroads in the ancient Near East, it was a place through which material and spiritual culture flowed to and from neighboring countries. Here, peoples, and everything that defined their identities, mingled in a vast and intricate mosaic. Throughout ancient history, the region of Mesopotamia—in whole or in part—was ruled by peoples that entered from the four corners of the ancient Near East: Elamites, Medians and Persians from the east; Sumerians, Chaldeans and Semites from the south; Kassites, Assyrians and Hittites from the north; Amorites and Greeks from the west, and others. The major problem facing the various rulers of Mesopotamia was twofold: unification and control of its interior regions on the one hand, while on the other keeping the next invader at bay. In fact, very few kingdoms were successful in doing so for long.

THE MEDITERRANEAN BASIN

Introduction

The lands of the ancient Near East were strung along the Fertile Crescent, balanced on either end by two thin river valleys and squeezed by the climactic uncertainties of the deserts and mountains that encroached along their entire length. In sharp contrast, the Mediterranean world can be seen as a vast amphitheater in which the sea draws the lands along its shore together, while an almost unbroken outer circle of mountains and deserts served to keep the enemies beyond at bay. These two worlds, east and west, are nevertheless tied together through geography, and from the earliest days their respective peoples were drawn to interact with each other for commercial and military interests.

It is only natural that a body of water as large and dominant as the Mediterranean would have been called by many names in the ancient world. For the Assyrians and Babylonians, this was the "Upper Sea" because of its location beyond the upper Euphrates River. The Old Testament speaks of the "Western Sea" (Deut 11:24; Joel 2:20) lying on the western horizon of Israel, a horizon which seemed to stretch toward infinity. Phoenicians and others (Num 34:6–7 *et passim*) called the Mediterranean the "Great Sea" as it was far larger than any other known body of water. For the Greeks this was the "Inner Sea," bounded by lands that they knew, unlike the foreboding Atlantic Ocean, an unfamiliar "External" or "Outer Sea." The Romans introduced the word "Mediterraneum" ("middle land," i.e., a sea surrounded by various lands of importance to the Romans). The New Testament calls the Mediterranean simply "the Sea" (Acts 10:32, 27:30), while for the Talmud this was "Okiyanus," the Ocean (Tosefta, *Terumot* 82).

Geological Structure and Topography

The Mediterranean Sea is part of a much larger east-west topographical basin that includes the lowlands of the north Arabian Desert, the Tigris and Euphrates river valley and the Persian Gulf. To the north lies a great mass of mountains stretching from the Alps eastward through the Balkans and Anatolia to the Zagros, Caucasus and Elburz mountains above Mesopotamia and Iran, then eventually to the Himalayas in central Asia. This jumbled mass of snow-capped mountains exhibits features of complex folding and faulting, and has a long geological history. Above this are the plains and tablelands of central Europe and the interior of Russia, a different world altogether in which the geological relief is largely defined by wide-spaced river valleys. From here the greatest invasions into the Mediterranean world would eventually take place, including those of the Huns (5th century A.D.) and Turks (11th–16th centuries A.D.).

The Mediterranean Sea itself is circumscribed on the north and east by a number of relatively low mountain chains (those of Greece, Lycia and Pamphilia; the Taurus Mountains and

The climate and soil of the high central Anatolian Plateau, heartland of the Hittite Empire, is well suited for grazing and for grain.

In the early second millennium B.C. the Assyrians established a trading center at Kanesh in this central Anatolian valley, and for over one hundred years controlled the historic route that ties Asia to Europe.

the Lebanon Range). The coastline is largely concordant, that is, it tends to follow the direction of these lines of coastal mountains. This is the case for most of the Italian Peninsula, the western and eastern coasts of the Balkan Peninsula, southern Anatolia, and most of the Levant. In many places the coastal mountains drop directly into the sea, and even when they run at some distance from the coast the straight-line direction of the overall topography offers few major natural harbors. The coastal plains, however, are typically fertile for agriculture and offer a decent base for permanent human settlement. In contrast, the only areas of discordant coasts, where the mountain chains run at right angles to the Mediterranean, are southern Italy, the very southern end of the Balkans (the Peloponnesus), western Anatolia, and the northwestern corner of the Levant. Here large areas of protected water in deep inlets provided ample opportunity for seaborne communication to develop. It is not surprising that it was in the Aegean and from northern Phoenicia that Mediterranean sea trade thrived.

Various areas of human settlement, then, sprang up around the Mediterranean, either in connection with natural harbors or centered on fertile coastal plains. The coastal mountains tended to separate these regions from each other on land, hence further prompting sea travel. Among the more important coastal plains are those of Cilicia (ancient Kue) and Attalia (modern Antalya) on the southern Anatolian coast, the river deltas of the Meander and Hermus

rivers in western Anatolia, the plain of Thessaly in eastern Greece, the Po river valley in northern Italy, and the plains along the western coast of Italy.

Anatolia is centered on a high plateau essentially isolated from the Mediterranean, Aegean and Black seas by rugged interior mountains. Here rainfall drains into the shallow, enclosed salt lake of Tuz Golu, with the great arc of the Halys River to the north circling to the Black Sea. This brutal landscape was the homeland of the Hittites, who used its natural defenses to launch an empire into the Levant in the late second millennium B.C. In the time of the New Testament this was the heartland of Galatia (Acts 16:6; Gal 1:2) and Cappadocia (Acts 2:1; 1 Pet 1:1). To the west, major drainage systems of Anatolia flowed into the Aegean, and here a gradual tapering in elevation provided numerous fertile agricultural valleys. This region, called Ionia by the Greeks but incorporated into the Roman Empire as Asia Minor, always maintained more suitable conditions for human settlement than the rest of Anatolia. Anatolia is separated from the Balkan Peninsula and Europe by a complicated depression forming the Bosphorus Strait (with an average width of only 1 mile), the Sea of Marmara and the Dardanelles (on average 3 miles [5 km] wide). Together these form one of most strategic and significant shipping channels on earth.

The Balkan Peninsula south of Mount Olympus (9,570 ft./2,920 m) was the heartland of ancient Greece, while to

31

These and many other "fairy chimney" formations of soft volcanic tuff were used as dwellings and monasteries from the ninth century A.D. on, in Cappadocia, central Anatolia.

the north lay the mountainous region of Macedonia. Due to prolonged and severe tectonic activity, the entire area of Greece is quite dissected and divided, and composed of an irregular series of mountain ranges all oriented more or less northwest-southeast, with many reaching elevations from 3,500 feet (1,100 m) to over 8,000 feet (2,400 m). Southern Greece, the Peloponnesus (properly Achaia in ancient Greek sources), a rough fig-leaf shaped landmass dangling into the Mediterranean by the narrow Isthmus at Corinth, is the most rugged of all both in terms of coastline and overall terrain in relation to size. Here no point inland is over 40 miles (65 km) from the sea. Altogether ancient Greece had an area of less than modern Portugal but a coastline longer than the entire Iberian or Italian peninsulas. The net result of the lay of the land in ancient Greece was twofold: (1) communities that sprang up in any of the numerous small intermountain valleys tended to be politically independent entities, while (2) the proximity to the sea prompted shared commercial and diplomatic interests.

Commercial interests centered on ports lining the western Anatolian and southeastern Greek coasts were pulled together by the islands of the Aegean Sea. Sailors in the Aegean are never out of sight of land until south of Crete, the largest of the Aegean islands, which is located in such a way so as to shelter the Aegean from the Mediterranean beyond. To the east is the island of Cyprus, from which the mountains of both Anatolia and Lebanon are visible, a line-of-sight which ensured that Cyprus would become a natural sea-bridge between the Mediterranean and the ancient Near East. For much of its history, then, Greece faced east, drawn by the islands and ports of the Aegean toward the eastern Mediterranean seaboard and beyond.

The boot-shaped Italian Peninsula slices deeply into the Mediterranean Sea, perfectly situated to dominate the east-west sea lanes that bind together the lands on the Mediterranean's perimeter. The straight-line backbone of the Italian Peninsula is formed by the Apennine Mountains that extend the full length of Italy. Although the Apennines rise to an average height of 4,000 feet (1,200 m), numerous mountain passes ensure that no area of settlement along the coastline is isolated from the others. Hence, the largely homogeneous character of the peninsula, in terms of geological structure but also climate, fertility and vegetation, served as a basis for political unification under Rome in the late first millennium B.C. In addition, the high wall of the Alps, rising dramatically from the fertile Po Valley in the north, provides an adequate defensive barrier for Italy's only land connection to the rest of the world. In spite of its lengthy coastline, Italy boasts few good natural harbors; the best in ancient times faced southwest. This fact, when combined with the reality that the best agricultural plains and hence largest cities (including Rome) were on the western coast, and the nearest islands—Corsica, Sardinia and Sicily—also lay to the west across the Tyrrhenian Sea, ensured that ancient Rome was first and foremost a western-oriented empire. With Greece facing east and Rome facing west, the Adriatic Sea dividing the Italian and Balkan peninsulas can be seen as an important east-west line in the Mediterranean.

Climate

The coastlands of the Mediterranean Basin largely share a similar climate, termed "Mediterranean," with cool, wet winters and hot, dry summers. Due to the prevailing rainfall, the western side of each region (western Italy, western Greece, western Anatolia, the western coast of the Levant) is wetter than its corresponding eastern side. Throughout, local variations in climate occur due to elevation and its effects on prevailing rainfall. In addition, annual rainfall amounts in any given region tend to vary dramatically, with a small margin any given year tipping the balance to feast or famine. The interior regions to the north are largely influenced by the climate of Europe. Hence, the cooler southern coast of the Black Sea (northern Anatolia) and upper Macedonia see precipitation throughout the year, with an autumn maximum and a spring minimum. This climate favors thick deciduous forests and heavy undergrowth, a rarity for the Mediterranean world. The high plateau of central Anatolia

is arid and cold, with steppe grasslands suitable for grazing and grain. The climate of the western slopes of Anatolia is more moderate, allowing a wide variety of agricultural pursuits elsewhere limited by the heat of the Mediterranean summer and the dry winter cold of the Anatolian interior. It was in this favored region that some of the largest cities of Anatolia took root during the period of Roman dominance, and here the growth of the early church during and just after the time of the New Testament was pronounced. As for the Italian Peninsula, only the Po Valley in the north sees rain throughout the year, a fact that enhances its role as Italy's primary agricultural land.

Natural Resources and Routes

The primary natural recourses of the Mediterranean Sea, its agricultural fertility and mineral deposits, together with the network of land and sea routes tying the region together and linking it to lands beyond, provided the basic material for the commercial success of its various peoples.

Due to the mountainous character of Italy, Greece, Anatolia, Crete and Cyprus, only a fraction of these lands are arable, with mainland Greece (at 20%) and Crete (around 12%, and that mostly in rocky terraces) having the least amount of cultivable land. In Greece and Crete only a few

CULTURE AND COMMERCE IN THE ANCIENT NEAR EAST

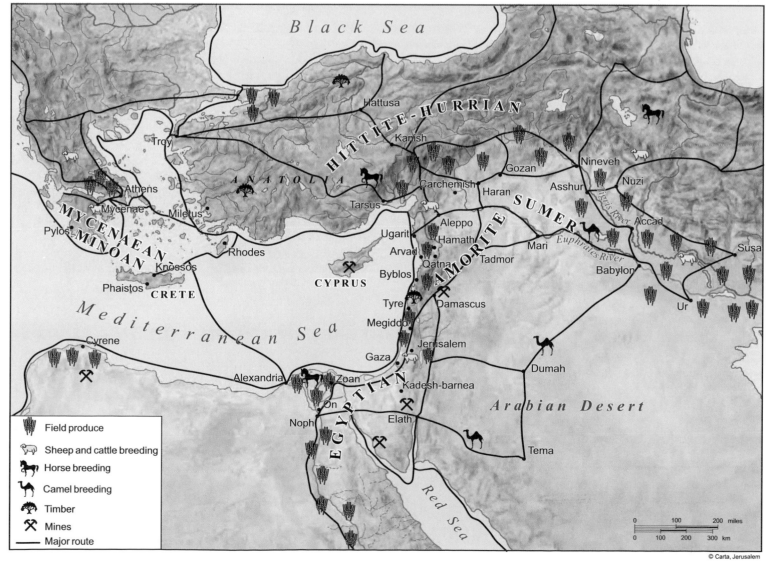

🌾	Field produce
🐑	Sheep and cattle breeding
🐎	Horse breeding
🐫	Camel breeding
🌴	Timber
⚒	Mines
—	Major route

© Carta, Jerusalem

This small harbor at the site of Alexandria Troas (Acts 16:7–11) on the far western coast of Anatolia, with the Aegean island of Bozcaada off-shore, represents the network of sea routes that drew the lands of the Mediterranean together.

valleys are more than a dozen miles long and a few wide, although erosion has filled them with fertile alluvial soil. Throughout the Mediterranean a mixed economy prevailed: olives, vines and wheat in the warmer, lower valleys and plains; sheep, goats and pigs on the mid-range slopes; with grain (especially barley) and large cattle characterizing the cooler steppe lands. In addition, certain regions gained fame for specialized commodities, such as the plains of Thessaly in Greece and Cilicia (Kue) in Anatolia for war horses (cf. 1 Kgs 9:28). In antiquity many of the hills throughout the

entire region were heavily forested, but already by the fifth century B.C. the effects of deforestation were felt in Greece as timber had to be imported from Macedonia and the southern Black Sea coast. The islands of Crete and Cyprus, their mountains largely denuded, have yet to recover their forests.

As for mineral deposits, silver mines near Athens helped to enrich the city as a center of learning and leisure, and from the earliest periods the silver, copper and iron deposits of Cyprus pulled that island into the trade network of the ancient Near East. Italy, too, had deposits of copper and iron, two commodities necessary for technological self-sufficiency in the ancient world. Marble can be found in Italy, Greece and Anatolia, with the green marble of eastern Greece most favored by the Roman emperors.

As for travel, the only river in the entire region that can truly be called navigable for any significant length was the Po, in the northern Italian Peninsula.

Greek merchant ship, 6th century B.C.

Others such as the Tiber, Meander and Hermus brought sea traffic inland to some extent, although the effects of silting over time tended to push their alluvial coastal plains out to sea; Ephesus, Miletus, Priene and Tarsus, all once port cities, are now inland as a result. Most watercourses, however, were narrow torrents, non-navigable in the winter because of the quick and violent flow of water and dry in the summer; during the summer, at least, their rocky beds could serve as local land routes. Among the strategic passes, none was more important than the Cilician Gates in southeastern Anatolia. Here, above Tarsus on the Cilician Plain, virtually all land traffic between Europe and Asia was funneled. In terrain as rugged as that which surrounds the Mediterranean, land routes were always difficult. Even after the advent of the Roman road system which greatly eased travel, a frequent traveler such as the Apostle Paul, a native of the great cosmopolitan center of Tarsus who traveled an estimated 15,000 miles (24,000 km) on his missionary journeys, would note:

> I have been on many journeys, in dangers from rivers, dangers from robbers . . . dangers in the city, dangers in the wilderness, dangers on the sea, dangers among false brethren. I have been in labor and hardship, through many sleepless nights, in hunger and thirst, often without food, in cold and exposure.   (2 Cor 11:26–27)

Navigation on the Mediterranean Sea

In spite of the dangers inherent to long-distance sea travel, the economic advantages that sea routes held over land routes launched people into the Mediterranean:

1. A ship moves easily and inexpensively, borne for the most part by the power of the natural ocean currents (in the Mediterranean, these flow in a counterclockwise motion along the coasts) and by the winds that fill its sails.

2. Ships can carry cargoes hundreds of times heavier and bulkier than can be loaded on the backs of animals or in carts.

3. A sea passage needs no preparation or upkeep as does a road.

Long-distance seafaring voyages in the eastern Mediterranean usually followed a counterclockwise route: if starting from the Peloponnesus, a ship would sail to Crete, then be pushed by the prevailing winds to Egypt or the southern Levant (Israel), then hug the shores of the Levant, Cyprus and Anatolia to Rhodes and island-hop the Aegean back to Greece. The larger Mediterranean islands are located no more than 40 miles (65 km) from shore, a reasonable daily distance covered by a ship under sail, and the islands of the Aegean are within quick and easy sailing distance from each other. Voyages were usually undertaken in daylight, although eventually many inhabited islands had lighthouses to help guide sailors by night. Long voyages required many intermediary stops, not only to spend as many nights as possible under safe anchorage but also to engage in commerce at ports of trade and replenish the ship's provisions (Acts 21:1–8). Even the longest voyage without landfall typically taken by sailboat, that from Crete to Egypt, usually took only four to five days.

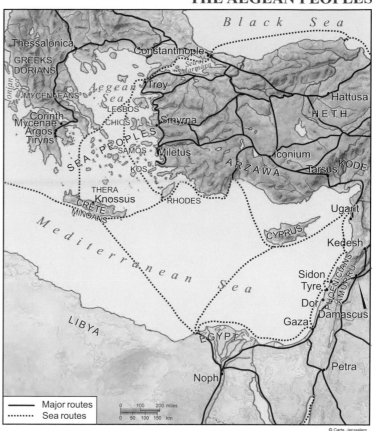

© Carta, Jerusalem

The Aegean Peoples and Their Cultures

One cannot overestimate the vital role that the Mediterranean Sea has played throughout history for the peoples who have lived along its shores. Domination of sea routes was imperative, not only in the economic and social development of nations, but also in their political and military history. It is not surprising that history is replete with the struggles of various nations over the right to rule the shores and parts of the sea; among these are Minoans, Mycenaeans, various Sea Peoples, Phoenicians, Greeks and Romans.

The Minoan Culture. Crete is the largest island on the Aegean Sea. With a comfortable climate it served as the main crossroads for shipping between the eastern Mediterranean—where sailing was relatively easy—and the central Mediterranean around the Italian Peninsula. The island's greatest length is 155 miles (250 km), with a maximum width of some 35 miles (55 km). Crete's mountains rise to 8,038 feet (2,450 m) above sea level, and were forested in antiquity with cypress, pine, and perhaps even cedar trees. Crops such as grains, grapevines, and olives were cultivated in the island's few arable areas, and the inhabitants engaged in fishing. Thus, Crete's sailors and farmers could supply provisions to the foreign ships that came from all directions and anchored at the island.

The Cretans, whose origins were evidently in Asia Minor and Greece, established their capital at Knossos (modern Heraklion), on the island's northern tableland, opposite the Greek mainland, a location that was safest in times of storm. A second important center was Phaistos, on the southern

In the mid- to late second millennium B.C. the Mycenaeans dominated the sea lanes of the eastern Mediterranean from their homeland in the hills and valleys of the eastern Peloponnesus, shown here.

coast facing Egypt. Thus the Cretans provided a link between Greece, Egypt and the Levant, but also had connections to Italy and Spain. Their commercial and military significance, then, becomes obvious.

The Minoan culture (named after their legendary king, Minos) that developed in Crete established commercial and cultural ties to Mesopotamia and Egypt in the third millennium B.C. Minoan culture reached its peak in the sixteenth century B.C., and is attested archaeologically in Cyprus, Ugarit and the Levant, Mesopotamia, Egypt, the Italian Peninsula, Sicily and Sardinia.

The Mycenaean Culture. The Mycenaeans appear to have been descendants of Achaean tribes that penetrated

A Mycenaean funerary mask of thin gold, found in a Mycenaean shaft grave, 1550–1500 B.C.

(below) A Mycenaean IIIA2 kylix, from Acco.

southward into the Peloponnesus from northern Greece. They farmed along river estuaries and mountain slopes, and later developed manufacturing. Archaeology has revealed evidence of distinctive Mycenaean products: enormous clay vessels for storing oil and wine, copper utensils from ore imported from Cyprus, and articles of ivory that have been found in Megiddo. Important Mycenaean cities included Mycenae, Corinth, Tiryns, and Argos.

During its height in the fifteenth and fourteenth centuries B.C., Mycenae was a strong competitor of Crete in maritime trade; with the fall of Knossos and the other Cretan cities in 1400 B.C., the Mycenaeans inherited control of the

THE ISLAND OF CRETE

Cape Spatha
Cape Kisamon
Mediterranean Sea
Kydonia
Polyrrhenia
Rethymna
Elyros
Leuka
Eleutherna
Knossos
Itanos
Phalanna
2456 m
Araden
Anopolis
Mt. Ida
Lyktos
Gortyn
Piranthos
Praisos
Phaistos
Oleros
Cape Erythraion
Rhytion

0   15   30 miles
0   25   50 km

© Carta, Jerusalem

THE MIGRATION OF THE SEA PEOPLES, 1174 B.C.

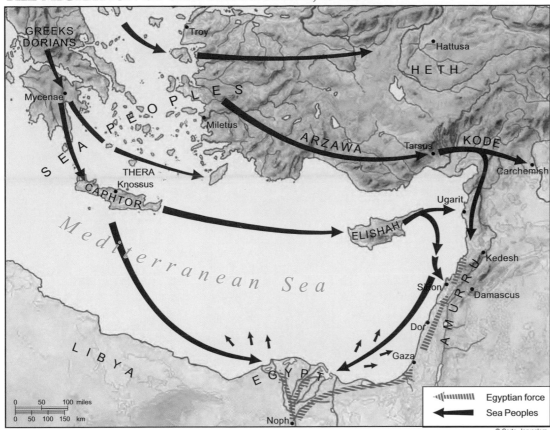

Prisoners from among the Sea Peoples, on relief of Rameses III (1195–1164 B.C.) at Medinet Habu, Egypt.

commerce of the eastern Mediterranean from Egypt to the Aegean. They controlled the islands of Rhodes and Cyprus and the port of Ugarit in the northern Levant, all of which served as settlements where the Mycenaeans traded with Mesopotamia and the Hittites. Mycenaean ships were constructed in the shipyards of Ugarit, and warehouses for importing and exporting goods were built in all the ports of the eastern Mediterranean. Mycenaean pottery, especially large storage vessels for oil and wine, has frequently been found in archaeological digs throughout the eastern Mediterranean, including many in Canaan/ Israel: Jaffa, Ashkelon, Gaza, Lachish, Beth-shemesh, Gezer, Jerusalem, Shechem, Taanach, Megiddo, Hazor, Beth-shean, and Jericho. These and other sites provide a "map" of Mycenaean commercial interests in the eastern Mediterranean. Mycenae was destroyed with the Dorian invasion from northern Greece in the twelfth century B.C.

The Sea Peoples. By the end of the thirteenth century B.C., the established power centers in the eastern Mediterranean began to break apart. While many factors surely contributed to this widespread decline in organized social and political structures, one that tends to be emphasized by all historians of the period is the movement of peoples from the region of the Aegean to the east and southeast. Who these people were, where they originated and why they left their homeland(s) are all debated. No doubt this was a prolonged process by many different groups for a variety of reasons. In any case, Egyptian sources of the mid-twelfth century B.C. speak of invasions into the Nile Delta and along the southern coast of the Levant by peoples from the sea,

hence the modern phrase "the invasion of the Sea Peoples" to label the entire phenomenon. Among the groups that ended up settling on the southern Levantine coast were the Philistines, whose original homeland, according to the prophet Amos, was Caphtor (=Crete; Amos 9:7). Other groups such as the Sherden and Tjekker apparently settled on the coast farther north. The Philistines, from whom the later geographical term "Palestine" is derived, established a loose confederation of city-states between Gaza and Ekron at the same time that Israel was settling the hill country to the east; their skirmishes over the region's limited resources is well attested in the Bible (Judg 13–16; 1 Sam 4–17).

The Phoenicians. The rise of the Phoenicians led to two historic changes in the eastern Mediterranean. For the first time in the history of the region, a Semitic people controlled the sea routes of the Mediterranean, and for the first time a people tiny in land area and population became a major maritime power, sailing not only the Mediterranean but the Red Sea (1 Kgs 9:26–28) and part of the Indian Ocean as well.

The name "Phoenicia" evidently derives from *phoinike*, a Greek word meaning "purple-red." Apparently the Phoenicians were among the first to perfect the technique of extracting and producing a rare and valuable purple-red dye from sea snails found on the northern Levantine coast. This dye was used to color fine-quality linen, wool, and silk cloth, and became a symbol for royalty.

Phoenicia was located along the narrow eastern coastlines of what are now Syria, Lebanon, and northern Israel, altogether nearly 300 miles (480 km) in length. Phoenician

37

The Economy of the Kingdom of Tyre, According to Ezekiel 27

Local Products

Natural Resources	Manufactured Products
Cypress from Senir	Lumber for building ships
Cedars of Lebanon	Masts for ships
Shipyards in Gebal	Shipbuilding
Purple and blue dyes	Dyed cloth, embroidered clothing
Ships and sailors from Tarshish	Ships for transporting metals
Fish	Fresh and salted fish

Cedars of Lebanon

Imports

Product	Origin	Manufactured Product and Commercial Use
Bashan oak	Bashan, in land of Israel	Masts for ships
Woven linen cloth	Egypt	Ship sails
Blue, purple dyes	Cyprus (Elishah)	Dyed sails
Metals	Spain	Silver, iron, tin, lead utensils
Copper	Asia Minor	Copper and brass utensils
Human beings	Asia Minor	Slave trade
Horses, mules	Togarmah—Anatolia	Pulling carriages
Ivory, ebony	Dedan in Arabia, East Africa	Art objects, statues
Woven cloth	Egypt	Clothing, rope, sails
Gemstones	Arabia	Jewelry
Grain, honey, balm, oil	Land of Israel	Food, cosmetics, offerings
Wine, wool	Damascus	Food, dyed woven cloth
Rugs, saddlecloths	Dedan in Arabia	Household use, riding
Lambs, goats	Arabia, Kedar	Woven wool clothing, dyed raw wool
Spices, precious stones, gold	Kingdom of Sheba	Cosmetics, jewelry

port cities at home included Arvad, Gebal (Byblos), Sidon and Tyre. The Phoenicians also established international ports at Cyprus, Rhodes, the Aegean Islands, Crete, Sicily, Malta, Sardinia, Utica, Carthage, and Cadiz in Gibraltar.

Limestone relief depicting the head of a Phoenician nobleman, from Dor.

Phoenician merchant ship, 7th century B.C.

With the high Lebanon Mountains protecting its back and a jagged, harbor-friendly coastline at its feet, Phoenicia faced the sea and developed a thriving trade economy that, by the mid-first millennium B.C. reached the western Mediterranean. Thus, Ezekiel called the Kingdom of Tyre "the merchant of the peoples" (Ezek 27:3) in a discourse that clearly recognized Phoenicia's role as a middleman for international trade in both practical and exotic goods (Ezek 27:12–25). Chief among trade products imported by the Phoenicians were basic foodstuffs grown in the land of Israel (Ezek 27:17; Acts 12:20), for Phoenicia didn't have enough agricultural land to support itself. Phoenicia's chief home-grown export was lumber (primarily cedar and cypress) cut from the Lebanon Mountains; biblical writers praised the strength of these forests (2 Kgs 19:23; Isa 14:8, 60:13) and both Solomon and the Egyptian pharaohs imported lumber for royal building projects (1 Kgs 5:7–10).

The political, economic, and maritime status of the Phoenicians required superior abilities of organization, planning, and administration. The inhabitants of Tyre in particular earned renown as skilled sailors who lived facing the Mediterranean at the "entrance to the sea"; their border was "in the heart of the seas" (Ezek 27:3–4). Tyrians were known to be adroit merchants with vision (Isa 23:8), brave and daring men of war (Ezek 27:10–11), and superb and resourceful craftsmen and artisans with great initiative (Ezek 27:16, 28:13).

Rabbi Shimon ben Lakish testified to the wealth of Tyre and its kingdom, to the abundance of its products and to the ease of life for its inhabitants when he said, "There is no 'land of the living' (Ps 116:9) but Tyre and its hinterland, and Cyprus and its hinterland, where things are inexpensive and there is plenty" (*Gen Rabbah* 74:1; J.T. *Kela'im* 9:4).

Greek City-states and the Spread of Hellenism. From the fall of the Mycenaean civilization around 1200 B.C. to the mid-eighth century B.C., Greece fell into a so-called "Dark Age" and was a minor player in the Aegean, while being nearly invisible on the larger world stage. It was during this time, however, that Greece absorbed and adapted important cultural traits from the ancient Near East, including the alphabet (from Phoenicia) and religious motifs that would form the basis of later classical Greek and Roman mythology. Seeds were sown for a pan-Hellenism that began to flower with the rise of independent, rival city-states during the Archaic Age (c. 750–500 B.C.); chief among these were Corinth, Athens and Sparta. This period saw the beginning of colonization throughout the Aegean and Ionia (western Anatolia), and in Cyrene in North Africa. The Classical Age (c. 500 B.C. to the rise of Alexander in 334 B.C.) was characterized not only by great cultural achievements in political science, literature, philosophy and the arts, but also by a resurgence of Greek commercial and military interests throughout the eastern Mediterranean. This "Triumph of Greece" was checked somewhat by a series of wars with the Persians on Greek soil in the early fifth century B.C. Alexander's push to the Indus Valley (334–323 B.C.) and

The strategic importance of the Dardanelles cannot be overestimated. Not only does this narrow channel separate Greece and Europe from Anatolia and Asia, it also provides the only sea route between the Mediterranean and Black seas.

the subsequent efforts to colonize various parts of the land that he had conquered spread the cultural grip of Hellenism throughout the rest of the eastern Mediterranean and the ancient Near East, while the wealth of the world flowed to the Aegean. The pendulum of commercial and cultural influence had swung to the West, where it was to remain for centuries.

Of particular relevance for the world of the Bible, many Jews followed the wake of these new social and economic opportunities into the lands of the Mediterranean; the result was a vibrant Jewish Diaspora that, among other things, provided avenues of contact for the emergent Church in the first and second centuries A.D. This contact with Hellenism also posed serious religious and social challenges to the Jews of Galilee, Judea and especially Jerusalem in their struggle to remain faithful to the "traditions of the ancestors" while becoming relevant to a changing world.

(left) Heinrich Schliemann dug this massive cut into the ruins of Troy in the 1870s, prompting a historic reassessment of the great Trojan War described by Homer in the Iliad. The Plain of Troy, ancient Greece's foothold in Anatolia, and the Aegean lie beyond.

(below) This white marble Temple of Trajan in Pergamum in western Anatolia represents Rome's economic, cultural and military hold on the Mediterranean world by the early second century A.D. For better or worse, the roads connecting the widely diverse geographical regions of the known world now all led to Rome.

Rome and the Legacy of the Mediterranean World

The relative latecomers, but eventual champions, in the entire ancient history of the Mediterranean were the Romans. The traditional founding of Rome dates only to 753 B.C., and while early attempts by Etruscans to create a viable urban fabric in the mid-Italian Peninsula were relatively successful, their efforts to unify the land politically were not. The Republic, centered on Rome, did gain political control over Italy during a long and difficult struggle in the fifth and fourth centuries B.C., and managed to secure their borders to the north (Gaul) and west. The third century B.C. saw a series of wars with Greece and Greek colonies such as Carthage, as Rome now had the resources and incentive to begin to forge an eastern empire. By the time of the New Testament, Rome had established control along the eastern Mediterranean seaboard, and by the early second century A.D. had taken the Arabian spice trade from the Nabateans and was able to exert a degree of control over the Parthians in Mesopotamia. From Britain and Spain to Egypt and Mesopotamia, Rome reigned supreme. While this new political reality carried some benefit for everyone—with *pax Romana* came economic opportunities, a relative ease of travel and the headiness of being a citizen of the world— there were clear drawbacks: the economic resources of far-flung lands such as Judea were bled for Rome's benefit, and peoples who preferred their own ancestral traditions over those of their conquerors were faced with difficult choices regarding loyalty and identity. The survival of Judaism and the spread of Christianity in the Roman world are testimonies to mankind's abilities both to adapt and to hold firm in the face of change in lands in which historical and cultural roots run deep.

Understanding
The Old Testament

Preface

Children hear their first Bible stories at home from their parents or grandparents, or in Sunday School from teachers whose names, too, are often biblical. As they grow older most children are introduced to Bible studies proper. Because of the vast scope of the work, such Bible studies usually concentrate only on selected books and chapters. These are often studied in depth and taught with great intensity or even by rote. Still, most adults end up remembering only a small portion of what they had learned: a few stories, prominent personages, or fragments of biblical passages. If asked to write down all that was remembered from hundreds of Bible lessons, sometimes it is doubtful whether all but a few pages could be filled, or if much accuracy could be retained.

How, then, despite the inexhaustible mine of information acquired, were all these hours of Bible teaching and study lost? One possible reason lies in the fact that the Bible is usually studied in a fragmentary manner, not within a comprehensive framework that is structured and organized from beginning to end. The importance of a structured framework may be somewhat exaggerated, but it can undoubtedly ease Bible study and make it more interesting and memorable. This Atlas provides just such a framework—a historical-geographical backdrop to the understanding of the Bible, providing the broadest background possible for placing the events and persons within a tangible framework of time and space.

We set forth the premise that the need for Bible study should not be subject to proof. The Bible is an inseparable part of Judaism, Christianity, and of Western culture in general. Remove the Bible from humankind, and all the cultures bound in Judaism and Christianity will lose the cornerstone of their foundations and a significant part of their meaning. Bible study, therefore, is a necessity.

Furthermore, the Bible reveals itself differently to different people, and can be studied in more than one manner. The Bible remains strong and firm despite the variant beliefs and extreme viewpoints ascribed to it, and, in this spirit, we present this Atlas.

In quoting the Bible, we intentionally used an old translation—the King James Version—and not one of the modern translations whose language is more attuned to modern times. The translation was completed at the beginning of the seventeenth century, in the days of William Shakespeare, by a group of scholars from among his circle. Its archaic language is in harmony with the Hebrew Bible both in its majesty and in its simplicity. There is no other translation that preserves the flavor of the Hebrew Bible better than this one. Of the King James Version, one is tempted to speculate that had the Bible originally been in English, this is the way it would have been written.

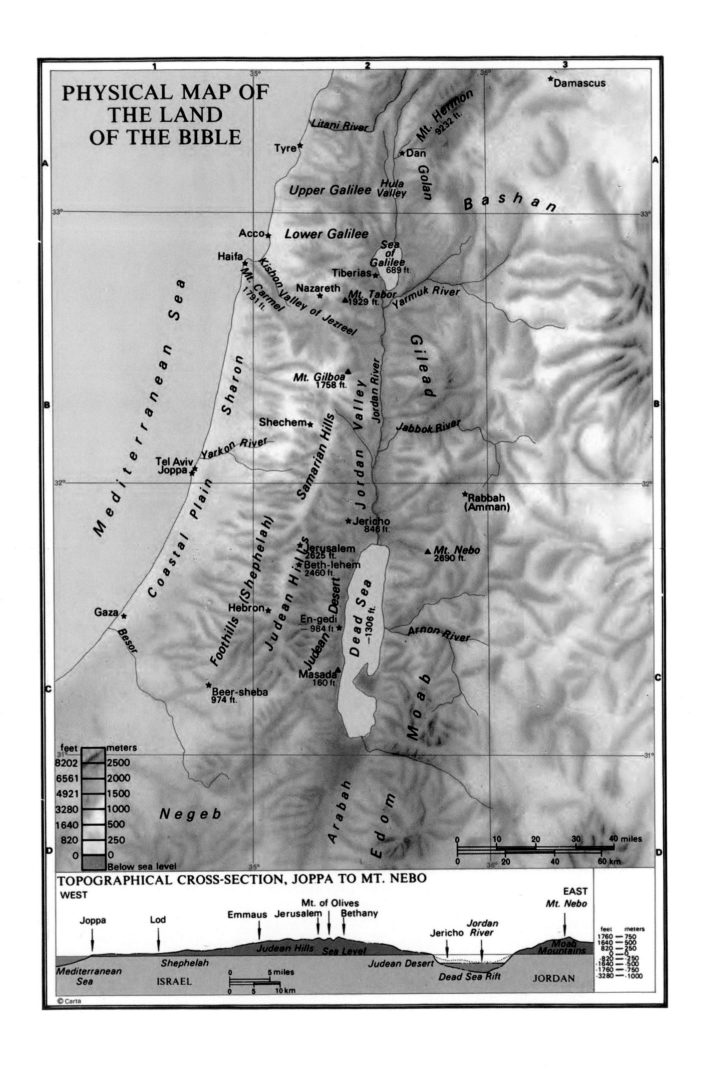

PHYSICAL MAP OF
THE LAND
OF THE BIBLE

★ Damascus

Litani River
Tyre ★
Mt. Hermon
9232 ft.
★ Dan
Golan

Upper Galilee Hula
Valley

B a s h a n

Acco ★ *Lower Galilee*
Haifa ★
Mt. Carmel
1791 ft.
Kishon Valley of Jezreel
Nazareth ★
Sea
of
Galilee
689 ft.
Tiberias ★
Mt. Tabor
▲ 1929 ft.
Yarmuk River

M e d i t e r r a n e a n   S e a

Sharon

Mt. Gilboa ▲
1758 ft.

G i l e a d

Shechem ★

Yarkon River
Tel Aviv ★
Joppa ★

Samarian Hills
Jordan Valley
Jordan River

Jabbok River

★ Rabbah
(Amman)

Coastal Plain

Foothills (Shephelah)

★ Jericho
846 ft.

▲ Mt. Nebo
2690 ft.

Jerusalem ★
2625 ft.
Beth-lehem ★
2460 ft.

Judean Hills

Gaza ★

Hebron ★

En-gedi
— 984 ft. ★

Judean Desert

Dead Sea
—1306 ft.

M o a b

Besor

Masada
160 ft. ★

Arnon River

Beer-sheba ★
974 ft.

feet	meters
8202	2500
6561	2000
4921	1500
3280	1000
1640	500
820	250
0	0
	Below sea level

N e g e b

A r a b a h

E d o m

0   10   20   30   40 miles
0   20   40   60 km

TOPOGRAPHICAL CROSS-SECTION, JOPPA TO MT. NEBO

WEST

EAST
Mt. Nebo

Joppa

Lod

Emmaus
Jerusalem
Mt. of Olives
Bethany

Jericho
*Jordan
River*

Judean Hills   Sea Level

Moab
Mountains

feet	meters
1760	750
1640	500
820	250
0	0
-820	-250
-1640	-500
-1760	-750
-3280	-1000

Mediterranean
Sea

Shephelah

Judean Desert

Dead Sea Rift

JORDAN

ISRAEL

0   5 miles
0   5   10 km

© Carta

44

The Hebrew Bible

The Hebrew word for Bible, *Tanakh*, is an acronym of the words *Torah* (The Five Books of Moses or Pentateuch), *Nevi'im* (The Prophets), and *Ketuvim* (The Writings or Hagiographa). These three sections of the Hebrew Bible are referred to as sacred texts or sacred writings in order to distinguish them from contemporary noncanonical works known as the Apocrypha. The Bible is also known in English as Scriptures, a term more or less parallel to the Hebrew *Mikra*, which means "reading," and refers to the fact that the biblical texts were written (not oral) and, therefore, read. The term *Mikra* serves also to distinguish the books of the Bible from the Mishnah and Midrash, which originally were not committed to writing. The Hebrew Bible is divided into 24 books (see below).

The selection of the books and their inclusion among the sacred writings began in the Second Temple period. The books that were not included, or were stored, were either lost or remained as part of the Apocrypha. The division into chapters and verses began in talmudic times, and developed gradually until it was finalized in the ninth century, with the addition of cantillation signs (*ta'amei ha-mikra*), which indicate the emphasized syllable of each word and the proper musical intonation as well as serving as a kind of punctuation mark. In the tenth century, the sages of Tiberias completed the work of the Masorah, i.e., the reading of each word of the Bible together with its vocalization (*nikkud*). The present division into chapters was established by Christian scholars in the Middle Ages. Jews adapted this division in the fourteenth century and it became widely known after the first Hebrew Bible was printed in Venice in the sixteenth century (apparently in order to facilitate the Jewish-Christian disputations of the time). In the Middle Ages the Pentateuch was also divided into the portions read weekly in the synagogue. This reading is done solely from a Torah scroll, a copy of the Pentateuch handwritten on parchment. Those qualified to produce such a Torah scroll are known as scribes (in Hebrew, *sofer stam*).

As the rank and file of the Jewish people became less knowledgeable of Hebrew, the need for translations of the Bible arose. Among the earliest and best known of these is the Greek translation known as the Septuagint, which was completed during the Second Temple period. There also exist a number of ancient translations into Aramaic, which was the spoken language of the Jews. Best known among these are *Targum Onkelos*, *Targum Jonathan*, and *Targum Yerushalmi* (Palestinian Targum). The Bible was later translated into Latin (the Vulgate) and, eventually, into almost every language in the world, with new and revised translations of the Bible being published all the time.

The Bible is the basis of all Jewish culture. The Mishnah (secondary work) and Talmud are based directly on the Pentateuch, and the entire Bible served as material for the *midrashim* (works of biblical exposition and homiletics that originated in the Second Temple period and continued to be produced until the twelfth century). Central to the Bible is the belief in the One God, who created the world and chose the people of Israel to be His model nation. The books of the Bible can be classified according to content: the Pentateuch—the story of the covenant the Lord made with the children of Israel; the Former Prophets—the realization of this covenant (by fulfilling God's commandments on the part of the people, and by settling the land of Israel on the part of God) and its fruition; the Latter Prophets—God's punishment of the nation for not obeying His orders and His guiding them toward salvation through prophecy; the Hagiographa—addressing God in prayer, individually or as a nation (Psalms), Wisdom Literature (Proverbs, Job, Ecclesiastes), memorial volumes (Daniel, Ezra and Nehemiah), the history of Israel (Chronicles), and the books known as the Five Scrolls. The books of the Bible were written in different forms, both structurally and linguistically: in narrative form, by historical account, verse or proverb, laws and statutes, parables, rebuke, and prayer. The means of interpreting the Bible are also varied, e.g., by means of plain, literal interpretation, fables, allegory, biblical criticism, literary analysis, and more.

The teaching of the Bible plays a central role in Western religious education, and is important in secular education as well. The Bible has been and continues to be used as a source of inspiration for religious, social and national movements, as well as for all types of art, especially literature. The Bible has immense influence on the three great monotheistic religions—Judaism, Christianity, and Islam and all the cultures associated with them. To this day the Bible is one of the most popular, revered, and most quoted books in the world.

TORAH (Pentateuch, The Five Books of Moses)	(The Latter Prophets)	KETUVIM (The Writings, Hagiographa)
1 Genesis בְּרֵאשִׁית	10 Isaiah יְשַׁעְיָהוּ	14 Psalms תְּהִלִּים
2 Exodus שְׁמוֹת	11 Jeremiah יִרְמְיָהוּ	15 Proverbs מִשְׁלֵי
3 Leviticus וַיִּקְרָא	12 Ezekiel יְחֶזְקֵאל	16 Job אִיּוֹב
4 Numbers בְּמִדְבַּר	13 **The 12 Minor Prophets:**	
5 Deuteronomy דְּבָרִים	Hosea הוֹשֵׁעַ	**The Five Scrolls:**
	Joel יוֹאֵל	17 The Song of Songs שִׁיר הַשִּׁירִים
NEVI'IM **(The Former Prophets)**	Amos עָמוֹס	
	Obadiah עֹבַדְיָה	
6 Joshua יְהוֹשֻׁעַ	Jonah יוֹנָה	18 Ruth רוּת
7 Judges שׁוֹפְטִים	Micah מִיכָה	19 Lamentations אֵיכָה
8 Samuel שְׁמוּאֵל	Nahum נַחוּם	20 Ecclesiastes קֹהֶלֶת
9 Kings מְלָכִים	Habakkuk חֲבַקּוּק	21 Esther אֶסְתֵּר
	Zephaniah צְפַנְיָה	
	Haggai חַגַּי	22 Daniel דָּנִיֵּאל
	Zechariah זְכַרְיָה	23 Ezra, Nehemiah עֶזְרָא-נְחֶמְיָה
	Malachi מַלְאָכִי	24 Chronicles דִּבְרֵי הַיָּמִים

The Books of the Bible

Pentateuch (The Five Books of Moses)

Genesis (*Bereishit* in Hebrew) opens with the verse: "In the beginning (*Bereishit*) God created the heaven and earth," whence the book's name. It has 50 chapters. The first eleven recount the story of the Creation up to the building of the Tower of Babel. The remaining chapters give an account of the lives of the Patriarchs until the descent into Egypt.

Exodus (in Hebrew, *Shemot*) opens with the verse: "Now these are the names (*shemot*) of the children of Israel, which came into Egypt." Its 40 chapters give an account of the enslavement in Egypt, the Exodus from Egypt, the Song at the Sea, the first wanderings of the Israelites in the wilderness, the Giving of the Law on Mount Sinai—the Ten Commandments, the building of the Sanctuary and its utensils and the priestly duties within the Sanctuary.

Leviticus (in Hebrew, *Vayikra*) opens with "And the Lord called (*Vayikra*) unto Moses…." The book's 27 chapters deal mostly with the Temple service and holy matters: sacrificial laws; the consecration of Aaron and his sons; laws concerning forbidden food, ritual uncleanliness and purity; the order of worship on Yom Kippur; laws of incest; consecration of the priests; laws concerning the Sabbath and festivals, vows and dedications, the Sabbatical and Jubilee years, and reward and punishment. The book is also known as the "Priest's Manual."

Numbers (in Hebrew, *Bemidbar*) begins with the verse: "And the Lord spake unto Moses in the wilderness (*bemidbar*) of Sinai…." It has 36 chapters, about a third of which continues with the historical record of Israel in the wilderness after the Exodus; the rest deals with the laws of the sacrifices and religious worship in the Temple. It is also referred to as the "*Hummash* (i.e., Pentateuchal volume) of the Numbered," for both at the beginning and toward the end of the book there is a census of the Israelites.

Deuteronomy (in Hebrew, *Devarim*) opens with "These be the words (*devarim*) which Moses spake…." It has 34 chapters. It is also referred to as *Mishneh Torah* (i.e., "the Repetition of the Torah," whence the Greek *Deuteronomion*—"Second Law"), because it repeats much of the laws previously recorded in the Pentateuch. It contains a survey of the Jews until their arrival at the plains of Moab, various laws and statutes, the blessing in reward for observing the Torah and the punishment for disobeying it, the account of Moses' final acts, his parting benediction to the tribes and his death.

The Former Prophets

Joshua gives an account of the acts and wars of Joshua, son of Nun, leader of the Israelites after the death of Moses. The book's 24 chapters deal with the conquest of the land of Canaan (chs. 1–12), the division of the land among the tribes and the establishment of the cities of refuge (chs. 13–22), and Joshua's final will and testament and his death (chs. 23–24).

Judges chronicles the period between the conquest of the land of Canaan and the establishment of the monarchy. During this time, leaders of the tribes, who were called Judges, occasionally rose to power, usually in times of danger, to defend their tribe or several nearby tribes against the enemy; after their successes the Judges would remain leaders also in times of peace, and some became leaders without any threat of war. The book contains 21 chapters.

Samuel is named after the last Judge and the only one who was leader of all the tribes of Israel. After the translation of the Septuagint and Vulgate editions, the book, because of its length, was divided in two: *I Samuel*, with 31 chapters, and *II Samuel* with 24. Based on the central figures there are three parts: the story of Samuel (I Sam. 1–12); Saul and his dynasty, until his death and burial (I Sam. 13–II Sam. 1); and the story of David's rule (II Sam. 2–24).

Kings is divided in two parts, *I Kings* (22 chapters) and *II Kings* (25 chapters). This division came relatively late and does not reflect the thematic contents of the book. The Book of Kings describes the last days of King David, the kingdom of Solomon, the split of the United Monarchy, the histories of the kingdoms of Judah and Israel (including lists of all the kings and the dates of their reign), the exile of the Ten Tribes, the end of the kingdom of Judah, and the Babylonian exile.

The Latter Prophets

Isaiah is, according to tradition, the prophecies of one prophet, Isaiah, son of Amoz. Most modern Bible scholars, however, suggest that while the first 39 chapters of the book are the work of Isaiah, who prophesied in the second half of the eighth century BCE, chapters 40 to 66 were written by another, anonymous prophet, who was active in the beginning of the seventh century BCE. Because both parts are arranged in one book, the second author has been named the second Isaiah (Deutero-Isaiah). According to its contents the book is divided into three parts. Chapters 1 to 35 include prophecies of calamitous suffering, future redemption, wrath and rebuke, and the end of days; chapters 36 to 39 describe events that occurred during the reign of King Hezekiah; and chapters 40 to 66 relate prophecies of redemption, as well as the end of days and Judgment Day.

Jeremiah is the book of the prophet Jeremiah, son of Hilkiah, who prophesied in Judah for about 40 years, from the reign of Josiah to the destruction of the First Temple. There are 52 chapters: chapters 1 to 25 relate prophecies of wrath and rebuke; chapters 26 to 45, various prophecies interspersed with biographical details; chapters 46 to 51, oracles against foreign nations; and the last chapter, 52, describes the final days of the kingdom of Judah and the history of King Jehoiachin in Babylon.

Ezekiel is the book of the prophet Ezekiel, son of Buzi the priest, who lived in the time of the destruction of the First Temple, and who was exiled to Babylon with King Jehoiachin (in 597 BCE), settling in Tel-abib, by the river Chebar. The book has 48 chapters. Chapters 1 to 24 tell of the call of the prophet and the prophecies of doom and destruction of Jerusalem; chapters 25 to 32 relate oracles of doom against foreign nations; chapters 33 to 39, prophecies of consolation and of Israel's restoration; and chapters 40 to 48 describe the complete restoration, plans for the future Temple, the laws of the priests, and the division of the land among the tribes of Israel.

The Twelve Minor Prophets

Hosea is the book of the prophet Hosea, son of Beeri, who prophesied in the days of Uzziah, Jotham, Ahaz, and Hezekiah, kings of Judah, and in the days of Jeroboam, son of Joash, king of Israel. His prophecies were mostly addressed to the northern kingdom of Israel. The book has 14 chapters, the first part of which (chs. 1–3) includes prophecies interspersed with biographical events. Chapters 4 to 14 contain prophecies of the crimes of Is-rael, their forewarned punishment, and of the coming redemption.

Joel is the book of the prophet Joel, son of Pethuel. The time of his prophecies was already disputed in the mishnaic and talmudic periods. Some maintain that Joel prophesied in the days of Jehoram, son of Ahab, while others suggest that he was active in the days of Manasseh. Modern scholars place him later, up to the time of the Return to Zion (late sixth–early fifth centuries BCE). The book has four chapters. The first two describe a plague of locusts and a call for repentance; the last two warn of punishment against the nations who have wronged the Jews and a promise of the return to Zion.

Amos is the book of the prophet Amos, a shepherd of Tekoa, who prophesied in the days of King Uzziah of Judah and in the days of Jeroboam, son of Joash, king of Israel. He was a contemporary of Hosea, Isaiah, and Micah. In the book's nine chapters, Amos demands justice and righteousness, fights against social injustice, and reproves the wealthy classes for pursuing their own pleasure while oppressing the poor, the people at large for worshiping idols, and those who would seek the help of foreign nations.

Obadiah is the book of the prophet Obadiah who, according to modern scholars, was active after the destruction of the First Temple. The book consists of one chapter with 21 verses. It prophesies that Edom would be destroyed as a result of its pride and hatred for Israel, and would be plundered by its enemies.

Jonah describes the mission of Jonah, son of Amittai, to Nineveh and all that he incurred. Jonah probably prophesied in the days of Jeroboam II, king of Israel. The book's four chapters describe the power of repentance and the greatness of God's mercy.

Micah is the book of the prophet Micah the Morasthite. He prophesied in the days of Jotham, Ahaz, and Hezekiah, kings of Judah, and was a contemporary of the prophets Amos, Hosea, and Isaiah. The book has seven chapters, dealing with the prophet's rebuke of corruption and oppression that will lead to destruction, and a prophecy of salvation that will bring a new and better world, based on universal brotherhood and peace.

Nahum is the book of the prophet Nahum the Elkoshite, who prophesied in Judah from the middle of King Manasseh's reign to the end of Josiah's rule. The book contains three chapters, which mainly envision the destruction of Nineveh.

Habakkuk is the book of the prophet Habakkuk. According to one tradition, the prophet lived in the time of Manasseh, king of Judah. Modern scholars, however, place him in the time of Jehoiakim; others suggest he prophesied after the destruction of the First Temple. The book has three chapters; the first two include a complaint about the evil that rules the world, a description of the victory of the Chaldeans, and their downfall. Chapter 3 is a psalm that describes the appearance of God bringing salvation to His people.

Zephaniah is the book of the prophet Zephaniah, son of Cushi, who prophesied in the days of Josiah. His prophecies were aimed at strengthening Josiah's religious and social reforms. The book has three chapters, dealing with the denunciation of idolatry in Judah, the Day of Judgment and Divine punishment, a prophecy concerning the neighboring nations, and the days of God's mercy after His anger subsides.

Haggai is the book of the prophet Haggai, in the days of the Return to Zion. The book's two chapters call for the completion of the Temple, compassion for the people, and the demand to keep the Temple sanctified; the book also prophesies the fall of the heathen kingdoms and God's choice of Zerubbabel, son of Shealtiel, to be His messenger.

Zechariah is the book of the prophet Zechariah, son of Berechiah, in the days of the Return to Zion. The book has 14 chapters. Chapters 1 to 8 contain visions of the building of Jerusalem, the nation's leaders, the purification of the land, the judgment of the world, and the beginning of the messianic era. Chapters 9 to 14 relate prophecies of the final days of Ephraim, Judah and several neighboring nations; these chapters are considered by some scholars to be the words of a different prophet (the "second Zechariah"), or even of two other prophets, who lived in the time of Antiochus' decrees and the Hasmonean revolt, or who lived much earlier, in the time of the First Temple.

Malachi is the book of the last prophet, Malachi, who lived in the days of Ezra and Nehemiah. The book's three chapters deal mainly with the prophet's fight against such negative phenomena as mixed marriages, nonpayment of tithes to the Temple, and oppression, in order to save the people from the danger of annihilation.

The Hagiographa

Psalms is a collection of 150 poems, most of which are hymns to God. The book is divided into five parts (chs. 1–41; 42–72; 73–89; 90–106; and 107–150). According to tradition, the authorship is ascribed to King David. Modern scholars suggest that some psalms were written before David, some were written in the time of David, and still others during the Babylonian exile. The psalms consist mainly of hymns of praise, elegies, but also wonderment and complaints. Many psalms were incorporated in the Jewish prayer book; Christian liturgy also makes extensive use of the psalms.

Proverbs belongs to the genre of Wisdom Literature and is attributed to King Solomon, "the wisest of all men." Some proverbs are ascribed to other sages. The proverbs appeal to man as a universal being, and not to the Israel nation in particular. Its 31 chapters deal with state and social matters, friendship and family relations, joy and sadness, commerce, trade, and other topics.

Job has as its central theme the issue of reward and punishment and, principally, the question of why "the righteous suffer while the wicked thrive." This book, like Proverbs, does not indicate a special relation to the nation of Israel. According to the book's content and structure, it is categorized as Wisdom Literature. The book contains 42 chapters. The date of its composition is generally ascribed to the Second Temple period (fifth–fourth centuries BCE).

The Five Scrolls

The Song of Songs is a collection of love poems between bride and groom. The book has eight chapters. Jewish tradition ascribes its composition to King Solomon and views the book as an allegorical description of the love between God and the nation of Israel. The Song of Songs is read during Passover.

Ruth recounts the story of Ruth the Moabitess, a model convert to Judaism from whom King David was descended. The book has four chapters and its story illustrates a number of Jewish laws: e.g., donations to the poor; *halitzah* (i.e., the act of "releasing" a childless widow for remarriage by the brother-in-law); and redemption of the lands. The story occurs during the harvest season and is thus read in the synagogue during the festival of Shavuot (Pentecost).

Lamentations (in Hebrew, *Ekhah*) derives its name from the first word in the opening verse ("How doth [*Ekhah*]…"). The author, traditionally ascribed to Jeremiah, laments the destruction of the First Temple. The book has five chapters, each with 22 verses (ch. 3 has 66 verses—22×3), the opening letters of which are arranged in Hebrew alphabetical order. Lamentations is read on the eve of the Ninth of Av, the fast day that commemorates the destruction of the Temple, and is reread during that day.

Ecclesiastes, like Proverbs and Job, belongs to the genre of Wisdom Literature. According to tradition, it was written by King Solomon in his old age. Bible scholars, however, date its composition to the Second Temple period. The book has 12 chapters. It is read in the synagogue during Sukkot (Feast of Tabernacles).

Esther recounts how the Jews of Persia and Media were saved from destruction in the days of King Ahasuerus (early fifth century BCE). This salvation is credited to Esther, who was married to Ahasuerus. To commemorate the event, the feast of Purim was established on the 14th and 15th of the Hebrew month of Adar, when the Book of Esther (ten chapters) is read in the synagogue twice, at both the evening and morning services.

Daniel tells the story of Daniel and his companions in the royal courts of Nebuchadnezzar, Darius, and Belshazzar, and the visions of Daniel concerning four symbolic kingdoms (referring to Baby-lon, Media, Persia, and Greece), which would be succeeded by a kingdom of heaven. Some of the book's 12 chapters are written in Hebrew (1:1–2:4; 8–12), the remainder in Aramaic (2:4–7:28). The time and place of its composition are unclear; according to some scholars, it was written in the time of Antiochus' decrees, in 167 BCE. Because the book deals with the end of days, it became a cornerstone in the development of Jewish mysticism, of the messianic concept, and the belief in the resurrection of the dead.

Ezra tells of the Return to Zion. The book has ten chapters: the first six describe the early stages of the return, from Cyrus' decree in 538 BCE to the dedication of the Temple in 515 BCE, in the time of Darius I; chapters 7 to 10 tell of Ezra's own return to the Holy Land, in the days of Artaxerxes until the banishing of the foreign wives (458–426 BCE). The books of Ezra and Nehemiah were originally a single book called Ezra, and only in the mid-fifteenth century were they divided in two; nevertheless, in Jewish tradition they are still considered a single work.

Nehemiah tells the story of Nehemiah, son of Hachaliah, who was appointed governor of Judah (444–437 BCE) by the Persian ruler, Artaxerxes I. The book has 13 chapters. Under Nehemiah's leadership, Judah was restored, the Jewish community was strengthened, the walls of Jerusalem were repaired, the number of inhabitants increased, the situation of the poor improved, the tax burden was eased, the Temple service was reinstituted, Sabbath observance intensified, and mixed marriages were banned.

Chronicles is, according to Jewish tradition, the last book of the Bible. The book is divided in two—*I Chronicles* (29 chapters) and *II Chronicles* (31 chapters)—in accordance with the Septuagint edition. Opinions differ as to the date of composition: according to some scholars, it was written in the fourth century BCE, together with the Book of Ezra. The book chronicles the history of the kings of Judah and their genealogies. Some discrepancies are found between Chronicles and the Former Prophets.

Aramaic translation, 5th century BCE, of Behistun Inscription of Darius I, recounting his many city conquests.

The Ancient Near East

The land to which Abraham came and to which Moses brought the Israelites after their Exodus from Egypt—the land of Canaan, namely, the land of Israel—is bound by the Great Sea, i.e., the Mediterranean Sea on the west, by hills and high mountains on the north and northeast, and by deserts on the east and south.

Physically, the land of Israel forms part of a block of lands that extend in a crescent-like shape from the Persian Gulf in the east, to Mesopotamia (Aram-naharaim) in the north, and to the Sinai peninsula in the west—the so-called Fertile Crescent. Its fertility stems from the great rivers of the Tigris and Euphrates that pass through the Mesopotamian lands, and the broad plains extending between and alongside those rivers and their tributaries. The land of Israel is less fortunate, for it is at the narrow and lean southwestern edge of the Fertile Crescent, with fewer and much shorter rivers and narrower and less fertile plains.

Another land of large rivers—Egypt, also nicknamed the "land of the Nile"—lies to the south of the land of Israel.

Great rivers supply water for sustenance and irrigation and serve as convenient arteries of communication, thus providing a nucleus and natural base for the development of organized, consolidated and regimented civilizations. Such civilizations arose already in the fourth millennium: the kingdoms of Sumer and Accad, Mitanni and Heth, Babylonia and Assyria, and Media and Persia, established on the banks of the Euphrates and the Tigris; and the kingdom of Egypt, along the Nile, which, because of its location, was more confined and homogeneous for development.

The geopolitical position of the land of Israel between these two civilizations—Mesopotamia and Egypt—determined its historical fate as a land-bridge and international crossroad, and often as an arena for battles between competing powers.

The general survey presented here describes the changes that the Middle East underwent in the second and first millennia, changes which are interwoven with the biblical period, from the time of the Patriarchs to the Return to Zion.

In the beginning of the second millennium, in the Euphrates and Tigris valley, there arose the Babylonian kingdom, which would subsequently know intermittent periods of expansion and secession. The Mari kingdom, in the middle Euphrates region, expanded its rule westward in the eighteenth century BCE, followed by the Mitanni kingdom, which grew and flourished in the area of the upper Euphrates.

In the second millennium, the Egyptian kingdom enjoyed two periods of power and expansion—that of the Middle Kingdom (12th Dynasty) in c. 1991–1786 BCE, and the New Kingdom (18th–20th Dynasties) in c. 1570–1150 BCE. Between these two periods, the Hyksos, a Semitic tribe, reigned over the land of Israel and extended their rule up to the Euphrates.

After the expulsion of the Hyksos, the Pharaohs of Egypt sought to expand their rule into the land of Israel and Syria. Egypt's rivals

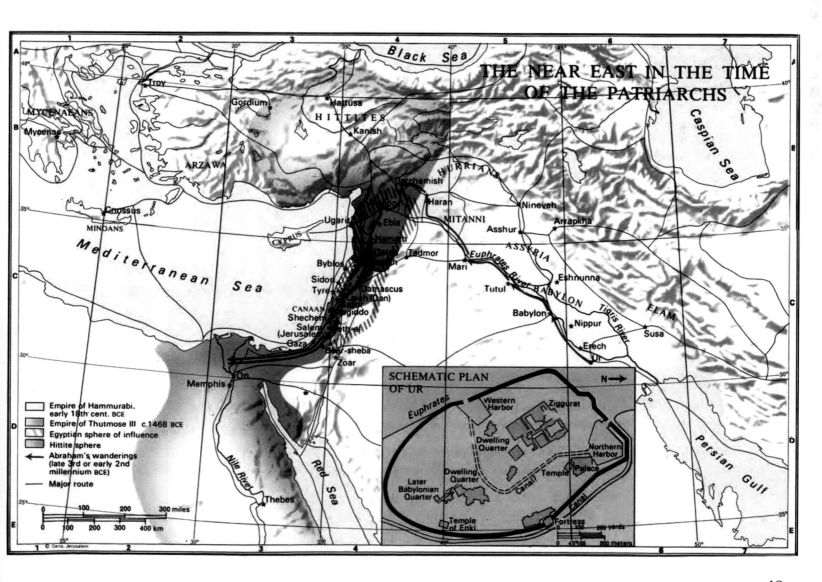

in the north were the Mitanni kingdom and, later, the Hittite kingdom, established in Asia Minor in c. 1800 BCE, which grew in power and expanded its rule to Syria, reaching its peak in the days of King Shuppiluliuma (c. 1380–1350 BCE). For stability and to prevent unrest, the Pharaohs occasionally set out on military campaigns. The best known of these were the campaigns of Thutmose III and the battle of Megiddo (fifteenth century BCE), the campaigns of Amenhotep (1431; 1429), Seti I (1303), Rameses II and the battle of Kedesh (1286), and the campaign of Merneptah (1220). Following the battle of Kedesh, a treaty was signed between Egypt and the Hittites, a treaty that was reinforced by the marriage of Rameses II to a Hittite princess. The Hittite kingdom collapsed in 1200 BCE, and Egypt again suffered a period of recession toward the end of the second millennium.

The period of the Patriarchs, as told in the books of Genesis and Exodus, began in about the middle of the second millennium. According to the biblical narrative, Abraham left Ur of the Chaldees, in southern Mesopotamia, and settled for awhile in Haran, east of the upper Euphrates. From there he wandered into the land of Canaan, where there was an abundance of city-states. The Patriarchs led their lives as nomadic shepherds. Once, because of drought and famine, Abraham descended into Egypt. His descendants kept ties with Haran but with the continuing drought, many of them also descended into Egypt, remaining there for four generations. The Exodus from Egypt, under the leadership of Moses, and the period of settlement in Canaan, under Joshua, mark the beginning of the history of the Israelites as a nation. The settlement of the land was an ongoing process, thought to have begun prior to the 13th century BCE and ending thereafter. Egyptian sources mention the name "Israel" on the Merneptah Stele (thus also called the Israel Stele) from 1220 BCE—testimony to the Israelites' existence in Canaan during that period.

During the period of conquest and settlement, the powers lying to the south and west of the land of Israel were in an extremely weakened state, leaving the Israelites to contend only with the city-states of Canaan and with the Sea Peoples, whose penetration reached its height at the beginning of the twelfth century BCE. In the beginning of the first millennium, the kings of Egypt once again sought to renew Egyptian rule in Canaan. In the days of King Rehoboam, the Egyptian king Shishak captured Jerusalem (in 924 BCE) and plundered the treasures of the Temple and the king's palace; still, he failed to establish his rule over the area he had conquered.

Between 1000 and 612 BCE, Assyria was the ruling power in the Middle East. In the battle of Qarqar in 853, the western kings attempted to form an alliance, headed by Hadad-ezer of Damascus, Ahab of Israel, and Irhuleni of Hamath, in order to halt the Assyrian army. However, after a few years, the Assyrians returned and proved invincible. One kingdom fell after the other: Damascus in 732, Israel (Samaria) in 722, and Judah became a subject-nation. At its height, Assyria's power spread over Elam, southeast Asia Minor, Syria, the land of the Philistines and, for a period, Upper Egypt, with its capital No-Amon (Thebes) plundered in 663 BCE.

Assyrian rule eventually fell to the Medes, in the east, and the Babylonians, in the south, who divided the former Assyrian territory among themselves. The capital of Nineveh was destroyed by the Medes in 612 BCE. The Babylonian kingdom reached its greatest extent in the days of Nebuchadnezzar II, who defeated the king of Egypt in the battle of Carchemish, in 605, and who brought an end to Assyrian rule in Elam, northern Syria, and in Asia Minor. In 598, Nebuchadnezzar ascended upon Jerusalem to suppress the rebellion led by Jehoiakim, king of Judah. He again returned to Judah, following Zedekiah's rebellion, at which time he destroyed one Judean city after another, burned Jerusalem and the Temple, and banished many of its inhabitants. Another exile occurred in 582 BCE, perhaps as a result of a further revolt.

The Median kingdom remained in power until 550 BCE, when it fell into the hands of the Persian king Cyrus, who annexed it to his kingdom. Within a few years, Cyrus succeeded in spreading his kingdom westward, to the Aegean Sea, and in 539 he captured Babylon. Cyrus, or "Cyrus the Great," is mentioned in the Bible thanks to his declaration allowing the exiled Jews of Babylon to return to their land. The land of Israel became a Persian province. Among its appointed governors were Zerubbabel, son of Shealtiel, and Nehemiah, son of Hachaliah, during whose time the Return to Zion had begun, the walls of Jerusalem were repaired, and the Temple was rebuilt. The Persian Empire, which remained in power for 200 years, extended from India to Cush (Nubia), until conquered by Alexander the Great in 331 BCE.

The Peoples and Lands of the Ancient Near East

Canaan is the ancient name of the land of Israel. It was promised to Abraham and his descendants, and was the land to which Abraham came from Haran. It was conquered by Joshua. Before and at the time of the conquest, Canaan was inhabited by seven nations: the Hittites, Perizzites, Amorites, Canaanites, Girgashites, Hivites, and the Jebusites. In some instances in the Bible, the name refers only to a Mediterranean coastal strip; in others, it refers to a large area that included Transjordan, southern Syria, and the eastern Sinai.

Amorites were a Semitic nation who settled in Syria and the land of Israel. At the end of the third millennium and the beginning of the second, they invaded Mesopotamia, captured Babylon, in whose culture they assimilated, and developed several small kingdoms. Many of the Babylonian kings were Amorites, among them Hammurabi (1792–1750 BCE), known for his famous law code. According to the Bible, they were mountain dwellers, contrary to the Canaanites, who settled in the valleys and on the coastal plain.

Hittites were an Indo-European-speaking nation who appeared in Anatolia and established the ancient kingdom of Heth (1700–1230 BCE), which, at its height, embraced most of the territory of Anatolia and Syria. Their capital was Hattusa, identified with Bogazkĩy. Like the Egyptians, they believed their king was an emissary of God and would turn into one at death. Their social structure was feudalistic and included slavery. Their language, though extinct, is known from hieroglyphic texts on documents and monuments, preserved for millennia in the royal archives at Hattusa. After the destruction of their kingdom, neo-Hittite kingdoms sprang up in Syria and southern Anatolia.

Edom is one of the neighboring nations of ancient Israel and close to it in origin. During the period of settlement and First Temple times, the Edomites dwelled on Mount Seir, south of the Dead Sea, but after the Babylonian exile, the desert tribes were driven away, moving to the Negeb and the Hebron hills. At the end of the First Temple period, the Edomites invaded Judah and speeded its destruction. They and their converts finally succumbed to John Hyrcanus the Hasmonean. Herod the Great was also an Edomite.

Moab was, according to the biblical narrative, the son of Lot by his eldest daughter, and chieftain of the Moabites, a Semitic nation, one of Israel's neighbors and foes who settled east of the Dead Sea. They had a highly developed culture. In the ninth century BCE, they rebelled against the Israelite conquest. The Mesha Stele, which was discovered at Dibon and dated to the ninth century BCE, bears a Moabite inscription that attests to the affinity of the Moabite script and language to those of Hebrew.

Ammonites were descendants of Ben-Ammi, the son of Lot by his youngest daughter. They lived in Transjordan, in the area of Rabbath-bene-ammon. Ammon was conquered by the tribes of Israel. The Ammonites attempted to rebel from time to time, but they were always defeated. Little evidence has been found about their culture. The few inscriptions that did survive revealed their language and script, like Moabite, are similar to Hebrew.

Amalek was a descendant of Esau, and chieftain of Edom. The ancient Amalekite nation apparently dwelled in the south and fought vigorously against the southern tribes of Israel. The Pentateuch throughout tried to eradicate the memory of this nation, and King Saul lost his throne because of his failure to do precisely that. They were finally destroyed in the days of King Hezekiah.

Assyria, an ancient kingdom in the upper Tigris valley, was named after its chief god, Asshur. The Assyrians, a Semitic nation, arrived in the Tigris valley in the middle of the third millennium, when, at first, they were a Babylonian protectorate. In the middle of the second millennium, Assyria became an empire, which was expanded in the days of Tiglath-pileser I (1120–1074 BCE), who captured the city of Babylon. In the days of Shalmaneser III (858–824), the land of Israel and Syria were also conquered. The Assyrian Empire reached its peak in the days of Tiglath-pileser III (754–725). Kings Sargon II, Sennacherib, and Esarhaddon were able to keep their domains intact, but in 612, the Babylonians and Medes captured the Assyrian capital of Nineveh and, in 609 BCE, Assyrian rule was put to an end.

Babylon is an ancient city and kingdom in the lower Euphrates valley. In the Bible, it also appears as Shinar, Chaldea, and Sheshach. The first known human culture—Sumer—developed in this area in the seventh millennium. The Babylonians were a Semitic people. The city of Babylon flourished between 2150 and 1740 BCE, in the days of the monarchical dynasty, among whose kings was Hammurabi. Afterward, it was under the threat of neighboring Assyria. The city was destroyed by the Assyrian king Sennacherib in 689, was rebuilt by Nebuchadnezzar II in 625, and was surrendered to King Cyrus the Great of Persia in 539. The kings of the new kingdom were Chaldeans, an Aramean tribe. Babylon played a significant role in the history of Israel: according to the Bible, Abraham came to Canaan from Ur of the Chaldees, Nebuchadnezzar conquered the kingdom of Judah (in 601) and exiled its people to Babylon (in 587), and, at the time of the Return to Zion by Ezra and Nehemiah, most of the people of Judah remained in Babylon.

Medes was one of the races descended from Japhet. The region southwest of the Caspian Sea was the site of the ancient kingdom of Media, whose inhabitants were seminomads. From the eighth to sixth centuries BCE, they united against Assyria and in 612, in the days of Cyaxares, they destroyed Nineveh with the help of the Babylonians. In 550, Media and Persia were combined in the expanding empire of Cyrus the Great, king of Persia.

Persia was an ancient kingdom between the Caspian Sea and the Persian Gulf. It became a large empire in the days of Cyrus the Great, in the mid-sixth century BCE. Cyrus allowed the exiled Jews to return to Judah (Zion) and to rebuild the Temple. The Book of Esther describes the events that occurred in the days of Ahasuerus (Xerxes); it is not clear, however, which Ahasuerus.

Midian was a son of Abraham and his wife Keturah, and progenitor of the Midianites, who dwelled south of the land of Canaan, between the Sinai and Edom mountains. Their origin is unknown. They wandered from the Arabian peninsula along two routes: the southern group settled on the banks of the Red Sea, in the region of Edom and south of it, while the others reached as far north as the Syrian desert. According to the Bible, the Midianites joined with the Moabites in preventing the Israelites from conquering their lands. Moses subdued them. The Israelites were under Midianite rule for seven years, until the judge Gideon rose up and expelled them, along with the Amalekites.

Aram is descended from Shem. It is the name for the Semitic peoples/tribes whose origins can probably be found west of the Euphrates. According to the Bible, the Arameans were related to the Patriarchs. Although they are first mentioned in the fourteenth century BCE, their presence increased only in the eleventh century BCE, when they spread out over extensive territories—from the Euphrates and Tigris valleys to southern Anatolia and from Armenia to northern Arabia. They established several kingdoms, over which their hegemony passed from one kingdom to the other. One of the most important was Aram-Damascus. Aramaic was an international language in the ancient world of the first millennium, until superseded by Greek. The Arameans adopted the Phoenician alphabet, from which the Hebrew square script and the Arabic script developed.

Philistines were a non-Semitic nation who arrived in Canaan in the beginning of the twelfth century BCE, repelled the attacks of the Israelites, and took control of the coastal area that was named after them—Philistia. Tradition has it that they were one of the Sea Peoples who left Crete. They were known as seafarers and for their belligerency. They remained in their kingdoms until their assimilation during the Hellenistic period.

Sea Peoples were seafaring tribes. In the thirteenth and twelfth centuries BCE, they wiped out the Hittite kingdom and settled in Asia Minor, the Aegean area, and North Africa. In 1170 BCE, they were almost completely destroyed by Rameses III, the king of Egypt. Some scholars identify them with the Achaeans, others with the Etruscans or the Philistines.

Chronology of the Old Testament

The first section of the Bible, the Pentateuch, opens with the creation of the world and ends with the death of Moses, a span of about 2,500 years, according to Jewish traditional chronological dating. The rest of the Bible (Former Prophets, Latter Prophets, Hagiographa) is placed within a period of about 800 years, from the conquest of the land of Canaan in the thirteenth century to the Return to Zion and the rebuilding of the Temple in the mid-fifth century.

Presented here is a table of the major events and their dates, some of which are conjectured, others estimated, and still others more or less exact. It should be noted that even the "exact" dates, based on one of several conventional dating methods, may differ from other such dates by a gap of ten years or less.

All the dates referred to below, and throughout this Atlas, are before the Common Era, thus precluding the need to append BCE to the year specified.

Period of the Patriarchs	1st half of 2nd
(Abraham, Isaac and Jacob)	millennium
Exodus from Egypt	1st half of 13th century
Wanderings of the Israelites	1st half of 13th century
The Israelite Entry into Transjordan	**Mid-13th century**
The Israelite entry into Canaan	Mid-13th century
Battle of Gibeon	Mid-13th century
The rise of Judah and the southern tribes	2nd half of 13th century
Conquest of the Shephelah districts	End of 13th century
Period of the Judges	**12th–11th centuries**
The war of Deborah	Beginning of 12th century
Battle of the Waters of Merom	Beginning of 12th century
Story of the concubine in Gibeah	1st half of 12th century
The war of Ehud	12th century
The war of Gideon	12th century
The kingdom of Abimelech	12th century
The war of Jephthah	End of 12th century
The deeds of Samson	1st half of 11th century
Battle of Eben-ezer	Mid-11th century
The wanderings of the Ark of the Covenant	Mid-11th century
The leadership of Samuel	2nd half of 11th century
Saul searches for his asses	2nd half of 11th century
The kingdom of Saul	1025–1006
David's duel with Goliath	1010
The kingdoms of David and Eshbaal	1006–1004
The battle by the pool at Gibeon David's	1005
conquest of Jerusalem	1004
The Philistine wars of David	1000
The Kingdom of David	**990–968**
David's campaigns in Transjordan	990
The conquest of Aram-zobah and Damascus	990
The conquest of Edom	990
The rebellion of Absalom	978
The rebellion of Sheba the son of Bichri	977
The Kingdom of Solomon	**968–928**
Division of the Monarchy	**928**

Kingdom of Judah		Kingdom of Israel		Wars/Military Campaigns	
Rehoboam	928–911	Jeroboam	928–907	Shishak's campaign	924
Abijah	911–908			Conquests of Abijah	911
Asa	908–867	Nadab	907–906	Zerah's campaign	900
		Baasha	906–883	Wars of Asa and	
				Baasha	855
		Elah	883–882	Ben-hadad I's campaign	
		Zimri	882	Conquests of Mesha,	
				king of Moab	
		Omri	882–871		
		Ahab	871–851	Ahab's wars in Aram	
					855–850
Jehoshaphat	867–851			Battle of Qarqar	853
Jehoram	851–843	Ahaziah	851–850		
		Jehoram	850–842		
Ahaziah	843–842				
Athaliah	842–836	Jehu	842–814	Shalmaneser III's	
				campaign	841
Joash	836–799	Jehoahaz	814–800	Hazael's campaigns	
					815–810
		Joash	800–785	Adad-nirari's	
				campaign	806
				Conquests of Joash and	
				Jeroboam II	790–770
Amaziah	799–786			Wars of Amaziah and	
				Joash	786
Uzziah	786–758	Jeroboam II	785–749	Uzziah's conquests	
					Mid-8th century
Jotham	758–742	Zechariah	749		
		Shallum	748		
		Menahem	748–737		
Ahaz	742–726	Pekahiah	737–735	Rezin and Pekah's	
		Pekah	735–731	campaign in Judah	734
		Exile of Israel	733		
		Hoshea	731–722		
Hezekiah	726–697	Fall of Samaria	722		
		Assyrian rule	722–628	Sennacherib's	
				campaign	701
Manasseh	697–642				
Amon	642–640				
Josiah	640–609	Josiah's rule	628–609		
Jehoahaz	609–608	Egyptian rule	609–604	Pharaoh Necho's	
				campaign	609
Jehoiakim	608–597	Babylonian		Nebuchadnezzar's	
		rule	604–539	campaign	605–604
Jehoiachin	597				
Zedekiah	597–587				
Exile of Judah	597				
Destruction of the				Nebuchadnezzar's	
First Temple	587			campaign	587
Babylonian					
rule	587–538				
Persian rule	538 ff.	Persian rule	538 ff.		
Cyrus' decree	538				
Return to Zion	538–445				
Zerubbabel governs					
Judah	522				
Building of the					
Temple	520–515				
Ezra	457–445				
Nehemiah	445–425				

The Patriarchs

According to the Bible, Patriarch is the traditional name given to each of the three fathers of the Jewish nation: Abraham, Isaac, and Jacob. In Jewish tradition it is customary to add the Hebrew epithet *Avinu* ("Our Father") to each name. They are seen as spiritual prototypes of the nation of Israel.

Abraham (in the beginning called Abram), the son of Terah, brother of Nahor and Haran, is the first of the three Patriarchs. He left the faith of his forefathers, who were idol worshipers, for the belief in one God. He abandoned his father's house and his homeland, Ur of the Chaldees, and descended into the land of Canaan. Through him was made the covenant between the nation of Israel and God, symbolized in the Jewish circumcision ceremony. God promised him that he would be the father of a multitude of nations and that his descendants would inherit the land of Canaan. Abraham and his wife Sarah are buried in the Cave of Machpelah, in Hebron.

Isaac, the son born to Abraham and Sarah in their old age, is the second of the three Patriarchs. He was destined to be sacrificed by his father Abraham at God's command (the "binding of Isaac"). He married Rebekah, the daughter of Bethuel, sister of Laban, of his father's family. He was the only Patriarch who lived his entire life in the land of Canaan. He and Rebekah, like his parents before him, are buried in the Cave of Machpelah.

Jacob, the son of Isaac and Rebekah, is the last of the Patriarchs. He bought the birthright from his twin brother Esau "for bread and pottage of lentiles" (Gen. 25:34). Jacob married Leah and Rachel, the daughters of Laban, son of Bethuel. His 12 sons were the progenitors of the tribes of Israel. In the years of drought, he descended with his sons into Egypt. He died in Goshen but his remains were brought for burial in the tomb of his forefathers, the Cave of Machpelah, where his wife Leah was buried before him (his second wife, Rachel, was buried on the way to Ephrath). Jacob was also called Israel, after which the nation, the children and the land of Israel were named.

The Matriarchs

Traditionally, Matriarch is the name given to each of the wives of the three Patriarchs: Sarah, the wife of Abraham; Rebekah, the wife of Isaac; and Leah and Rachel, the wives of Jacob. In Jewish tradition it is customary to add the Hebrew epithet *Imenu* ("Our Mother") to each name. Sarah, Rebekah and Leah were buried alongside their husbands in the Cave of Machpelah; Rachel was buried in the way to Ephrath ("Rachel's Tomb").

Sarah (in the beginning called Sarai) was the wife of Abraham and the first of the four Matriarchs. She was barren and gave her handmaid Hagar to Abraham so that he would be granted offspring, but when Hagar gave birth to Ishmael, Sarah decreed their banishment. At the age of 90, she became pregnant with Isaac, so called because she laughed at the news that she would be giving birth to a son (*Yitzhak*, i.e., Isaac, derives from the Hebrew root *tz-h-k*, "to laugh").

Rebekah, the daughter of Bethuel, son of Nahor, brother of Abraham, was the wife of Isaac, son of Abraham, and the second of the four Matriarchs. About 20 years after her wedding, she gave birth to twins, Esau and Jacob. She favored Jacob over

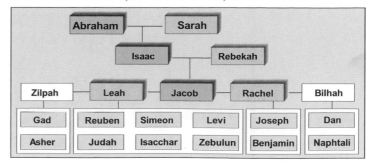

Esau, and cunningly misled Isaac so he would bless Jacob with the blessing of the first-born, instead of his elder son, Esau.

Leah, the daughter of Laban, son of Bethuel, brother of Rebekah, was the third of the four Matriarchs. Jacob first married Leah instead of her sister Rachel, through her father's trickery. She bore Jacob six sons (Reuben, Simeon, Levi, Judah, Issachar, and Zebu-lun) and one daughter (Dinah). She gave to Jacob her handmaid Zilpah, who in turn bore Jacob two sons (Gad and Asher).

Rachel, the daughter of Laban, son of Bethuel, brother of Rebekah, was the last of the four Matriarchs and the beloved wife of Jacob. She was the mother of Joseph and Benjamin. She gave to Jacob her handmaid Bilhah, who bore Jacob two more sons (Dan and Naphtali). She died while giving birth to Benjamin and was buried on the way to Ephrath ("Rachel's Tomb").

The Exodus from Egypt and the Entry into Canaan
(Beginning of the 13th century–mid-13th century)

The route taken by the Israelites after their Exodus from Egypt, under the leadership of Moses, until their entry into the land of Canaan is not altogether clear, because most of the places and way stations described in the Bible have not been identified with certainty.

Migdol and Baal-zaphon, mentioned at the start of their journey, are known from Egyptian sources as fortresses at the northeastern edge of the Nile Delta. Because the Israelites did not choose the Way of the Sea (also called for a time the Way of the Philistines), along which Egyptian fortresses and way stations were scattered, they probably detoured this route from the south, in the area of the Red Sea, which they crossed on dry ground.

In the third month of the Exodus from Egypt there occurred the "revelation at Mount Sinai," in which the Law was given to the people of Israel through Moses.

In the wilderness of Sinai, the Israelites built a tabernacle (in Hebrew, *mishkan*)—the Tent of the Meeting, also known as the Tent of the Congregation—in which was placed the Ark of the Covenant, containing the stone tablets of the Law that were given to Moses during the Revelation on Mount Sinai. The portable tabernacle served as the focal center for God's work during the years of wandering in the wilderness and in the period of settlement in Canaan, until the building of Solomon's Temple in Jerusalem, to which the Ark of the Covenant and the rest of the Sanctuary's utensils were transferred.

The locations of the numerous way stations, through which the Israelites passed in their wanderings in the Sinai wilderness, are based on conjecture only. Only Kadesh-barnea has been identified with certainty—an oasis rich in springs, on the border of the Sinai and the land of Canaan. Kadesh-barnea was the

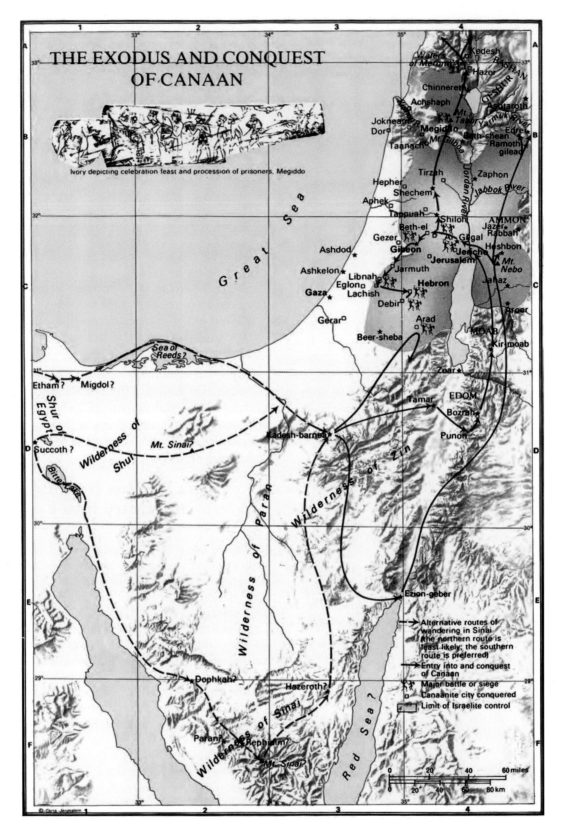

THE EXODUS AND CONQUEST OF CANAAN

Ivory depicting celebration feast and procession of prisoners, Megiddo

Legend:
- Alternative routes of wandering in Sinai (the northern route is least likely; the southern route is preferred)
- Entry into and conquest of Canaan
- Major battle or siege
- Canaanite city conquered
- Limit of Israelite control

focus of the Israelites in their wanderings. From here the spies set out to scout the land of Canaan, and here the tribes organized their penetration into the land. The story of the spies is mainly linked to Hebron and its environs, but their final objective was actually Lebo-hamath, at the northern edge of Canaan.

The first attempt to invade the land of Canaan, which was made south of the Negeb and the Judean hills, failed as a result of strong resistance from the Negebites, the Canaanites and the Amalekites, headed by the king of Arad.

According to the Bible there were two routes by which the Israelites had penetrated the land of Canaan, both of which passed through Transjordan. Settled in the southern sections of Trans-jordan were a number of nations close in origin to Israel—Edom, Moab, and Ammon—as well as the Amorite kingdom of Heshbon, which spread between Moab and Ammon. Sihon, the king of Heshbon, fought against the king of Moab and conquered the entire plain of Moab up to the river Arnon. Moses, wishing to take advantage of this situation, turned to the kings of Edom and Moab and requested permission for the Israelites to pass through their lands in order to reach the land of Sihon; but the kings of Edom and Moab refused, and Moses was forced to retreat as far south as Elath (Ezion-geber), bypassing

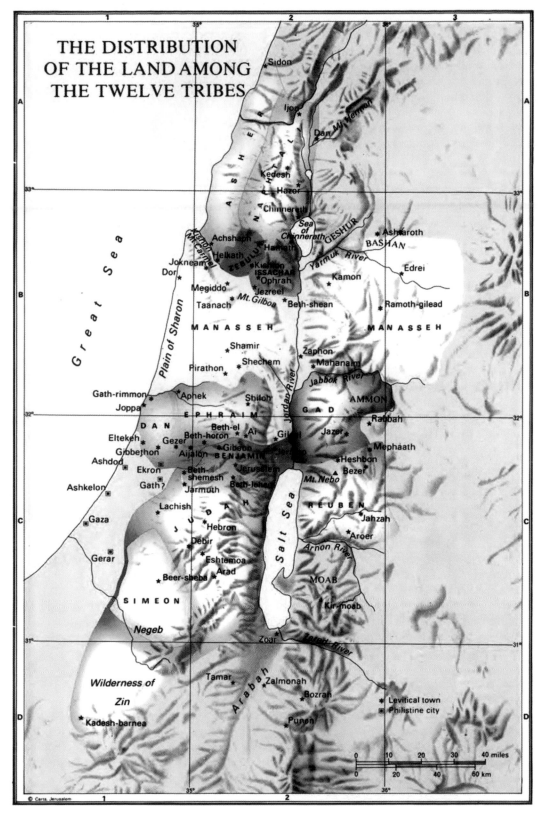

THE DISTRIBUTION
OF THE LAND AMONG
THE TWELVE TRIBES

Edom and Moab to the east, and invade Sihon's kingdom from the wilderness of Kedemoth.

The other route, which is indicated from the list of wilderness stations, passes through the heart of Edom and Moab, reaching the plains of Moab, opposite Jericho.

The life and deeds of Moses end in the plains of Moab. The story dramatically recounts the elderly leader viewing from the top of Mount Nebo the land he so longed for and yet did not reach.

Moses was the son of Amram and Jochebed, of the tribe of Levi, and the leader of the Israelites in their Exodus from Egypt and in their wanderings in the wilderness. He received the Ten Commandments on Mount Sinai, also known as the Law of Moses. He is considered the progenitor of the Prophets. He is a central figure in the books of Exodus, Leviticus, Numbers, and Deuteronomy. According to the biblical narrative, he gained closer communion with God than any other man. He is also described as a military leader: he defeated Amalek, Sihon the Amorite, and Og, the king of Bashan, and endowed Israel with Transjordan. He himself was forbidden to enter the Promised Land, as punishment for disobeying God's command at Marah by smiting a rock to obtain water instead of speaking to it as he had been commanded. His burial place is unknown.

Aaron the High Priest was the son of Amram and Jochebed, of the tribe of Levi, the brother of Moses, his spokesman and right-hand aide in leading the Israelites through the wilderness. He succumbed to the demands of the multitude by making the golden calf. He was the first High Priest and progenitor of the priesthood. The priests, descended from Aaron the High Priest, are also known as "the sons of Aaron" or "the house of Aaron." He died on Mount Hor and, like Moses, was forbidden to enter the Promised Land because of disobeying God's command at Marah.

Joshua, the son of Nun, of the tribe of Ephraim, had served Moses since the time of his youth. He accompanied Moses on his ascent up to Mount Sinai. He led the warriors against Amalek and was one of the 12 spies sent by Moses to scout the land of Canaan. He became leader of the Israelites after Moses' death, during the period of conquest and settlement of the land, as related in the Book of Joshua. He conquered Jericho and Ai, and defeated the southern kings and the allied northern kings. After the conquest he divided the land of Israel among the tribes and turned Shiloh into a spiritual center. He was buried within his own allotment, at Timnath-serah.

The Conquest and Settlement
(Second half of the 13th century–12th century)

The conquest of the land of Canaan is described in the books of Joshua and Judges. However, the versions are not always identical—the deeds of one tribe are occasionally ascribed to Israel as a whole, while the same acts attributed to Joshua are sometimes ascribed to one of the Judges as well. Events were given mostly partial, fragmentary descriptions or sometimes none at all. Moreover, the order of events remains somewhat obscure and, as a result, any descriptive survey is of necessity conjectural.

The conquest of the land of Canaan begins with the crossing of the river Jordan at Gilgal, but it should be noted that not all the tribes crossed the river. Some continued to move northward, in Transjordan, capturing the Amorite lands, where the tribes of Gad, Reuben, and the half-tribe of Manasseh remained and settled. Nevertheless, the main body of tribes did cross the Jordan westward and after capturing Jericho and Ai, they penetrated into the heart of the hill country.

The inhabitants of the land were Canaanite, mostly Semitic peoples, who are mentioned in the Bible in various connections: the Canaanites, the Hittites, the Hivites, the Perizzites, the Girgashites, the Amorites, and the Jebusites. They dwelled in independent city-states that sometimes banded together, primarily for the purpose of warring against a common enemy. In the beginning of the twelfth century, the land was invaded by a non-Semitic nation—the Philistines—who took control of the coastal area that was named after them, Philistia. Apparently, they were one of the Sea Peoples, a nation who had defeated the Hittite kingdom in the thirteenth and twelfth centuries; settled in Asia Minor, in the Aegean coastal area and in North Africa; and were almost destroyed by Rameses III, the king of Egypt, in 1170. The traces of their remains are scattered throughout the land of Israel.

The Bible describes the conquest of the land as a single campaign under the leadership of Joshua, son of Nun, a campaign that began with the capture of Jericho and that ended with the great battle against Jabin, the king of Hazor, by the Waters of Merom.

According to the Book of Joshua, the land of Canaan was conquered in stages. During the stage of penetration, Jericho

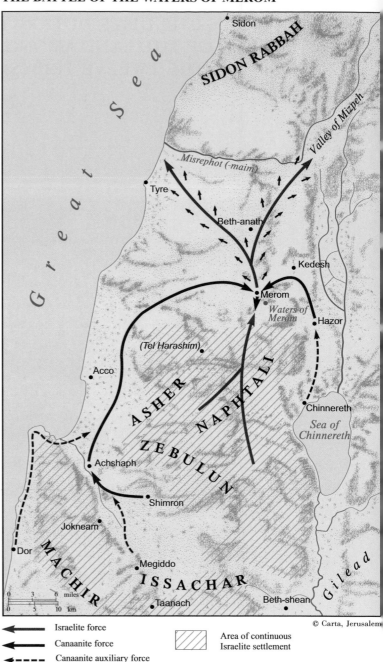

THE BATTLE OF THE WATERS OF MEROM

© Carta, Jerusalem

⟵ Israelite force

⟵ Canaanite force

◀- - - Canaanite auxiliary force

▨ Area of continuous Israelite settlement

and Ai were captured, and a pact was made with the Gibeonites. The main event of the next stage was the battle of Gibeon. The Israelites rallied around Joshua to come to the aid of their allies, the Gibeonites, after the king of Jerusalem called up his allies to punish the Gibeonites for making a covenant with Israel. The Canaanite forces were routed, thereby creating conditions for the next stage—the rise of the southern tribes of Judah and Simeon. The tribes of Judah and Simeon probably came from the north, the Judahites settling in the Judean hills and the Simeonites, in the Shephelah (lowlands) and the Negeb. On the other hand, the Calebites and the Kenizzites, who were incorporated in the tribe of Judah, probably came from the south, capturing Hebron and Debir and settling in the area of Arad. The war of Deborah and the battle of the Waters of Merom—both aimed against the king of Hazor, Jabin—brought about the consolidation of the northern tribes.

In the twelfth century, at the end of the period of settlement of the tribes, the principal rival peoples in the land of Israel had become well established in their respective areas: the Canaanites

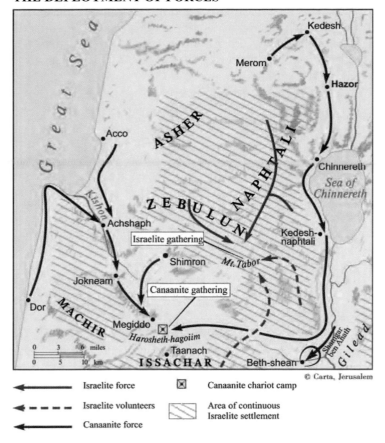

Israelite force — Canaanite chariot camp ☒

Israelite volunteers ◄ - - -

Area of continuous Israelite settlement ▨

Canaanite force ◄

© Carta, Jerusalem

The Tribes of Israel

The twelve tribes of Israel, descendants of the sons of Jacob born to him by Leah and Rachel and Bilhah and Zilpah, are Reuben, Simeon, Levi, Judah, Issachar, Zebulun, Dan, Naphtali, Gad, Asher, Joseph, and Benjamin. The tribe of Joseph split into two tribes—Ephraim and Manasseh—resulting in the number of tribes actually reaching thirteen. Nevertheless, only twelve tribes were allotted territories in the land of Israel (the tribe of Levi, who earned its livelihood from donations and tithes received from the other tribes, did not receive a territory of its own and its cities were dispersed among the remaining tribal allotments).

The ties among the tribes after the period of settlement were rather weak, with their sole link found in the spiritual center they shared at Shiloh. Sometimes they did not join forces even when warring against a common enemy. Each tribe, or group of tribes, would for the most part fight separately. At times, they even fought among themselves, as, for example, in the days of Jephthah or following the incident of the "concubine in Gibeah" (Judg. 19–21). With the establishment of the monarchy, the differences among the tribes grew fainter, a process that was accelerated when the Assyrians exiled the ten northern tribes in the eighth century. The remaining remnants gathered in and around the area of Judah (the tribe of Simeon had already been incorporated in the tribe of Judah). Eventually, all the Israelites who did not assimilate into other nations were named "Jews." Only the tribe of Levi, because of its sacred status, kept its lineage.

The Period of the Judges
(12th–11th centuries)

The period of the Judges is the period between the death of Joshua and the establishment of the monarchy. The tribes of Israel continued to consolidate, each in their own territory, while the ties between them remained weak. The central sanctuary, which was located at Shiloh, within the tribal allotment of Ephraim, contained the Ark of the Covenant, the symbol of national unity, but its power as a unifying force was limited. The wars during this period were mainly ones against neighboring

in the northern valleys and plains, the Philistines on the southern coastal plain, and the tribes of Israel in the hill country and in Transjordan. The unconquered territories remained as foreign enclaves within the tribal allotments. The Book of Joshua calls the regions included within the borders of the Promised Land and not conquered during the period of settlement "the land that yet remains"—Philistia, in the south, and Phoenicia, Lebanon and the Lebanon valley, in the north.

THE WAR OF EHUD

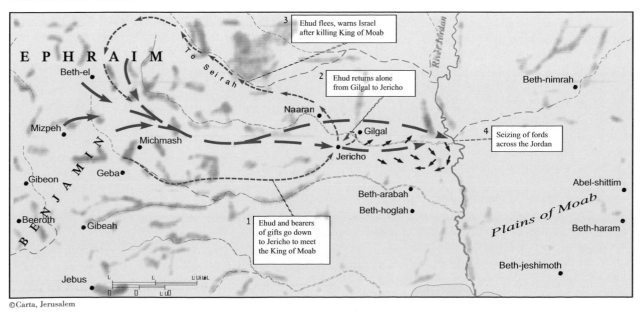

3 Ehud flees, warns Israel after killing King of Moab

2 Ehud returns alone from Gilgal to Jericho

4 Seizing of fords across the Jordan

1 Ehud and bearers of gifts go down to Jericho to meet the King of Moab

Israelite force ◄
Moabites ◄ - ◄ -

© Carta, Jerusalem

THE WAR OF GIDEON

© Carta, Jerusalem

wonderful wanderings was the Ark returned to Kiriath-jearim, remaining there until King David brought it to Jerusalem.

A special chapter in the period of the Judges is the story of the three-year kingdom of Abimelech. Abimelech attempted to succeed his father, Gideon Jerubbaal, as ruler, and to turn his leadership into a kingdom with the help of the Shechemites,

THE BATTLE OF EBEN-EZER

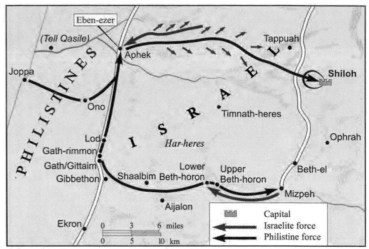

© Carta, Jerusalem

powers or incursors who infiltrated the land to pillage and destroy. Under these conditions there developed a system of rule by local leaders who were called "Judges."

The judge was chieftain of a tribe, or of several neighboring tribes. Usually, he was called on to lead in an hour of great danger, and after he succeeded in overcoming the enemy and distancing the threat, he would be recognized as a leader even in times of peace, to "judge Israel." However, there were also judges who did not start out as war heroes. Recounted in the Book of Judges are Othniel, son of Kenaz; Ehud, son of Gera; Shamgar, son of Anath; Deborah the Prophetess; Gideon, son of Joash; Abimelech; Tola, son of Puah; Jair the Gileadite; Jephthah the Gileadite; Ibzan; Elon the Zebulunite; Abdon, son of Hillel; Samson; Eli the Priest; and Samuel the Prophet.

The "great" Judges, considered to be saviors, were Othniel, Ehud, Shamgar, Deborah the Prophetess, Gideon, Jephthah the Gileadite, Samson, and Samuel the Prophet. Othniel, Ehud, Gideon, and Jephthah fought mainly against the neighboring nations in Transjordan, who attempted to infiltrate Israel, and against desert marauders who would pillage the land's cities and produce. Othniel defeated the king of Aram-naharaim, an invader from Mesopotamia. Gideon defeated the Midianites. Ehud repelled the attempts of the Moabites to expand their borders at Israel's expense, and Jephthah repelled similar attempts made by the Ammonites.

The names of Shamgar, Samson and Samuel are associated with the wars against the Philistines, who dwelled along the southern coast of the land of Israel and who, because of their administrative and military superiority, attempted to subdue the tribes of Israel.

The most serious confrontation between Israel and the Philistines occurred in the mid-eleventh century, between Aphek and Eben-ezer, known as the "battle of Eben-ezer." The war ended with the defeat of the allied tribes of Israel. The Ark of the Covenant, which had been brought from Shiloh to the battlefield, fell into Philistine hands, and Shiloh itself was destroyed and ceased being a spiritual center. Only after some

who considered him one of their own because of his mother's lineage. However, the people of Shechem refused to accept his rule as king of Israel. Abimelech destroyed Shechem and died during the siege of Thebez.

The Book of Judges ends with the narrative of the "concubine in Gibeah." This is the story about the fraternal war between the tribe of Benjamin and the other Israelite tribes. The war was bloody and the tribe of Benjamin was almost completely annihilated. The tribe was returned to the fold and was restored only after a way had been found to provide wives for the remaining Benjaminites, who had fled to the wilderness "unto the rock Rimmon."

The last of the Judges was Samuel the Prophet, whose story is told in the biblical book named after him. He was also the only judge to be described as the leader of all Israel and symbolized the transition toward the establishment of the monarchy. He anointed King Saul, and afterward replaced him with King David.

THE WANDERINGS OF THE ARK OF THE COVENANT

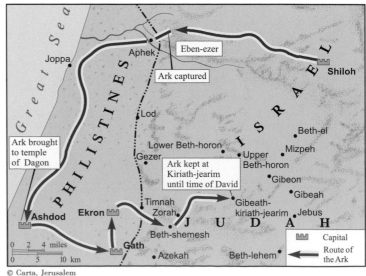

© Carta, Jerusalem

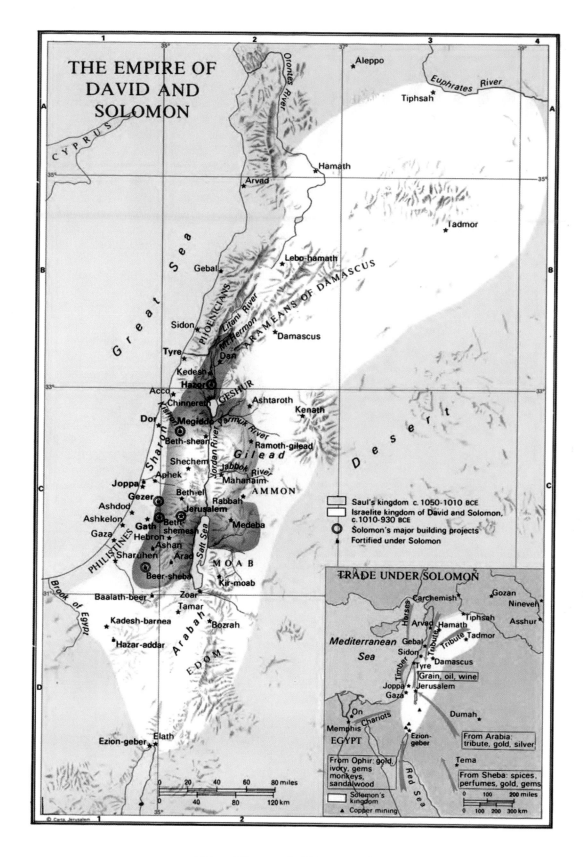

THE EMPIRE OF
DAVID AND
SOLOMON

Saul's kingdom c. 1050-1010 BCE
Israelite kingdom of David and Solomon, c. 1010-930 BCE
Solomon's major building projects
Fortified under Solomon

TRADE UNDER SOLOMON

Grain, oil, wine

From Ophir: gold, ivory, gems, monkeys, sandalwood
Solomon's kingdom
Copper mining

From Arabia: tribute, gold, silver

From Sheba: spices, perfumes, gold, gems

© Carta, Jerusalem

The United Monarchy
(End of 11th century–end of 10th century)

The United Monarchy is the term ascribed to the kingdom of Israel in the days of Kings Saul, David, and Solomon. Unlike the Judges before them and the kings of Judah and Israel after them, these three kings ruled over all the twelve tribes of Israel. The monarchy arose as a result of the people's demand to crown a king, apparently in order to cope with the Philistine threat. The United Monarchy lasted for about one hundred years and was divided after the death of Solomon.

Saul, the first king of Israel, was the son of Kish of the tribe of Benjamin. His reign is described in the Bible in three versions: in the beginning, he was secretly anointed king by Samuel the Prophet, then he was chosen (by the casting of lots) at Mizpeh to reign over the tribe of Benjamin, and, after the victory at Jabesh-gilead, he was coronated at Gilgal to rule over the whole of Israel. He reigned from approximately 1025 to 1006. Saul began with a war against the Philistines, driving them from the

THE KINGDOMS OF DAVID AND ESHBAAL

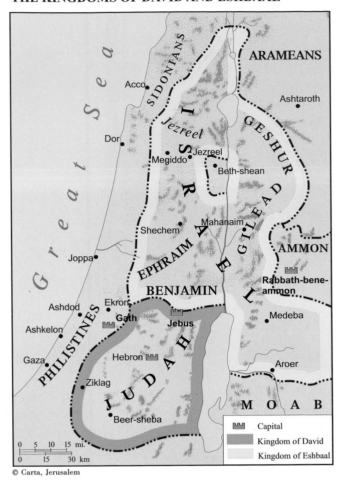

© Carta, Jerusalem

broke off alliances at will. During his reign (1004–968), David completed Israel's war with the Philistines and defeated them, conquered Jerusalem from the Jebusites and made it the capital of Israel (1004), set up a monarchical regime and expanded its borders, organized the administration of the new state, and established a large, disciplined and well-equipped army. Apart from all this, he was also a spiritual man and a "sweet psalmist of Israel," as tradition has it. Apart from his lamentations about Saul and Jonathan and Abner, the son of Ner, tradition also accredits him as a psalmist. His image is inscribed in the people's consciousness as a symbol for a warrior who redeemed his people from the hands of their enemy, an admired king who established the Israelite monarchy, built Jerusalem, and brought security and glory to the nation.

Solomon succeeded his father David as king of Israel (968–928). The days of his reign and those of David are considered the Golden Age of the Israelite monarchy. He organized the kingdom and divided it into districts, built cities and fortresses, founded numerous enterprises and established commercial ties with states both near and far, and he built the Temple in Jerusalem. To finance all this, he imposed heavy taxes that caused increasing unrest among the people and brought about the division of the kingdom after his death. Tradition ascribes Solomon with the composition of the books of Proverbs, The Song of Songs, Ecclesiastes, and Psalm 72 in the Book of Psalms. His image, wealth and wisdom are praised in the Bible and in Jewish legend (and following that, also in Christian and in Muslim legend), and he was granted the epithet, "the wisest of all men."

hill country and continuing to fight them throughout his reign (until he was defeated at the battle of Gilboa). Saul also inflicted heavy defeats on the aggressive neighbors of Israel in the east (Ammon, Moab, Edom) and on Zobah in the north and Amalek in the south. Saul's victories lifted the people's spirit and laid the cornerstone for the mighty kingdom that was to follow.

Saul was the first to establish a regular Israelite army—3,000 soldiers in all—and to command them personally, or with the help of his son Jonathan. However, he was unable to consolidate all the tribes into a single nation. During the war with Amalek, a rift formed between Samuel and Saul, because Saul had spared King Amalek and not killed him as God commanded. Saul's situation became even more complicated in the war with David, as related in the Book of Samuel, in the beginning because of jealousy, and later because of a power struggle. Saul is described as a tragic figure given to volatile moods. When he was defeated at the battle with the Philistines on Mount Gilboa, he fell on his sword and died.

After Saul's death, the kingdom split in two for the first time: Abner, the son of Ner, proclaimed Eshbaal (Ish-bosheth), one of Saul's surviving sons, as king of Israel, at Mahanaim beyond the Jordan, while the elders of Judah proclaimed David as king, at Hebron. Eshbaal and David's kingdoms existed side by side for about two years (1006–1004), until David overpowered Eshbaal and combined the kingdoms of Israel and Judah into one.

David, the son of Jesse, is the founder of the Davidic dynasty—the House of David. He was already active in the days of Saul's kingdom. He fought Goliath, was appointed commander-in-chief by Saul, aroused Saul's wrath and jealousy, established for himself a private army of warriors, organized incursions, and

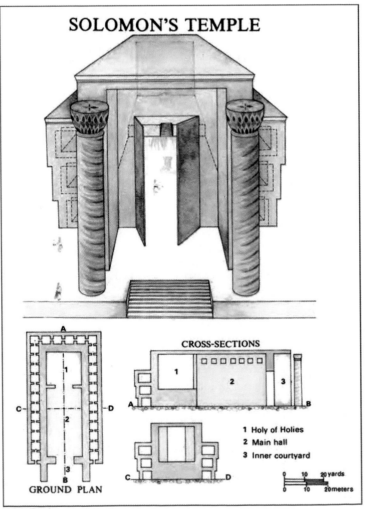

SOLOMON'S TEMPLE

CROSS-SECTIONS

1 Holy of Holies
2 Main hall
3 Inner courtyard

GROUND PLAN

© Carta, Jerusalem

60

The Kingdom of Israel

The northern kingdom of Israel arose after the division of the United Monarchy of Israel. It embraced the tribal territories not included in the kingdom of Judah. It existed from 928 until the destruction of Samaria (in c. 722). During this period, it was ruled by kings of various dynasties. Jeroboam, the son of Nabat and founder of the kingdom, rebelled against King Solomon and, in the days of Solomon's son Rehoboam, was crowned at Shechem. He built royal sanctuaries at Beth-el, in the southern part of his kingdom, and at Dan in the north, in order to divert the ten tribes from their pilgrimage to the Temple in Jerusalem. There was constant friction between the kingdom of Israel and Aram in the north and with the kingdom of Judah in the south. Omri made Samaria his capital, made a covenant with Tyre, and introduced Baal worship to the land, which grew in the days of his son Ahab. The prophets (Elijah, Elisha, and Micaiah, the son of Imlah) zealously opposed Omri and Ahab. Together with Aram, Ahab succeeded in defeating the Assyrians in the battle of Qarqar (in 853) and his regnal years saw a period of prosperity. Jehu destroyed the House of Omri and cleansed the land of Baal worship. However, he lost the support of Tyre and was forced to pay a levy to Assyria in return for aid in his struggle with the Arameans. In the days of Jeroboam II, the kingdom of Israel enjoyed its second, and last, period of growth. Aram was repelled and the kingdom of Israel spread to the Bashan and the Golan and, in Aram, up to Lebo-hamath. The last kings of Israel were unable to halt the Assyrians' thrust toward Egypt. After two failed revolts, the kingdom of Israel was conquered by the Assyrians, who exiled some of the Israelites eastward, replacing them with inhabitants brought from other districts of the Assyrian kingdom (the Cuthites). The history of the kings of Israel is told mainly in the Book of Kings and in I Chronicles.

The Kings of Israel

928–907	Jeroboam (son of Nabat)
907–906	Nadab (son of Jeroboam)
906–883	Baasha
883–882	Elah (son of Baasha)
882	Zimri
882–871	Omri
871–851	Ahab (son of Omri)
851–850	Ahaziah (son of Ahab)
850–842	Jehoram/Joram (son of Ahab)
842–814	Jehu
814–800	Jehoahaz (son of Jehu)
800–785	Joash/Jehoash (son of Jehoahaz)
785–749	Jeroboam II (son of Jehoash)
749	Zechariah (son of Jeroboam)
748	Shallum
748–737	Menahem
737–735	Pekahiah (son of Menahem)
735–731	Pekah
731–722	Hoshea

The kings of Israel numbered 19—two from the house of Jeroboam, two from the house of Baasha, four from the house of Omri, five from the house of Jehu, two from the house of Menahem, and four individual kings.

Jeroboam, son of Nabat, was the first king of Israel (928–907) after the division of Solomon's kingdom. He served under Solomon and rebelled against him. When Solomon ordered him put to death, Jeroboam fled to Shishak, the king of Egypt. After Solomon's death, he was proclaimed king over the ten tribes, as prophesied by Ahijah the Shilonite. He made his capital at Shechem, then at Penuel beyond the Jordan, and finally at Tirzah. He reinstated cult worship of the two golden calves and established altars for them in Beth-el and Dan, after which pagan worship continued in the kingdom of Israel until its destruction. His kingdom suffered from incursions by the Egyptian king Shishak and from the hostile acts of Rehoboam and Abijah, the kings of Judah.

Nadab, son of Jeroboam, was king for two years (907–906). During the siege of the Philistine city of Gibbethon, Baasha, son of Ahijah, conspired against Nadab, had him put to death, and seized the throne.

Baasha, son of Ahijah, of the house of Issachar, was the third king of Israel (906–883). He rebelled against Nadab, the son of Jeroboam, destroyed his entire family, and seized the throne. Throughout his reign he battled against Asa, king of Judah, and for this purpose he allied himself with King Ben-hadad I of Aram-Damascus. However, Asa bribed Ben-hadad, who broke off his ties with Baasha.

Elah, son of Baasha, reigned for less than two years (883–882). He was killed by Zimri, one of his two commanders of the chariots, who tried to seize his throne after destroying the entire house of Baasha.

Zimri was the fifth sovereign of Israel (882). He was commander of half the chariots of Elah, and killed the king and his family in an attempt to gain the throne. When the army heard of Elah's murder, the soldiers proclaimed their general, Omri, king, who in turn marched his army against Zimri at Tirzah. The self-crowned Zimri retreated into the late king's palace, set it on fire, and perished in its ruins after only seven days of rule.

Omri was the sixth king of Israel (882–871) and founder of the Omri dynasty. He was an army general at the time of Elah's murder. After the murder, a revolt broke out over the rule between Omri, who was coronated by his army, and Tibni, the son of Ginath, whom "half the people" desired to raise to the throne. Omri prevailed and consolidated his rule. In the middle of his reign, he established Samaria, which was the capital of Israel until its fall. Omri made a covenant with Tyre and with the king of Judah, and in his time the kingdom of Israel stabilized and the political-military situation improved.

Ahab, son of Omri, the seventh king of Israel (871–851), continued the covenant with Tyre and married Jezebel, the daughter of Ethbaal, king of Tyre and the Sidonians. He made a covenant with Judah and married his daughter Athaliah to Jehoram, the son of Jehoshaphat king of Judah. He captured and returned to Israelite rule all the cities that had been taken by Aram. He headed the royal alliance against Shalmaneser III, king of Assyria, during the battle of Qarqar. Ahab fell in Ramoth-gilead, in the war with Aram. During Ahab's reign, Israel knew prosperity and growth, but the "incident of Naboth" and Ahab's benevolent attitude toward Baal worship raised the ire of the prophets, in particular, Elijah.

Ahaziah, son of Ahab and Jezebel, succeeded his father as king of Israel (851–850). The defeat of Israel by Aram, the attacks of

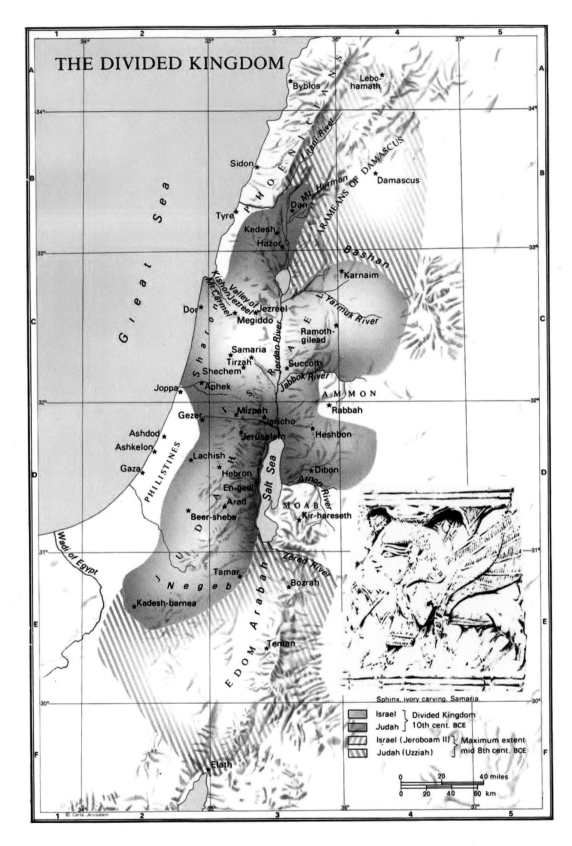

THE DIVIDED KINGDOM

Sphinx, ivory carving, Samaria

Israel	Divided Kingdom
Judah	10th cent. BCE
Israel (Jeroboam II)	Maximum extent
Judah (Uzziah)	mid 8th cent. BCE

© Carta, Jerusalem

King Mesha of Moab, and the weakening of the covenant made between Israel and Judah caused the weakened military and political situation in the kingdom of Israel during his reign. Baal worship continued to spread, apparently under the influence of his mother Jezebel. He was wounded in an accident and died of his injuries. Because he had no sons, his brother inherited the throne.

Jehoram/Joram, son of Ahab, ascended to the throne (850–842), succeeding his brother Ahaziah. With the help of Jehoshaphat, king of Judah, and the Edomite army, he defeated the invading army of Mesha, king of Moab. During

his reign, Hadad II, king of Aram, invaded Israel and besieged Samaria, but the Aramean army fled when the rumor spread that the Egyptian army was coming to the aid of Israel. Jehoram was wounded in the war with Hazael and returned to Israel to recuperate. Meanwhile, Jehu, his military minister, had been secretly anointed by command of the prophet Elisha. Jehu conspired against the king and had him killed.

Jehu, son of Jehoshaphat son of Nimshi, was founder of the Jehu dynasty and tenth king of Israel (842–814). He was a commander in King Jehoram's army, was anointed secretly by a disciple sent by the prophet Elisha, plotted against Jehoram, killing him and destroying the entire house of Ahab. He abolished Baal worship, but continued to practice the ritual of the golden calves, first insti-tuted by Jeroboam, son of Nabat. He had the support of the army, the common people and the prophets, but was condemned by the prophet Hosea. He paid a levy to Shalmaneser III, king of Assyria, thereby avoiding a confrontation with King Hazael of Aram.

Jehoahaz was the son and successor of Jehu, and eleventh king of Israel (814–800). The period of his reign was a low point in Israel's history. Hazael, the king of Aram, invaded Israel and made Jehoahaz his subject and subject of his son Ben-hadad.

Joash/Jehoash, son of Jehoahaz, was the twelfth king of Israel (800–785). Taking advantage of the Assyrian king Adad-nirari's campaign against Aram, he attacked Aram and freed the kingdom of Israel from its yoke. He defeated Amaziah, king of Judah, in the battle between the army of Judah and the army of Israel, near Beth-shemesh, and took him prisoner. He invaded Jerusalem, looted the treasures of the king's palace and the Temple, razed sections of the city wall as a sign of surrender, and took away hostages.

Jeroboam (Jeroboam II), son of Jehoash, expanded and consoli-dated the kingdom of Israel as in the days of David and Solomon. His reign (785–749) was a period of prosperity and growth. In this respect he was counted among the great kings of Israel. Never-theless, according to the Bible, he did evil in the eyes of God and the prophet Amos, who reproved him for the social woes and pagan worship that prospered under him, and predicted his doom. The prophets Hosea and Jonah also prophesied during his time.

Zechariah was the son of Jeroboam II. He reigned for about half a year (in 749), until he was murdered by Shallum, son of Jabesh. His murder marked the end of the Jehu dynasty.

Shallum, son of Jabesh, conspired against Zechariah, son of Jeroboam, king of Israel, killed him, and reigned for 30 days (in 748), until he was slain by Menahem, son of Gadi.

Menahem, son of Gadi, slew Shallum, son of Jabesh, and seized his throne (748–737). He paid a heavy tribute to Tiglath-pileser III, king of Assyria, and ruled for about ten years, until his death.

Pekahiah, son of Menahem, succeeded his father to the throne for two years (737–735), until he was murdered by his captain, Pekah, son of Remaliah, who seized the throne.

Pekah, son of Remaliah, was a captain of King Pekahiah of Israel. He conspired against his king, killed him, and seized the throne (735–731). He made a covenant with Rezin, king of Aram, against the kingdoms of Judah and Assyria. The armies of Israel and Aram invaded Judah and besieged Jerusalem. The situation changed with the appearance of Tiglath-pileser III in Galilee. He invaded the hills of Ephraim and posed a threat to Samaria. According to the Bible, Hoshea, son of Elah, conspired against Pekah, killed him, and seized the throne.

Hoshea, son of Elah, was the nineteenth and last king of Israel (731–722). He conspired against his king Pekah, son of Remaliah, killed him, and seized the throne. He paid a heavy tax to Tiglath-pileser III, king of Assyria, and during his reign, Assyria annexed most of the territory of the kingdom of Israel. For a time, Hoshea, apparently together with other allies, rebelled against Assyria, and discontinued the levy. Hoshea was arrested by Shalmaneser III, king of Assyria, Samaria was placed under siege and, after about three years, was captured. The conquest put an end to the kingdom of Israel.

The Kingdom of Judah

The southern kingdom of Judah arose after the division of the United Monarchy of Israel. It extended over the tribal allotments of Judah, Benjamin, and Simeon. The kingdom existed from 928 until the destruction of the First Temple (in 587). During this period, it was ruled by 20 kings, 19 of them from the House of David. The kingdom of Judah conducted continuous wars with the kingdom of Israel and sometimes even called for the help of foreign states. In general, it lost on the battlefield and, in the days of Amaziah, it even became a subject-nation of Israel. In the days of Jehoshaphat, Jehoram and Ahaziah, a covenant was made between the two brethren kingdoms. Judah reached the height of its greatness in the days of Uzziah, who built roads to the Mediterranean and the Red Sea, and fortified the land. In 722, Samaria fell to Assyria, marking the end of the kingdom of Israel. Judah too became a subject-nation of Assyria in the days of Ahaz, but rebelled against it in the days of Hezekiah. King Josiah, taking advantage of Assyria's decline in the days of Sennacherib, succeeded in expanding his kingdom northward and possibly even westward. During his rebellion Jerusalem was captured. Jehoiachin was exiled, and Zedekiah was crowned king. Zedekiah also rebelled and in suppressing the revolt, the Babylonians destroyed the First Temple and exiled thousands to Babylonia. The history of the kingdom of Judah is recounted in the Book of Kings and in II Chronicles.

The Kings of Judah

928–911	Rehoboam	758–742	Jotham
911–908	Abijah/Abijam	742–726	Ahaz
908–867	Asa	726–697	Hezekiah
867–851	Jehoshaphat	697–642	Manasseh
851–843	Jehoram/Joram	642–640	Amon
843–842	Ahaziah/Jehoahaz	640–609	Josiah
842–836	Athaliah	609–608	Jehoahaz
836–799	Joash/Jehoash	608–597	Jehoiakim/Eliakim
799–786	Amaziah	597	Jehoiachin
786–758	Uzziah	597–587	Zedekiah

There were 20 kings of Judah, all of whom belonged to a single dynasty—the House of David—with the exception of Athaliah, the daughter of Ahab, king of Israel, who married Jehoram, king of Judah, and seized the throne after the death of his son Ahaziah.

Rehoboam, the first king of Judah (928–911) after the division of Solomon's kingdom, was the son of Solomon and Naamah the Ammonitess. After Solomon's death, representatives of the tribes complained to Rehoboam about the burden of the heavy taxes they had to bear. His answer ("my father hath chastised you with whips, but I will chastise you with scorpions" [I Kg. 12:11]) raised the wrath of the people, and the kingdom split in two. Rehoboam built fortresses in the Shephelah (the lowlands) and around Jerusalem, and throughout his reign he was in battle with the king of Israel. Also during his reign, Shishak, king of Egypt, invaded Judah and plundered its cities.

Abijah/Abijam was the second king of Judah (911–908) and successor of his father Rehoboam. He battled against Jeroboam, son of Nabat, and captured several of his cities. According to the Book of Kings, he followed in his father's sinful ways; according to Chronicles, he endeavored to recover the kingdom of the Ten Tribes and to restore the centrality of the Temple in Jerusalem.

THE WARS OF AMAZIAH AND JOASH

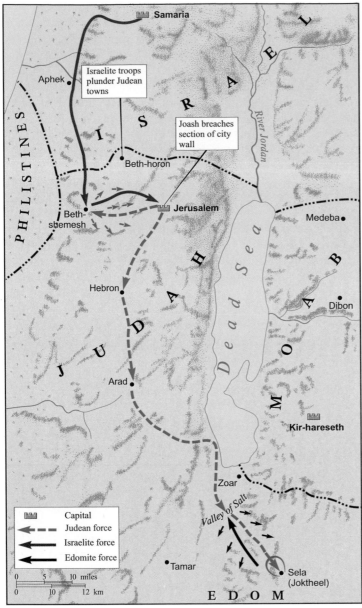

© Carta, Jerusalem

Asa succeeded his father Abijah and was the third king of Judah (908–867). Like his father, he also attempted to reunite Judah and Israel. He fought the house of Jeroboam and especially Baasha, but in the end he was defeated. He wished to cleanse the land of idol worship. He repelled the incursions of sheep and camel herdsmen, led by Zerah the Cushite, who were forced to retreat to the southern boundaries of Judah.

Jehoshaphat, son of Asa, was the fourth king of Judah (867–851). He fortified existing cities, established new ones, and strengthened his army. He imposed a levy on the Philistines, and defeated the Ammonite and Moabite armies. Toward the close of his reign, with the help of King Ahaziah of Israel, he built a navy designed to sail to Tarshish. His plan failed after the ships were wrecked at Ezion-geber.

Jehoram/Joram, the fifth king of Judah (851–843), was the eldest son of Jehoshaphat, his predecessor. He married Athaliah, daughter of Ahab, king of Israel, and Jezebel the Sidonian. Under her influence, he killed his six brothers and several of his ministers. The priestly city of Libnah rebelled against him, as did Edom. The prophet Elijah admonished him. The Philistines and Arabians invaded Judah, plundered its property, and took Jehoram's wives and children hostage (only Ahaziah, the

youngest son, was able to escape). He himself died of a serious illness, and was not buried in the Tombs of the Kings.

Ahaziah/Jehoahaz was the youngest son of Jehoram, king of Judah, and the only one to survive him. During his one-year reign (843–842), he followed the ways of his mother, Athaliah, in cult matters and reinforced the covenant with the house of Omri. He came to visit his uncle Jehoram, king of Israel, who had been wounded in war, and was killed in his flight from Jehu, who seized the rule in Israel.

Athaliah was the daughter of King Ahab of Israel and Jezebel the Sidonian. She married Jehoram, king of Judah, and persuaded him to kill his brothers and to go to war against Aram. After the death of her son Ahaziah, she killed all the possible inheritors to the throne and seized it herself (842–836). Jehosheba, Ahaziah's sister, succeeded in hiding her nephew Joash for six years, and in the seventh year, he was anointed king by the high priest Jehoiada. Athaliah was killed while trying to flee.

Joash/Jehoash, son of Ahaziah, was the eighth king of Judah (836–799). For six years he was concealed by his aunt Jehosheba, wife of the high priest Jehoiada, in order to save him from the hands of his grandmother, Athaliah, who had killed all his brothers and seized the throne. Joash was coronated by Jehoiada and the Davidic dynasty was renewed. In the days of Joash, the priestly status was reinforced, Jerusalem was cleansed of Baal worship, and the Temple was restored. Toward the close of his reign, he surrendered to Hazael, king of Aram, and was forced to send him the treasures from his palace and the Temple. He was murdered by conspirators from among his servants after the murder of Zechariah, the son of Jehoiada, who ordered the assassination.

Amaziah, son of Joash, was the ninth king of Judah (799–786). He punished the murderers of his father but did not harm their sons. He established an army for war with Edom and requested the participation of Israel's army, but abandoned that plan. After his victory over Edom, the strife between Judah and Israel grew. He declared war on Joash, king of Israel, was defeated and fell into captivity, and Jerusalem was captured and its treasures from the king's palace and the Temple were looted. During the last years of his reign, a breach apparently formed between him and the clan leaders, and Amaziah was murdered after his flight to Lachish.

Uzziah, son of Amaziah, was the tenth king of Judah (786–758). He was crowned king after his father's murder, and continued his policy of reinforcing Judah. He controlled several Philistine cities, fortified Jerusalem, built fortifications in Judah, and strengthened his army. Following his achievements, he wished to also assume the crown of the priesthood and, according to the narrative in Chronicles, he became afflicted with leprosy. Apparently, while still alive he placed his son Jotham in power, but it is not known precisely how many years before Uzziah's death this occurred. The prophets Isaiah, Amos and Hosea were active during his time.

Jotham succeeded his father Uzziah and was eleventh king of Judah (758–742). According to some calculations, he was regent also during the lifetime of his father, who was afflicted with leprosy, and perhaps did not rule independently. Jotham continued his father's policies: he fortified Jerusalem, established fortified cities and fortresses in Judah, apparently also ruled over Elath (Ezion-geber), subdued the Ammonites, and expanded the border of Judah eastward. At the close of his reign, Rezin, king of Aram, and Pekah, king of Israel, began to plot against Judah.

Ahaz was the son of Jotham and king of Judah (742–726). Part of his rule was as regent under his father and perhaps even his grandfather, Uzziah. He refused to join forces with Aram and Israel against Assyria. Aram and Israel attacked Judah and besieged Jerusalem. Against the advice of the prophet Isaiah, he t...
He reinstat...
the time of...
Philistines t...
in the Nege...

Hezekiah...
He inherite...
guidance c...
abolished p...
against Ass...
armies, an...
After Senn...
army besie...
the advice...
baladan, k...

Manasseh...
of Judah (...
reigned for...
built altars...
for Molech...
abominatio...
captive by a...
sins, returned to his kingdom and remedied all.

Amon was the son of Manasseh and king of Judah. He followed in the ways of his father and, according to the narrative in Chronicles, was worse than Ahaz and Manasseh. He ruled for two years (642–640) and was murdered in a conspiracy by his courtiers. The people avenged him by putting all the conspirators to death, and secured the succession to his youngest son, Josiah.

Josiah was the son of Amon and king of Judah. He was coronated at the age of eight, and his regnal years (640–609) are considered the last Golden Age in the history of Judah. In his days the book of the Law of the Lord (i.e., Deuteronomy), which was stored deep inside the Temple, was found, he destroyed the pagan altars, reinstated the Divine service, made Jerusalem the single religious center, and led a religious revival movement. The decline of Assyria paved open the way for national independence, too, and Josiah was the only king of Judah who set out against Egypt. He was wounded and died while attempting to block the path of the army of Pharaoh Necho, king of Egypt, who attacked Assyria.

Jehoahaz was the son of Josiah and king of Judah. He reigned for only three months (in 609–608). Pharaoh Necho took him prisoner and brought him to Egypt, where he died.

Jehoiakim/Eliakim was the son of Josiah and king of Judah (608–597). He was coronated by Pharaoh Necho after the latter deposed his brother, Jehoahaz. He was a tyrant and wicked man who oppressed his people and persecuted Jeremiah and anyone else who predicted for him hard and difficult times. At the start of his reign, Judah was a subject-nation of Egypt, and after the battle of Carchemish, it became subject to Babylon. Jehoiakim rebelled against the Babylonian king Nebuchadnezzar. In the end, Nebuchadnezzar ascended upon Jerusalem, forcing its surrender. According to the Book of Chronicles, Jehoiakim was bound in fetters and carried off to Babylon.

THE CONQUESTS OF JOASH AND JEROBOAM II

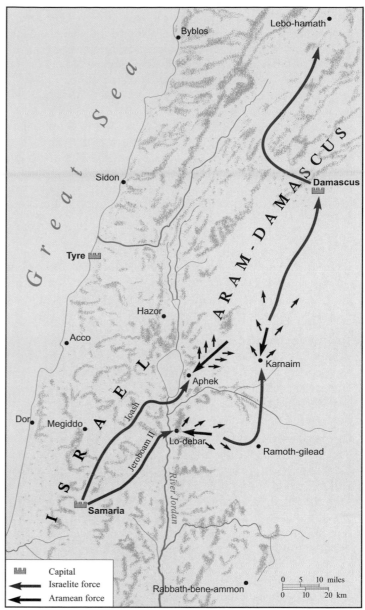

Byblos
Lebo-hamath
Great Sea
Sidon
Tyre
Hazor
Acco
Damascus
ARAM-DAMASCUS
ISRAEL
Karnaim
Aphek
Dor
Megiddo
Joash
Jeroboam II
Lo-debar
Ramoth-gilead
River Jordan
Samaria
Rabbath-bene-ammon

Capital
Israelite force
Aramean force

0   5   10 miles
0   10   20 km

© Carta, Jerusalem

Jehoiachin, successor of his father Jehoiakim and king of Judah, rose to the throne during the rebellion against Babylon. He reigned for three months (in 597), until Nebuchadnezzar exiled him to Babylon along with his mother, members of his family, his ministers, and ten thousand soldiers. His life was spared and he remained in Nebuchadnezzar's court prison, until he was released in the days of Evil-Merodach, the Babylonian king's successor. From among his descendants arose the leaders during the Babylonian exile and the Return to Zion.

Zedekiah was the third son of Josiah and Hamutal, and the last king of Judah (597–587). He was coronated in the days of Nebuchadnezzar, who, on the same occasion, changed his name from Mattaniah to Zedekiah. Zedekiah was persuaded to rebel against Babylon, despite the warnings of the prophet Jeremiah. Nebuchadnezzar's army invaded Judah, besieged Jerusalem, and breached its walls. Zedekiah escaped but he was caught by the Chaldeans. His sons were slaughtered before his eyes, his own eyes were then blinded, and he was bound in fetters and brought to Babylon, where he died.

The Prophets

The prophet of the Bible was an emissary of God and the intermediary between the Divine Will and individuals, people, or the Gentile nations. His mission was forced upon him: he was chosen to be a prophet, sometimes against his will. In some instances in the Bible, the prophet is called either "a seer," "a visionary" or a "man of God," all of which are identical in meaning.

The sages listed 48 prophets and seven prophetesses, beginning with the patriarchs Abraham, Isaac and Jacob, and ending with Malachi, in the days of the Return to Zion. However, only the prophecies relevant to future generations are included in the Bible. The sages also counted seven prophets who prophesied to the Gentile nations, among them Balaam and Job.

The division between the Former Prophets and the Latter Prophets is designated by the order of their appearance in the Bible. Based on their character, status and deeds, the prophets can be divided into three categories, a division that also fits the periods of their activity: the "leader" prophets, the court prophets, and the classical prophets.

The first of the **"leader" prophets** was Moses. Miriam, the sister of Moses, was called a prophetess. Among the Judges were a few prophet-soothsayers, but only Deborah was called a prophetess. In the period of the Judges there were bands of prophets, but these were probably groups formed for their own purposes. Samuel was the last "leader" prophet.

Court prophets were active in the days of David and Solomon and in the days of the Divided Monarchy of Judah and Israel. Gad and Nathan were court prophets in the days of David and Solomon. The "man of God" Shemaiah and the "seer" Iddo recorded the chronicles of Rehoboam and Abijah. Ahijah the Shilonite, Jehu, son of Hanani, and Micaiah, son of Imlai, opposed the deeds of their kings and prophesied their doom. Elijah and Elisha were prophets who were forceful and decisive in their opinions and deeds, and they interfered in political, social and religious matters. The advice of Huldah the Prophetess was required by Josiah, king of Judah.

Classical prophets are the literary prophets: each one is associated with a book counted with the books of the Bible. Three of these are books of the Major Prophets (Isaiah, Jeremiah, and Ezekiel) and twelve are books of the Minor Prophets. The classical prophets are distinguished also for their religious fervor, their moral and social views, their historical outlook, and their power of rhetoric. They were not in need of fortune-telling or miraculous deeds, which were a separate part of the work of the Former Prophets.

Below are short biographies of the court prophets (the classical prophets are mentioned above in connection with the books named after them; see above, "The Books of the Bible").

Gad was a court prophet in the days of David. He joined David's regiment before David was king. David turned to him for God's advice. On the prophet's advice, David built an altar for God on the threshing floor of Araunah.

Nathan was a court prophet in the days of David and Solomon. He promised the House of David an eternal monarchy. He notified David about the postponement of building the Temple until the days of Solomon. He reproved David for the act of Bathsheba and Uriah (the parable of "the poor man's lamb"; II Sam. 12:1–4).

THE WANDERINGS OF ELIJAH

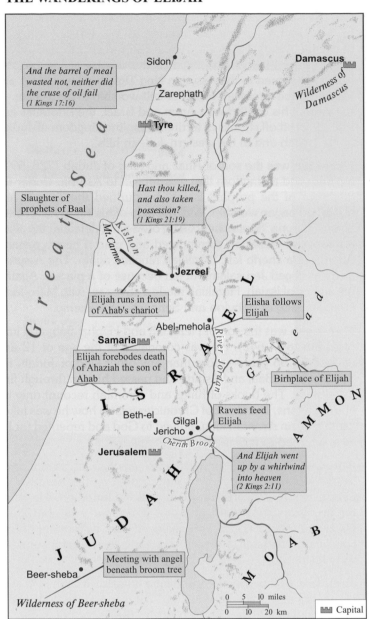

And the barrel of meal wasted not, neither did the cruse of oil fail (1 Kings 17:16)

Slaughter of prophets of Baal

Hast thou killed, and also taken possession? (1 Kings 21:19)

Elijah runs in front of Ahab's chariot

Elisha follows Elijah

Elijah forebodes death of Ahaziah the son of Ahab

Birhplace of Elijah

Ravens feed Elijah

And Elijah went up by a whirlwind into heaven (2 Kings 2:11)

Meeting with angel beneath broom tree

Wilderness of Beer-sheba

0   5   10 miles
0   10   20 km

🏛 Capital

© Carta, Jerusalem

Ahijah the Shilonite was a prophet in the days of Solomon and Jeroboam. He was among the prophets who opposed Solomon because of the burden his heavy taxes imposed and because of the pagan cults he allowed to exist. He prophesied Jeroboam's reign over Israel, and realized his prophecy in a symbolic manner (he had rent Jeroboam's garment into 12 strips, gave ten to Jeroboam and left one for the House of David).

Shemaiah was "a man of God" in the days of Rehoboam, king of Judah. He passed on God's word of warning to the king not to go to war with Jeroboam, son of Nabat. He and the "seer" Iddo recorded the chronicles of Rehoboam and his wars.

Iddo was a "seer" in the days of Rehoboam and Abijah, kings of Judah. He recorded the chronicles of Rehoboam (with Shemaiah) and those of Abijah.

Jehu, son of Hanani, was a prophet in the days of Baasha, king of Israel, and Jehoshaphat, king of Judah. He reproved Baasha for his evil deeds and prophesied his doom.

Elijah the Prophet (also called "the Tishbite" and "the Gileadite") was a popular and powerful prophet, who lived in the

THE ACTIVITIES OF ELISHA

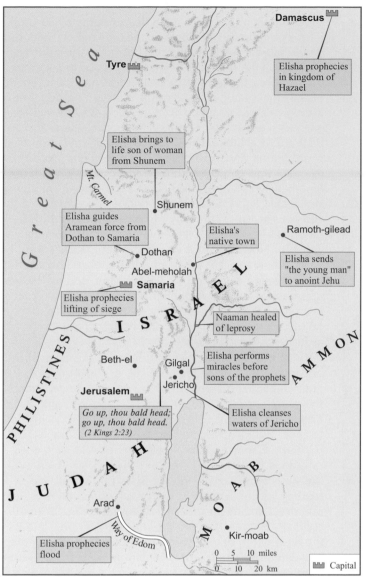

Damascus

Elisha prophecies in kingdom of Hazael

Tyre

Great Sea

Mt. Carmel

Elisha brings to life son of woman from Shunem

Shunem

Elisha guides Aramean force from Dothan to Samaria

Elisha's native town

Ramoth-gilead

Dothan

Elisha sends "the young man" to anoint Jehu

Abel-meholah

Samaria

Elisha prophecies lifting of siege

Naaman healed of leprosy

Beth-el

Gilgal

Elisha performs miracles before sons of the prophets

Jericho

Jerusalem

Go up, thou bald head; go up, thou bald head.
(2 Kings 2:23)

Elisha cleanses waters of Jericho

I S R A E L

A M M O N

J U D A H

M O A B

PHILISTINES

Arad

Way of Edom

Elisha prophecies flood

Kir-moab

| 0 | 5 | 10 miles |
| 0 | 10 | 20 km |

🏰 Capital

© Carta, Jerusalem

Elisha, son of Shaphat, was a prophet in the kingdom of Israel in the days of Kings Jehoram, Jehu, Jehoahaz, and Joash. Elijah cast his mantle on Elisha, thus anointing him prophet. He was active in political life, forceful in his opinions, and brave in his acts. He prophesied to the Israelite monarchy, on his command Jehu was anointed, he led the soldiers of Aram from Dothan to Samaria, and prophesied the lifting of the siege of Samaria. Many stories and miraculous deeds are associated with him: the story of the 42 children who were preyed upon by two bears ("Go up, thou bald head; go up, thou bald head"), the resurrection

THE CITIES OF THE PROPHETS

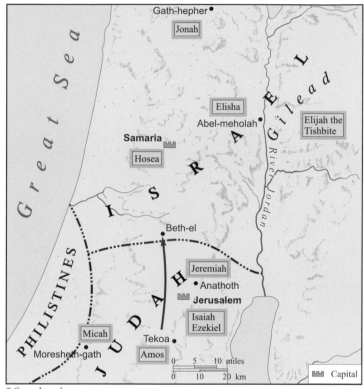

Gath-hepher

Jonah

Great Sea

Elisha

Abel-meholah

Samaria

Hosea

River Jordan

Elijah the Tishbite

I S R A E L

G i l e a d

Beth-el

Jeremiah

Anathoth

Jerusalem

Isaiah Ezekiel

Micah

Tekoa

Moresheth-gath

Amos

PHILISTINES

J U D A H

| 0 | 5 | 10 miles |
| 0 | 10 | 20 km |

🏰 Capital

© Carta, Jerusalem

of the son of a Shunammite woman, the cure of Naaman from leprosy, purifying the waters of Jericho, and more.

Huldah was a prophetess in the days of Josiah, king of Judah. Hilkiah, Ahikam, and Abdon turned to her upon the king's request to demand God's word, and upon her advice, the king acted.

The Latter Prophets by their periods: Amos and Hosea prophesied during the Israelite monarchy, in the eighth century, before its destruction. Isaiah, Joel, Micah, Nahum, Habakkuk, Zephaniah, and Jeremiah prophesied during the Judahite monarchy. Obadiah prophesied after the destruction, Ezekiel prophesied during the exile of Judah, and Haggai, Zechariah, and Malachi prophesied after the Return to Zion.

False prophets arose in Israel alongside the prophets of God. They misled the people for the sake of monetary gain, and were among those who preached Baal and Astarte worship. Jezebel of Tyre had installed the prophets of Baal and of Astarte. In the Book of Nehemiah, a false prophetess is also mentioned—Noadiah of Sanballat's community—who incited against Nehemiah.

kingdom of Israel and was active in the days of Kings Ahab and Ahaziah. He was a zealot for the belief in one God and fought vigorously against Baal worship. He was pursued in the days of the monarchy and often sought refuge in hiding places, but he would return in times of need. He argued with the prophets of Baal and had them slaughtered. He performed miracles and experienced miracles himself: the ravens fed him, he resurrected a dead boy, stopped the rain, and went up by a whirlwind into heaven. He consecrated Elisha as his disciple and, upon his instructions, Hazael was proclaimed king over Aram and Jehu, king over Israel. Already in the days of Malachi, the belief spread that Elijah would return before the Day of Judgment. Many legends are woven around him, among them the legend that he would herald the coming of the Messiah. During the seder on Passover eve, it is customary to place a cup of wine in his honor ("Elijah's cup").

Micaiah, son of Imlah, was a prophet in the days of Ahab, king of Israel, and Jehoshaphat, king of Judah. Ahab despised him because he always prophesied his doom. After one of his harsh prophecies, Zedekiah, son of Chenaanah and one of the false prophets under Ahab, rose and struck his face, and sent him to prison.

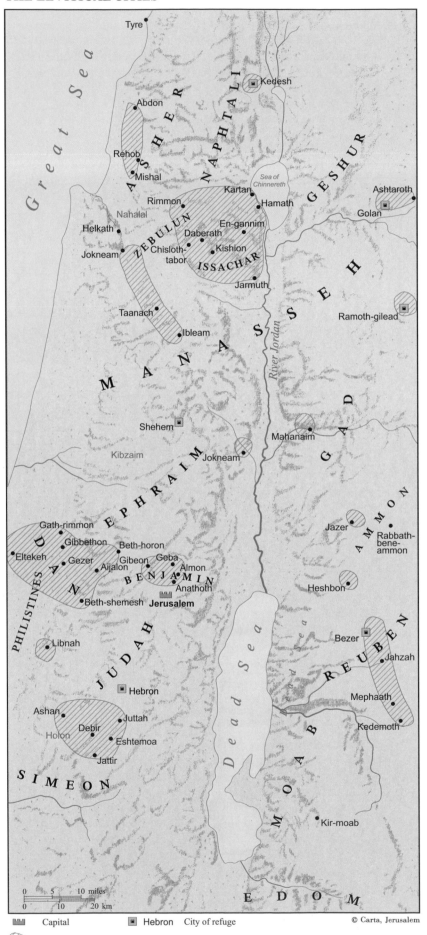

| Capital | Hebron | City of refuge |
| Area of Levite cities | Holon | Conjectured site |

© Carta, Jerusalem

The Priests, Levites, and Israel

Priests (*kohanim*) were male descendants of Aaron the High Priest, brother of Moses, of the tribe of Levi, and were consecrated to serve in the priesthood of the Tabernacle and later in the Temple. Their tasks included the offering of the sacrifices, the burning of the incense, and the arranging of the shewbread. They did not receive an allotment of their own since they earned their livelihood from priestly gifts, such as parts of sacrifices, firstborn flocks and cattle, firstfruits, and tithes. Their status also imposed upon them prohibitions and restrictions, such as being forbidden to come into contact with a dead person or to marry a divorced woman. At the head of the priestly hierarchy stood the High Priest, whose special duties included the Temple service on the Day of Atonement (Yom Kippur). Essentially, the priest's duties were confined to matters of worship. However, in the period of the Judges and the First Temple, he was assigned additional responsibilities: he conveyed the word of God to the nation; he was approached regarding queries to God; he was a teacher instructing the nation in the Torah; he rendered judgment on questions of ritual purity and impurity; and he served as judge in legal matters.

(In the days of the Second Temple, the High Priests became political leaders but, as a consequence, lost their status as interpretors of Jewish law, as teachers of the people, and as spiritual guides. Today, only a few distinguishing signs of the *kohanim* remain: guarding their lineage, as, for example, expressed in the family name [Cohen, Cahane, Katz (acronym for *kohen tzedek*— righteous priest), etc.]; reciting the priestly blessing in the synagogue; and being the first to be called up to the reading of the Torah. Of the priestly gifts, all that have remained are the custom of redeeming the firstborn male child [in Hebrew, *pidyon ha-ben*] and, in holy matters, the prohibition of marrying a divorced woman. *Kohanim* are also forbidden to come in contact with the deceased or to enter a cemetery.)

Levites are members of the Levite tribe not included in the order of priests. Like the priests, they were chosen by Moses to serve in the Tabernacle as a reward for their loyalty to him regarding the golden calf. During the wanderings in the wilderness, they were charged with carrying the Tabernacle and its holy vessels, and helping the priests. During the period of settlement in Canaan, the Levites did not receive territories of their own but were allotted 48 cities, and subsisted from the tithes they received from the people. When the First Temple was built and the wanderings of the Tabernacle ceased, the Levites were divided into 24 watches that they served in the Temple, coinciding with the 24 watches of the priests. Among the Levites were appointed judges, officials, public teachers of the Torah, and scribes.

(In the Second Temple period, their duties in the Temple [and later in the synagogue] were confined to those of singers, musicians, gatekeepers, and public servants. The Levites were ranked second to the priests in the social hierarchy, and above the rank of Israel. Some of them have also kept their lineage through their family names—Levi, Halevi, Levine, Leviteh, etc.)

Israelite refers to someone who is neither a priest nor a Levite.

THE CLOSING YEARS OF THE KINGDOM OF JUDAH

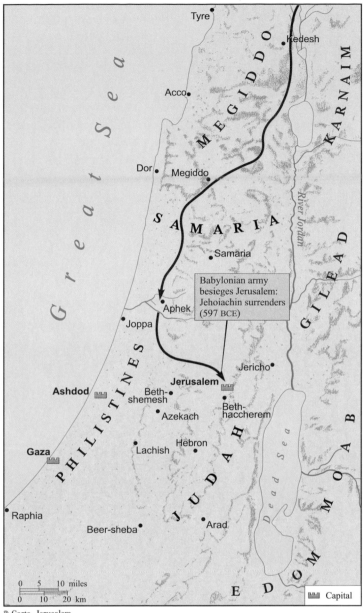

© Carta, Jerusalem

The Destruction and Exile

Exile refers to the banishment of the people of Israel from their land and their resettlement in foreign lands. In the "reproof section" of the Bible (Lev. 26; Deut. 28–30), exile is mentioned as the gravest of all punishments the people of Israel could expect if they did not observe God's commandments. However, the exiles are promised to return to their land if they repent for their evil ways.

It is customary to list a number of exiles in the history of Israel. **Egyptian exile**, when all the Jewish people dwelled among a foreign nation in enslavement. **Assyrian exile:** the exile of the northern tribes of Israel and those living in the cities along the Jordan by King Tiglath-pileser of Assyria in 733. After some 12 years, King Sargon of Assyria captured Samaria and exiled the rest of the tribes (only the kingdom of Judah remained). **Babylonian exile:** in 597, Nebuchadnezzar, king of Babylon, exiled King Jehoiachin and all his ministers and soldiers from Jerusalem, and coronated his uncle Zedekiah instead. Zedekiah also rebelled against Babylon, and Nebuchadnezzar returned and ascended upon Jerusalem. In c. 587, the city was destroyed, the Temple was burned, and many more Judahites were exiled to Babylon.

(The term "exile" is also used for the "exiles" of Zion after the destruction of the Second Temple. For example, the Edomite exile is the name for the enslavement of Israel by the Romans; the Ishmaelite exile—name for the exiles of Israel in the Islamic countries; the Spanish exile—expulsion of the Jews from Spain and Portugal at the end of the fifteenth century CE; and, in general, the dispersion of the majority of the Jewish people in the Diaspora, outside Israel.)

The Return to Zion

The Return to Zion refers to the return of some of the Babylonian exiles to the land of Israel following the decree of Cyrus in 538. The returnees left in summer and before the Hebrew month of Tishri, they established the altar and instituted the sacrificial ser-vice. In the second year in the Hebrew month of Iyyar, the con-struction of the Temple began. The first group of returnees arrived under the leadership of Zerubbabel and numbered 42,360 people. The list of returnees included descendants of the families who had been exiled to Babylon. Close to the mid-fifth century, with the second

THE EXILE FROM JUDAH

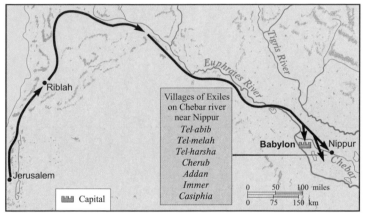

© Carta, Jerusalem

THE FINAL CAMPAIGN OF NEBUCHADNEZZAR AGAINST JUDAH

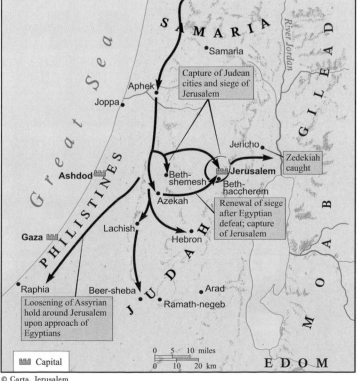

© Carta, Jerusalem

THE LAND OF JUDAH IN THE DAYS OF THE RETURN

return, under Ezra, about 5,000 people arrived. Altogether, about half of Babylonian Jewry had returned.

The building of the Temple began in 520 and was completed in 515. The costs of the sacrifices were borne by the authorities. The hardships of absorbing such a large migration and the sparse number of residents in the land strengthened the rule of the upper classes and increased the social tension. The shortage of women among the returnees (the first return included 30,000 men and only 12,000 women and children) resulted in many mixed marriages. The prophet Malachi complained of this phenomenon, and the Book of Ezra reveals that this custom even extended to priestly circles. Close to the return of Ezra, Nehemiah (who some predate to Ezra) arrived to build the walls of Jerusalem. He, like Ezra, was alert to social and religious reforms.

The returnees at first settled in the vicinity of Jerusalem, in an area whose size was only a fifth of the former kingdom of Judah. They found here a sparse Jewish community. It was these returnees who determined the character of Jewish settlement in the land, according to the modes of life they had adopted for themselves in Babylon. The national framework uniting the nation into a single unit had somewhat the character of a religious community, especially in its segregation. Aramaic was the official language of the Persian kingdom, and it was the language to which the returnees from Babylon were accustomed. In the same period, the Aramaic script was apparently adapted to the Hebrew one and gradually replaced the ancient Hebrew script, although the latter was not discarded completely. Similarly, this also occurred in the realm of the spoken word and ever since, Aramaic and Hebrew have been used side by side.

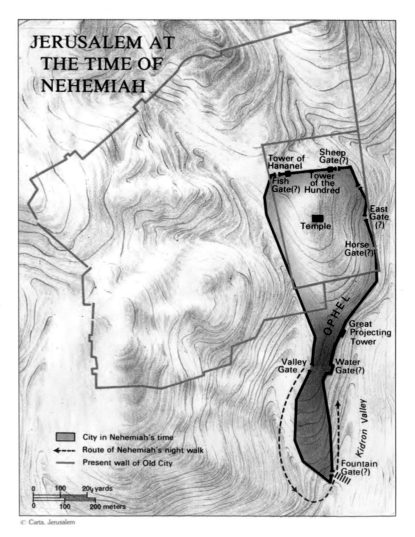

JERUSALEM AT THE TIME OF NEHEMIAH

City in Nehemiah's time
Route of Nehemiah's night walk
Present wall of Old City

© Carta, Jerusalem

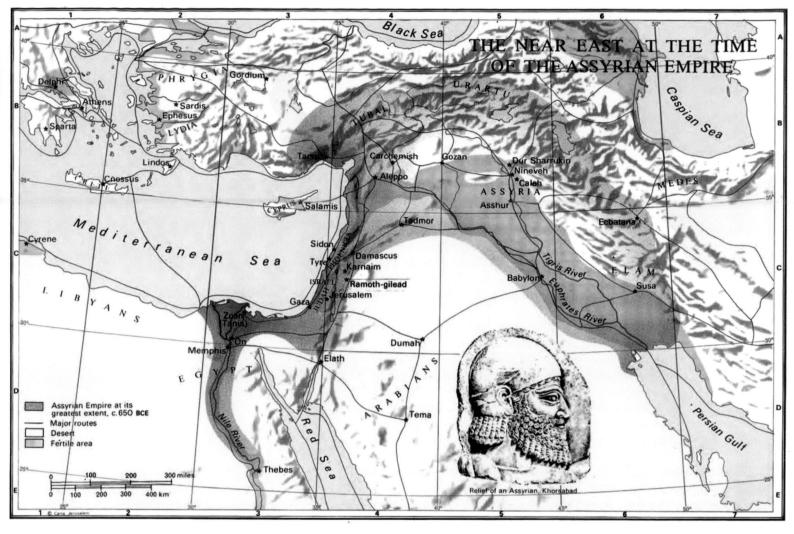

THE NEAR EAST AT THE TIME OF THE ASSYRIAN EMPIRE

Delphi
Athens
Sparta
Cnossus
CRETE

PHRYGIA
Gordium
Sardis
Ephesus
LYDIA
Lindos

Black Sea

URARTU

Caspian Sea

MEDES

Tarsus
Carchemish
Gozan
Aleppo
Dur Sharrukin
Nineveh
Caleh
ASSYRIA
Asshur

Ecbatana

CYPRUS
Salamis

Tadmor

Mediterranean Sea

Sidon
Tyre
PHOENICIA
Damascus
Karnaim
ISRAEL
Ramoth-gilead
JUDAH
Jerusalem
Gaza

Babylon
Euphrates River
Tigris River
ELAM
Susa

CYRENE

LIBYANS

Zoan
(Tanis)
On
Memphis

EGYPT

Elath

ARABIANS

Dumah

Tema

Persian Gulf

Nile River
Red Sea

Assyrian Empire at its
greatest extent, c. 650 BCE
Major routes
Desert
Fertile area

0   100   200   300 miles
0   100   200   300   400 km

Thebes

Relief of an Assyrian, Khorsabad

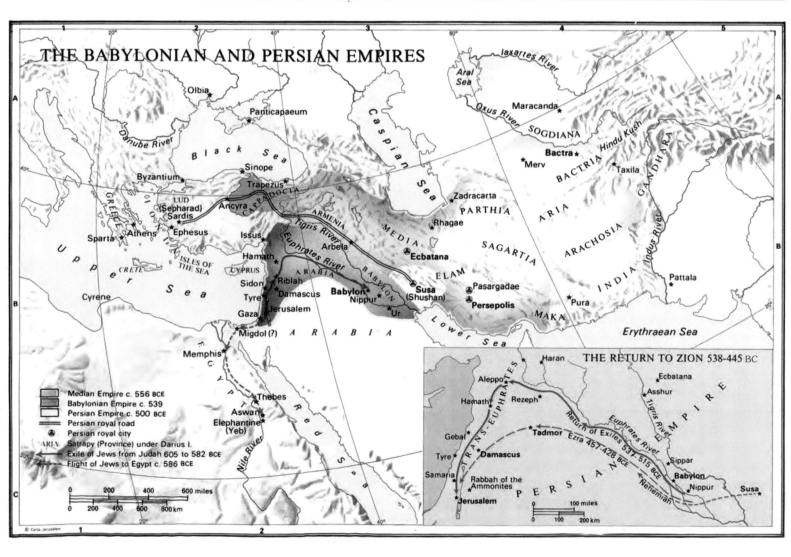

THE BABYLONIAN AND PERSIAN EMPIRES

Olbia
Panticapaeum

Danube River
Black Sea

Caspian Sea

Iaxartes River
Aral Sea

Oxus River
SOGDIANA
Maracanda

Bactra
BACTRIA
Hindu Kush
Taxila
GANDHARA

Byzantium
Sinope
Trapezus
CAPPADOCIA

Merv
ARIA

LUD
(Sepharad)
Sardis
Ancyra
ARMENIA
Tigris River
Zadracarta
PARTHIA
Rhagae

GREECE
Sparta
Athens
Ephesus
CRETE
ISLES OF
THE SEA
CYPRUS

Issus
Hamath
Euphrates River
Arbela
MEDIA
Ecbatana

SAGARTIA

ARACHOSIA
INDIA
Indus River
Pattala

Upper Sea

ARABIA
Sidon
Riblah
Tyre
Damascus
Gaza
Jerusalem
Migdol (?)

BABYLON
Babylon
Nippur
Ur

ELAM
Susa
(Shushan)
Pasargadae
Persepolis

Pura

MAKA

Cyrene

ARABIA

Lower Sea

Erythraean Sea

Memphis

EGYPT

Thebes

Aswan
Elephantine
(Yeb)

Median Empire c. 556 BCE
Babylonian Empire c. 539
Persian Empire c. 500 BCE
Persian royal road
Persian royal city
ARIA Satrapy (Province) under Darius I.
Exile of Jews from Judah 605 to 582 BCE
Flight of Jews to Egypt c. 586 BCE

Nile River
Red Sea

0   200   400   600 miles
0   200   400   600   800 km

THE RETURN TO ZION 538-445 BC

Haran
Aleppo
Hamath
Rezeph
EUPHRATES
TRANS-EUPHRATES
Gebal
Tyre
Damascus
Samaria
Rabbah of the
Ammonites
Jerusalem

Tadmor
Return of Exiles 537-515 BCE
Ezra 457-428 BCE
Euphrates River
Tigris River

Ecbatana
Asshur

EMPIRE

Sippar
Babylon
Nippur
Susa

PERSIAN
Nehemiah

0   100   200 miles
0   100   200 km

© Carta, Jerusalem

The Hebrew Alphabet

The Hebrew lettering system consists of 22 characters. In biblical times, Hebrew was written in a script inherited from the Phoenicians. At the time of the Second Temple, the so-called "Jewish" script developed, based on the Aramaic script, from which further writing styles eventually developed.

It is believed that the early Hebrew script developed its own style in the ninth century BCE. The first appearance of the script is on the stele of King Mesha of Moab (c. 850 BCE). Other important evidence, dating from the eighth to sixth centuries BCE, was found in the Samaria ostraca (inscribed sherds), the Siloam inscription, the Arad letters, and the Lachish letters. Further light on the history of the ancient Hebrew alphabet is revealed on fragments of stone inscriptions, inscriptions on clay jars and seals from the First Temple period, a few Dead Sea Scrolls, dating from about the third century BCE, as well as single words in scrolls otherwise written in the "Jewish" script, and Hasmonean and Bar Kokhba coins. A version of this ancient Hebrew writing is still used by the Samaritans to this day.

From the seventh century BCE, Aramaic had become the official language of the Persian Empire; it was written in Aramaic script, which had Phoenician roots. In the Hellenistic period, the different countries of the former empire developed variations of this script for writing the local languages. The Jews who lived in the far-flung parts of the empire also adopted the Aramaic script, and a local variant of it developed in Judah. Passages in this modified script date from the end of the third century BCE. The "Jewish" script, also known as the Assyrian or square script, continued to develop and supersede the early Hebrew script, a process that ended in the second century CE.

From the time the "Jewish" script came into use, it was possible to distinguish separate paths of alphabet development. Scripts such as ornate square, intermediate, and cursive were distinguished for their various uses. After the destruction of the Temple and the dispersion of the Jewish people, various communities formed writing styles of their own: e.g., "Eastern," Sephardi, Ashkenazi, Italian, Yemenite, Persian, Byzantine and Karaite.

The two major document findings of the "Jewish" script and scripts which evolved from it are the Dead Sea Scrolls (c. 300 BCE to 70 CE) and the manuscripts in the Cairo Genizah (the earliest of which date from the eighth or ninth century CE).

With the invention of printing, certain main types became dominant and were used all over Europe. In Israel today, mainly the Ashkenazi and Sephardi script styles prevail.

Vocalization (in Hebrew, *nikkud*) is the system of signs or points accompanying the letters in Hebrew as aids for grammatically correct pronunciation. The pointing system accepted in today's Hebrew is the Tiberian system of vowel pointing, which includes 13 vowel signs placed mostly beneath the letters. Other pointing systems are the Palestinian system, which includes seven vowel signs (above and in between the letters); the simple Babylonian system, including six vowel and one half-vowel (*schwa na'*) signs (mostly above the letters); and the ornate Babylonian system, which also indicates hard and soft consonants. All these vowel systems probably developed between the seventh and mid-ninth centuries.

Transliteration Guide

Letter	Name	Latinized	Pronounced
א	aleph	'	orig. glottal stop; now silent in the middle of words if it has no vowel; otherwise pronounced according to accompanying vowel sign
ב	beth	b	
ב	bheth	v	
ג	gimel	g	hard, as in "good"
ג	ghimel	gh	orig. as gh; now like hard g
ד	daleth	d	
ד	dhaleth	dh	orig. as th in "this"; now like d
ה	he	h	
ו	vav	v, w	(consonant)
ז	zayin	z	
ח	cheth	ch	as ch in Scottish "loch" but guttural
ט	tet	t	
י	yod	y	
כ, ך	kaph	k	
כ, ך	khaph	kh	as ch in Scottish "loch"
ל	lamed	l	
מ, ם	mem	m	
נ, ן	nun	n	
ס	samekh	s	
ע	ayin	'	strong guttural sound; now usually treated in the pronunciation like an *aleph*
פ	pe	p	
פ	phe	ph	
צ, ץ	tzadhe	tz, ts	as ts in "tse-tse"
ק	koph	q	guttural k
ר	resh	r	
ש	shin	sh	as sh in "sheet"
ש	sin	s	
ת	tav	t	
ת	thav	th	orig. as th in "thing"; now like t

Vocalization Guide

	Vowel form	Name	Latinized	Pronounced
1) Long vowels	ָ	qamatz gadhol	ā	as a in "far"
	ֵ	tzeré	ē	as ai in "rain"
	ִ	hiriq gadhol	i	as i in "machine"
	ֹ	holam	ō	as o in "fork"
	וּ	shuruq	ū	as u in "true"
2) Short vowels	ַ	patah	a	as a in "far"
	ֶ	seghol	e	as e in "them"
	ִ	hiriq qatan	i	as i in "pin"
	ָ	qamatz qatan	o	as o in "gone"
	ֻ	qubbutz	u	as u in "put"
3) Half vowels	ְ	schwa (na')	e	as e in "agent"
	ֲ	hataph patah	a	like a very short patah
	ֱ	hataph seghol	e	like a very short seghol
	ֳ	hataph qamatz	o	like a very short qamatz qatan

Chronological Chart of the Alphabet

Phoenician					Hebrew					Samaritan
c. 1000 BCE	8th–7th cent. BCE	c. 800 BCE	7th–1st cent. BCE	New Punic	c. 1000 BCE	(Moabite) c. 850 BCE	7th cent. BCE	6th cent. BCE	2nd cent. BCE	13th cent. CE

Aramaic				"Jewish"			Latin
(Assyria) 7th cent. BCE	(Lapidary) 4th cent. BCE	5th–4th cent. BCE	3rd cent. BCE	"Herodian" c. 100 BCE	1st cent. BCE	Modern Hebrew	

73

The Hebrew Calendar

In the Hebrew calendar, the days are reckoned from sunset to sunset, the months are calculated according to the moon, and the years according to the sun. As the lunar year consists of about 354 days and the solar year has about 365 days, the lunar cycle must be adjusted yearly to the solar calendar. Without this modification, the Jewish festivals would come 11 days earlier each year. This adjustment, first made public by the talmudic sage Hillel II in the year 359, is made by having a leap year seven times in each 19-year cycle—years 3, 6, 8, 11, 14, 17 and 19, a leap year being the intercalation of an extra month of Adar (Adar II) into the calendar.

The oldest known Hebrew calendar is the tenth-century BCE Gezer Calendar, from the start of the monarchical period. It is a calendar in which the names of the months are based on an annual cycle of agricultural activities beginning with a month of gathering, a month of sowing, a month of late sowing, one month of flax harvest, one month of barley harvest, a month of wheat harvest, a month of vine pruning or of vintage, and the month of picking or drying of figs. In the Bible, the months are generally referred to serially, Nisan being called "the first month," Iyyar "the second month," and so forth. There are four months which have special designations: Nisan (Abib—spring), Iyyar (Ziv—splendor), Tishri (Ethanim—strength), and Marheshvan (Bul—produce). The present names of the months, which are of Akkadian, Assyrian or Babylonian origin and whose meanings are often unclear, first appear in Jewish sources during the period of the Babylonian exile, and have since been known in the following order: Tishri, Marheshvan, Kislev, Tevet, Shevat, Adar, Nisan, Iyyar, Sivan, Tammuz, Av, and Elul.

The Gezer Calendar opens with the season of gathering, but the Bible intimates clearly that the year was first counted from the month of Nisan, marking the start of the Exodus from Egypt; then for awhile the New Year (Rosh ha-Shanah) was counted from the month of Tishri and, according to the Mishnah, the 1st of Tishri was considered the New Year "for the years and for the fallow years and for the jubilee years and for the planting and for the vegetables," while the 1st of Nisan was considered as the New Year "for the kings and for the pilgrim festivals." After the destruction of the Temple, which brought about the end of royal life, Nisan was generally replaced by Tishri as the start of the New Year.

The Hebrew chronology conventionally begins with the creation of the world based on Jewish tradition. The Jewish year is calculated by adding 3760 to the civil year and, conversely, the civil year is obtained by subtracting 3760 from the Jewish year.

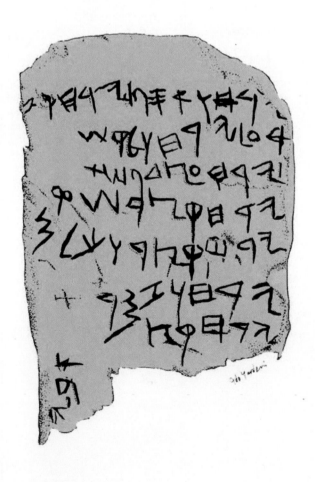

The Gezer Calendar, 10th century bce, and facsimile (right).

Months and Festivals in the Hebrew Calendar

Hebrew month	(Civil month)	Alternative monthly order	Name source and meaning	Duration (in days)	Zodiac sign	Jewish/Israeli holidays and their dates in Hebrew calendar
1 Tishri	(Oct./Nov.)	1st month of Hebrew year, 7th from Nisan	Accadian *Tashritu* ("beginning"). In Bible called "Ethanim" (strength)	30	Libra	**1–2** Rosh ha-Shanah; **3** Fast of Gedaliah (commemorates murder of Gedaliah [II Kg. 25:25]); **10** Yom Kippur; **15–21** Sukkot; **21** Hoshana Rabbah; **22** Shmini Atzeret and Simhat Torah
2 Marheshvan	(Nov./Dec.)	2nd month from Tishri, 8th from Nisan	Accadian *Varhu samnu* ("eighth month"). Abbreviated name, Heshvan. In Bible called "Bul" (produce)	29 or 30	Scorpio	
3 Kislev	(Dec./Jan.)	3rd from Tishri, 9th from Nisan	Accadian *Kislimu, Kislivu*	29 or 30	Saggitarius	**25** Chanukkah (lasts 8 days, until 2nd or 3rd of Tevet)
4 Tevet	(Jan./Feb.)	4th from Tishri, 10th from Nisan	Accadian *Tebeitu* (perhaps "month of sinking in")	29	Capricorn	**1–3** last days of Chanukkah; **10** Fast of 10th of Tevet (commemorates the start of Nebuchadnezzar's siege on Jerusalem)
5 Shevat	(Feb./Mar.)	5th from Tishri, 11th from Nisan	Accadian *Shabatu* ("month of the beating rain")	30	Aquarius	**15** New Year for Trees
6 Adar	(Mar./Apr.)	6th from Tishri, 12th from Nisan	Accadian *Addaru* (perhaps "month of threshing")	29; in leap year — 30 in Adar I, 29 in Adar II	Pisces	**7** birth and death of Moses, marked also as Memorial Day for the Unknown Soldier; **13** Fast of Esther; **14** Purim; **15** Shushan Purim
7 Nisan	(Apr./May)	1st month of Jewish religious calendar, 7th from Tishri	Accadian *Nisannu*; in Bible called "Abib" (spring)	30	Aries	**14** Passover eve; **15–21** Passover; **16** counting of the Omer begins (continues 49 days, until Shavuot); **27** Holocaust Memorial Day
8 Iyyar	(May/June)	8th from Tishri, 2nd from Nisan	Accadian *Ayaru*; in Bible called "Ziv" (splendor)	29	Taurus	**4** Memorial Day for Israel's Fallen Soldiers; **5** Israel's Independence Day; **18** Lag ba-Omer
9 Sivan	(June/July)	9th from Tishri, 3rd from Nisan	Accadian *Simanu*	30	Gemini	**6** Shavuot (Feast of Weeks or Pentecost), commemorates Giving of the Law on Mount Sinai and Festival of the Firstfruits
10 Tammuz	(July/Aug.)	10th from Tishri, 4th from Nisan	Babylonian	29	Cancer	**17** Fast of 17th of Tammuz (commemorates breaches of the walls of Jerusalem by the Babylonians)
11 Av	(Aug./Sept.)	11th from Tishri, 5th from Nisan	Accadian *Abu*, also called "Menahem (=Consoler) Av"	30	Leo	**9** Fast of 9th of Av (commemorates destruction of First and Second Temples); **15** Feast of the Vineyards
12 Elul	(Oct./Nov.)	12th from Tishri, 6th from Nisan	Accadian *Elulu* ("harvest, time of harvest")	29	Virgo	

Understanding
The New Testament

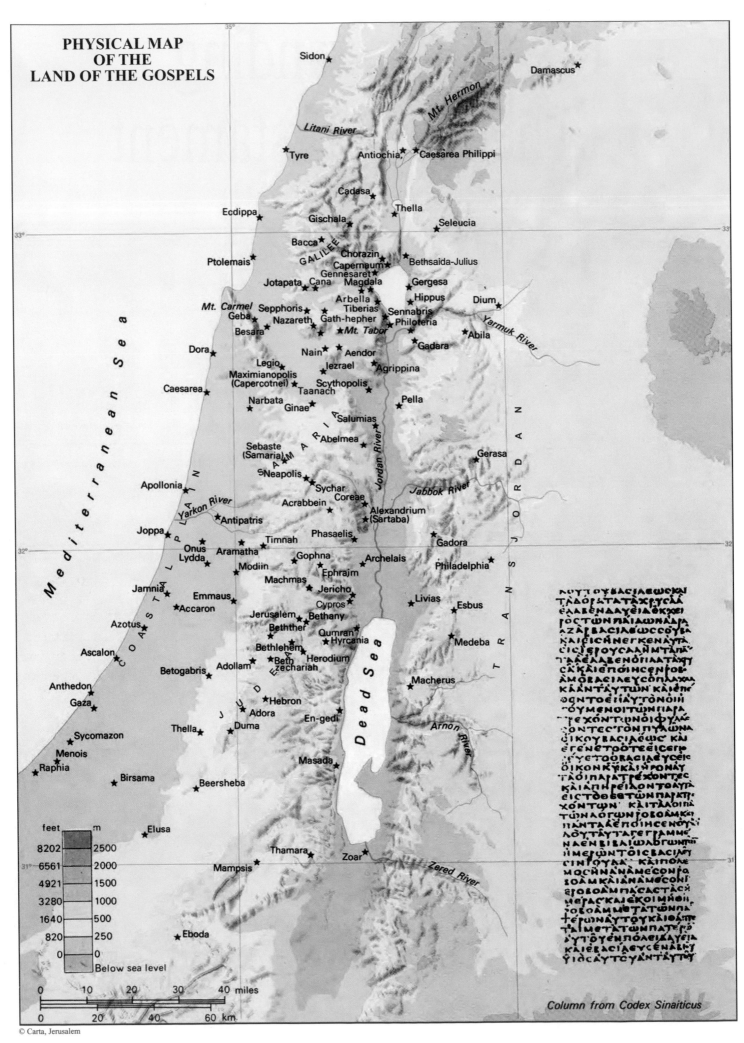

PHYSICAL MAP
OF THE
LAND OF THE GOSPELS

Sidon

Damascus

Mt. Hermon

Litani River

Tyre

Antiochia

Caesarea Philippi

Cadasa

Thella

Ecdippa

Gischala

Seleucia

Bacca

GALILEE

Chorazin

Ptolemais

Capernaum

Bethsaida-Julius

Gennesaret

Jotapata

Cana

Magdala

Gergesa

Hippus

Dium

Arbella

Mt. Carmel

Sepphoris

Tiberias

Sennabris

Geba

Nazareth

Gath-hepher

Philoteria

Besara

Mt. Tabor

Abila

Yarmuk River

Dora

Nain

Aendor

Gadara

Legio

Iezrael

Agrippina

Maximianopolis
(Capercotnei)

Scythopolis

Taanach

Caesarea

Narbata

Ginae

Pella

Salumias

Abelmea

Sebaste
(Samaria)

Gerasa

SAMARIA

Neapolis

Apollonia

Sychar

Coreae

Jabbok River

Jordan River

Yarkon River

Acrabbein

Antipatris

Alexandrium
(Sartaba)

Joppa

Phasaelis

Gadora

Onus

Timnah

Lydda

Aramatha

Gophna

Archelais

Philadelphia

Modiin

Ephrajm

Machmas

Jericho

Jamnia

Emmaus

Cypros

Livias

Esbus

Accaron

Jerusalem

Bethany

Azotus

Bethther

Medeba

Ascalon

Qumran

Hyrcania

Bethlehem

Herodium

Betogabris

Adollam

Beth
zechariah

Anthedon

Macherus

Gaza

Hebron

Adora

En-gedi

Arnon River

Thella

Duma

Sycomazon

Menois

Masada

Raphia

Birsama

Beersheba

Mediterranean Sea

COASTAL PLAIN

JUDEA

TRANS JORDAN

Dead Sea

feet   m

8202   2500
6561   2000
4921   1500
3280   1000
1640   500
820   250
0   0
        Below sea level

0   10   20   30   40 miles

0   20   40   60 km.

Elusa

Thamara

Zoar

Zered River

Mampsis

Eboda

Column from Codex Sinaiticus

The New Testament: Text and Context

The Christian Scriptures are composed of the New Testament (containing 27 books), the Old Testament (with 39 books, counted as 24 in the Hebrew Bible) and, in the Catholic tradition, the Apocrypha (usually numbering 15 books). Written by a handful of men over the course of several decades in the mid- to late first century A.D., the New Testament contains a record (or, more properly, multiple records) of the life of Jesus Christ and the birth and early growth of Christianity. Although each of the books of the New Testament possesses a character and flavor of its own, the group as a whole is unified around a single overarching theme: Jesus of Nazareth is the long-awaited Jewish Messiah, and because of his life, death and resurrection the community of people who believe in him (the Church) can find favor with God.

The New Testament was written in Koine Greek, the common dialect of the vast Greek-speaking world of the first century A.D. This allowed the writings of the New Testament to be read and understood widely, and the Gospel, or "good news" of Jesus Christ, to be carried throughout the Mediterranean basin and beyond. However, linguistic and literary evidence found in Matthew, Mark, and Luke suggests that at least these three gospels (the Synoptic or "look-alike" gospels) were rooted deeply in the Jewish world of first-century Palestine.

For two thousand years, Bible readers have looked to the words of the New Testament to find meaning and direction for life. Those who seek to understand the message that it holds for today quickly come to realize that it is also important to study its original context, the world in which the authors of the New Testament lived and wrote. Questions related to the meaning of a passage, its style and idiom, are clarified by looking at the larger literary context within which the passage appears (the paragraph, chapter or New Testament book in which it is found, and the Bible as a whole), but also by considering background of the text itself. Why was a gospel or epistle written, and for whom? What specific need was the author trying to address? What did he assume his original audience already knew? Why did he choose to say what he did in the way that he did?

An important part of context is place. For all of the rela-tive ease of travel that characterized the Roman world of the first century A.D., most people stayed pretty close to home. The role that a person's hometown played in defining his or her personal, social and religious identity cannot be overestimated. A Jewish peasant farmer living high in the hill country of Judea viewed the world quite differently than did an urban gentile born and raised on the edge of the Aegean Sea. A Hellenized Jew from Alexandria, a religious Jew from western Galilee and a villager native to Galatia were all part of the larger Roman and New Testament world; while each sought peace, security and the good life for himself and his family, each defined what that meant in very different ways.

The New Testament was written by, to and about real people living in real places. The writers of the New Testament had an intimate knowledge of place, and of the particular challenges that living in this or that place held for life. Moreover, the events and images described by the writers of the New Testament are grounded in an assumed knowledge of particular places or of specific aspects of the geographical or physical world in which individuals lived. The lands of the Bible have been aptly described as the "stage" on which the people who grace the pages of the New Testament moved, or as the "playing board" for which the "instructions" for people living there (the New Testament itself) were given. By understanding the dynamic of place, we open a window into other aspects of personal and communal life: political, economic, social and religious.

In looking at the world of the New Testament, many Bible readers focus on the words of the Apostle Paul found in Galatians 4:4: "But when the fullness of time had come, God sent forth his Son. ..." The phrase "fullness of time" points to the religious, social, and cultural conditions that fostered the rise and spread of Christianity, first in Palestine and then in the Greco-Roman world. But it is also proper to speak of a "fullness of place," of the geographical realities of the first-century world in which the Gospel spread. By learning about these places and the historical interconnections between them, Bible readers can enter more deeply into the pages of the Bible and the divine message that it contains.

The Books of the New Testament

Historical Books (The Gospels and Acts)

Matthew. In several ways, the Gospel of Matthew bridges the gap between the world of the Old Testament and that of the New. First, the book opens with a genealogy of Jesus that is tied into the royal line of Judah. Second, the author repeatedly states that Jesus fulfilled Old Testament messianic prophecies. Third, with a geographical sweep that includes everything from Mesopotamia (the visit of the Magi) to Egypt (the flight of the Holy family), the Gospel implies that the world of Abraham and his descendants (cf. Gen 11:31–12:10) has become the world of Jesus and his followers. Five major discourses by Jesus dominate the book, suggesting that the divine word has once again come to the people of the land of Israel. The book's author, Matthew (also called Levi—cf. Mk 2:14), a tax-collector from Capernaum, became one of the twelve Apostles.

Mark. The Gospel of Mark, which begins with the baptism rather than the birth of Jesus, is a fast-moving, tightly packed account of Jesus' ministry in Galilee that culminates in his journey to Jerusalem and the cross. Throughout, the gospel focuses on action rather than word, noting Jesus' ready ability to rub shoulders with his fellow countrymen and meet whatever needs they might have. The book's author, Mark (also called John Mark—cf. Acts 12:12), a man who may have had family ties to Jerusalem, was a long-time traveling companion of the Apostle Paul (2 Tim 4:11).

Luke. The Gospel of Luke is the most universal of the gospels in scope, covering the sweep of Jesus' life from conception to resurrection and following his journeys throughout Judea, Samaria, Galilee and the surrounding regions. Luke's gospel includes a number of stories not mentioned by the other gospels (ch. 9–18). Of particular note is Luke's emphasis on marginalized or peripheral elements of Jewish society: women, lepers, and foreigners. That the book's author, Luke, was a well-educated physician (cf. Col 4:14) is attested by the gospel's heart-felt compassion and attention to detail.

John. As the last gospel written, John presents the most complete picture of Jesus' humanity and his divinity. Selected events from Jesus' Galilean and early Jerusalem ministries (ch. 1–11) serve to provide the background for his climactic last week in Jerusalem (ch. 12–21). Because John mentions three Passover festivals (2:13; 6:4; 11:55), most interpreters conclude that Jesus' public ministry lasted three years. The book's author may have been John the Son of Zebedee, a Galilean fisherman who became Jesus' closest disciple and one of the most prominent Apostles.

The Acts of the Apostles. Following Jesus' charge that his disciples should be his witnesses "both in Jerusalem, and in all Judea, and in Samaria, and unto the uttermost part of the earth" (1:8), the Acts of the Apostles tracks the earliest years of Christianity from Jerusalem to Rome. On the way, disciples such as Peter, Stephen, Philip and Paul (Saul of Tarsus) carry the Gospel message to a variety of Jewish and gentile audiences. Based on style and content, it is reasonable to conclude that Acts was written by Luke.

Epistles

Romans. The Apostle Paul's greatest epistle was written to the local church in Rome, a church that held a special place in his heart even though it was founded by someone else. For Paul, the fact that there were disciples of Jesus in Rome—the world's bastion of wealth, imperial might, and paganism—was proof of the power of the Gospel. Paul's epistle to the Romans is a well-reasoned argument of how the death and resurrection of Jesus provides justification and righteousness for all who have faith in him. Paul concludes his epistle by urging the church in Rome to demonstrate their new-found righteousness by their deeds.

1 and 2 Corinthians. Paul founded the church at Corinth during his second missionary journey (cf. Acts 18:1–17). The church grew significantly during his 18-month stay in Corinth, and counted among its members Crispus, the leader of the local synagogue (cf. Acts 18:8). But Corinth was a bustling seaport dominated both by the rougher elements of life and the appeal of Greco-Roman paganism, aspects of life that for the Corinthian church were too seductive. Paul's first letter to the Corinthians, probably written when he was at Ephesus on his third missionary journey, addresses a number of these problems and urges the Corinthian Christians to live lives worthy of the love of Christ. Paul's second letter to the Corinthians expresses his joy upon hearing that many Corinthian believers had turned from following teachers who had maligned him, and urges that his authority be acknowledged by the rest.

Galatians. Paul's epistle to the Galatians was written to churches sprinkled throughout Galatia, the high mountainous interior of Asia Minor, including those he founded on his first missionary journey (Antioch, Iconium, Lystra and Derbe; cf. Acts 13–14). Written before he penned his epistle to the Romans, Galatians can be considered Paul's primer on justification by faith, arguing that righteousness before God is based on grace, not works.

Ephesians. Paul spent nearly three years in Ephesus (cf. Acts 20:31), an important commercial city on the Aegean coast of the Roman province of Asia. His subsequent letter to the Ephesians—which was probably intended to be circulated among churches throughout Asia—is a mature treatise on the blessings and responsibilities of living the Christian life.

Philippians. Philip of Macedon, father of Alexander the Great, founded the city of Philippi on a fertile plain just north of the Aegean Sea. By the first century AD Philippi was one of the most important cities in northeastern Macedonia, and it was here that Paul planted the first church on European soil (cf. Acts 16). Paul enjoyed an especially close relationship with this church, and his letter to the Philippians, written when he was in prison in Rome, radiates his joy and confidence in their life in Christ.

Colossians. Colossae was a rather insignificant town lying in the Lycus River valley, nestled in a beautiful mountainous area in southwestern Asia Minor one hundred miles east of Ephesus. Previously an important commercial center, by the first century A.D. the city had been eclipsed by the nearby cities of Laodicea and Hierapolis (cf. Col 4:13). The epistle to the church at Colossae, as well as that to the church at Laodicea (Col 4:16), were intended to be read in churches throughout the region. Although the Apostle Paul never visited Colossae, he knew its church well enough to direct his letter against a syncretistic heresy which threatened his teaching on the uniqueness of Christ.

Mountains edging the Lycus Valley, viewed from the mound of Colossae.

1 and 2 Thessalonians. Paul's first two epistles were written to the church at Thessalonica, the capital of Macedonia and an important Aegean port city on the Egnatian Way, Rome's principle highway to the east. Paul founded the Thessalonian church on his second missionary journey (cf. Acts 17:1–9), but had to flee the city in the face of persecution before the church had a chance to grow in its faith. Later during his journey, perhaps when he was in Corinth, Paul wrote his first epistle to the church in Thessalonica, a wide-ranging, practical letter aimed at encouraging the church to continue to mature in spite of ongoing persecution and to answer questions about the second coming of Christ. In his second letter, Paul corrects certain misunderstandings about Christ's second coming which had arisen from comments he had made in his first.

1 and 2 Timothy. Timothy, whose mother was Jewish and father was Greek, came to faith in Christ in his home church of Lystra (cf. Acts 16:1–2), a city in southern Galatia. As Paul passed through the city on his second missionary journey, Timothy joined the apostle on his travels. Timothy remained a faithful and committed traveling companion of Paul and eventually spent significant time as the young pastor of the influential church in Ephesus (1 Tim 1: 3). Paul's first letter to Timothy warns against unorthodox teaching and provides instruction for administering the growing Ephesian church. His second letter, written while awaiting execution in a Roman prison, urges Timothy to remain strong and, if possible, travel to Rome to visit his aging spiritual father.

Titus. Titus, who was Greek, was a tireless traveling companion of Paul. He served Paul as an ecclesiastical trouble-shooter, going to Corinth and Crete to sort out problems in the churches there (cf. 2 Cor 8:6, 16–17; Titus 1:5). Titus's travels also took him as far as Dalmatia (modern Croatia and Bosnia; cf. 2 Tim 4:10) and Jerusalem (Gal 2:1). Paul's pastoral epistle to Titus urges Titus to appoint qualified leaders for the Cretan church, preach sound doctrine and encourage good works.

Philemon. Philemon was a well-to-do resident of Colossae who offered his home as a meeting place for the local church there. He was also a slave owner, and one of his slaves, Onesimus, had run away to Rome after causing Philemon financial harm, only to come to faith in Christ under the ministry of Paul. Paul's letter to Philemon, a window into issues of domestic concern, urges him to accept Onesimus back as a Christian brother.

Hebrews. The epistle to the Hebrews, an anonymous book, reflects a stage in the development of the early Church in which the Church was starting to pull away from Judaism. The author argues that the revelation of God through Jesus was superior to that of angels, prophets and even Moses himself. For this reason, believers in Jesus should hold fast to what they have been taught and, like the great men and women of the Old Testament, remain faithful to the end in spite of persecution. This epistle was apparently written to Jewish believers in Jesus, but their location, whether in Israel or the Roman world, is unknown, and the letter is largely lacking in geographical information.

James. The epistle of James, more a sermon than a letter, was written to "the twelve tribes in the dispersion" (1:1), a broad reference to Jewish believers in Jesus scattered across the known world. This universal audience is matched by the universal theme of the letter, namely, that faith, or belief in God, is useless without an accompanying display of faithfulness, i.e., good works. Tradition holds that the author of this epistle was James the brother of Jesus (cf. Mk 6:3), who became the head of the Jerusalem church (cf. Acts 15:13). This is supported by the large number of teachings in the book that parallel the words of Jesus.

1 and 2 Peter. The first epistle of Peter, a Bethsaida-born fisherman turned chief Apostle, was written to "pilgrims of the dispersion" in Pontus, Galatia, Cappadocia, Asia and Bithynia, districts in northern and western Asia Minor (1:1). Peter wrote from "Babylon" (5:13), a cryptic allusion to Rome, where tradition holds he was martyred. In this letter, Peter urges his audience to stand fast in the face of persecution. Peter's second epistle, written to Christians generally, warns against the dangers of false prophets and speaks of future judgment at the second coming of Christ.

1, 2 and 3 John. Identified only as "the Elder" in 2 and 3 John and not at all in 1 John, early Church tradition has long held that the writer of these epistles was Jesus' beloved disciple John, author of the fourth gospel. According to this tradition, John became the leader of the church in Ephesus after the fall of Jerusalem. John writes as a loving elder statesman, building on the teachings of his gospel and prompting his readers to love each other with the fellowship and love of Christ.

Jude. Tradition holds that Jude's epistle was written by Judas the brother of Jesus and James (cf. Mk 6:3). There is no geographical information in Jude's letter which would help to identify its audience, nor is it clear whether Jude was writing to Jewish believers in Jesus or gentile Christians. Jude refers to several events—some from the Old Testament and others known only from Jewish apocalyptic literature—to illustrate the danger of following false teachers and accepting their aberrant, almost fantastic, beliefs.

Prophecy
The Revelation of John. The Apocalypse (or, "Revelation") of John was written to Christians "to show things which must shortly take place" (Rev 1:1). The language throughout is cryptic, symbolic and highly graphic, apparently intended to conceal as well as to reveal. The author, the Apostle John, Jesus' beloved disciple, draws heavily on imagery from the Old Testament and Jewish apocalyptic literature as he describes terrible trials which will someday face the Church. John opens his book with a personal challenge to seven churches in western Asia (Ephesus, Smyrna, Pergamum, Thyatira, Sardis, Philadelphia and Laodicea), and ends with a glorious picture of a new heaven and new earth, a new Jerusalem that brings the perfection of Eden to the now triumphant universal Church.

The Land of the Gospels

The land of the Gospels—the land that Jesus walked—is a narrow strip wedged between the Mediterranean Sea and the upper reaches of the vast Arabian Desert. The great trunk road that has connected Mesopotamia and Egypt since antiquity bisects this land from north to south. During the time of the Old Testament this road brought the merchants and armies of the world's great empires to the doorstep of ancient Israel. By the time of the New Testament the geopolitical center of the world had shifted westward to the Aegean and Rome, and the homeland of the Jews was reduced to a far-flung corner of the Roman Empire. Nevertheless, Jesus' travels in his ancestral land brought him into contact with peoples representing everything that the Roman world had to offer.

The land of the Gospels can be divided into five basic geopolitical divisions: Judea, Samaria, the Coastal Plain, Galilee, and Transjordan. For comparative purposes, the modern state of Israel, including the West Bank, is about the same size as New Jersey and slightly smaller than Wales. Yet this small region contains a variety of landforms and changes in climate similar to that found in California. Far from uniform in shape, style and substance, the land of the Gospels provides a fitting stage for the weave of stories of the New Testament world.

Judea

The heartland of Judea consists of the rugged limestone hill country lying within a day's walk of Jerusalem. Elevations reaching over 900 meters (2,950 feet) provide the land with cold, wet winters and summers that, though sunny and hot, are usually cooled by mid-afternoon Mediterranean breezes. With the primary exceptions of the city of Jerusalem and the town that grew up next to Herod's winter palace at Jericho, this was a land of villages and farms, with terraces of grapevines and olive, fig and pomegranate trees embracing the hills. The land's ruggedness tended to isolate the people of Judea from its more open neighbors on every side, fostering a degree of conservatism more prevalent here than in the surrounding regions.

Dropping out of the hill country to the east, one encounters the chalky wilderness of Judea, an arid land best suited for flocks of sheep and goats. Beyond is the Dead Sea, the lowest spot and saltiest body of water on the face of the earth. On its western shore, between Jericho and En-gedi, grew the Roman world's supply of balsam.

To the west of the hill country the broad valleys of the Shephelah, or foothills, open the land of Judea to the coastal plain. Here conditions are favorable for agriculture, and the alluvial soil, ample rainfall and warmer overall temperatures prove ideal for fields of wheat and barley. In the days of the New Testament the southern section of the Shephelah was called Idumea, with a population that traced its roots to the Edomites, descendants of Esau who settled there after the fall of the Old Testament kingdom of Judah.

Samaria

In terms of soil and water—its best natural resources—the hill coun-

Olive trees on the terraced hillsides of Judea.

Northern Samaria, viewed from Mount Gilboa.

try of Samaria surpasses that of its southern Judean neighbor. This was the region of the Old Testament tribes of Ephraim and Manasseh, a land that the biblical writers described as the most blessed of all the tribal inheritances (Gen 49:22–26; Deut 33:13–17). It was also the heartland of the northern kingdom of Israel. Elevations in Samaria rarely exceed 750 meters (2,460 feet), which results in moderate wintertime temperatures. A network of broad alluvial valleys run through the center of the hill country, giving Samaria a mixed and fertile economic base. The natural routes connecting these valleys also join Samaria to the outside world, opening its people to foreign religious and cultural influences. Samaria's population in the first century was mixed Samaritan and gentile, and Jews traveling between Jerusalem and Galilee preferred to avoid the region altogether.

The Coastal Plain

A broad, north-south plain separates the hill country of Judea and Samaria from the Mediterranean Sea. Here rich alluvial soils washed down from the hills mix with North African sand, brought ashore by the continual action of current and waves. The southern part of the plain (Old Testament Philistia) is a flat, fertile agricultural land that has always supported a relatively large population and, from the beginning of the historic period, true cities. In the north (the Sharon Plain), several long, low ridges of *kurkar* (solidified sand dunes) parallel the shore, impeding the flow of runoff water to the coast and resulting in a relatively soggy land that never attracted a large population.

The international flavor of the Coastal Plain is primarily a result of the land route connecting Egypt with Asia and Europe that runs its length, and by the time of the New Testament the cultural influences of Hellenism were well entrenched along its length. In contrast, the plain's long, gently arched coastline, with no decent breaks to form a natural harbor except at Joppa (modern Tel Aviv), failed to draw the populations of Judea and Samaria into the Mediterranean world. Eventually Herod's massive man-made harbor at Caesarea remedied this, and provided the region the necessary port to interact freely with the West.

Galilee

Galilee, a diverse region in the northern part of the land of the Gospels, was the focal point of most of Jesus' ministry. The region is separated from the hills of Samaria by the vast Jezreel Valley, a geological basin which serves not only as the agricultural breadbasket of the entire area but also as a wide-open corridor channeling international traffic between West and East, between the lands of the Mediterranean and those of Transjordan. Jesus' boyhood home of Nazareth was located high on a limestone ridge overlooking the Jezreel Valley from the north; no doubt the valley's rich and storied history helped to shape his messianic awareness.

The limestone hills of Galilee are high and rugged in the north (over 600 meters/1,970 feet, hence the term "Upper Galilee"), and lower in the south ("Lower Galilee"). Upper Galilee resembles the higher parts of the hill country of Judea in many respects, particularly in its agricultural base and general isolation from the larger world around, although Upper Galilee is wetter and more productive. Lower Galilee is characterized by a series of parallel hilly ridges separated by broad, fertile valleys, and it is here that most of the population of first-century Galilee lived. The relatively low terrain of Lower Galilee makes for fairly easy travel throughout, and serves to pull the region together as a self-contained unit while at the same time linking it to its neighbors. Nestled among basalt hills to the east lies the jeweled Sea of Galilee, the only freshwater lake

83

The Golan region (ancient Gaulanitis) with Mount Hermon in the background.

of any consequence on the entire eastern Mediterranean seaboard and the primary natural resource of all of Galilee.

Transjordan

The lands of Transjordan are separated from Judea, Samaria and Galilee by the Rift Valley, a massive geological tear on the surface of the earth that extends from southern Turkey deep into East Africa. The northernmost part of Transjordan (today's Golan, opposite Galilee) is a well-watered area of basalt that rises eastward to form a high plateau that was intensively farmed for wheat in Roman times. To the south, and east of Samaria, looms the high limestone dome of Gilead with mountainous slopes terraced for grapevines, olives and figs. Farther south yet, above the Dead Sea, rises a chalky plateau best suited for grazing land, the homeland of the Old Testament kingdom of Moab. And in the deep south beyond lie the arid, high and somewhat mysterious mountains of Edom which, by the time of the New Testament, were dominated by the Nabateans, a kingdom of camel caravaneers who controlled the spice route coming out of the Arabian Peninsula. The lands of Transjordan are connected by an international highway, a landed eastern route paralleling that along the Mediterranean coast. The Roman Empire's southeastern frontier never pushed beyond Transjordan; farther east, the vast Arabian Desert lay untamed even by the power and resources of Rome.

Roman remains of Gerasa (modern Jerash), one of the cities of the Decapolis in Transjordan.

Peoples and Lands of the New Testament World

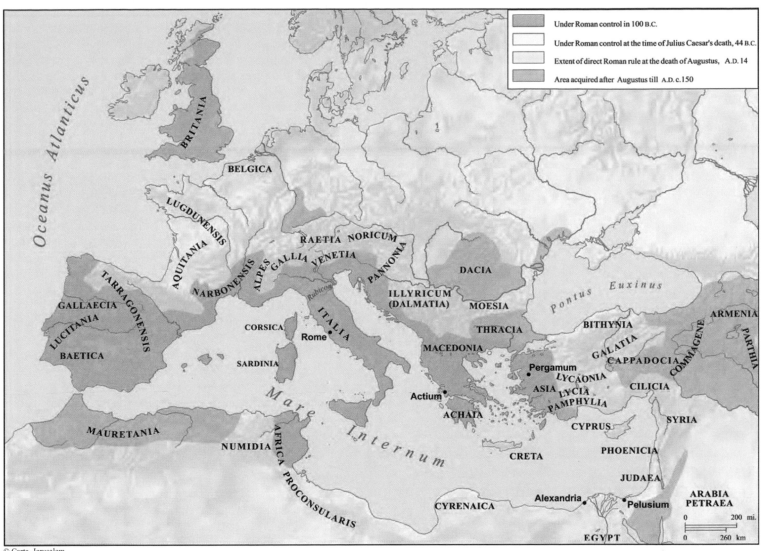

	Under Roman control in 100 B.C.
	Under Roman control at the time of Julius Caesar's death, 44 B.C.
	Extent of direct Roman rule at the death of Augustus, A.D. 14
	Area acquired after Augustus till A.D. c.150

© Carta, Jerusalem

The world of the New Testament was a Mediterranean world. The march of Alexander the Great through the ancient Near East, from Macedonia to India, awoke the lands of the Old Testament to the emerging world of Hellenism, and eventually to Rome itself. With it, the center of the world swung west to the Mediterranean basin, bringing new social, economic and religious opportunities—and the accompanying challenges that followed close behind.

The lands of the ancient Near East hung along the Fertile Crescent, crowded by the looming mass of the Arabian Desert and balanced on either end by the river valleys of the Nile to the west and the Tigris and Euphrates to the east. By contrast, the Mediterranean basin was a vast amphitheater, a circle of lands and peoples drawn together by the closeness of the sea and protected from lands beyond by a wider, almost unbroken circle of mountain and desert. The peninsulas of Italy and Greece; the large islands of Cyprus, Crete and Sicily; a scattering of smaller islands filling the Aegean; innumerable bays, inlets, estuaries, seas and coves—these natural geographic features within the Mediterranean basin connected sea and land, providing an expanding network of routes that hurried both armies and commerce to the farthest corners of this new world. By the end of the first century A.D. the lands of the Mediterranean basked in Pax Romana, the "Peace of Rome," as the military priorities that build the Roman Empire gradually gave way to the social and economic benefits that came in its wake.

A list of peoples who visited Jerusalem for the Jewish festival of Shavuot (Pentecost) seven weeks after the crucifixion and resurrection of Jesus is found in Acts 2:9–11. This list is a sampling of lands and peoples of the Mediterranean—including a few from the ancient Near East—and provides a first-century "Table of Nations" (cf. Genesis 10) ripe for the spread of the Gospel. More Mediterranean lands are mentioned in other writings of the New Testament. Taken together, those that played the most prominent role in the story of the New Testament are listed below, in counterclockwise geographical order.

Syria (Syro-Phoenicia). The large Roman province of Syria encompassed most of what is today modern Syria and Lebanon, in addition to parts of southeastern Turkey (Asia Minor). During at least part of the time of the New Testament, Syria also exercised some control over Judea and Galilee (cf. Lk 2:1–2). The capital of Syria was Antioch, a beautifully situated city nestled near the northernmost bend of the Orontes River. It was here that the followers of Jesus were first called "Christians" (Acts 11:19–26; 15:22–23). Syria was an extremely hellenized part of the Roman Empire. Many established cities here had already been given Greek names during the Hellenistic period and were eventually rebuilt according to classic Greco-Roman architectural lines, becoming important centers of Greek philosophy and literature. Hellenism first gained a foothold in

Syria through cities such as Tyre and Sidon, old seafaring ports that hugged the rocky Phoenician (Lebanese) coast. In part the Greeks and Romans simply took advantage of the role that these cities had already played in the Mediterranean world, for by establishing trading colonies throughout the Mediterranean as early as the eighth century B.C., Tyre and Sidon had forged close economic and political ties with the west long before the rise of Rome.

Cyprus. Cyprus, an island rich in natural resources, is noted especially for its copper mines (which were controlled in the late first century B.C. by Herod the Great) and timber. On a clear day it is possible to see both southern Turkey and the Lebanese mountains from the northeastern part of the island, and this close proximity to the mainland made Cyprus a cultural crossroads in the eastern Mediterranean throughout antiquity. Tied to both Greece and Phoenicia from its earliest days, Cyprus lay astride some of the most active shipping lanes in the Mediterranean (cf. Acts 21:3, 27:4). Historically the island was inhabited by Minoans and then Greeks, and in intertestamental times was controlled alternatively by Persia, Ptolemaic Egypt, and Rome as each in turn sought to gain strategic advantage in the eastern Mediterranean. Apparently there was a large and vibrant Jewish population in Cyprus by the first century A.D.; there was, for instance, more than one synagogue at Salamis, the main port on the eastern side of the island (Acts 13: 4–5). Barnabas, a native of Cyprus (Acts 4:36), joined the Apostle Paul and John Mark on their first missionary journey, visiting synagogues the length of the island from Salamis to Paphos (Acts 13:4–6). When the island's procounsul Sergius Paulus embraced Christianity as a result of Paul's preaching, Cyprus became the first Roman territory to be governed by a Christian (Acts 13:6–12).

Cilicia. The province of Cilicia was located in Asia Minor at the northeastern corner of the Mediterranean Sea. A large, fertile plain dominated the eastern end of Cilicia, and was home to a thriving Greek and Jewish population at the time of the New Testament. The easternmost city on this plain, Issus, was the site of Alexander the Great's decisive battle against Darius the Persian in 333 B.C., which opened the east to Hellenism. Tarsus, on the western end of the plain, was a center of education rivaling Alexandria and Athens, and also the hometown of the Apostle Paul. Behind this plain towered the Taurus Mountains, a rugged 10,000-foot wall separating continental Asia from Asia Minor. These mountains were punctured by the narrow Cilician Gates, a formidable pass above Tarsus that carried most of the traffic between west and east. The Apostle Paul navigated the Cilician Gates on his second and third missionary journeys (Acts 15:41, 18:23).

Cappadocia. Cappadocia was a rugged, barren province in east central Asia Minor, occupying much of the heartland of the ancient Hittite Empire. Elevations up to 3,960 meters (13,000 feet) made for an extreme climate and harsh living conditions, and the hardy residents of Cappadocia, like their Hittite predecessors, raised mostly sheep and horses. Hellenism was not particularly attracted to these conditions, and the relatively small, largely rural population of Cappadocia tended to resist outside influences. Nevertheless, there were Jewish residents of Cappadocia, and "sojourners scattered throughout Cappadocia" were among the recipients of the first epistle of Peter (1 Pet 1:1).

Bithynia and Pontus. Bithynia and Pontus were originally two neighboring regions in northwestern Asia Minor lying along the southern coast of the Black Sea. Scant agricultural land, a noticeable lack of good harbors and frequent earthquakes conspired to hold back the progress of the area. In addition, high mountains in the south tended to isolate the coastal cities of Bithynia and Pontus from the interior of Asia Minor, and the tough inhabitants of these regions remained largely independent until they were incorporated into the Roman Empire as a single province in the first century B.C. Even though the Apostle Paul was "not permitted by the Spirit of Jesus" to visit Bithynia (Acts 16:7), the early Church did take root there (1 Pet 1:1), probably first among the regions' Jewish population which counted among its natives Aquila, one of Paul's closest companions (Acts 18:1; cf. Acts 2:9).

Galatia. In the third century B.C. bands of migrating Gauls from Europe settled on the high mountainous plateau of north central Asia Minor, establishing there the independent kingdom of Galatia. In 25 B.C. this kingdom, along with its mountainous southern neighbors Pisidia (Acts 14:24), Lycaonia (Acts 14:11) and parts of Phrygia (cf. Acts 2:10), were incorporated into the Roman Empire, becoming together the Roman province of Galatia. This was a wild and rugged land, inhabited—at least from the point of view of Rome—by people of a similar temperament. Neither Hellenism nor, it is assumed, Judaism, took deep root in the northern part of the province and fared only a little better in the south, and Rome's occupation throughout was primarily military. Nevertheless, the Apostle Paul traveled through the southern, Pisidian part of Galatia on all three of his missionary journeys, establishing a handful of churches there in spite of ongoing travel dangers (cf. 2 Cor 11:26). Timothy, perhaps Paul's favorite disciple, was a native of Lystra in Pisidian Galatia (Acts 16:1–2).

Pamphylia. The Roman province of Pamphylia consisted of an alluvial plain that followed the curve of a vast arc on the south Asia Minor coast tucked between two massive outcroppings of the Taurus Mountains, with Cilicia to the east and Lycia (Acts 27:5) to the west. With a pleasant year-round climate and ample water supplies, this fertile plain produced orchard and field crops in abundance, and supported five large Hellenistic port cities. Of these, the Apostle Paul passed through Perga (Acts 13:13–14) and Attalia (Acts 14: 25; modern Antalya) on his first journey into Galatia. Squarely facing the Mediterranean, Pamphylia was home to a wide variety of peoples (the name Pamphylia means "of all peoples"), yet served more as a port for regional pirates than for cosmopolitan Rome. Even though Pamphylia had an established Jewish population (Acts 2:10), the New Testament records little of Paul's work to establish churches there.

Asia. The Roman province of Asia filled the entire western third of Asia Minor, including numerous islands off its coast. Asia was oriented westward, with several large rivers slicing the province from east to west and draining into the Aegean Sea. Fertile river valleys and a mountainous interior combined to form a pleasant land, with a strong, mixed economy and a large, relatively prosperous population. Many influential Greek cities were sprinkled throughout Asia, and three—Ephesus, Pergamum and Smyrna—held the official title "First of Asia." Of these, the primary city was the capital Ephesus, and it was from here that the gospel spread throughout the entire province, "among both Jews and Greeks" (Acts 19:10). Intensive missionary activity by the Apostles Paul and John, among others, resulted in a strong Christian presence throughout Asia by the late first century A.D. (note the "seven churches" of Revelation 1–3).

The temple of Hephaistos, the Agora at Athens, Greece.

Macedonia. The rugged, mountainous land of Macedonia sat astride the southern Balkan Peninsula just north of Achaia (Greece). Except for its southeastern exposure to the Aegean, Macedonia was not particularly oriented toward the sea. Because of its physical connection to the Balkans, growing conditions were affected more by the harsher climate of eastern Europe than that of the Mediterranean, and livestock and grains rather than grapes, olives and figs, provided its agricultural base. The entire ancient history of Macedonia was a history of conflict—both military and cultural—between the Macedonian and Greek populations of the lower Balkan Peninsula. Macedonia was the launching pad for the conquests of Alexander the Great, a native of that land who united the peninsula and then the known world under a blended, though predominantly Greek, culture known as Hellenism. Setting the stage for the New Testament, Caesar Augustus formally separated Macedonia from Achaia in 27 B.C. (cf. Acts 19:21), its more prominent and refined rival to the south. Two of Macedonia's main cities, Thessalonica and Philippi, figured prominently in the journeys of the Apostle Paul (Acts 16:9–12, 18:5), who founded important Christian churches among the Greek and Jewish populations of the region.

Achaia (Greece). Originally a small land lying just north of the Corinthian Gulf, Achaia by Roman times was enlarged to include the whole of Greece, including over two hundred islands scattered throughout the Aegean Sea. Achaia's most prominent region was the Peloponnesus, a tumbled peninsula shaped something like a mulberry leaf dangling into the Mediterranean by the narrow Isthmus of Corinth. The highly irregular coastline of Achaia brought the sea close to the land's dissected interior, providing vistas and

venues that came to characterize the entire Greco-Roman world. With a mild climate but little in the way of natural resources, Achaia's prominence and wealth was found in its control of the shipping lanes of the eastern Mediterranean. City-states such as Athens, Corinth and Sparta, which for centuries had been fierce rivals for the body and mind of ancient Greece, were brought together into the Roman Empire in the second century B.C., while continuing to clamor for attention and privilege from Rome. The Apostle Paul was eagerly drawn into this challenging world and visited a number of Achaean cities on his second and third missionary journeys, focusing his work in particular in Athens and Corinth (Acts 17:16, 18:27–28; 2 Cor 1:1).

Crete. The large island of Crete, forming the southern boundary of the Aegean Sea, is strategically positioned as a bridge between the lands of the eastern and central Mediterranean basin. During the third and second millennia B.C. Crete was home to the pre-Greek Minoan civilization, but with the Minoan collapse the island lay awash a vast movement of peoples and cultures. Crete can probably be identified with biblical Caphtor, original homeland of the Philistines (Amos 9:7). Though always tied to the Greek mainland historically, Crete became a separate Roman province in 67 B.C. when, instead, it was joined administratively to Cyrene on the north African coast. In the first century A.D. Crete, like Achaia, boasted a large Greek population with a significant Jewish minority (Acts 2: 11), but unlike the inhabitants of the classical mainland, Cretans had a low reputation in the ancient world (Titus 1:12, quoting the Cretan poet Epimenides). Crete is almost entirely covered with high mountains which were heavily forested in ancient times, and has only a few areas suitable for agriculture. The best harbors are on the northern shore. Paul's Rome-bound ship was unable to find suitable a winter harbor at Fair Havens, a rocky inlet midway along Crete's southern side where the island's mountains typically rise right out of the sea (Acts 27:8–13). Paul sent Titus to Crete to guide the growing churches there (Titus 1:5).

Illyricum. The Roman province of Illyricum lay along the eastern coast of the Adriatic Sea, from today's Albania to Croatia. With a cold, mountainous interior and a warm, inviting coast, the people of this region looked historically as much to Europe as to the Mediterranean. The region of Illyricum had been colonized as early as the eighth century B.C. by the Greeks yet lay largely outside of effective Greek control, and it harbored elements renowned for piracy on the Adriatic. Rome conquered the region in the mid-second century B.C., but the unrepressed nature of its inhabitants slowed full incorporation of the province into the Roman Empire until the first century A.D. The Romans divided the province of Illyricum into two major administrative sections; the more important of the two, Dalmatia, was visited by Titus (2 Tim 4:10). Illyricum's remoteness from the eastern Mediterranean world represents the far-flung distance that Paul traveled to preach the gospel (Rom 15:19). The extent of a Jewish presence there is unknown.

Italia (Rome). The boot-shaped Italian peninsula—probably the most distinctive coastline in the world—slices through the central Mediterranean Sea perfectly positioned to control the entire Mediterranean basin. The towering Alps have isolated the peninsula from mainland Europe, while the irregular, 3,220-kilometer (2000-mile) coastline provided ample harbors, especially in the southwest, to confirm Italy's destiny as a sea power from the beginning of its history. The Apennines, running the spine of the peninsula, are not particularly high mountains and did not provide a barrier to unification in antiquity. The mixture of climate, soil and water is good, blessing the inhabitants of the peninsula with the basic necessities of life. The magnificent city of Rome, straddling the Tiber, the only navigable river in the central peninsula, became synonymous with the vast empire that filled the Mediterranean basin by the first century B.C., washing ashore in Judea in the year 63. The adage "all roads lead to Rome" properly notes the intricate imperial highway system that was still expanding in the first century, although most transport always moved by sea. Mediterranean ports controlled by Rome were, by definition, the chief cities of the known world. A notable Jewish and emerging Christian presence was counted among Rome's cosmopolitan population in the first century A.D., and when Paul finally reached that city (Acts 27:1, 28:16) he was able to foster the growth of what was to become the most influential church in Christendom (Rom 1:7; cf. Heb 13:24).

Cyrenaica. The land of Cyrenaica stretched along a great bend of the north African coastline west of the Nile Delta, comprising a portion of both ancient and modern Libya. Because Cyrenaica backed up against the wasteland of the vast Saharan Desert, the attention of its inhabitants was directed toward the Mediterranean. This was a fertile land, and its excellent soil and pleasant climate combined to give the region a reputation known for bountiful grain fields and strong livestock. The region's main city, Cyrene, was founded by Greek colonists by the early sixth century B.C., only to be incorporated into Ptolemaic Egypt three hundred years later. It was under Ptolemaic rule that Cyrene became a renowned center of learning and medicine. The Romans officially joined the region to Crete in 67 B.C., uniting both lands into a single province named Cyrenaica, governed from Cyrene, the provincial capital. A large Jewish population had taken root in Cyrene during Ptolemaic times. During the first century A.D. the Jews of Cyrene maintained close ties to Jerusalem (Mt 27:32; Acts 2:10, 6:9), many no doubt coming into contact with the Gospel there. Christians from Cyrene helped to foster the growth of the early church in Antioch (Acts 11:20, 13:1).

Egypt. Perhaps no land in the ancient or classical world was better defined by its natural resources than was Egypt, the "Gift of the Nile." The immensely fertile Nile River valley, replenished each year by a new layer of rich flood-deposited silt, was only 10 to 26 kilometers (6 to 16 miles) wide, yet provided a steady crop of grain and vegetables to feed large portions of the Roman world. In the late second millennium B.C. Egypt was the strongest empire on earth, but its fortunes spiraled downward throughout the time of the Israelite monarchy. Ptolemaic Egypt (late fourth through first centuries B.C.) saw a meek attempt to revive past Egyptian glory, with Egyptian-based control extending over Cyrenecia and Syro-Palestine. With the suicide of Cleopatra VII (*the* Cleopatra) in 30 B.C., the last vestige of Pharaonic Egypt passed to Roman rule. Important Jewish colonies had been founded at Elephantine (Aswan), and especially in Alexandria on the Mediterranean coast, where Jews enjoyed a certain measure of autonomy. During the time of the New Testament, Alexandria was the greatest center of commerce and learning in the eastern Mediterranean, and Jews played an important role in both activities. This was fertile ground for Christianity as well, and the early Church took deep root in Egyptian soil (Acts 2:10, 18:24–28).

Arabia Petraea. The Arabia of the New Testament world consisted of a thin band of high rocky desert in what is today eastern and southern Jordan (including the ancient homelands of Moab and Edom) and the southern Sinai. This was the geographical and cultural seam between the peoples and lands of the eastern Mediterranean and those of the Arabian Peninsula. Traditionally home to a number of fiercely independent desert tribes, this region became dominated in the centuries leading up to the New Testament by the Nabateans. From their fabulous and fabled capital city of Petra, carved out of the red sandstone cliffs above the Rift Valley, the Nabateans dominated the great spice route that brought frankincense and myrrh from the recesses of the Arabian Peninsula into an eager Roman world. Nabatean control under Aretas IV, father-in-law of Herod Antipas, extended as far north as Damascus (2 Cor 11:32–33), and it was into this territory that the Apostle Paul retreated after becoming a follower of Jesus (Gal 1:17). When the Romans under Trajan were finally able to seize the Nabatean-held lands in A.D. 106, Arabia Petraea became the Empire's southeastern frontier.

The Intertestamental Period

Alexander the Great. Alexander of Macedon launched his campaign to conquer an aging Persian Empire in 334 B.C. Fearless and dynamic, the 20-year-old Alexander rode the rising tide of Hellenism, an equally vibrant way of life that would forever change the world. After sweeping through Asia Minor in just one year, Alexander fought his first major battle at Issus on the Cilician Plain, where the daring general routed the Persian king Darius. While Darius fled east, Alexander turned south, conquering Tyre in 332 B.C. after a seven-month siege and then easily subduing the remaining petty city-states that hugged the eastern Mediterranean seaboard. After being crowned Pharaoh in Egypt, Alexander retraced his steps up the eastern seaboard of the Mediterranean before catching up with Darius at Gaugamela in northern Mesopotamia. Here was the decisive battle, and after his ringing victory Alexander faced little real

Alexander the Great (left) from a mosaic found at Pompeii.

resistance as he marched all the way to the Indus Valley and the steppes of Central Asia. When he died at the age of 32 in Babylon, the seeds of a new world order had been sown across the entire ancient Near East. Alexander's soldiers settled down in his wake, establishing Macedonian colonies and cities throughout the former Persian Empire, including one in Samaria.

The Successors to Alexander. Upon his death, the fruit of Alexander's conquests passed to his generals. After two initial decades of war during which each general sought to gain advantage over the others, the world from Greece to Persia fell into an uneasy peace. The land of Palestine, including the Phoenician coast and Transjordan, came under the control of the Ptolemies, a long line of successors of Alexander's general Ptolemy who ruled from Egypt. The lands from Damascus to the Indus River were ruled by Seleucus, another of Alexander's generals, and his successors, most of whom were named Seleucus or Antiochus. The Seleucid kings in particular encouraged a policy of establishing a series of military colonies and Greek cities—many named Seleucia or Antioch—throughout the territory under their control. These served several purposes: to bind together an otherwise diverse and divisive land, to foster loyalty to the king, and to disseminate Hellenism among the native populations of the empire. During the third century B.C., Greek language and customs took deep root in Seleucid soil, finding life among many people—including Jews—who were attracted to new economic and cultural opportunities now available to them.

At the same time, the lands bordering the eastern seaboard of

THE ROUTE OF ALEXANDER THE GREAT, 334–323 B.C.

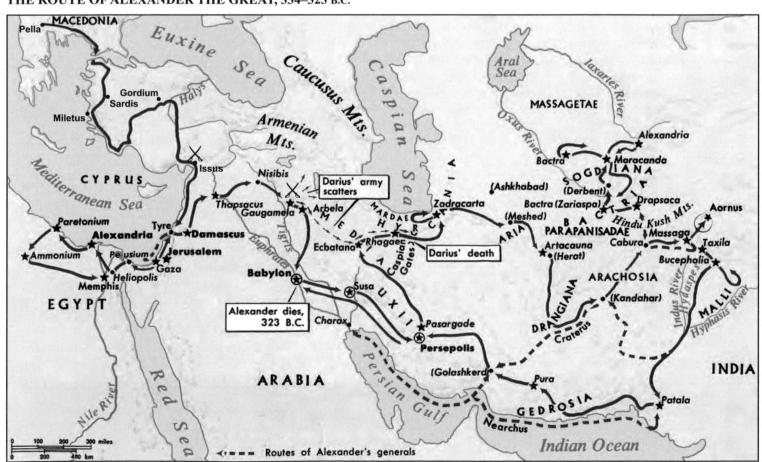

89

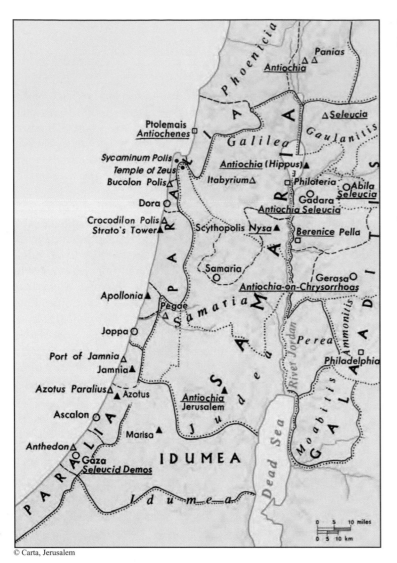

© Carta, Jerusalem

THE GREEK CITIES IN PALESTINE
312–167 B.C.

Seleucid war elephant.   *Seleucid coin with Apollo on reverse.*

———	Border of Seleucid eparchy
- - - -	Border of Ptolemaic city
....	Border of Ptolemaic hyparchy
PARALIA	Seleucid eparchy
Judea	Ptolemaic hyparchy
<u>Seleucia</u>	City given Seleucid dynastic name
□	City given Ptolemaic dynastic name
O	City with municipal rights under Ptolemaic rule
△	Town given Greek name
▲	City given Greek name

the Mediterranean were buffeted by five Syrian wars as Seleucids fought Ptolemies for dominance over the region. With the Battle of Panias in 201 B.C., the border of Seleucid control was finally pushed south to Gaza. The Jews of Jerusalem welcomed the Seleucid king Antiochus III, who granted them rights and privileges that allowed relatively free expression of Jewish religious practices. Ominously, within a decade Antiochus III lost his holdings in Asia Minor to Rome, an emerging world power already poised to sweep into the lands of the Eastern Mediterranean.

The Maccabean Revolt. Antiochus IV took the Seleucid throne in 174 B.C. as Roman war clouds gathered on the western horizon. To meet this rising threat, Antiochus sought to strengthen his own far-flung empire by uniting its diverse lands and peoples under the religious and cultural flag of Hellenism, integrating all gods under the supremacy of Zeus. Certain elements among the population of Jerusalem accepted these decrees, while most, of course, resisted. At the highest levels, the office of the high priesthood was "purchased" by Jason, an ardent hellenizer, and then by Menelaus (2 Macc 4), two powerful men who tried to use their position to bend the cultural and religious loyalty of the Jews toward Hellenism. When Antiochus IV invaded Egypt to try to forge a single political unit out of all of the eastern lands, Rome stepped in. Humiliated and frustrated on the world stage, Antiochus turned his wrath against the Jewish population of Jerusalem, who had largely rebuffed his earlier attempts to hellenize their city and bring it into his cultural and political fold. Antiochus forbade the exercise of religious practices essential to Judaism (such as keeping the Sabbath and yearly feasts, offering

sacrifices and circumcision) and in December 167 B.C. he turned the Temple into a sanctuary of Zeus, offering on its altar sacrifices unclean according to Jewish law (1 Macc 1:41–64).

With this the Jews mounted an armed revolt, prompted by Mattathias, a priest of the Hasmonean family who hailed from the village of Modiin, located on the edge of Palestine's hellenized coastal plain. Mattathias's son Judas Maccabeus ("the hammerer") waged what amounted to a guerrilla war against the Seleucid army, which was trying to link with the Hellenistic forces in Jerusalem and crush the Jewish revolt. A brilliant battle tactician, Judas routed the Seleucid forces at each attempt, finally taking his own army into Jerusalem. In December 164 B.C. Judas cleansed and rededicated the Temple (1 Macc 2–4); the festival of Hanukkah ("Dedication"; cf. Jn 10: 22–23) commemorates this event.

Not content with rescuing the Temple from Seleucid hands, Judas launched a series of defensive campaigns aimed at strengthening the Jewish position in their historic homeland. Judas himself fell in battle in 161 B.C., but over the next two decades his brothers Jonathan and Simon gained decisive victories over the Seleucids in Samaria, Galilee, Transjordan (Gilead and Syria) and even the coastal plain, long a stronghold of Greek culture and power (1 Macc 10–15). The Seleucid king formally recognized Judea's independence under Simon in 142 B.C. (1 Macc 13:33–42), signaling the rise of the first independent Jewish state since the fall of Judah to the Babylonians in 586 B.C. In response, the Jews granted Simon the title "leader and high priest forever, until a trustworthy prophet should arise" (1 Macc 14:25–49).

The Hasmonean State. With its newly won political and religious independence in hand, the Jewish state began to consolidate and expand power in its ancestral homeland. John Hyrcanus succeeded his father Simon in 135 B.C. and, with the tacit approval of Rome, formally conquered Medeba in Transjordan, Samaria (where he destroyed the Samaritan temple on Mount Gerizim) and Idumea, thereby securing for Judea the lands which were best placed strategically for later territorial expansion. Toward the end of his reign Hyrcanus sided with the Sadducees over against the Pharisees in inter-Jewish religious affairs, signaling a gradual shift toward hellenization within the ruling administration of Judea (as the party of the wealthy Jewish aristocracy, the Sadducees were more in touch with the social and economic opportunities that arose with Hellenism than were the more conservative Pharisees). That Hyrcanus gave his sons (and successors) Greek names (Aristobulus and Alexander Janneus) is a further indication of the inter-Jewish religious and cultural strife that lay ahead.

Hyrcanus was succeeded by his older son Aristobulus in 104 B.C. During his one-year reign Aristobulus was able to conquer Galilee, reportedly forcing its inhabitants to be circumcised. His successor, Alexander Janneus, pushed the borders of the Hasmonean kingdom to their greatest extent, to include essentially the same territory that had been controlled by David and Solomon. Of particular importance was the conquest of all of the Greek cities on the coastal plain (except Ascalon). In internal affairs, however, the Judean king was less successful. Janneus's favor for things Hellenistic, combined with gross personal moral failings, brought him into open conflict with the Pharisees, who represented the conservative masses of the population. Janneus suppressed the Pharisees with cruel force, at one time crucifying 800 of them.

Janneus's queen, Salome Alexandra, succeeded him as ruler in 76 B.C. Her largely peaceful reign was marred by conflict between her two sons and heirs-apparent, Hyrcanus II (favored by both the Pharisees and the queen) to whom she granted the high priesthood, and Aristobulus II (favored by the Sadducees) who controlled the army. Upon her death in 67 B.C., the brothers waged civil war. Both Hyrcanus II and Aristobulus II asked Rome to intervene on their behalf. Rome was all too happy to oblige; using the chaos of the time as an excuse, the army of Pompey entered Jerusalem in 63 B.C. and the Hasmonean kingdom came to an ignoble end.

Herod the Great. Pompey reorganized the lands of the now defunct Hasmonean kingdom in order to incorporate its territory into the fold of the Roman Empire. Greek cities occupied by the Jews since the days of Hyrcanus—those on the coastal plain, Sebaste in Samaria, Scythopolis and various cities in Transjordan, together with their agricultural hinterlands—were made into autonomous units under the supervision of the Roman proconsul in Syria. The Transjordanian cities were then joined into a league called the Decapolis, filling a territory strategically located to guard Rome's eastern frontier against its political and cultural foes. The Jews retained areas most densely settled by them: Judea, a large portion of Galilee and, across the Jordan, Perea. Hyrcanus II was appointed as high priest over this shell of his former kingdom, but administrative control was given to Antipater the Idumean, who had acted as the behind-the-scenes power broker during the last years of Hasmonean rule. Antipater appointed his older son Phasael governor of Jerusalem and his younger son, Herod, as governor of Galilee.

For two decades various factions vied for control of the land, some struggling to revive the forces of Jewish nationalism, others opting for a form of Roman supremacy. Throughout, Herod maintained a firm, if ruthless, grip on Galilee. This struggle grew to

© Carta, Jerusalem

a climax with the murder of Antipater in 43 B.C. and the invasion of Jerusalem by the Parthians three years later. The Parthians, who controlled Mesopotamia, were Rome's greatest enemy to the East. The Jews who remained in Mesopotamia after the Babylonian Exile represented an important minority population within Parthian controlled lands. They supported the Parthian invasion of Jerusalem as a means of reestablishing an independent Jewish state in Judea. Herod, facing his match, fled to Rome where the Senate responded by appointing him king of all Judea. Eager to reclaim his throne, Herod landed his army at Ptolemais, the port of Galilee, in 39 B.C., then embarked on a series of ferocious campaigns against forces loyal to the Hasmoneans. Within two years he had subdued the land, emerging as the sole, undisputed and largely unloved ruler of Judea. Certain territorial additions on the coast and in Transjordan were added over the next couple of decades, giving Herod a territory, with some modifications in northern Transjordan, reminiscent of that of Alexander Janneus.

A megalomaniac by nature, Herod was restrained from further territorial expansion by Caesar Augustus. Instead, he directed his enormous energies inward, in a personal building campaign that was unsurpassed in the ancient world. Each of his projects, including Jerusalem's Temple Mount, was built in an architectural style that proclaimed the glorious presence of Rome.

- Herod's most prominent building projects were in **Jerusalem**. Here Herod built for himself a sumptuous palace in the north-

91

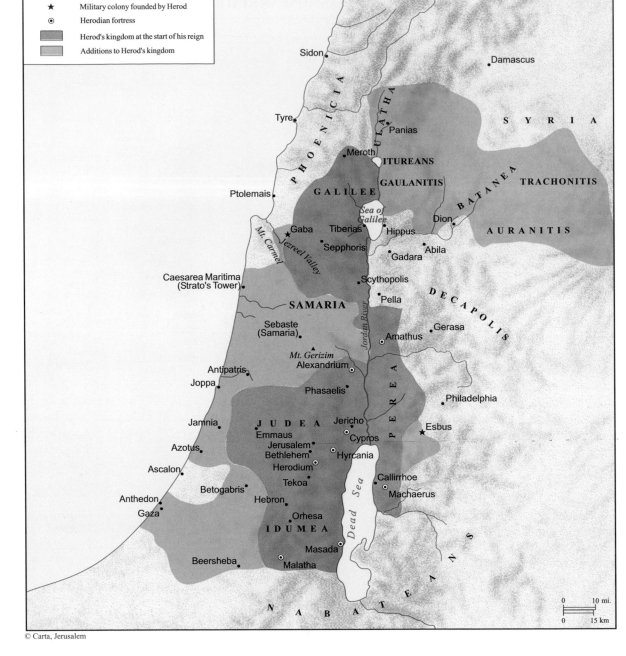

★	Military colony founded by Herod
⊙	Herodian fortress
	Herod's kingdom at the start of his reign
	Additions to Herod's kingdom

© Carta, Jerusalem

Coin of Herod the Great.

western corner of the Upper City (the area of today's Jaffa Gate), guarded by three massive towers. The Temple Mount was doubled in size and encircled by a massive portico. The Temple itself was rebuilt entirely, and the Antonia Fortress constructed to overshadow the Temple Mount from the north. Herod also built a theater and a stadium in the city, and strengthened its fortifications.

- Herod founded **Caesarea** (cf. Acts 8:40, 10:1, 18:22, 21:8), a new port city on the Sharon Plain, to provide better sea access to both Judea and Galilee. Well planned and developed, the city boasted a theater and an amphitheater, a magnificent palace on the sea, a temple dedicated to Caesar, an aqueduct and, most importantly, a harbor projecting far into the Mediterranean that was held together by underwater mortar.

- Herod built a number of palace fortresses in the rugged wilderness east and southeast of Jerusalem, both to secure his back flank into Judea and to provide places of refuge during times of unrest. These included **Herodium**, **Hyrcania**, **Alexandrium**, **Cypros**, **Masada** and, east of the Dead Sea, **Machaerus**. Some of these fortresses had previously served the Hasmonean kings. At Masada Herod especially expressed his grandeur, bring-

ing all the comforts of Rome to an otherwise totally inhospitable corner of his kingdom.

- Herod also rebuilt and enlarged the old Hasmonean palace complex at the oasis of **Jericho**. Here he could escape the winter chill of Jerusalem and banquet in decadent splendor amid pools, fountains, baths, gardens and columned courtyards. The opulence of Herod's Jericho attracted both rich opportunists (cf. Lk 19:1–8) and the desperately poor (cf. Lk 18:35–43).

- Caesar Augustus granted to Herod the city of Samaria (cf. Acts 8:5, 15:3), a bastion of Hellenism since the days of Alexander, and in gratitude Herod renamed the city **Sebaste** (Greek for Augustus). Herod refortified the site, settled foreign mercenaries there and built a temple to Caesar Augustus so colossal that it could be seen by ships on the Mediterranean.

- Augustus also gave Herod the region northeast of Galilee that included the springs of the Jordan River. The easternmost spring was already a center of worship for the Greco-Roman god Pan, and it was here that Herod built a temple faced with white marble, also dedicated to Augustus. In 2 B.C. Herod's son Philip renamed the site **Caesarea Philippi** (cf. Mt 16:13).

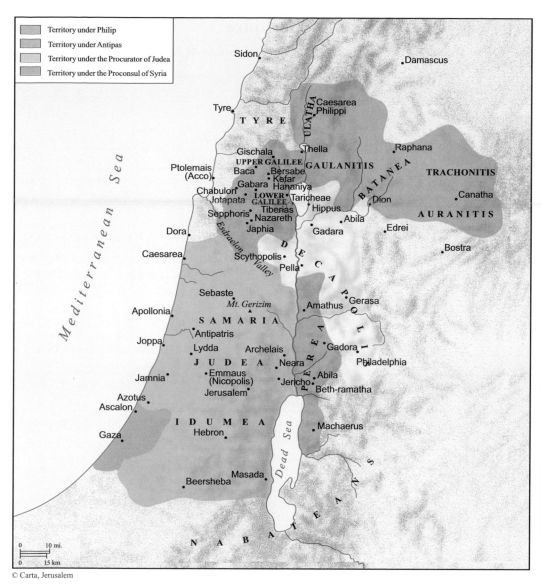

Legend:
- Territory under Philip
- Territory under Antipas
- Territory under the Procurator of Judea
- Territory under the Proconsul of Syria

© Carta, Jerusalem

Site of Caesarea Philippi (modern Banias).

Through these building projects, Herod sought to appease his insatiable ego, to secure his rule, to provide his people with work and to entice their loyalty and devotion to him.

The end of Herod's reign was filled with civil and domestic unrest, much of it fostered by his own family as various sons fought to inherit the throne. Into this volatile fray came Magi from the East (probably from Parthia, Herod's old nemesis who had already driven him from Judea once, at the beginning of his reign), looking for the legitimate king of the Jews (Mt 2:1–12). Herod's response to kill the babies of Bethlehem was overreaching, yet true to form.

Upon Herod's death in 4 B.C., Augustus divided the kingdom between Herod's three surviving sons. Archelaus was appointed ethnarch over Judea, Idumea and Samaria. Herod Antipas was given two primarily Jewish areas, Galilee and Perea. Herod Philip received lands in northern Transjordan including Gaulanitis, where relatively new Jewish settlers mixed with a deeply rooted Hellenistic population. Antipas and Philip stayed in office throughout the lifetime of Jesus (cf. Lk 3:1, 3:19). In contrast, Rome banished Archelaus (Mt 2:22) to Gaul in A.D. 6 for gross incompetence, preferring instead to rule Judea through a string of procurators such as Pontius Pilate (A.D. 26–36; cf. Lk 3:1).

Jewish Religious and Political Parties at the Time of the New Testament. In the first century Judaism was multi-faceted and sectarian, with various parties competing for the allegiance of the people of Judea. Of these, Josephus mentions four groups:

Pharisees, Sadducees, Essenes and a "fourth philosophy" which was probably the Zealots. Although their origins are lost in time, by the time of the New Testament these parties were deeply rooted in the old clash between Jewish nationalism and religion on the one hand and various forces of Hellenism—including the occupying might of imperial Rome—on the other.

- **Pharisees.** The Pharisees were the leading Jewish party in Jesus' day and held great influence over the general populace. Like the scribes, the Pharisees were scholar-teachers and could be found scattered among the towns and villages of Judea and Galilee, wherever there was a Jewish community large enough to support a synagogue. Pharaisaic authority was grounded in a scrupulous adherence to the Oral Law, the Torah-based "tradition of the elders" which had been handed down faithfully since the time of Moses. The Pharisees maintained a system of strict religious practices, holding others accountable for not adhering to the same. Opposed to the forces of Hellenism, the Pharisees were also champions of Jewish political freedom. Jesus' teachings were more closely aligned to the Pharisees than to any other religious party (Mt 23:2–3), and the Apostle Paul was trained as a Pharisee (Phil 3:5–6).

- **Sadducees.** Though smaller in number than the Pharisees, the Sadducees exerted greater influence at the higher levels of religion and politics since they represented the Jewish urban, landed aristocracy. Based in Jerusalem, the Sadducees controlled the high priesthood and other influential positions in the

93

Early Caesars of the Roman Empire

Caesar	Years of Reign	New Testament References	Selected Notes of New Testament Significance
Julius Caesar	49–44 B.C.	—	—
Second Triumvirate (Mark Antony, Octavian, Lepidus)	44–31 B.C.	—	—
Augustus (Octavian)	31 (27) B.C.–A.D. 14	Luke 2:1	Patron of Herod the Great; Caesar at Jesus' birth
Tiberius	A.D. 14–37	Matthew 22:17, 22:21; Luke 3:1, 23:2; John 19:12, 19:15	Caesar during Jesus' ministry; namesake of Herod Antipas' capital on the Sea of Galilee
Caligula (Gaius)	A.D. 37–41	—	—
Claudius	A.D. 41–54	Acts 11:28, 17:7, 18:2	Caesar during Paul's first two missionary journeys
Nero	A.D. 54–68	Acts 25:11–12, 26:32, 27:24, 28:19; Phil 4:22	Caesar during Paul's third missionary journey and Roman imprisonment; executed Paul and Peter
Galba, Otho and Vitellius ("the year of the three emperors")	A.D. 68–69	—	—
Vespasian	A.D. 69–79	—	As general, led Roman forces against the Jewish Revolt in A.D. 66–69
Titus	A.D. 79–81	—	As general, defeated Judea and destroyed Jerusalem in A.D. 70
Domitian	A.D. 81–96	—	Caesar during John's exile in Patmos; great persecution of the church
Nerva	A.D. 96–98	—	—
Trajan	A.D. 98–117	—	Annexed the Nabatean realms in A.D. 106
Hadrian	A.D. 117–130	—	Suppressed the Second Jewish (Bar Kochba) Revolt

The Herods

Name	Relationship to Herod the Great	Greatest Extent of Territory Ruled	Title and Dates of Reign	New Testament References
Antipater I	Grandfather of Herod the Great	Idumea	Governor during the reign of Alexander Jannaeus	—
Antipater II	Father of Herod the Great	Greater Judea (including Idumea, Samaria, Galilee and Perea)	De facto administrator from 63–55 B.C.; procurator from 55–43 B.C.	—
Herod I (the Great)	—	Greater Judea (including Idumea, Samaria, Galilee, Perea, Gaulanitis and surrounding regions)	King from 37–4 B.C.	Mt 2:1–22; Lk 1:5
Archelaus	Oldest son of Herod the Great	Judea, Samaria and Idumea	Ethnarch from 4 B.C.–A.D. 6	Mt 2:22
Herod Philip	Son of Herod the Great	Gaulanitis and surrounding regions	Tetrarch from 4 B.C.–A.D. 34	Lk 3:1
Herod Antipas	Son of Herod the Great	Galilee and Perea	Tetrarch from 4 B.C.–A.D. 39	Mt 14:1–11; Mk 6:14–29; Lk 3:1, 3:19, 13:31–33, 23:7–12
Herod Agrippa I	Grandson of Herod the Great	Greater Judea (same land as ruled by Herod the Great)	King from A.D. 37–44	Acts 12:1, 12:18–23
Herod Agrippa II	Great grandson of Herod the Great	Chalcis (southeastern Lebanon); Gaulanitis and surrounding regions; parts of Galilee and Perea	King of Chalcis from A.D. 48–53; Tetrarch of Gaulanitis and surrounding regions and parts of Galilee and Perea from A.D. 53–c. 100	Acts 25:13–26:32

Remains of the Essene settlement of Qumran, looking east toward the Dead Sea and the mountains of Moab.

government of Jewish affairs. The Sadducees were generally wealthy, well-educated, and eager to advance their standing through contacts with the outside world, all characteristics that tended to separate them from the masses. As a whole, the Sadducees sought to build a Hellenistic state on a Jewish national foundation, a combination that was rejected by most Jews in Jesus' day.

- **Essenes**. The Essenes devoted themselves to an aesthetic, monastic lifestyle emphasizing ritual purity, communal meals, study and prayer. Viewing the high priesthood and Jerusalem Temple worship as corrupt, the Essenes withdrew, under the leadership of the Teacher of Righteousness, from normative Jewish society to await the dramatic, foreordained intervention of God on their behalf at the end of time. The Essenes looked to the coming of two Messiahs, a priestly Messiah "from Aaron" who would redeem Temple worship and a royal Messiah "from Israel" who would retore the Davidic line. Most Essenes lived communally in and around the settlement of Qumran on the northwestern shore of the Dead Sea; their writings, the Dead Sea Scrolls, are an important window into their own community as well as into the world of the Gospels. There is evidence that some Essenes also lived in Jerusalem and other towns and villages in Judea.
- **Zealots**. The term "Zealot"—reflecting more a way of thought than a formal party—encompassed a number of independent groups whose overall goals were to restore political independence to Judea and to improve the socioeconomic plight of the masses. Toward this end, Zealot bands attracted persons who not only squirmed under the heavy hand of Rome, but also suffered injustices perpetrated by wealthy and powerful Jews, especially by Jews who collaborated with the Romans. Galilee in particular was a fertile breeding ground for nationalistic movements due largely to its position as an open Jewish frontier, and during the first century A.D. several messiah figures arose from Galilee to try to overthrow Roman rule in the land (cf. Acts 5:37). The last defenders of Masada were Zealots, let by the Galilean Eleazar.

Jesus counted a Zealot among his twelve disciples (Mk 3:18).

The vast majority of first-century Jews, however, did not formally belong to any of these parties—they were simply *am haaretz*, "people of the land." This multitude, largely composed of lower class peasants—regular folks just trying to get by—often felt alienated in their own land (cf. Jn 7:49). Not particularly well-educated and suffering under a tax burden estimated to be between 50 and 70 percent of personal income, the multitudes simply wanted to live quiet and secure lives, much like people do everywhere. Caught between the "traditions of the fathers" and new ways of the world, these were people who sought the ways of God amidst the challenges of everyday life.

> And so Jesus went about all the cities and the villages, teaching in their synagogues and proclaiming the gospel of the kingdom, and healing every kind of disease and every kind of sickness. Seeing the multitudes, He felt compassion for them, because they were distressed and downcast like sheep without a shepherd.
>
> (Mt 9:35–36)

The Gospels

The Birth and Early Years of Jesus. The Gospel story opens with Luke's account of the births of John the Baptist and Jesus in the last days of the tumultuous reign of Herod the Great (Lk 1–2). John was born into a priestly family which, according to tradition, lived in Ein Kerem, a small village nestled in the rugged hills just west of Jerusalem. Mary, a poor peasant girl from the Galilean village of Nazareth, three-days' journey to the north, visited John's mother Elizabeth while she herself was pregnant with Jesus. She returned to the region some months later with Joseph, giving birth to Jesus in the city of David, Bethlehem of Judea, Joseph's ancestral home. Geographically, Bethlehem lay equidistant between Herodium—Herod's desert fortress representing the intrusive world of Rome—and Jerusalem, the world center of Judaism. Lying in the shadow of both and rooted in the royal line of David, Bethlehem was a fitting birthplace for a baby destined to usher in the Kingdom of God.

Jesus' first visitors were simple shepherds from nearby fields (Lk 2:8); that they were tending their flocks on ground that would normally be sown with grain between November and April suggests that the Christmas story probably took place in the summertime, when Judean sheep and goats typically grazed on field stubble. The subsequent visit to Bethlehem of Magi "from the east" (Mt 2: 1–12) indicates that, like Solomon (cf. 1 Kgs 9:26–10:29; cf. Isa 60: 6), Jesus was a king worthy of receiving the tribute of the world. The Magi's gifts—gold, frankincense and myrrh—were typical of the commodities entering the Roman world through Palestine via the Nabatean-controlled Arabian spice route.

Mary, Joseph and Jesus subsequently fled to Egypt to escape the wrath of Herod (Mt 2:13–18), no doubt finding shelter among the large Jewish population there. Coptic tradition identifies several sites visited by the Holy Family while in Egypt. Sometime after the death of Herod in 4 B.C. Joseph took his family back to Judea, then on to Nazareth in Galilee, preferring to live under the rule of Herod's more even-handed son Antipas rather than in a Judea controlled by Archelaus, a king who had inherited much of his father's temperament (Mt 2:19–23).

Joseph settled in Nazareth, a small, nondescript village in a chalky basin high atop a limestone ridge that overlooks the Jezreel Valley from the north. Nazareth was a village largely lacking in economic opportunities (Mt 2:23; cf. Jn 1:46). Jesus, like all grow-ing boys in the first century, learned his family trade, in this case the specialized skills of a "carpenter," a worker in wood and stone, the local building materials (cf. Mt 13:55). It is likely that jobs were scarce in Nazareth and therefore possible that both Joseph and Jesus honed their skills in Sepphoris, Galilee's capital city in the Beth Netofa Valley five miles north of Nazareth. Here jobs were plentiful, as the city was undergoing a massive rebuilding campaign financed by Herod Antipas.

Jesus was also raised in the Jewish "tradition of the elders" (cf. Lk 2:52). One might imagine that as a boy he often gazed into the vast Jezreel Valley from high atop the Nazareth Ridge, recalling to mind God's great redemptive acts of old that took place there, nearly at his doorstep—the battles of Deborah, Barak (Judg 4–5) and Gideon (Judg 6–8) and the ministries of Elijah (1 Kgs 17–19) and Elisha (2 Kgs 4–5). In addition, Gath-hepher, hometown of the prophet Jonah (2 Kgs 14:25; Jonah 1:1), was an hour's walk northeast of Nazareth. One might also suppose that Jesus' awareness of such Galilee connections helped to shape his resolve later in life. In the spring when he was twelve, Jesus traveled to Jerusalem with his parents to celebrate the Passover festival. He stayed behind when his parents began their return trip home; retracing their steps to Jerusalem, they found him in intense debate with teachers in the Temple (Lk 2:41–51).

Jesus' Baptism and Move to Capernaum. Based on data provided in the Gospels, it is not possible to establish a definitive chronology of Jesus' ministry, or to be certain of his travel itineraries or even the number of times that he visited Jerusalem. Jesus began his ministry when he was about thirty years old (Lk 3:23), and most interpreters reconstruct a three-year ministry based on the number of Passover festivals mentioned in the Gospel of John (2:13, 6:4, 11:55).

John the Baptist began preaching "a baptism of repentance for the forgiveness of sins" in the fifteenth year of Tiberius Caesar, A.D. 27–28 (Lk 3:1–3). John's activity was concentrated in the Jordan Valley, from the south at Bethabara (i.e., "Bethany beyond the Jordan"; Jn 1:28)—just a day's walk for the multitudes of Jerusalem (Mt 3:1–12; Lk 3:4–17)—to Aenon near Salim, east of Samaria (Jn 3:23). His bold message has been likened to those of both Elijah and the Essenes, and was part of the spiritual fervor that gripped Judea in his day. The beginning of Jesus' public ministry was marked by his baptism by John (Mt 3: 13–17; Lk 3:21–22). Immediately afterward Jesus spent forty days in seclusion in the wilderness of Judea, probably in the empty hills above Jericho. Throughout history this desolate terrain has been a place of retreat and refuge, and it was here that Jesus successfully overcame the temptations of Satan (Lk 4:1–13). For his part, John eventually ran afoul of the authorities. He was arrested and beheaded by Herod Antipas—in Machaerus, according to Josephus—for criticizing Antipas's marriage to his brother Philip's wife (Mt 14:1–12; Lk 3:19–20).

The wilderness of Judea, above Jericho, where Jesus spent forty days in seclusion.

JESUS IN GALILEE

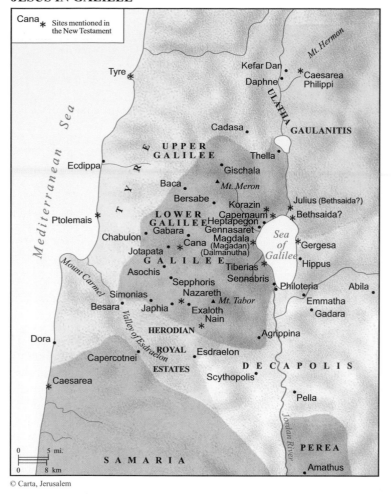

Cana* Sites mentioned in the New Testament

© Carta, Jerusalem

Jesus' initial Galilean ministry appears to have been based in Nazareth, with travels taking him throughout the region to villages such as Cana and Capernaum. He soon attracted a significant crowd of followers, including members of his own family (Lk 4: 14–15; Jn 2:12). The Gospels provide various accounts of Jesus' calling of his twelve disciples (Mt 4:18–22; Mk 1:16–20, 2:14, 3: 13–19; Lk 5:1–11; Jn 1:19–51). Most of his disciples were from villages that bordered the northern shore of the Sea of Galilee such as Capernaum and Bethsaida, and several were fishermen. James and John, sons of Zebedee, probably stood to inherit a rather profitable fishing business (cf. Mk 1:20). Notable also were Matthew (Levi), a tax collector, and Simon the Zealot, Matthew's socio-economic rival. The name "Iscariot" may have indicated that Judas was the lone Judean of the group (from the village of Kirioth), or that he was a member of the radical Zealot group Sicarii ("assassins"). In any case, it is clear that together, Jesus' small band of disciples represented a cross section of the peoples of Galilee.

Jesus performed his first miracle at Cana, a village on the northern edge of the Beth Netofa Valley three hours' walk from Nazareth. Here, at a wedding, he turned water into wine (Jn 2:1–11), the first of several instances in which Jesus seemed to pattern his ministry after that of Elisha (Elisha's first miracle was to make bad water good; cf. 2 Kgs 2:19–22; Jesus' first miracle was to turn already good water better). On a later visit to Cana Jesus healed the son of a royal official, a man who was probably attached to the court of Herod Antipas (Jn 4:46–54).

Jesus steadily gained a following throughout Galilee, but had less success back home in Nazareth. There he met resistance in the local synagogue when he unfavorably compared his nationalistic townsfolk to the Sidonians and Syrians, Israel's cultural and political

enemies during the days of Elijah and Elisha (Lk 4:16–30; cf. Mt 13: 53–58). This was a particularly sensitive issue in Galilee, a Jewish frontier land bordering these regions. Escaping from Nazareth with his life, Jesus moved to Capernaum for good (Lk 4:31). The prophet Isaiah had known that because of its location, Galilee would always face the dark threat of invasion and so coined the phrase "Galilee of the *Gentiles*" (Isa 9:1). Citing Isaiah in this regard, Matthew notes that with Jesus' move from Nazareth to Capernaum, a light was now dawning on a land overshadowed by death (Mt 4:12–17).

Jesus' Galilean Ministry from Capernaum. It should not be supposed that Jesus' move to Capernaum was an attempt to withdraw from the limelight and spend quiet time along the shores of a gentle sea. Rather, in the first century A.D. three distinct political units bordered the Sea of Galilee. By focusing his ministry around this sea, Jesus was able to come into contact with people who represented the full scope of religious, social and political identities found in first-century Palestine.

- **Galilee** proper, on the west side of the Sea, was under the control of Herod Antipas. Galilee included towns such as Capernaum, Magdala and Tiberias (Jn 6:23), Herod Antipas's newly founded capital city (since A.D. 17). Galilee was primarily a Jewish region, with some corridors of Hellenism.
- **Gaulanitis**, rising from the northeast corner of the Sea, included Bethsaida and Caesarea Philippi. Governed by Herod Philip, Gaulanitis was an area of decidedly mixed Jewish-Hellenistic sentiments.
- The region of **Decapolis** touched the southeastern quarter of the Sea. This was an "in-your-face" bastion of Hellenism and Roman imperial might, established to guard Rome's eastern frontier.

In addition, geographical, archaeological and textual evidence suggest that Capernaum, Jesus' adopted hometown (Mt 9:1), was a bustling population center. The city lay astride the main highway linking Galilee's coast to Damascus. Capernaum was the last town in Galilee before reaching Gaulanitis, and so it was appropriate that there was a tax office alongside the road (cf. Mk 2:14). Moreover, with at least eight large stone piers—the most of any town on the Sea of Galilee in Jesus' days—Capernaum was a center of fishing and related industries (boat- and net-manufacture, fish processing and distribution). The outlying regions of Capernaum were devoted to agriculture, as was the case for every town and village in Galilee (cf. Mk 2:23, 4:1–9), but the city was also apparently a center for

Remains of the Late Roman period synagogue at Capernaum.

97

Modern Kursi (Gergesa), on the eastern shore of the Sea of Galilee.

manufacturing heavy food-processing equipment such as grain mills and olive presses. Finally, a Roman garrison was based in Capernaum; its commander fronted the money to build the town's synagogue (Lk 7:2–5). In all, it is certain that in Capernaum, Jesus faced the busyness and challenges of life no less than did his contemporaries. Occasionally, however, he withdrew in the early morning to "a lonely place" (Mk 1:35)—probably the rocky basalt hills above Capernaum—to gaze out over the awakening world of the Sea and pray in solitude.

Except for a few journeys, Jesus' entire ministry before his final departure to Jerusalem took place around the northern half of the Sea of Galilee (also called the Lake of Gennesaret—Lk 5:1; or the Sea of Tiberias—Jn 6:1, 21:1; cf. Mk 2:13, 4:1). Here, along pathways connecting villages, in homes and in fields, Jesus found numerous illustrations for his parables of the kingdom, stories with teaching points grounded in everyday life (e.g., Mt 5:13–16, 7:13–23, 12:1–7, 13:1–52; Lk 13–16). Large multitudes from the entire area seemed to follow his every move; most were Jewish (from Galilee, Judea, Jerusalem, Idumea and Perea—Mk 3:7–8), but others hailed from Gentile regions (the vicinity of Tyre and Sidon—Mk 3:8). Initially, Jesus' ministry focused on the "lost sheep of the house of Israel" (Mt 10:6), and so he sent his own disciples into the towns and villages of Jewish Galilee to preach, teach, heal (Mt 10:1–23; Mk 6:7–13) and, like him, to "go about doing good" (Acts 10:28). Eventually his ministry—and theirs—reached into Gentile areas as well.

Jesus performed most of his miracles in Capernaum, Bethsaida and Chorazin (Mt 11:20–24; cf. Lk 10:13–16), three towns forming a triangle on the northern shore of the Sea of Galilee. We can only surmise what most of these miracles may have been, since the Gospels mention only a very few in the vicinity of Bethsaida and none at all in Chorazim (cf. Jn 21:25).

The Gospels record several visits of Jesus to synagogues in Nazareth, Capernaum, Jerusalem and elsewhere (Mt 12:9, 13:54; Mk 1:21, 3:1; Lk 4:16; Jn 6:59, 18:20). We can assume that Jesus attended the synagogue every Sabbath, in whatever town or village that he happened to be in at the time. There is abundant literary evidence that many towns and villages throughout Judea, Galilee and the world of the Diaspora had synagogues during the time of the New Testament. Synagogues from the first century A.D. have

been found at Masada, Herodium and Gamala, and a recently excavated building at Jericho that was probably a synagogue dates to the first century B.C. The synagogue was the main public institution for Judaism, where the community met every Sabbath day and on holy days to read the Torah and *Haftorah* (prophetic writings), to pray and listen to sermons or homilies. Jesus was often invited to read from the Scriptures and deliver the sermon when he attended synagogue. He soon gained a reputation for teaching "with authority" (Mt 7:28–29; Mk 1:22), with the result that he often locked horns with the local religious establishment (e.g., Mt 21:23; Lk 4:16–30; Jn 9:22–23).

Jesus often traveled across the sea by boat and these journeys could end unpredictably, if, for instance, a powerful storm churned up the lake, a frequent occurrence during the winter months. While waves on the sea rarely exceed 1.5 meters (4 to 5 feet) in height in even the fiercest storms, Galilean fishing boats in the first century A.D. were not particularly large (the "Jesus boat" at Ginnosar, an Israeli kibbutz on the northwestern shore of the Sea of Galilee, measures 8 meters/27 feet in length) and could easily be swamped if heavily loaded. Such a storm caught Jesus' disciples off guard one evening as they were sailing from Capernaum to the other side of the lake, probably intending to land, as they often did, in the territory controlled by Herod Philip (Mk 4:35–41). Jesus, asleep in the stern, was awakened by his frantic disciples and promptly calmed the sea, rebuking the evil chaos that ancient Israel had long pictured as deep, churning waters (v. 39; cf. Gen 1:2; Ps 107:29; Jonah 1:4–16; Rev 21:1).

The boat reached shore in the country of the Gergasenes (Mt 8:28; Mk 5:1; some versions read Gadarenes or Gerasenes). While some scholars place the following event in the region of Gadara (a Decapolis city whose territory touched the southern end of the sea) or even in Gerasa (i.e., Jerash, another Decapolis city high in the Transjordanian hills), geographical logic suggests that the boat was blown into the harbor of Gergesa (modern Kursi), a small fishing village just on the Decapolis side of the border with Gaulanitis, Philip's territory. Here Jesus healed a wild, animal-like man possessed by demons, sending the demons into a large herd of pigs which promptly ran down a cliff and were drowned in the sea—returning to the chaos, as it were, from which they came (Mk 5:2–17). A rather steep hill drops directly into the sea about 1.5

kilometers (1 mile) south of Kursi, providing a convenient location for the miracle. Jesus instructed the man whom he healed to spread the good news of God's mercy to his gentile countrymen (Mk 5: 18–10), and the next time that Jesus returned to the Decapolis he was met by an eager crowd (Mk 7:31–37).

Tradition places the Feeding of the Five Thousand, the only Galilee miracle recorded in all four Gospels, at Tabgha (Heptapegon, lit. "seven springs") on the northwestern shore of the sea near the Plain of Gennesaret. Certain textual evidence (e.g., Lk 9:10), however, suggests that this miracle took place in the vicinity of Bethsaida, on the sea's northeastern shore. The location was a lonely, desolate spot, somewhat at a distance from any town or village (cf. Mk 6: 32, 6:36), yet within fairly easy walking distance from Capernaum (cf. Mk 6:3). While either of the two locations is possible on this account, the clues in the following episode (in which Jesus walked on water) suggest that the region of Bethsaida was the more likely location. It was the time of Passover (Jn 6:4), when the springtime grass was at its most luxuriant stage of growth (Jn 6:10). The five loaves that fed the multitude (Jn 6:9) were made from barley, the first harvest of spring. The yearly Passover celebration, a festival celebrating Israelite freedom from Egypt, fueled the Jews' longing to be freed from Roman oppression. Perhaps it was this hunger that prompted those whom Jesus fed to proclaim him to be "the Prophet who is to come into the world" (Jn 6:14), apparently a reference to the coming prophet foretold by Moses (Deut 18:15, 18:18). It is noteworthy that Elisha performed a similar miracle, multiplying fresh barley loaves for a small crowd (2 Kgs 4:42–44); like the miracle at Cana (cf. Jn 2:1–11), Jesus again surpassed his predecessor.

Jesus' disciples intended to return that evening to Capernaum by boat. Again a storm blew up, this one suddenly, as is typical in the unstable weather of springtime (Mt 14:22–33; Jn 6:16–21). While the disciples were straining to row westward against a strong west wind (Mt 14:24), Jesus came to them, walking on the water. Peter's attempt to mimic his Master was thwarted by the fierceness of the storm and his own lack of faith. The boat landed on the Plain of Gennesaret where again Jesus was met by the needy multitude (Mt 14:34–36; cf. Jn 6:25).

Jesus' travels took him to many towns and villages throughout Galilee (Mt 4:23; Lk 8:1), although only a very few other than those

JESUS' MINISTRY—SIDON TO JERUSALEM

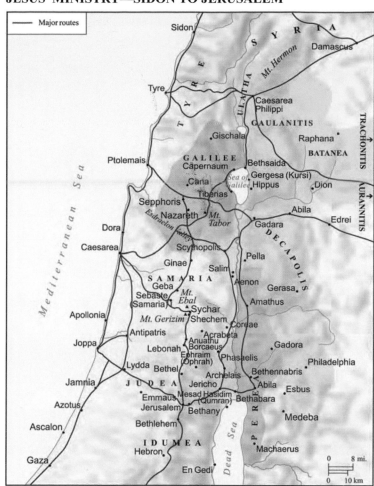

© Carta, Jerusalem

The name "Jesus," as written in Hebrew on an ossuary.

The Plain of Gennesaret with the cliffs of Arbel and the Horns of Hattin in the background.

The northern Jordan Valley, looking east toward the hills of Transjordan (the Decapolis and Perea).

hugging the northern shore of the sea are mentioned by name: Cana (Jn 2:1, 4:46), Nazareth (Lk 4:16) and Nain (Lk 7:11–17). It was at Nain that Jesus brought back to life the only son of a widow as the lad was being carried out of the city for burial. Nain was a relatively small village on the northwestern slope of the Hill of Moreh, perched at the southern border of Galilee overlooking the Esdraelon (Jezreel) Valley. Eight hundred years earlier the town of Shunem had dominated the southwestern slope of the same mountain. It was here that Elisha had raised another son, also an only child, from the dead (2 Kgs 4:8–37). By the time of the New Testament Shunem was gone, but apparently the people of Nain still remembered the prophet who had visited their mountain centuries before. Upon witnessing Jesus' miracle at the entrance to their city, the mourners exclaimed, "A great prophet has arisen among us! God has visited his people [again]!"

In addition to his visits to the Decapolis, the Gospels record only one journey of Jesus into Gentile territory: his trip with his disciples to the district of Tyre and Sidon (Mt 15:21–28; Mk 7:24–30). This journey probably took Jesus through a number of Jewish towns and villages nestled in the rugged hills of Upper Galilee, then into a very foreign land lying along the Phoenician coast. Here, as far from his "comfort zone" as Elijah was from his when he ministered to a poor widow and her son at Zarephath (1 Kgs 17:8–16), Jesus touched the lives of a poor woman and her daughter. In them, he found faith in the God of Israel among the Gentiles.

Jesus' Travels to Jerusalem. Two routes connected Galilee with Jerusalem. One passed through the Jordan Valley, crossing the Decapolis from Scythopolis to Pella, then ran along the eastern, spring-fed side of the valley through Perea, an area of Jewish settlement that, like Galilee, was governed by Herod Antipas. This route then ascended to Jerusalem via Jericho. Although the Jordan Valley was insufferably hot in the summertime, it was the preferred route for Jews who wished to avoid Samaria. The other route passed through Samaria. Jews who traveled this latter route north from Jerusalem typically spent the first night at Anuathu Borcaeus at the northern border of Judea and the second in the Esdraelon Valley, so as not to have to stay overnight in Samaria.

John records that Jesus traveled from Galilee to Jerusalem at least three times prior to his final Passover journey that led to the Cross:

- John 2:13–25 notes that Jesus overturned the money-changers' tables in the Temple precinct during the Passover festival. Many scholars suggest that John placed this event—which probably happened only once, during Jesus' last Passover journey (cf. Mt 21:12–17)—at the beginning of his Gospel in order to set the stage for an account of Jesus' life that emphasized his ministry in Jerusalem. Immediately following his narrative of the Cleansing of the Temple, John records Jesus' nighttime visit to Nicodemus, an influential Pharisee from Jerusalem who was a member of the Sanhedrin (Jn 3:1–21). Nicodemus became a follower of Jesus, advocating on his behalf during a later visit to Jerusalem (Jn 7:45–53) and helping to prepare his body for burial (Jn 19:38–42).
- Returning to Jerusalem for an unnamed festival, Jesus healed a man at the Pool of Bethesda who had been lame for thirty-eight years (Jn 5:1–17). The Pool of Bethesda was a huge public water reservoir lying just outside the city wall north of the Temple Mount. Archaeological investigation suggests that this was also a site dedicated to Aesclepius, the Greco-Roman god of healing, and no doubt served the Roman soldiers garrisoned at the nearby Antonia Fortress. Perhaps the lame man had been

hedging his bets, hoping for mercy from any deity who happened along. By healing the man, Jesus showed that he could meet the needs of not only the upper crust of Jerusalem society (e.g., Nicodemus), but also the down-and-out.

- Jesus also traveled to Jerusalem to celebrate the fall festival of Succoth (the Festival of Booths—Jn 7:1–39). It is not clear whether he made this visit after he had left Galilee for the final time before his crucifixion, or whether he returned to Galilee after the trip. In any case, his visit was made without fanfare, not wanting to take the risk of running afoul of the authorities. On the last, climactic day of the Succoth festival Jesus likened himself and his followers to fountains of living (i.e., spring) water (v. 37–38), a powerful image for the residents of Jerusalem whose own cisterns were nearly dry at the end of the summer drought. It was apparently also on this trip that Jesus healed a man who had been born blind, asking him to wash in the Pool of Siloam (Jn 9:1–12; cf. 2 Kgs 5:10).

After the trip to Jerusalem during which he was visited by Nicodemus, Jesus returned to Galilee by way of Samaria. On the second day of his journey he rested from the noontime heat at Sychar (Jacob's Well), near the ruins of the Old Testament city of Shechem, in the heart of Samaria (Jn 4:1–6; cf. Gen 33:18–19). Sychar lay beneath Mount Gerizim, the site of a Samaritan temple that had been destroyed by the Hasmonean king John Hyrcanus in 108 B.C. (Jn 4:19–20). Hyrcanus's destruction was one of many factors that had bred antagonism between the Jews and the Samaritans over the centuries (cf. 2 Kgs 17:24–41; Neh 4:1–9). Like the Jews, the Samaritans considered themselves to be the true guardians of the pure Mosaic faith, basing this belief on the ties that Abraham (Gen 12:6–7), Jacob (Gen 33:18–19; Josh 24:32) and Moses (Deut 11: 26–32; Josh 8:30-35) had to the region. Jesus remained in Samaria for two days—much to the consternation of his disciples—and many believed in him (Jn 4:39–42).

Jesus' Last Year: The Way of the Cross. During the early part of his ministry, Jesus preferred to avoid the limelight that would invariably accompany messianic claims and instead simply went about towns and villages, preaching the good news of the Kingdom of God and healing people who were sick or demon-possessed. He spoke in parables to prevent anyone from jumping to conclusions about his objectives and goals (Mt 13:10–17; Mk 4:33–34), and often told his followers not to spread the word about his miracles (Mt 8:4, 9:30; Mk 3:12) or mention that he was the Messiah (Mt 16: 20). Slowly, methodically and with an eye to the future, the ground was prepared and the seed sown.

Then the time was ripe. Jesus took his disciples into the region of Caesarea Philippi, in the northern reaches of Gaulanitis. This was an area where Hellenism had taken deep root among a scattering of Jewish villages, a region that represented in microcosm the Jewish Diaspora in the Roman world. The city of Caesarea Philippi (modern Banias), lying at the foot of Mount Hermon awash in the headwaters of the Jordan River, was a pagan cult site devoted to the worship of the god Pan and the Nymphs. Here Herod the Great had built a temple to the divine Caesar, Augustus, out of which a powerful spring of living water flowed. Jesus chose this context to question his disciples, "Who do you say that I am?" (Mt 16:13–16). Peter affirmed that Jesus was the Messiah, the Christ, and Jesus replied by giving him the keys to the kingdom of heaven (Mt 16: 17–19). Here Jesus also mentioned the church, the first of only two times that this concept, so integral to the spread of the Gospel in the Roman world, appears in the Gospels (cf. Mt 18:17). With Peter's confession, Jesus made the first of three Passion predictions: that

"HE RESOLUTELY SET HIS FACE TOWARD JERUSALEM" (LK 9:51)

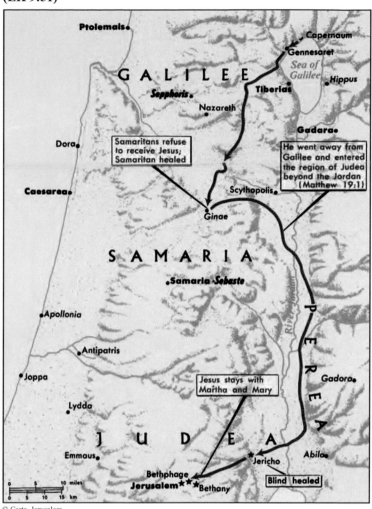

© Carta, Jerusalem

he had to go to Jerusalem, that he had to suffer and be killed, and that he had to be raised on the third day (Mt 16:21–23, 17:22–23, 20:17–19). The die was cast; the disciples, for the most part, were unwilling and afraid (cf. Mt 16:24–28).

Six days later, to confirm his role as the divine God-man, Jesus took Peter, James and John, the "inner three" of his disciples, to a high mountain where he was transfigured before them. There, in the presence of Moses and Elijah, a voice from heaven pronounced Jesus to be "My beloved Son with whom I am well pleased; listen to him!" (Mt 17:1–8). One early Church tradition places the Transfiguration on Mount Tabor, a dramatic mountain near Nazareth looming over the northeastern corner of the Jezreel Valley. Another, attested by Eusebius in the early fourth century A.D., prefers to locate this event somewhere on Mount Hermon, since Jesus and his disciples were already in the vicinity of Caesarea Philippi. If the location of Mount Hermon is correct, then Jesus' last, triumphal journey to Jerusalem can be seen as beginning here, at the farthest extent of the Holy Land. From Mount Hermon Jesus embarked on a final long, circuitous journey that took him one last time to each of the regions in which he had focused his ministry (Mt 17:24, 19:1–2, 21:1; Lk 9:52, 17:11) before cresting the Mount of Olives on the Sunday before Passover.

So Jesus "resolutely set his face toward Jerusalem" (Lk 9:51). He spent most of the winter prior to his final Passover in Perea, the "Judea beyond the Jordan" governed by "that fox," Herod Antipas (Mt 19:1–2; Lk 13:32). Here he had greater contact with the religious authorities from Jerusalem than he had had in Galilee, and it is likely that many of their confrontations recorded in the middle

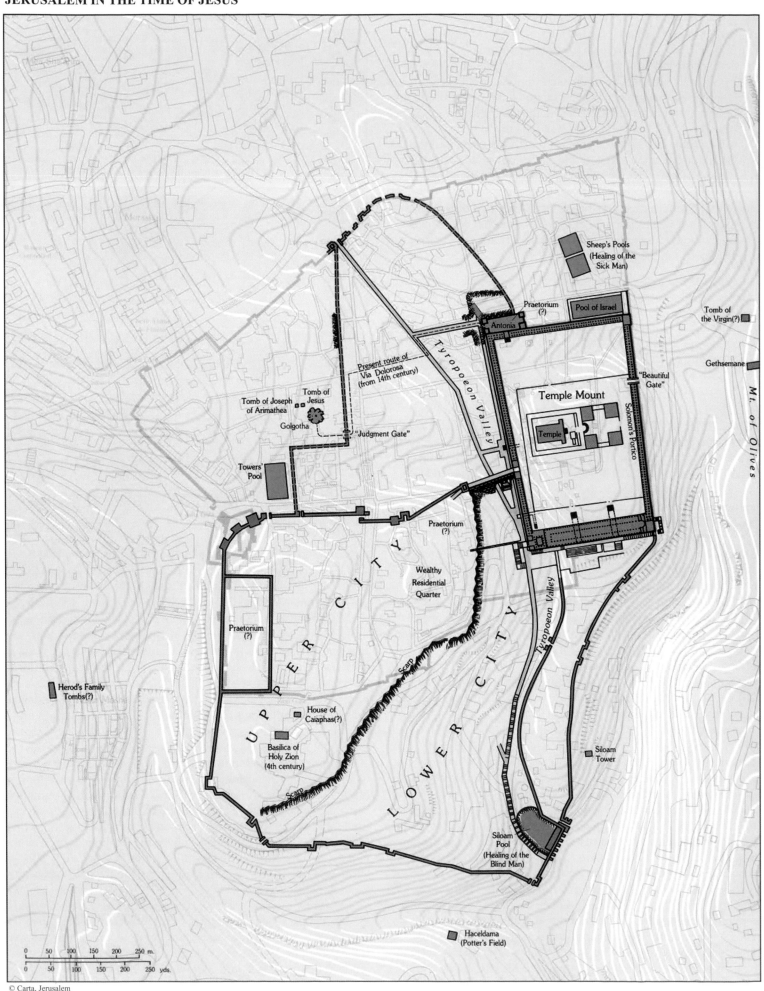

Sheep's Pools
(Healing of the
Sick Man)

Praetorium
(?)

Pool of Israel

Tomb of
the Virgin(?)

Antonia

Gethsemane

Present route of
Via Dolorosa
(from 14th century)

"Beautiful
Gate"

Tyropoeon Valley

Temple Mount

Tomb of Joseph
of Arimathea

Tomb of
Jesus

Mt. of Olives

Temple

Golgotha

Solomon's Portico

"Judgment Gate"

Towers'
Pool

Praetorium
(?)

U P P E R   C I T Y

Wealthy
Residential
Quarter

Praetorium
(?)

Scarp

Tyropoeon Valley

L O W E R   C I T Y

Herod's Family
Tombs(?)

House of
Caiaphas(?)

Siloam
Tower

Basilica of
Holy Zion
(4th century)

Scarp

Siloam
Pool
(Healing of the
Blind Man)

| 0 | 50 | 100 | 150 | 200 | 250 m. |
| 0 | 50 | 100 | 150 | 200 | 250 yds. |

Haceldama
(Potter's Field)

© Carta, Jerusalem

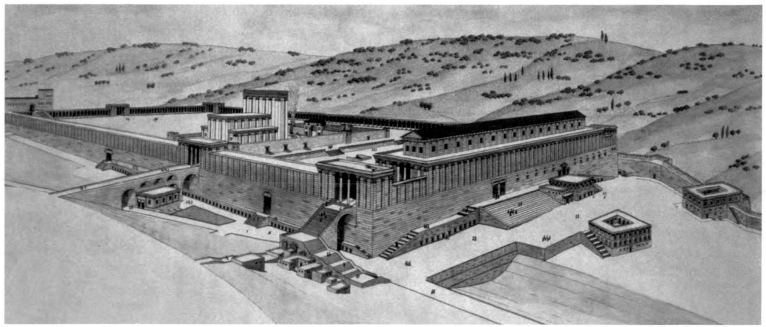

Reconstruction of the Temple Mount in the time of Herod the Great.

chapters of the Gospel of Luke would have taken place at this time, as Jesus' ministry was approaching its climax (Lk 10:25–29, 11:14–26, 11:37–54, 13:31–35, 14:1–6, 15:1–2, 16:14, 18:18–30). Perea also provided a fitting setting for Jesus' parables of the Good Samaritan (Lk 10:30–37) and the Prodigal Son (Lk 15:11–32), since the region lay adjacent to Samaria and the Decapolis (where a man might eat with the pigs), and his audience would have often traveled the Jerusalem-Jericho road.

Jesus himself traveled up to Jerusalem from Perea at least twice before completing his final journey to the Cross. The first was to attend the Feast of Dedication (Hanukkah), which celebrates the cleansing of the Temple by Judas Maccabeus in 164 B.C. (Jn 10:22–42). When pressed by the people to declare himself the Messiah, Jesus answered, "I and the Father are one" (Jn 10:30). Jesus' second trip was to Bethany, a small village on the eastern slope of the Mount of Olives where, in a touching scene revealing the depths of his humanity and divinity, Jesus raised Lazarus, brother of Mary and Martha, from the dead (Lk 11:1–53).

Jesus' final journey to Jerusalem, like his previous ones, took him through the oasis city of Jericho where he passed under the shadow of Herod's elegant winter palace. As a border town, a hub of routes and a market for balsam trade, Jericho was a tax-collection center where agents like Zacchaeus, under the patronage of Rome, made a fine living cheating the residents of the area (Lk 19:1–10). Jericho's wealth attracted the desperately poor as well, persons such as Bartimaeus, a blind roadside beggar (Lk 18:35–43). True to form, Jesus encountered both men and by the time he left town to climb to Jerusalem both had become his followers.

As was his custom, Jesus made the village of Bethany his home while he was in Jerusalem (cf. Mt 26:6). He spent the upcoming Sabbath there, then on Sunday morning sent his disciples to the nearby village of Bethphage to secure a colt for his triumphal ride into Jerusalem (Mt 21:1–11; Lk 19:28–36). Cresting the Mount of Olives, Jesus wept over the city, mixing tears of sorrow over its coming destruction with the crowd's cheers of victory: "Hosanna!" ("Save now!"—Lk 19:37–44; cf. 2 Sam 15:23, 15:30). Jesus entered the city from the east and then, in his strongest messianic statement yet, overturned the money-changers' tables in the Temple precinct, cleansing its courts for proper worship and prayer (Mt 21:12–17; Lk 19:45–46). Jesus spent the next day or two boldly teaching in and around the Temple courtyard, a popular place for rabbis to gain and hold a hearing—or, to lose one (Mt 21:23–23:39).

Messianic expectations ran high in Jerusalem on the eve of the Passover and the city was crowded with pilgrims from across the Roman world. Jesus' presence in the city at this time was a threat to the Temple authorities and they planned to seize him quietly, fearing civil unrest (Mt 26:1–4). Longing to celebrate the Passover with his disciples (Lk 22:15), Jesus instructed Peter and John to prepare a room for the meal (Lk 22:7–13). Tradition, as well as archaeological and literary evidence, points to a large, well-to-do home or institution on the highest point of the Upper City of Jerusalem—today's Mount Zion—as the location for the Last Supper. The setting was formal, proper and solemn (Mt 26:20–29; Lk 22:14–23). Judas, having arranged beforehand to turn Jesus over to the Temple authorities (Lk 22:3–6), left the meal early (Jn 13:21–30).

Late in the evening, after the meal, Jesus and the rest of his disciples walked to Gethsemane ("olive press") in the Kidron Valley, at the foot of the Mount of Olives. There they sought solitude and divine strength for the events to come (Mt 26:30, 26:36–46). Jesus was arrested, abandoned by his disciples and taken back to the Upper City of Jerusalem to the home of Caiaphas, the high priest, for interrogation (Mt 26:47–57; Jn 18:1–11). Jesus was questioned first by Annas, the former high priest, and then by Caiaphas himself, who presided over a tribunal composed of members of the Sanhedrin, Jerusalem's supreme religious governing body (Lk 22:66–71; Jn 18:12–24). As members of the Sadducean aristocracy, Annas and his son-in-law Caiaphas looked unfavorably upon popular messianic unrest against Rome. Meanwhile Peter, secretly listening to the proceedings from an outer courtyard, denied three times that he knew Jesus when pressed by onlookers to identify himself (Lk 22:54–62; Jn 18:15–18, 18:25–27).

Jesus' statements before Caiaphas were seen as blasphemous (Mt 26:57–68; Jn 18:19–24), but the tribunal was not able to inflict the death penalty. For this, Jesus was taken to Pontius Pilate, the Roman governor of Judea. Pilate's official residence was in Caesarea on the Mediterranean coast, but his responsibility to suppress any hint of insurrection in Judea had brought him to Jerusalem during the Passover. Jesus faced Pilate in the Praetorium, where his accusers presented him as the "King of the Jews," an upstart bent on fostering a rebellion against the emperor (Mt 27:11–26;

Panoramic view of Jerusalem, looking southeast. In foreground, the Temple Mount with the Golden Dome of the Rock and el-Aqsa Mosque.

Lk 23:1–3; Jn 18:28–19:15). Luke's Gospel includes an additional hearing before Herod Antipas, who was also in Jerusalem for the Passover (Lk 23:6–12).

After being scourged and mocked by the Roman garrison in the Praetorium, Jesus was led through the streets of Jerusalem to Golgotha ("the Place of the Skull") where he was crucified (Mt 27: 27–56; Lk 23:26–49; Jn 19:16–30). The route of the Via Dolorosa ("Way of the Cross") can be determined only in relation to the location of the Praetorium and Golgotha. Tradition places the site of the crucifixion at the Church of the Holy Sepulchre, which at the time of Jesus' crucifixion lay outside a northwestern bend in the city wall, near a road leading into the city and in an area used as both a garden and a cemetery (cf. Jn 19:41–42). The Praetorium—Pilate's residence while in Jerusalem—may have either been within the Antonia Fortress adjacent to the northwestern corner of the Temple Mount, or in Herod's Palace in the northwestern corner of the Upper City. Because the Sabbath was approaching, Jesus was buried in a newly hewn tomb nearby (Lk 23:50–56; Jn 19:38–42).

The Resurrection took place early the next Sunday morning (Mt 28:1–10; Lk 24:1–12; Jn 20:1–10). Jesus appeared first to Mary Magdalene as she stood weeping at the tomb (Jn 20:11–18; cf. Lk 8:2; Mk 15:40, 15:47), then late that afternoon to two men on the road to Emmaus (Lk 24:13–35). Four sites have been proposed for Emmaus; the one that makes most sense geographically is in the vicinity of modern Mozah, a village in the Judean hills less than two hours' walk west of Jerusalem. Later that evening Jesus appeared to his disciples in Jerusalem, perhaps back in the Upper City (Lk 24:36–49; Jn 20:19–25), and then to them again, eight days later (Jn 20:26–29; cf. 1 Cor 15:3–8). Jesus also appeared to seven of his disciples on the northern shore of the Sea of Galilee, where he found that they had returned to fishing (Jn 21:1–3). In an act that echoed their initial call, Jesus foretold Peter's miraculous catch of fish, then commissioned him to "feed my sheep" (Jn 1:4–17; cf. Lk 5:1–11).

Forty days after his resurrection, Jesus led his disciples to the top of the Mount of Olives where, after declaring them to be his witnesses "in Jerusalem, and in all Judea and Samaria, and even to the uttermost part of the earth," he ascended into heaven (Acts 1:1–11). Jesus' earthly ministry was over; that of his disciples was just beginning.

The Garden of Gethsemane, at the foot of the Mount of Olives.

The Growth of the Early Church in the First Century A.D.

The spread of the Gospel from Jerusalem and subsequent growth of the early church must be seen in the larger context of the Diaspora, the "dispersion" of Jewish communities across the known world. While small Jewish communities existed as far west as central Italy in the first century A.D. and a strong Jewish presence still remained in Babylon, now under Parthian control, the largest concentration of Jews lived in lands in the eastern half of the Roman Empire: Greece, Asia Minor, Egypt, and Syro-Palestine. Each of these Jewish communities was centered around a synagogue and enjoyed certain privileges granted by the Romans that allowed them to maintain their Jewish identity and govern their own internal affairs. On the whole these communities were prosperous and peaceful, and desired to maintain good relations with their Gentile neighbors. The missionary journeys of the Apostle Paul and other early evangelists focused on this region, where many of these Jewish communities provided pockets of receptivity for the Gospel message. As a Jew, Paul had ready access to synagogues wherever he went and his teachings, often controversial, were met with mixed reactions. When he left one town for another, the small group of believers left behind formed the core of a new local church.

The outworking of Jesus' commission to his disciples to "be My witnesses in Jerusalem, and in all Judea and Samaria, and even to the uttermost part of the earth" (Acts 1:8) can be traced in the book of Acts and provides a convenient geographical outline of the spread of the Gospel message: first in Jerusalem (Acts 2–7), then to Samaria and the coastal plain (Acts 8–10) and finally across the Mediterranean world to Rome (Acts 11–28). Surprisingly, almost nothing is mentioned in Acts about the growth of the church in Galilee, the focal area of Jesus' ministry (cf. Acts 9:31). Moreover, Luke, the author of Acts, included only a small selection of events in his work that took place in the decade between Jesus' crucifixion and the death of Herod Agrippa I, grandson of Herod the Great, in A.D. 44 (cf. Acts 12:20–23). What is mentioned, however, is adequate to help readers determine the general nature of the challenges and opportunities that faced those who believed in Jesus as Messiah during these crucial early years, and to set the stage for the missionary journeys of the Apostle Paul into the Roman world.

"You shall be My witnesses in Jerusalem...." Most Jews living in the Diaspora maintained close contacts with Jerusalem, their spiritual home. While the journey was often difficult and expensive, many tried to make a trip to Jerusalem at least once in their lifetime for one of the three *hagim*, or pilgrimage festivals, mandated by Mosaic law: Pesach ("Passover"), Shavuot ("Weeks" or "Pentecost") and Succoth ("Tabernacles" or "Booths") (cf. Ex 23:14–17; Deut 16:1–17). During these festivals Jerusalem took on a lively, cosmopolitan air as pilgrims from across the known world crowded into the city. So it was at the first Shavuot after Jesus' resurrection, when the Holy Spirit descended "as tongues of fire" upon the disciples gathered together in Jerusalem's Upper City. The disciples began speaking in the native languages of the Diaspora Jews who were in Jerusalem for the festival, persons who hailed from lands from Mesopotamia to Rome (Acts 2:1–13). Many scholars see this New Testament "Table of Nations" as a kind of reversal of the Tower of Babel incident recorded in Genesis 11. Seizing the opportunity, Peter preached a sermon declaring Jesus the Nazarene to be "both Lord and Christ," and about three thousand hearers believed (Acts 2:14–42).

Word about Jesus continued to spread when Peter and John

healed a lame man at the Beautiful Gate, probably the same gate through which Jesus had passed into the Temple precinct on his Triumphal Entry (Acts 3:1–10; cf. Mt 21:12). More miraculous healings in Jerusalem followed, to the extent that persons living in towns and villages of Judea near Jerusalem brought many who were sick and demon possessed to the disciples for healing (Acts 5:12–16; cf. Mt 4:23–24).

The early success of Peter and John in gaining converts among both native and hellenized Jews aroused the same kind of controversy that had dogged Jesus' ministry (Acts 4:1–22, 5:17–42). It culminated in Jerusalem with the stoning of Stephen—a deacon in the Christian community and its first martyr—for blasphemy (Acts 6:8–7:60). Stephen's execution unleashed a strong reaction against the church, driving many converts out of the city and into the countryside of Judea and Samaria (Acts 8:1), and others as far as Phoenicia, Cyprus and Antioch (Acts 11:19). As the church dispersed, it continued to grow (Acts 8:4).

"...and in all Judea and Samaria...." Another deacon, Philip, fled Jerusalem north through Samaria to "the city of Samaria" (Acts 8:5), perhaps Sebaste, site of the Old Testament capital city of Samaria. The city was now largely gentile, having been settled by mercenaries in the days of Herod the Great. Philip's miracles there attracted the attention of one Simon Magus, a magician who also came to believe in Jesus, although apparently through impure motives. Simon was reprimanded by Peter and John in Sebaste (Acts 8:6–24). By the second century A.D. a spurious tradition had arisen claiming that Simon Magus was the father of Gnosticism, an early heresy that claimed the superiority of a spiritual form of higher knowledge not readily available to the common man.

Peter and John traveled back to Jerusalem through the towns and villages of Samaria, preaching the Gospel to the Samaritans on the way (Acts 8:25). Philip, on the other hand, was prompted by the Spirit to travel south to a "desert" (or, "pastureland"; cf. Heb. *midbar*) road connecting Jerusalem to Gaza, Palestine's gateway to Africa (Acts 8:26). In Late Roman times this route would become an important artery in the network of paved Roman roads in the region. Somewhere along its length Philip met a eunuch, a high-ranking official in the court of Candice, queen of Ethiopia (modern northern Sudan). The eunuch, who was a Jewish proselyte, believed in Jesus and was baptized, then carried his newly found faith back to his homeland (Acts 8:26–39). For his part Philip turned north, preaching the Gospel along the coastal plain from Azotus to Caesarea (Acts 8:40). The cities of the coast, though only one or two days' walk from Jerusalem, were largely incorporated into the Hellenistic world and as such lay light-years away from the conservative hills of Judea culturally. For this reason, Philip's journey up the length of the coast was the boldest statement yet by a follower of Jesus.

One of the most vehement opponents of the church in Jerusalem was Saul, a native of Tarsus in Cilicia. Saul had been trained as a Pharisee in Jerusalem by Gamaliel (Acts 22:3, 23:6, 26:5; cf. Gal 1:11–14; Phil 3:5–6), a highly respected teacher of the Law who earlier had advocated a reasoned approach toward the growing church (cf. Acts 5:33–34).

Saul traveled to Damascus, which at the time was controlled by the Nabatean governor Areatas (cf. 2 Cor 11:32–33), to search out members of the synagogues who believed in Jesus and bring them back to Jerusalem. As he neared Damascus, Saul was blinded by a great light and heard a divine voice—the voice of Jesus himself,

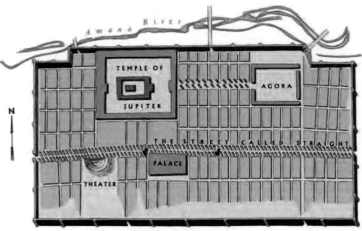

DAMASCUS IN THE TIME OF SAUL

© Carta, Jerusalem

Location of the ancient port of Caesarea.

Saul would later say (Acts 22:8, 26:15; cf. 1 Cor 15:8). Saul was led into Damascus to the home of a believer named Judas, who lived on a street called Straight, the main thoroughfare in the city. Three days later Saul was met by Ananias, a leading disciple in Damascus, who welcomed him into the growing church (Acts 9: 1–22). After spending three years in Arabia (Nabatean-controlled Transjordan—Gal 1:17), probably to sort out the ramifications of his new faith in Jesus, Saul returned to Damascus where his boldness aroused much opposition among the hellenized Jews. Returning to Jerusalem, he was welcomed into the church by Barnabas—no easy task, given Saul's previous reputation. Vehemently opposed by the hellenized Jews in Jerusalem, Saul fled for his life to Caesarea, then sailed to Tarsus, his hometown (Acts 9:23–30).

In the meantime, Peter's preaching and healing ministry had taken him to Lydda (Lod) and Joppa, two cities on the coastal plain that had historical connections to Jerusalem (Acts 9:32–43; cf. 2 Chron 2:16; Ezra 2:33, 3:7; Neh 7:37, 11:35). For Peter, a conservative man, a trip to this part of the coastal plain was relatively risk-free, since he was able to move about primarily in Jewish circles. It was quite another thing for him to go to Caesarea, to the household of Cornelius, a Roman centurion who, although a God-fearer (a Gentile who kept certain Jewish laws but was not circumcised), represented both the imperial might of Rome and the Hellenistic world generally. Yet Peter did so, after his nighttime vision of unclean animals, with the result that the household of Cornelius believed and received the Holy Spirit (Acts 10:1–48). It was thus at the Mediterranean port of Caesarea, where Herod the Great had placed Rome's most dramatic footprint in the land, that the Gospel first reached the Gentiles (Acts 11:1–18). The city would become the launching point of the Gospel to the world.

"... and even to the uttermost part of the earth." The first city to see large numbers of Gentiles come to faith in Jesus as the Messiah was Antioch in Syria, the third largest city in the Roman Empire. The church in Jerusalem sent Barnabas, an emerging leader in the church, to Antioch to assess the situation (Acts 11: 19–25; cf. Acts 4:36–37). As a Levite of Cypriot birth, Barnabas would have the proper sensitivities to understand the challenges that a large influx of Gentiles would bring to a phenomenon that so far had been primarily Jewish (cf. Acts 11:19). Barnabas in turn brought Saul from Tarsus, who readily spent a full year in Antioch bearing fruitful ministry (Acts 11:26). It was here that the believers were first called "Christians," followers of "Christos," the Messiah (the "anointed one").

The church in Antioch provided economic relief to the church in Jerusalem during a famine early in the reign of the Emperor Clau-

dius (Acts 27:30). Classical writers mention that Claudius's entire reign (A.D. 41–54) was plagued by widespread food shortages and general distress. Such offerings were gladly received in Jerusalem, where a marginal resource base ensured that the church would never become economically self-sufficient even though its members gave generously to each other (cf. Acts 2:44–45, 4:36–37, 5:1–2, 6:1, 24:17; 1 Cor 16:1–4).

The book of Acts notes the dramatic death of "Herod the king" (Herod Agrippa I) in Caesarea (Acts 12:20–23). It is known from classical sources that Agrippa I died in A.D. 44. Acts 12 then provides a firm chronological peg around which to hang other events described in the first half of the book of Acts. Agrippa's extravagant and reckless lifestyle earned him the reputation as the black sheep of the Herodian family, although once he became king he was largely faithful in observing Jewish law. Agrippa severely persecuted the church in Jerusalem, killing James the brother of John and imprisoning Peter (Acts 12:1–19).

Throughout their time of rule over Syro-Palestine, the Romans found the Jewish population of the land to be particularly difficult to control and tried various methods to enforce subservience to the emperor:

- Initially (63–40 B.C.), Rome allowed the Hasmonean family and its supporters (Hyrcanus II and Antipater, an Idumean) to remain in power in a vassal status, hoping that this buffer would win the allegiance of the people to Rome.
- Antipater's son, Herod the Great, reigned as "king of the Jews" (in reality, "king of Judea") from 40–4 B.C. He divided the land among his sons at his death: Archelaus, Antipas and Philip, although none were given the title "king."
- Rome removed Archelaus from control over Judea, Idumea and Samaria in A.D. 6 for incompetence, preferring instead to govern the province directly through a series of procurators (governors). These men were a mixed lot, though generally self-serving, cruel and corrupt, and typically ruled for three to four years before being promoted (or removed) to a position elsewhere in the Roman Empire. Of the procurators, Pontius Pilate governed the longest (A.D. 26–36). The church historian Eusebius claimed that Pilate committed suicide after being dismissed as procurator. Other procurators mentioned in the New Testament are Antonius Felix, who was a freed slave (A.D. 52–60; Acts 23:24–24:27), and Porcius Festus (A.D. 60–62; Acts 24:27–26:32).
- Agrippa I, grandson of Herod the Great, inherited the lands that had been under the control of his half-uncles Philip (who had died in A.D. 34) and Antipas (who was banished to Gaul in A.D. 39 for self-indulgence). The Emperor Claudius gave Judea,

EXPANSION OF THE EARLY CHURCH IN PALESTINE AND SYRIA

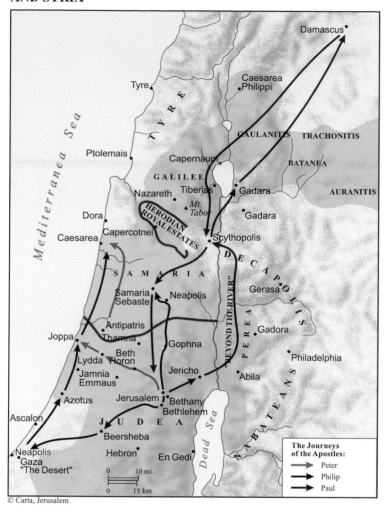

© Carta, Jerusalem

Samaria and Idumea to Agrippa in A.D. 41 as well, effectively returning the Herodian royal family to full power in the land. Agrippa I extended the city wall of Jerusalem northward, enclosing a large area of suburban estates—and the site of Jesus' crucifixion—in its arc. Agrippa's brief reign (he died suddenly in A.D. 44) was the last hurrah of the Second Temple period before the nation fell to destruction.

- At the death of Agrippa I, Rome reinstated procurator rule in Judea, Samaria, Idumea and much of Galilee. A quick run of several thoroughly corrupt procurators helped to prompt the Jewish revolt that led to the destruction of Jerusalem and the Temple in A.D. 70. It was during this time that the Apostle Paul made his three great missionary journeys, as well as his trip to Rome (Acts 13–28).

- When he came of age in A.D. 48, Agrippa's son, Agrippa II, was given territory in the north and, by A.D. 61, controlled most of Perea, the eastern half of lower Galilee, and the lands that previously had belonged to Philip. Agrippa II survived the destruction of Jerusalem and remained in power until his death sometime around the year A.D. 95.

Coin of Agrippa I.

Paul's First Missionary Journey (c. A.D. 46–48). The church in Antioch had a true international flavor and its leadership, hailing from lands across the eastern Mediterranean, chose Saul of Tarsus (now known as Paul the Apostle), Barnabas and John Mark to carry the Gospel into the Roman world (Acts 13:1–3). Paul's first missionary journey took him and his companions initially to Cyprus, the homeland of Barnabas. They traveled the length of the island from Salamis to Paphos, stopping in synagogues along the way and counting among their converts Sergius Paulus, the island's Roman proconsul, or governor (Acts 13:4–12).

From Paphos Paul sailed northwest to Perga, a large port city in Pamphylia, where John Mark decided to return to Jerusalem (Acts 13:13; cf. Acts 15:36–38). From there Paul and Barnabas crossed the rugged Taurus Mountains to Pisidian Antioch, a moderate-sized city in southern Galatia lying a hard ten-days' walk from the coast (Acts 13:13–14). It has been suggested that the "perils of rivers" and "perils of robbers" mentioned in 2 Corinthians 11:26 may refer to this part of Paul's travels—or certainly something similar. Paul preached in the synagogue in Pisidian Antioch on several occasions; his message was met with mixed feelings by the Jews, but was well received by a gentile audience (Acts 13:15–49). Facing opposition in Pisidian Antioch, Paul and Barnabas fled southeast along the main trade route that connected the province of Asia with Syria, to Iconium, where his *modus operandi*—and the results—were the same (Acts 13:50–14:5).

From Iconium Paul and Barnabas continued farther southeast to Lystra. No synagogue is mentioned in Lystra, although Paul's most-beloved disciple Timothy would come from this town (cf. Acts 16:1–2). There Paul and Barnabas healed a man who had been born lame and were promptly hailed as Greek gods (Acts 14:6–18). Paul's opponents from Antioch and Iconium followed him to Lystra, driving him farther east to Derbe and the surrounding region. After making many disciples in Derbe, Paul boldly retraced his steps through Lystra, Iconium and Pisidian Antioch, strengthening the churches that he and Barnabas had planted there (Acts 14:19–23). Tracking back through the Taurus Mountains, Paul and Barnabas sailed from Attalia (modern Antalya) to Syrian Antioch where they were well received by their sending church (Acts 14:24–28).

Paul's success among the Gentiles prompted a heated discussion within the Jerusalem church about the relationship between Gentile converts and matters of Jewish law, particularly circumcision. In response, Paul and Barnabas traveled to Jerusalem for the Jerusalem Council, where they argued for the full inclusion of Gentiles into the body of believers. After much deliberation, the Council decided to place only minimal Jewish legal demands on Gentile believers; by not including circumcision among them, the way was paved for the development of a truly universal church. Carrying the Council's written decision, Paul and Barnabas, together with Judas Barsabbas and Silas, two church leaders from Jerusalem, returned to Antioch (Acts 15:1–35).

Paul's Second Missionary Journey (c. A.D. 49–52). Desiring to strengthen the churches that he had founded on his previous journey, Paul, this time with Silas, traveled overland from Antioch to Derbe. Their route followed the international highway through Tarsus and the Cilician Gates. Barnabas and John Mark, meanwhile, revisited Cyprus (Acts 15:36–41). Timothy joined Paul and Silas in Lystra and the three continued on to Pisidian Antioch, then turned north through Phrygia. Skirting Bithynia, they headed west through Mysia, a northern district of Asia, to Troas, a Roman colony that owed its prosperity to its location as the terminus of a major eastern trade route on the Hellespont (Acts 16:1–8). There the three were joined by Luke, author of the book of Acts.

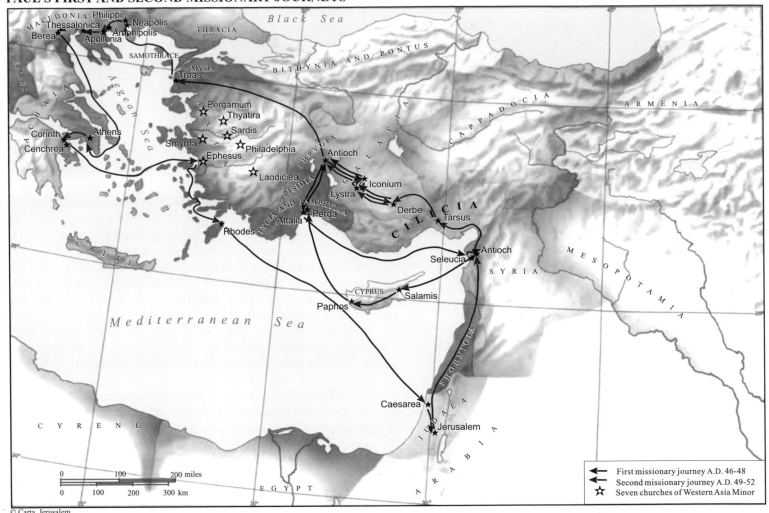

Black Sea

THRACIA

MACEDONIA
Philippi
Thessalonica
Berea
Apollonia
Amphipolis
Neapolis

SAMOTHRACE

MYSIA
Troas

BITHYNIA AND PONTUS

ARMENIA

EPIRUS

Aegean
Sea

Pergamum
Thyatira
Sardis
Smyrna
Philadelphia
Ephesus
Laodicea

CAPPADOCIA

Corinth
Cenchrea
Athens

ACHAIA

PHRYGIA
GALATIA

Antioch
Iconium
Lystra
Derbe

Tarsus

CILICIA

PISIDIA
LYCIA AND PAMPHYLIA
Attalia
Perga

Rhodes

CRETE

Seleucia
Antioch

SYRIA

MESOPOTAMIA

CYPRUS
Paphos
Salamis

Mediterranean   Sea

CYRENE

PHOENICIA

Caesarea

JUDAEA

ARABIA

Jerusalem

EGYPT

0   100   200 miles
0   100   200   300 km

← First missionary journey A.D. 46-48
← Second missionary journey A.D. 49-52
☆ Seven churches of Western Asia Minor

© Carta, Jerusalem

At Troas Paul had a vision compelling him to travel to Macedonia to preach the Gospel on European soil (Acts 16:9–10), thus irrevocably altering the course of the growth of the early church. He and his companions sailed across the northern Aegean to the Macedonian port of Neapolis, then made their way inland to Philippi, a thriving city proud of its Roman heritage (cf. Acts 16:20–21). Paul's first convert in Europe was Lydia, a prosperous businesswoman and God-fearer who opened her home to Paul and his companions (Acts 16:11–15). As usual, opposition followed close at hand. As a result of a commotion that arose when Paul healed a demon-possessed slave girl, he and Silas were jailed overnight on charges that, as Jews, they were "throwing the city into confusion" (Acts 16: 16–24). That night the Philippian jailer and his family came to faith in Christ when an earthquake destroyed the cell in which Paul and Silas were being held. The following morning, upon learning that they had imprisoned Roman citizens, the Philippian magistrates urged Paul and Silas to leave the city, hoping to put the matter behind them. Paul and Silas obliged, apparently leaving Luke in Philippi to minister to its growing, much-beloved church (Acts 16: 25–40; cf. Phil 1:3–11).

Paul, Silas and Timothy traveled overland to Thessalonica where they quickly established another church, then just as quickly were run out of town by a mob who opposed their message (Acts 17: 1–9). They found greater success in nearby Berea, where a number of Jews and influential Gentiles embraced the Gospel. Leaving Silas and Timothy in Berea, Paul continued on to Athens by ship, one step ahead of the opposition that persistently dogged his path (Acts 17:10–15).

Paul's stay at Athens was relatively brief and he failed to make

The Erechtheum, on the acropolis of Athens, Greece.

significant inroads among its sophisticated population. No longer the political capital of Greece (Achaea), Athens nevertheless retained its reputation for culture and learning that it had gained in the fifth century B.C., the Golden Age of classical Greece. Paul's famous defense of the Gospel before Epicurian and Stoic philosophers of the Areopagus, in which he used the Athenian altar "to an unknown god" as a springboard to speak of the God of the Jews and the resurrected Jesus, gained a mixed reaction: some sneered while others asked for another hearing (Acts 17:16–34). It can be assumed that Paul planted a church in Athens although the New Testament fails to mention one there.

Ruins of the Temple of Apollo at Corinth, with the city's acropolis, the rocky Acrocorinth, in the background.

The climax of Paul's second missionary journey was at Corinth, the capital and main shipping center of Achaea, where he stayed for eighteen months (Acts 18:1–18). Here he was joined by Silas and Timothy. Initially Paul based his ministry out of the home of Aquila and Priscilla, Jewish believers who, like him, were tent-makers by trade (cf. Rom 16:3–4). The church grew quickly after Crispus, the leader of the synagogue, believed the Gospel message (Acts 18: 8–10; cf. 1 Cor 1:14). Many of the new Corinthian converts came from disadvantaged life circumstances while others were undisciplined extremists, and Paul remained concerned about the moral state of the Corinthian church for some time (cf. 1 Cor 1:26–29, 5: 9–13, 6:9–11; 2 Cor 7:5–16). Paul probably wrote his two letters to the Thessalonian church during his extended stay at Corinth.

Paul finally left Corinth to return home. He, along with Aquila and Priscilla, sailed from Cenchrea, Corinth's port facing the eastern Mediterranean (Acts 18:18; cf. Rom 16:1–2). After a brief stop at Ephesus where he left Aquila and Priscilla, promising to return "if God wills," Paul sailed under the prevailing Mediterranean winds across the open sea to Caesarea. Back in Palestine, he first reported to the church in Jerusalem, then returned to Antioch (Acts 18: 19–22).

Paul's Third Missionary Journey (c. A.D. 53–57). After spending some time in Antioch, Paul headed west once again to build and strengthen the churches of Asia Minor, Macedonia and Achaia. He probably began by following the same overland route into Galatia that he had taken on his previous journey, no doubt visiting for a third time the churches which he had founded in Derbe, Lystra, Iconium and Pisidian Antioch. Paul then continued west to Ephesus (Acts 18:23, 19:1). His route probably would have taken him through Colossae and Laodicea (but cf. Col 2:1); later in life, when he was in prison in Rome, Paul wrote letters to churches in these two cities (Col 1:2, 4:10, 4:15–16).

Making good on his promise to return to Ephesus, Paul remained in the city for up to three years (Acts 19:8, 19:10, 20:31; cf. Acts 18:20–21). Here he found "a wide door for effective service" (1 Cor 16:8), and used Ephesus as a base of operations to reach people from all areas of the province of Asia (Acts 19:10). The city of Ephesus was well positioned for this as it lay at the juncture of two important overland routes through Asia (one east-west, the other north-south) and was the province's main Aegean harbor. For most of his time in Ephesus Paul spoke daily in the "school of Tyrannus," perhaps renting use of the hall every midday after its normal classes had finished and after spending the mornings himself making tents (cf. Acts 18:3). Paul wrote First Corinthians (1 Cor 16:8) and probably also a prior letter to the Corinthian church (cf. 1 Cor 5:9) during this stay in Ephesus, and he may have even made a quick trip to Corinth in order to attend to some pressing matters there (cf. 2 Cor 12:14, 13:1). He also dispatched Timothy and Erastus from Ephesus to minister to the churches of Macedonia (Acts 19:22). Opposition to Paul's preaching and healing ministry in Ephesus climaxed in a riot in the city's huge theater, where the worshipers of the fertility goddess Artemis (Diana), the chief deity of the Ephesians, had gathered to exert their claim on the religious sensibilities—and economic loyalty—of the city's residents. Soon afterward Paul left for Macedonia, probably by way of Troas (Acts 19:23–20:1; cf. 2 Cor 2:12–13).

It is not possible to trace with certainty Paul's subsequent travels through Macedonia and Achaia (Acts 20:1–3). One might suppose that he visited churches that he had previously founded there. Paul stayed in Achaia—almost certainly at Corinth—for three months, and it is likely that he wrote Second Corinthians on his way there. He may also have taken a side trip sometime during this journey across Macedonia into Illyricum (Rom 15:19). It is also probable that Paul wrote his grand epistle to the Romans at this time, noting to the believers in Rome his longing to visit their city and even travel on to Spain (Rom 15:22–25; cf. Acts 19:21).

But his heart longed for Jerusalem, and so Paul retraced his steps around the Aegean to Philippi where he celebrated the Passover, then on to Troas where he again met Luke who accompanied him to Jerusalem (Acts 20:3–12). Paul and Luke threaded their way by ship through the islands off the coast of Asia to Miletus—a glorious springtime journey—where they met with the elders of the church of Ephesus for a final farewell (Acts 20:13–38). Hurrying to be in Jeru-

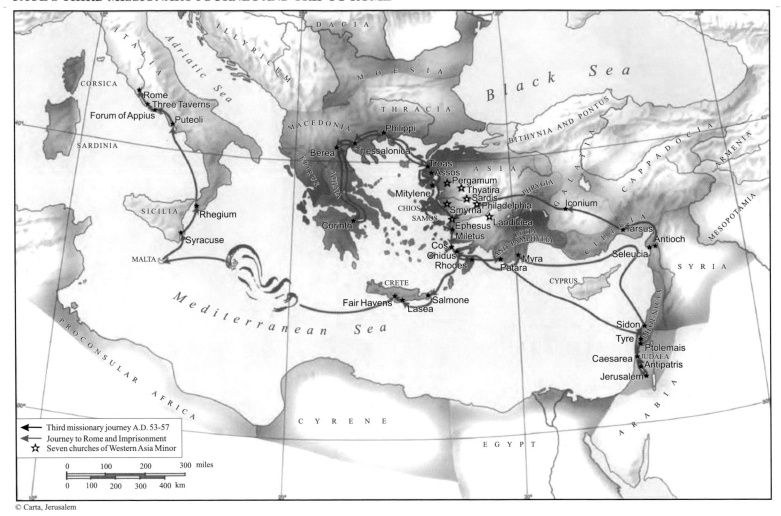

© Carta, Jerusalem

salem for the festival of Shavuot (Pentecost), Paul sailed around the southern end of the province of Asia to Patara, then straight across the Mediterranean to the ports of Tyre, Ptolemais and Caesarea. From there Paul climbed to Jerusalem, where he gave a glowing report of the spread of the Gospel among the Gentiles to James and the elders of the church (Acts 21:1–20). In the quarter century since the believers had first been empowered by the Holy Spirit at Pentecost, the church had grown with remarkable success.

Paul's Arrest and Journey to Rome (c. A.D. 59–62). On each of his journeys, Paul faced the issue of how closely Jews who were living in the Gentile world and who came to believe in Jesus should adhere to normative Jewish religious practices. Now, so as not to cause undue offense to the Temple authorities, Paul completed the proper purification rites for a vow that he had made, then entered the Temple precinct for Pentecost (Acts 21:20–26; cf. Acts 18:18). Toward the end of the festival he was falsely accused of bringing a Gentile into the Temple, thus defiling the sanctuary. Paul was arrested, gave a defense of his actions before the crowd that had gathered in the Temple courtyard, and then taken before the Sanhedrin (Acts 21:27–23:11). Hearing of an attempt on Paul's life, the Roman garrison commander in Jerusalem ordered his evacuation to Caesarea, the provincial seat of government (Acts 23:12–35). The initial leg of that journey, through the rough hills from Jerusalem to Antipatris, was made with a heavy armed guard under the cover of darkness, apparently to lessen the threat of ambush.

After a formal hearing in Caesarea, Felix, the procurator, kept Paul in open confinement for two years, in part hoping that the prisoner would bribe his way to freedom (Acts 24:1–27). When Festus,

Felix's successor, granted Paul another hearing at the beginning of his term of office, Paul exercised his right as a Roman citizen and appealed directly to Caesar (Acts 25:1–12; cf. Acts 22:25–28). King Agrippa II held a third hearing in Caesarea after which both he and Festus agreed that had Paul not appealed to Caesar, he could have been set free (Acts 25:13–26:32).

Paul, again accompanied by Luke, began his long journey to Rome under armed guard on a small trading ship heading back to its home port of Adramyttium on the west Asian coast. The boat sailed west against the prevailing winds, hugging the coast of Cilicia, Pamphylia and Lycia. At Myra, Paul was put aboard a large Alexandrian freighter loaded with over seventy tons of Egyptian wheat bound for Rome (Acts 27:1–6). It was late in the shipping season, well past "the fast" (i.e., Yom Kippur, the Day of Atonement —Acts 27:9), and the onset of sudden winter storms posed a real risk to travel on the high seas. Failing to find safe winter anchorage at Crete, the ship was caught by a violent wind and driven against the waves for two weeks until finally running aground and breaking up on the tiny island of Malta (Acts 27:7–44).

Although the ship and its cargo were lost, all of the passengers made it safely to land and spent the winter on the island. In the spring Paul continued by ship to Italy, touching briefly at Syracuse in Sicily and Rhegium on the tip of the Italian "boot" before landing at the port of Puteoli. There Paul met with believers who escorted him up the Appian Way to Rome. The book of Acts ends with Paul under house arrest in Rome, where for two years he preached the Gospel of Jesus to all who would hear (Acts 28:1–31).

Tradition, supported by some New Testament textual evidence (eg. Philem 22), holds that Paul was released from custody in Rome

THE JEWISH REVOLT AGAINST ROME, A.D. 66–70

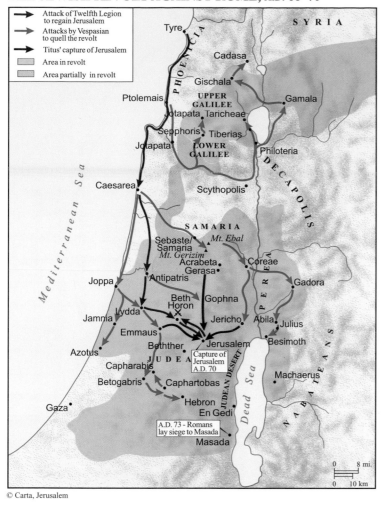

Legend:
- Attack of Twelfth Legion to regain Jerusalem
- Attacks by Vespasian to quell the revolt
- Titus' capture of Jerusalem
- Area in revolt
- Area partially in revolt

© Carta, Jerusalem

The Jewish Revolt Against Rome (A.D. 66–73). The growth of the early Church in the middle of the first century A.D. should be viewed against the backdrop of the uneasy relationship between the Jews and the cultural and military forces of the Roman Empire. Diaspora Jews lived as a minority—albeit a rather significant one—in a vast sea of Hellenistic culture and, although they were granted certain important privileges that allowed them to maintain a degree of self-autonomy, they had no desire to establish political control in the lands in which they lived. Not so for the Jews living in their historic homeland, the hills of Judea and Galilee. Here, in spite of a thin aristocratic upper crust that preferred to maintain its socio-economic position by not rocking the Roman political boat, the hope for real freedom beat strong within the heart of the vast majority of the people. The more Rome clamped down on the Jews, the stronger the desire for freedom grew, fueled by increasingly corrupt procurators who repeatedly offended Jewish religious sensitivities. The inevitable result was open revolt.

This drive for political freedom was spearheaded by the Zealots and a fanatical fringe group called the Sicarii—assassins—who resorted to kidnapping and murder to force Jewish political independence. When a large number of the Pharisees joined the Zealot cause, opposition to Roman rule gained widespread popular support. The spark that led to revolt flashed first in Caesarea with a clash between Greeks and Jews that resulted in the Jews being expelled from the city (A.D. 66). When news of this reached Jerusalem, riots there only fanned the flames. Neither the procurator Gessius Florus—who earlier had robbed the Temple treasury and now fled for his life back to Caesarea—nor Agrippa II could calm the situation. When Eleazar, a leading Temple official in Jerusalem, ordered that the hated sacrifice for the emperor cease, it signaled open revolt against Rome. Seizing the opportunity, Zealot groups captured the city's strongholds and by the end of the summer all of Jerusalem was under Jewish political control. As the revolt spread, the Jews captured the outlying Herodian fortresses of Masada, Cypros and Machaerus and seized the approaches to Judea. In Galilee and on the coast the Greek and Jewish populations fell on each other savagely.

Rome's response was swift and sure. Because the procurator had no legionary troops at his disposal, the governor of Syria, Cestius Gallus, intervened. Driving the Twelfth Legion to Jerusalem, he entered the city but shortly withdrew to find reinforcements. The Jewish forces followed up by ambushing and routing Gallus's troops at the descent of Beth-horon. With the immediate threat of Roman intervention gone, the Jewish rebels established a wartime government which collected revenue, minted coins and set up military districts. Of these, Galilee, the most vulnerable, was placed under the command of Josephus Flavius, the future historian, a scholar-priest with little military experience.

Tragically, the initial rebel victories were marred by bloody political infighting among numerous Jewish splinter groups. Lacking a unified front, the Jewish forces had no real chance against the renewed Roman onslaught. Nero appointed Vespasian, his best general, to the task. Vespasian brought three full legions to Ptolemais from which he attacked Galilee with a vengeance. The Roman troops easily overwhelmed Josephus's defenses in Galilee and the Jewish commander surrendered after a lengthy siege at Jotapata. By the end of A.D. 78 mopping-up operations had secured the area of the Sea of Galilee and, after a heroic Zealot stand at Gamala, Gaulantis.

Gamala in the Golan (Gaulanitis).

and traveled to other parts of the Mediterranean, including Crete (Titus 1:5). In his epistle to the Corinthians (c. A.D. 96), Clement of Rome noted that Paul "went to the limit of the West," which may be a reference to Spain (cf. Rom 15:23–24). A second imprisonment, probably during the reign of Nero, is implied in 2 Timothy 4:6–18. It is thought that both Paul and Peter met their deaths in Rome in A.D. 67–68 during Nero's persecution of the Christians. As a Roman citizen, Paul would have been beheaded with the sword.

Triumphal parade with Temple vessels, the Arch of Titus, Rome.

© Carta, Jerusalem

Vespasian then turned his eyes to the south, quickly overrunning Samaria and the coastal plain. To isolate Jerusalem, he marched next through Perea, capturing all but the stronghold of Machaerus. Tightening the noose, Vespasian stationed the Fifth Legion at Emmaus (modern Imwas) from which he crushed the cities of the Shephelah and Hebron. After conquering the southern Jordan Valley—including the Essene settlement at Qumran—Vespasian headquartered the Tenth Legion, together with the main body of the Roman army, at Jericho. By the spring of A.D. 69, the Jewish forces controlled only the hills surrounding Jerusalem, the Judean wilderness from Herodium to Masada, and a pocket of rocky hills around Machaerus; all access beyond lay in Roman hands.

Facing revolt in the western provinces and unrest at home, Nero committed suicide in A.D. 68. After a tumultuous "year of three emperors" (A.D. 69), the Roman army in Alexandria and Caesarea proclaimed Vespasian emperor. Vespasian's son Titus was dispatched from Alexandria to Jerusalem to finish his father's task. With a combined force of four Roman legions, Titus attacked Jerusalem from the north, the city's most vulnerable approach, in the spring of A.D. 70. The Jewish defenders, finally united in their struggle, were no match for the Roman assault. Systematically and relentlessly, the Romans breached each of the city's defenses, burning the Temple on the Ninth of Ab (28 August). The Upper City of Jerusalem held out for another month. When it finally fell, Titus ordered the entire city to be leveled with a vengeance uncharacteristically fierce even for the Romans. Only the three towers that had guarded Herod's palace remained standing; around these the Tenth Legion, assigned to guard the city, now camped. Follow-up operations took the fortresses of Herodium, Macherus and finally, in A.D. 73, Masada, after the celebrated confrontation between the Roman general Silva and the Zealot commander Eleazar.

The threefold tragedy of the destruction of the Temple, the cessation of sacrifices and the dissolution of the high priesthood shook Judaism to the core, but by focusing inwardly on the "tradition of the fathers" Jewish life found a renewed and fruitful expression through the local synagogue. The Sanhedrin reconstituted itself as the official authoritative body of Judaism, first at Jamnia (Jabneh) just before A.D. 100 and later in Galilee, and in the following centuries gave Judaism its normative, rabbinic shape through the compilation of the Mishnah. Christianity, still a fledgling movement, was affected as well. On the eve of the siege of Jerusalem the Christian community fled to Pella, in the Decapolis beyond the Jordan. With the Jerusalem

Herod's northern palace at Masada, overlooking the Dead Sea.

Remains of the Arcadian Way leading to the theater at Ephesus.

church now scattered, leadership passed to the churches in Antioch, Alexandria, Ephesus and elsewhere, a process of decentralization that eventually undercut Christianity's Jewish roots while allowing the church to adapt to local—and sometimes pagan—conditions. Partly because the Christians did not take part in the revolt against Rome, the Romans ceased viewing the movement as a Jewish sect and withdrew from it the official Diaspora privileges that it had previously enjoyed while under the umbrella of Judaism. By the mid-second century A.D., most Christians no longer hailed from a Jewish origin. For better or worse, the church was now weaned from its parent to come of age in a Gentile world.

The Seven Churches of Revelation. At the end of the first century A.D. the church faced intense persecution at the hands of Domitian, a particularly cruel emperor who insisted that all of his subjects address him as "Lord and god." The Apostle John, elderly and imprisoned on the island of Patmos during Domitian's reign, saw the ramifications of the new world that now faced the Church in a series of remarkably vivid visions which he recorded in the book of Revelation. At the beginning of his book, John addressed seven churches located in the province of Asia. He encouraged their members to be faithful in the face of persecution and warned them about dangerous heresies that threatened their existence (Rev 1:4–3:22). The problems and promises that these seven churches faced are typical of those that have confronted Christians in many parts of the world for centuries.

The letters to these seven churches are ordered in the book of Revelation in a clockwise geographical sequence starting with Ephesus.

- **Ephesus**. Strategically located on the west Asia coast, Ephesus was the political and commercial center of the region and the hub from which Christianity spread to the province of Asia and the Aegean. The island of Patmos, where John was imprisoned, lay 50 miles (80 kilometers) out to sea to the southwest. Extensive archaeological remains can be seen at the site of ancient Ephesus today, although most postdate the time of the New Testament. John commended the Ephesian church for its steadfastness, but noted that its members had lost their first love (Rev 2:1–7).

- **Smyrna**. Smyrna is modern Izmir, the third largest city in Turkey, and the ancient site is so built over today that little archaeology is possible. With a sweeping harbor and control of immensely fertile agricultural lands, first-century Smyrna felt itself to be the true center of the province and, like both Ephesus and Pergamum, claimed the title "First of Asia." The Smyrna church was commended for its perseverance in the face of persecution, and exhorted to be faithful even unto death (Rev 2:8–11).

- **Pergamum**. The ancient city of Pergamum was draped over a 305-meter (1,000-foot) high hill above a large, fertile valley and enjoyed a magnificent view of the Bay of Lesbos on the Aegean 24 kilometers (15 miles) to the west. Today the site (above the modern city of Bergama) boasts wonderful standing ruins, many of which date to the second century B.C., and is a real treat for visitors. Renowned as a center of art and literature, Pergamum was the official cult center for emperor worship in Asia. John noted the faithfulness of many in the church of Pergamum who faced unusually intense temptation—situated as they were at "Satan's throne"—but condemned those who had fallen into immorality and self-indulgence (Rev 2:12–17).

- **Thyatira**. The ancient site of Thyatira is located under the modern city of Akhisar making excavation difficult, and only meager remains have been found, none of which date to the first century A.D. Although militarily indefensible, the site was located on the imperial post road linking Mesopotamia to Syria and so developed an important role in international commerce. The residents of Thyatira were famous in antiquity for establishing highly organized trade guilds, many of which serviced workers in various types of cloth (cf. Acts 16:14). John commended the Thyatirian church for its growing faith and service, but condemned certain members who tolerated the apostate teachings of the "prophetess Jezebel" (Rev 2:18–29).

- **Sardis**. Rich in historical associations, Sardis had held strategic military and commercial value since the beginning of the thirteenth century B.C. The ancient city dominated the region of the Hermus River, the broadest and most fertile of all the river basins in Asia Minor. The extensive ruins of Sardis, located just south of the modern village of Sart, date primarily to the second and third centuries A.D., although the remains of a fourth-century B.C. temple to Artemis imitating the Artemis temple in Ephesus (cf. Acts 19:23–28) are noteworthy. John sounded a stern "wake-up" call to the apathetic church in Sardis, noting that only a few

of its members had remained faithful (Rev 3:1–6).

- **Philadelphia**. Although located in an arm of the same valley as Sardis and occupying a spot on the imperial post road, Philadelphia was a second-rate city in the first century A.D. with little to boast of other than its position as a beneficiary of the financial patronage of the emperor. Today the small town of Alasehir is located on the same site, and no excavation of the ancient city has taken place. John had nothing negative to say about the church in Philadelphia. He commended its faithfulness despite its "little strength" and noted that the church faced "an open door which no one can shut" (Rev 3:7–13).

- **Laodicea**. One hundred miles (62 kilometers) upriver from Miletus (cf. Acts 20:15–38), Laodicea and its neighbor Colossae were situated at a great hub of routes, ensuring prosperity and opportunity for their residents. Laodicea was a banking center and boasted a famous medical school. The remains of the city cover hundreds of acres, but little excavation has been done. Among the finds is a sophisticated aqueduct carrying water from springs 10 kilometers (6 miles) away; unlike the hot springs bubbling up at neighboring Hierapolis and the cool springs watering Colossae, the water of Laodicea was lukewarm by the time that it reached the city. John had nothing favorable to say to the church at Laodicea. Though its members were privileged (cf. Col 4:13–16), he compared them to lukewarm water, apathetic and stale, and urged them to renew their commitment to Christ (Rev 3:14–22).

Remains of the Temple of Artemis at Sardis.

Canadian Native Art

Frontispiece
Photo: The National Museum of Canada

A face carved in the trunk of a spruce tree in Northern British
Columbia, said to have been carved by the Tlingit to mark their
southernmost territorial limit. The delicate marks of the adze are still
visible on the face, which emerges from the form of the tree in an
image of metamorphosis.

Nancy-Lou Patterson

Canadian Native Art

Arts and Crafts
of Canadian Indians
and Eskimos

Collier-Macmillan
Canada, Ltd.

Design: Carl Brett
Cover photo of Haida
Transformational Mask·
National Museum of Man,
and The National Gallery
of Canada

Library of Congress
Catalogue Card Number:
73-8039

SBN:
02.975610.3

Collier-Macmillan Canada, Ltd.
1125 B Leslie Street, Don Mills, Ontario
Macmillan Publishing Co., Inc.
New York
Printed and Bound in Canada

For Mildred and Louis Gellermann

Contents

List of Illustrations

Acknowledgements

I wish to express particular thanks to
Mrs. Kay Desrochers
of the National Museum of Man
and Mr. Steven Long
of the Pollock Gallery
for their gracious assistance and
personal courtesy;
to Mr. Michael J. Banks
for allowing me to study
"The Reluctant Bride;"
to Mr. Basil Johnston
and Dr. Helmuth Fuchs
of the Royal Ontario Museum
for their helpful advice
on the manuscript;
to Mr. David Norman
and Miss Martha Lawrence,
students of mine
who provided photographs;
to Mrs. Terry MacLean,
Mrs. Judy Treischl,
and Mrs. Beverly Bald
of the University of Waterloo
for endless and able assistance
in the preparation of the manuscript
and illustrations;
and to my husband Palmer,
whose unfailing support, advice,
and encouragement,
made the whole thing possible.

Introduction

The late nineteenth and early twentieth centuries saw the discovery of primitive art. That is, artefacts made by cultures with simpler technologies than those of Europe were seen for the first time as art. This involved a change in sensibility and of the idea of art; thus the discovery is a part of the history of modern art. Originally it was based on a romantic nostalgia for paradise (which saw primitive art as naïve, innocent, irrational, or unself-conscious). Today there is a desire to recover the sense of the sacred which fills much native art: this art is no longer seen as the expression of a childish faith, but of a mature spirituality.

The artefacts that at first seemed refreshingly crude and free of specialization now seem to draw their aesthetic power from an exact relationship between form and need. They are seen to express specific movements (of the hunt, for instance) as extensions of the self. Writing in a significant and prophetic essay in *Canadian Art* in 1947, Doris Shadbolt described the increasing sympathy in the twentieth century for primitive art. She suggested the following causes: first, a taste (perhaps romantic) for the primitive; second, an attraction for the supposedly naïve, as in Gauguin; third, a reaction against specialization and the restriction of too much training; and fourth, a reaction against the realism inherited from the Renaissance. She listed the chief qualities of primitive art as formal organization, emotional expressiveness, and simplicity of form, adding that the art functioned within a community which shared a common idea. The simplicity of form was due to the strength of purpose, for the simplification is not one of looseness but of intense con-

centration. She suggested that moderns were losing confidence in technology and felt the need of an art which was symbolic in its true sense.

Nineteenth-century artists in Canada often depicted the Indian and the Eskimo and took an interest in native artefacts. The influence of primitive art in Europe (upon Picasso, Modigliani, Matisse, etc.) is well known; in Canada its influence may have been felt by the early twentieth-century Canadian nationalists and certainly is expressed in the art of Emily Carr. More recently Doris Shadbolt and others have originated a series of exhibitions of native art which have won world-wide attention.

It is significant that many of the finest works of West Coast and Prairies native art were made during contact times; that is, at the same time as the works of European-born or -descended artists who are usually listed as Canadian. According to Frantz Fanon, it is typical of colonialism to downgrade the pre-colonial past, to show the colonizers as a light in darkness, a mother who saved her colonized children from themselves. The native is forced to re-establish the grandeur of his own past. In Mexico and South America, *Indianismo* is an attempt to recover that past for all citizens, whether of native of non-native descent. Youth's identification with this other "indigenous past" is an expression of their radicalization.

One may ask whether Canada is really solely European. Native art preceded that of Europeans in North America. It continued to exist and even to flourish superbly in response to the new presence. It has begun to nourish and enrich the art and the

lives of the new "Canadians". The development of Eskimo sculptors and graphists since the 1950s, and of contemporary Indian painters like Norval Morriseau, indicates that native art continues to develop in association with the art and presence of the majority. Thus native art is a living and essential part of Canadian art and must be given its due place in that history by teachers, students, and writers in Canada.

A quarrel burns continually among students of primitive art, fired by historical factors as well as by differences of temperament. The dispute is between those who study primitive art for its aesthetic quality, and those who insist that it must be understood in terms of its cultural context. The word "primitive" is itself in question, and may show what has touched off the fire. The word suggests inferiority, but it is used for a reality. Moderns are becoming uncomfortable with ideas about "European superiority," and would like to find new language to express new equality.

The word "primitive" causes trouble in the following way. A work of primitive art has been made in a culture whose technology is less complex than that of the writer who uses the term "primitive." However, the object of primitive art—its purpose and function—is certainly no less complex than the purposes and functions of art in a society with an elaborate technology. This difference between a limited *means* and a complex *end* has not always been recognized by the technique-proud West in looking at artefacts from outside Western culture.

Similarly, Europeans did not understand the sophisticated and fully developed religious systems expressed in individual and communal practices—including dancing, singing, and the making of objects of plastic and graphic art. The early missionary thought he had come to fill a void or to replace a benighted superstition. The European sophisticate, on the other hand, thought that North American religion was child-like, and free of doubt, hesitation, insecurity. He saw it as being paradisaical in its elemental force. Native art thus became the object of a projection of the European's own myth of spring.

Furthermore, the whole idea of collecting and admiring objects of non-Western origin is a Western concept; giving approval to such objects—making them, as it were, subjects of moral or ethical judgement—is a characteristically Western activity. Whether the non-Western object is admired for its aesthetic power or studied to gain understanding of the culture which produced it, the admiration or examination is carried out by a Western mind (whatever the colour of the student's skin). This does not mean that we cannot learn to appreciate or understand this art, of course. Quite the contrary. To appreciate or understand it in this sense is to see it with a Western eye. If there is a rescue from this dilemma (and perhaps only a Westerner could feel *guilty* about having a culture of his own), it lies at a level deeper than the part of us which makes aesthetic judgements, moral pronouncements, statements of opinion, and formulations of historical perspective or contextual analysis.

What we see is influenced to a great degree by what we expect to see. The visual language of our own culture—the conven-

tions of style at work in our own times—affects our *ability* to see what is before us, and the *way* in which we see it. In our extremely eclectic age we run through a style every ten years or so, then come out hungry for a new one. This desire for newness perhaps accounts for the "discovery" in the late nineteenth century of "primitive" art. Westerners have brought back objects from areas of exploration, conquest, and colonization for a long time, but for the first time they saw such objects as *art*. This discovery, based on the idea of "art for art's sake," promoted objects which had not, with rare exceptions, been made for their own sake, to the status of independent objects whose merit lay solely in their aesthetic qualities. This is not to say that "primitive" societies do not recognize aesthetic values or the value of the "well-made" object. They do. But the making of artefacts for this end alone is as rare in primitive non-Western societies as it was in mediaeval Western society.

The usual division of hand-made objects into "art" (painting and sculpture) and "minor arts" (drawing, printmaking) or "crafts" (pottery, weaving, and other techniques of making useful things) breaks down when the art of the Indian and Eskimo is to be considered. These categories place an unnecessary limit upon the range of native objects, each of which may be called beautiful. At a time when artists find even painting and sculpture increasingly invalid and irrelevant, it is absurd to cling to such definitions in dealing with non-Western cultural patterns. There is a constant tension in contemporary criticism;

should one regard functional artefacts as objects of aesthetic significance, or as forms whose meaning lies within and is validated by function? This question is the basis of the whole quarrel about primitive art.

The objects of "expressive form" (to use Suzanne Langer's definition of art) produced by members of the native population in the geographical area which is now called Canada have interested European collectors for many years. Numbers of these objects have been preserved only because of their presence in these collections. They were seen partly as curiosities and partly as evidence for the anthropologist. It is interesting, though, that when Paul Kane, a Romantic painter who travelled west in the 1840s, stuffed his shoulderbag with what he regarded as bizarre objects, he was clearly attracted to beautiful ones as well. The following remarks, recording an essentially negative judgement, show the context within which he analysed Indian crafts:

The Chinooks evince very little taste, in comparison with some of the tribes on the eastern side of the Rocky Mountains, in ornamenting either their persons, or their warlike or domestic implements. The only utensils I saw at all creditable to their decorative skill were carved bowls and spoons of horn, and baskets made of roots and grass....

The words "ornamenting" and "decorative" show what Kane looked for, and his collection includes examples of objects which met this criterion. The present writer has ex-

amined an elegant horn digging stick, used to uproot camas bulbs, that Kane carried away from his encounter with the Chinooks; it is handsomely decorated with drilled circles in a polka-dot pattern.

"Arts of the Raven," the 1967 exhibition of objects of West Coast art at the Vancouver Art Gallery, and the exhibition of "Masterpieces of Indian and Eskimo Art in Canada" at the National Gallery in 1970, have been heralded as bringing Canadian native art into proper perspective. The arts of the Eskimo took a world-wide tour in 1972 in the show, "Sculpture of the Inuit: Masterworks of the Canadian Arctic." The aesthetic standards applied in the choice of objects exhibited in these collections were no less Western than (and perhaps not altogether different from) those of Paul Kane.

It is common in journalistic reports of these exhibits to use words like "surprising" and "remarkable" as if amazement were the appropriate response to the discovery that Canadian Indians and Eskimos have been capable of producing beautiful forms. There is a smell of paternalism to this tendency. It implies the fundamental confusion between technical means and cultural ends discussed above. Beautiful objects made by hand have been produced by native Europeans — why not native Canadians? But journalists love surprises. The fact that European travellers have been delighted by Canadian native arts for centuries does not deter them. Even the pronouncement that West Coast Indian and Eskimo sculptures are equal to those of Egypt seems a little late to be precisely surprising.

Besides these recent enthusiasts, some scholars have been working in the field for many years. One thinks immediately of Marius Barbeau, omitting equally distinguished names only for lack of space. The work of these writers is indispensable to the student for its combination of deep knowledge and profound empathy. Painstaking and exhaustive work such as theirs could be applied to the arts of every Canadian native group, and art history in Canada owes such men a significant debt. Surveys like this book would be impossible without the patient labours of the specialist. Certainly the beauty of native art has not come as a recent surprise to men like Barbeau.

The whole idea of progress is to blame for the journalist's astonishment. Progress is a nineteenth-century concept that has done infinite mischief in the attempt of the races to see one another as brothers. In art it is equally disastrous. The undoubted ability of technology to improve by development has led many observers to think that non-Europeans who adopt European technology are somehow becoming Western in thought as well, and to think that such Westernization is a desirable, or even possible, thing. In fact, what occurs in contact between any two cultures (short of genocide, which in Canada was the fate of the Beothuks) is *synthesis*. New technology and, to some extent, new ideas are accepted just so far as the previous cultural forms and context will admit them. In Canada, for example, those groups who had previously practised agriculture took quite readily to European agricultural techniques, and made a strong impression on missionaries and government

officials by doing so. Little girls who came from a culture where the painstaking craft of quillwork was practised delighted their Ursuline teachers by showing great skill at European-style embroidery with silk thread.

This trait of cultural synthesis isn't unique to Indians and Inuit, of course. What is more, it has not been confined to intercourse with Europeans; any given group shows cultural traits which have been borrowed from its neighbours. This phenomenon occurs not only in space, but in time, for no native culture had remained static before its encounter with Europeans. A long history of adaptation to changing climate, geography, and economic base, of cultural borrowing and interchange, of evolution of technology, lay behind every one of the groups who met, at varying points in time, the white newcomers who were to conquer them, by economic and medical as well as by military means.

It is the time dimension that is particularly important for an understanding of Canadian native art. There is no "pristine" native art in the sense of art which has never undergone change or influence. The superb arts of the West Coast and the Prairies are due in significant measure to pressures and influences of European presence and technology, sometimes exerted from a great distance. It is difficult to set a convenient date at which native art suddenly becomes "post-contact"; the processes are far too complex for that. This book is only a very late example of what has been a long and extremely involved process of cultural interchange. The following chapter will outline in a general way the course of these events.

Chapter 1

The Original People

Hand-made objects consist of natural materials found in their primary form and modified by hand to a usable state. These materials are usually found nearby, in the immediate environment, but sometimes they are trade goods or materials brought from a considerable distance, such as the abalone shell used as inlays by the Haida, traded from the warm seawaters of California. Perhaps the most recent example would be the use of fine Japanese rice paper by Inuit printmakers of the 'seventies. Still, materials reflecting the immediate environment are most common.

Environment also influences the function of objects. Here the psychic environment is brought to bear, for the spiritual world in which people live is as important as the physical in determining which objects are needed and preserved. Much of early Inuit art (in the Dorset culture), for instance, seems to have been spiritual in intention; various amulets and shaman's instruments have been explained in this context.

In addition the environment shapes the economic base of life, and thus in part determines which objects of a culture are preserved for the archaeologist. The burial practices of a people also help to determine what is left behind. These factors have operated in North America, and to an extreme degree in Canada, to limit the nature and scope of objects preserved from ancient times, since the first men came into the New World by crossing a land bridge which opened from time to time across what is now the Bering Strait.

The fluted point, made of flint, is a good starting point for an examination of the arts of Canadian native peoples. Artefacts of leather or wood have not survived, but hands capable of such delicate work in flint could have used organic material as well, and in such a climate they undoubtedly did. The makers were big game hunters; their prey was the mammoth, far bigger and more terrifying than the buffalo of later times. Stone quarries where the flint was obtained and shaped give us significant insights into the relationship of maker to material. Individual styles can be recognized; finds of abandoned carcasses show that the hunters worked in teams and used points which differed sufficiently so that they must have been unmistakable to men who had grown up and hunted together for life. The fluted point is an independent North American variation on the points of the Old World. It suggests the influence of long isolation after the original immigrants made their way down the icy corridor between the two major glaciers. The word "beautiful" can be applied to these points, with the slender flute and the graceful outline differing from industry to industry, identifying Folsom from Clovis or other varieties. From this mute and limited evidence we can detect not only individual variation but distinct industries, styles, periods, and all the paraphernalia of art history.

The first wave of migration to the New World took place at least forty to thirty-five thousand years ago. These firstcomers made crude stone tools, difficult to recognize except by the trained eye. During a period from twenty-eight to twenty-five thousand years ago, the makers of the Llano complex of projectile points found their way over most of the Americas. At last the fluted point developed; several styles

are found in Canada on sites dating from thirteen to nine thousand years ago. Between the second movement and a third which is dated at thirteen to ten thousand years ago, there was a vast period in which no passage across the strait was easy or perhaps even possible. This third period of connection between the continents has been called the "American Epi-Gravettian" by scholars who see it as an extension of Old World culture; it showed a characteristic tendency to produce small implements. This is the origin of the Eskimo culture, just as the earlier movements were precursors of the Paleo-Indians whose life-styles underlie those of Canadian Indian culture.

During the periods described above, and following the slow withdrawal of the ice to its present polar position, the climate and environment changed several times. The weather, the vegetation, the surface of the land were altered. The people were hunters throughout this period, but their game, their vegetable food, and their materials changed repeatedly. The response of the various peoples—some of them settled, some part of migratory movements—was to change their life mode to suit the new realities. Sometimes they borrowed concepts and methods from their neighbours, sometimes from new contacts. There is no period in which life can have been entirely static, though the difference between styles in the north is not so great as that which developed further south, for hunting does tend to produce certain similar habits and points of view. Some of these are found in the so-called "hunter style" or "animal style" of Central Asia, which at different times in-

fluenced Chinese, Eastern European, and Muslim art. Aspects of this style can be seen at work in the art of Eskimo and West Coast peoples and attenuated versions are recognizable in eastern hunting cultures as well. Two of the outstanding traits are the *X-ray style*, showing the bone-structure and sometimes other organs on the surface of the bodies of animals and men; and the *metamorphic forms*, in which men, animals, and spirits are blended together to produce composites or groups of interlocked forms.

The alternative to hunting in the ancient world, and a way of life which gradually replaced it in some cultures, was agriculture. The Neolithic revolution seems to have occurred spontaneously, or at least in great isolation, at about the same time in the New World as in the Old, though a few recent studies suggest that its earliest origins may lie in Southeast Asia. This way of life produced superb theocratic civilizations in Mexico, Central America, and the Andes of South America. Agriculture slowly moved north from Mexico, producing the complex life-styles of the American Southwest and Southeast. Ultimately farming arrived in Canada, to be practised in parts of the Great Lakes region and the St. Lawrence Valley. Along with methods of cultivation—chiefly of corn and tobacco—came various practical and cultural elements: pottery, smoking implements, burial mounds, and various practices related to the seasons, orientation to the four directions, and sacrifice of war prisoners.

The case of pottery is particularly complex, for it is part of a pottery tradition found in the northern forested zones of

Europe and Asia as well as North America. Perhaps the pottery was diffused from Siberia to North America, but it came a roundabout route to the Great Lakes, because it appears at an earlier date in the East than it does in the Great Lakes region. The greatest glories of agricultural culture were represented by the Hopewellian culture of the American Great Lakes region. The fading of this classical period of ancient American culture was followed in Canada (after AD 800) by the Lalonde culture of Ontario, where inland villages grew corn, beans, squash, and sunflowers, supplementing these domestic vegetable foods by hunting. These people, with their pipes, pottery, and mass ossuaries for burial, are probably the ancestors of the various Iroquoian groups, especially the Huron.

Such were the varying patterns of life in Canada when the first Europeans arrived, probably Vikings who settled briefly in Labrador during the Middle Ages; the Thule people may have been the Skraelings described in the Vinland Sagas. The first white men of a continuous stream were probably fishermen off the Grand Banks in the fifteenth century. As certain land-based techniques for preserving fish evolved, the fishermen began to spend time ashore, at the same time beginning the process of taking over the land from its original owners.

Gradually settlement began in various parts of North America, and the effects of white presence travelled well ahead of the newcomers themselves. One of these was disease; hitherto unknown diseases, such as smallpox and measles, to which Indians had no immunity, raced across the land, wiping out whole villages. No area was unaffected, and in many cases the population was halved or even quartered, with consequences to the culture and creative life which can only be imagined. No people were untouched by the time settlers reached their area. A second influence, and one ultimately far more important, since the population had since recovered itself, was that of the new trade goods which the Europeans brought with them. Women were glad to give up pottery for iron cooking vessels, and the trade bead became a quick substitute for the painstaking technique of quillwork. Some groups became engaged as middlemen in the new trade, and sought advantage in a changing form of economy. None of the groups who had used agriculture practised it exclusively, and in this early period the pressure was to hunt, to obtain the furs the traders wanted.

The changes in the physical side of Indian life in the sixteenth, seventeenth, and eighteenth centuries were very great. The effects on the psychic life, however, were not so marked, for several reasons. One is that the group structure remained, and mothers brought up their children in the traditional ways. The traders were glad to see the hunting life maintained, for it provided the goods they wanted. Indian-white relations were cordial except where the Indian groups were forced to take sides in European-versus-European conflicts, notably between the French and English. Urged on by their European allies, some groups took part in the bitter competition, earning themselves an ugly reputation among whites who saw in Indians traits they could not admit seeing in themselves.

Moving slowly from the American Southwest, the descendants of Spanish horses eventually arrived in Canada in the eighteenth century. This, too, brought change. Men who ventured out only occasionally on the great prairies, travelling on foot and with the dog-pulled *travois*, and returning to their forest life again in regular cycles, found that the horse was a much superior beast of burden. Groups began to live permanently in the wide and previously hostile environment. Buffalo hunters could thunder over the open prairie and drive their prey before them, attacking swiftly and taking many more animals than before. In such a situation men grew rich; elaborate ceremonials, paraphernália, and objects of wealth-display accompanied this rapid cultural expansion. Even the periodic waves of disease which left ghost villages here and there could not prevent the culture from producing a splendid art of chivalry. This elegant culture was only curbed when settlers began to settle on the land and confine the proud buffalo hunters to reservations, out of the way of the agricultural thrust of nineteenth-century European culture. The last free buffalo herds disappeared in the 1870s. At the same time missionaries and government officials began their eager attempts, with schools, hospitals, and thick rule-books, to change these Indians, too, into whites.

By this time the Indians of the East Coast had been under the rule of Europeans for almost two hundred years. Yet despite all the European teaching and persuasion (some far from gentle), they remained recognizably Indian, much to the frustration of their mentors. The same thing is true of the people of the Six Nations, whose ancestors came to Canada after the Revolutionary War, to land granted in reward for their loyalty to the British. After four hundred years of practising agriculture (based upon their previous agricultural ways) and the close presence of whites, they remain recognizably Indian. Many still worship in the Longhouse and speak their native language; most are proud of their identity.

The most recent Indian cultures to undergo contact are those of the West Coast. Here an extremely rich environment and mild weather formed the background of an equally rich and favoured culture. But nearly all of the artefacts we have to show this cultural wealth were made since the arrival of the iron axe and adze. The gigantic heraldic poles were made with metal tools. (As well, the elaborate potlatches showed a strong influence of competition brought about by the trading of the white man.) These most splendid of all Canadian art objects exist partly because of European influence during a period before it became overwhelming. What underlay such splendour can only be reconstructed in part from the stone implements and ceremonial vessels of prehistoric West Coast culture; much of the less permanent portion lies rotting in the rainforests of the Coast and is but faintly suggested by the stone objects which have survived.

The Athapaskan peoples of the Mackenzie River area in the huge hunter's interior of the Territories are less touched by white presence than Eastern groups. Nevertheless they too have undergone influence from trade goods, which they eagerly seek in the towns and trading centres even while

they continue their life in the bush. These peoples have long puzzled observers and come under negative judgement for the simplicity of their life. They are to this day relatively free of structure, following a highly individualistic style of independent hunting wherever possible, though Athapaskans, too, are coming into the city today. They have led a life of extreme hardship and ever-threatening hunger, with little time, perhaps, for the making of elegant artefacts; yet they do produce beadwork and leatherwork for trade. Though their material culture is far less dependent upon display than that of the Prairies or the West Coast, their supply of traditional mythological narratives and complex social games (such as the Dogrib Hand Game) suggests that their psychic life is far from meagre. Other Athapaskan peoples moved south hundreds of years ago to become, among others, the much-admired Navajo, borrowing the traits of the surrounding Pueblo dwellers and learning herding from the Spanish. Those who remained in the north gladly took over white goods and adhered to the new religion, but they still hunt much as before, free of heavy white settlement in their empty and difficult land.

North of them are the Eskimo, descendants of the Thule culture which supplanted the rich Dorset culture around AD 1000. The Dorset population had developed *in situ* about 800 BC from the Arctic Small Tool Tradition which began in the Bering Strait region about 4000 BC. They produced tiny objects of sculpture whose purpose we can only surmise and whose beauty would match Kwakiutl sculpture in

"plastic superiority" could they be enlarged to the same scale. The Thule people came in contact with the first Europeans at short-lived Viking settlements, but their descendants, the Eskimo, were in long contact in the Eastern Arctic. The art of the Eskimo seems to have become confined to tourist art, collected by whaling ship crews and missionaries over the long years of the nineteenth century. From this seemingly unlikely background, a rich flowering has taken place within the last few decades. Under the influence of James Houston and others, new styles of Eskimo stone carving and printmaking have been introduced both to the artists who make them, such as Kenojuak, Kiakshuk, Paloosie, Lukta, and Pudlo, and to the eager collectors of southern Canada.

Another recent development has been the appearance and public recognition of Canadian Indian artists. Some work in conventional contemporary styles and subjects, and some, such as Norval Morriseau, Francis Kagige, Jackson Beardy, Carl Ray, and Gerald Tailfeathers, have drawn upon their own psychic tradition to produce forms of great power. These latest responses to changing realities can be seen as the most recent and accelerated in a series of responses to change over a period of forty thousand years by descendants of peoples who have challenged and survived the vast and hostile north. They met the tide of European settlement and cultural onslaught with courage, resourcefulness, and a level of expressive creativity the equal of any in world history.

Chapter 2

Hunters of the Eastern Woodlands and Subarctic

Figure 1. Plainview Point, Brohm Site, near Thunder Bay, Ontario.
Photo: The National Museum of Canada

After about 8000 BC, lanceolate points began to replace the earlier fluted points. The Plainview Point is a northern example of the type used by Aqua-Plano Culture hunters who moved along the shores of enormous glacial lakes.

In the Great Lakes Region, one of the first areas to be inhabited in Canada, a fairly clear record of continuous change emerges. Both the size and number of the lakes have varied considerably over the past thirteen thousand years. Before 7000 BC in the region itself, and until 4500 BC north of Lake Superior, the ice made all life impossible. Once the lakes were stabilized, however—and the inhabitants of the region must have had boats in 700 BC—the waterway became the major highway. The land bore a thick forest cover of hardwood, changing to pine forest in the north. A rich variety of animal life included bear, deer, and, in the northern areas, moose and caribou. The human population was relatively sparse, but it must have comprised ten per cent of North American people at the time Europeans arrived.

The glaciers began their slow retreat about 11,000 BC, but by 8500 BC deglaciation speeded up, followed apace by the expanding forest, home for the great mammoths and other gigantic game. Men came following the game: Paleo-Indians with their fluted points. At this time the forest was all spruce and fir, and a few of the hunter's points were left behind to mark their presence, during a period of about 10,000 to 7000 BC.

After about 8000 BC the fluted point of the earliest Big Game Hunters were gradually replaced by the lanceolate points, so-called because of their long, graceful shape. These are generally larger than the Folsom type, and a characteristic one found in Ontario is the Plainview point. Its style seems to show its derivation from the earlier fluted form; its base is concave and its basal edge has been ground and thinned to aid in hafting it. This kind of point, used by bison hunters, is very widespread in North America. The style forms a part of the Plano series, which is thought to have a somewhat northerly origin; in Ontario it is part of the Aqua-Plano culture where the hunters moved along the shores of enormous glacial lakes. The Brohm site, which has yielded some of these finds (Figure 1), is about twenty-five miles northeast of Thunder Bay, at Pass Lake, Ontario, in the region of Thunder Cape. There Richard S. MacNeish found Aqua-Plano artefacts in layers of clay and pebble beach deposits. The Indians of this period lived along the beach of Lake Minong, which was 224 to 230 feet above the present level of Lake Superior. The date is estimated to be about 7000 to 6000 BC. A number of other stone artefacts, suitable to a hunter's life, were also found.

Peoples of two different life-styles followed these early hunters: the Boreal Archaic Indians, who arrived about 5000 BC, and the Old Copper Indians, the first people in North or South America to make objects of metal. They worked cold copper, which they formed into tools and weapons of various elegant forms as well as jewellery and hair ornaments which give evidence of a certain luxury in life-style.

Implements of the Old Copper type are found among northern hunting peoples north of the frost line (the prehistoric agricultural limit) or near its southern margin; in Canada these include the Athapaskans near the Alaskan border, the Eskimo, and the Laurentian peoples in the East, according to Suzanne Miles. The sources

Figure 2. Birdstone, Elgin County, Ontario.
Photo: The National Museum of Canada

A typical birdstone of green slate, found in a Boreal Archaic site
(before 500 BC). It may have been an ornament, for it is perforated,
and it may have had some magical intention, but its streamlined
shape and conventionalized form give it an intrinsic attraction.

of native copper are outcroppings of lumps of pure copper in a weathered matrix; the lumps are either dug out or are scattered as a result of glacial action. The main Canadian site is the Copper Mountains near the mouth of the Coppermine River. Old Copper people of Southern Ontario acquired their copper from the area south of Lake Superior.

Sharing the region with them were the Boreal Archaic Indians, who continued their hunting culture up to 500 BC, making and using objects of ground and polished stone. They must have taken excellent advantage of the increasingly deciduous forest, judging by the array of woodworking tools they left behind, but their carvings have not been preserved. A common, and highly conventionalized, object of this period is the birdstone (Figure 2), which occurs in forms which are more or sometimes emphatically less birdlike. Some are perfect images in miniature of the same forms used today as wooden decoys, but some are fitted with ears and similar unbirdlike parts. A typical birdstone, found in Elgin County, Ontario, is made of greenish slate, the layers of which can be seen on the smooth surface. The hole through the tail is typical. The function of these mysterious objects is not known, but some writers call them ornaments because the perforation suggests that they were strung upon or fastened to something. Perhaps, as George Quimby proposes, they were handles or weights for spear throwers. Their bird/animal form may imply some magical intention as they resemble their makers' game. Their streamlined shape, smoothness, and intriguing anonymity give them attraction as objects in their own right.

The Early Woodland peoples were the first to use fired pottery, during a period from 500 to 100 BC; they made burial mounds as well. In the Middle Woodland period, from 100 BC to AD 800, the Hopewell culture enriched the regions south of the Great Lakes, though few such riches have been found in Canada. These people were the farmers whose culture derived from Mexico. The Late Woodland period lasted until 1600, after which the presence of Europeans brought about numerous additional cultural changes. During this period the Indians developed increasingly different life styles. Their descendants, who combined hunting and farming or were only partially hunters, include the Ottawa, the Huron, the Ojibwa, and the Potawatomi.

Those who remained primarily hunters were the peoples of the Maritimes—Beothuks, Micmacs, and Malecites; the Subarctic groups of eastern Canada, the Montagnais and Naskapi; and the northern peoples of the central subarctic, the Ojibwa, Cree, and Mistassini-Cree. Of the Indian peoples mentioned here, all but the Huron are Algonkian-speakers. The region inhabited by the Eastern Woodland and Eastern Subarctic peoples who are part of the Algonkian-speaking group is so large that it will be discussed in smaller areas, beginning in the East Coast, and touching in detail primarily upon the larger groups.

When Europeans first began to spend a portion of their time ashore in the eastern tip of Canada, there may have been a hundred thousand "Indians"—to use the misnomer coined by Christopher Columbus. The People (or "the human beings" or "the original people") as they called themselves in their various languages, made responses

to this new presence according to the behaviour of the visitors. Easternmost of all Canadian natives were the Beothuks ("Human Beings"). Their practice of smearing their bodies and clothing with red ochre for religious and practical reasons (it helped discourage insects) is responsible for the name of "Red Indians" being given to their fellow aborigines over the rest of the continent. The fate of the Beothuks was harsh. The French placed a bounty on their heads and the European fisherman shot them as if they were foraging deer. The Micmacs of the eighteenth century, having acquired the gun, cooperated with the Europeans, and the last of the Human Beings died in 1829.

In 1776, however, there were five hundred of them, fishing and sealing in parts of Newfoundland where they could avoid white fishermen. Painted all over with ochre, they wore poncho-like shirts laced with sinew through awled holes. In 1612 a European observer described one of their summer houses, made of poles placed in a circle, meeting overhead at the centre and covered with caribou skins. In the same year a square, roofed log dwelling with moss chinking was also seen. In 1768 a cone-shaped house with a birchbark cover was reported. Their canoes were twenty feet long, four-and-a-half feet wide at the beam; over ribs of conifer wood, birchbark was sewn with split roots. The vessels had a V-shaped cross section and the seams were caulked with ochre, oil, or pitch. Contemporary reports give the impression that both dwellings and watercraft were rather austere and utilitarian.

The Beothuks did, however, leave in burials certain striking artefacts which can be considered as art objects: numerous bone pendants of many forms, including one-, two-, and three-pronged, meticulously engraved with abstract motifs of considerable delicacy and complexity. Little else of Beothuk manufacture seems to have been so adorned. Many of them have a hatched double line down the centre, sometimes interrupted, suggesting to this writer a "heart-line" (see below for the use of this motif in boulder arrangements in Manitoba) or X-ray style backbones, as in Dorset and other hunting art. Triangles, zigzags, and lozenges (frequently inside one another and of diminishing size), and every sort of linear and hatched form abound. Although the shapes fall into classes, nearly every one is different in its detail.

James Howley thought that the fact that so many of them were found in burials suggested their symbolic or talismanic significance. He pointed out their presence on the garment of a little Beothuk boy's robe, and in a drawing made by Shanawdithit of a dancing woman. Probably the last surviving Beothuk, Shanawdithit, called Nancy by her captors, was captured in 1823 and died of tuberculosis in St. John's, Newfoundland, in 1829 at the reported age of twenty-nine. It is reported that Shanawdithit never told the story of the death of her family without weeping. The image of this talented woman artist, forlornly recording her lost heritage in meticulous drawings with a white man's pencil and paper, touches us almost unendurably.

She drew maps of great accuracy, and made careful depictions of the *mamateek* (winter wigwam), and of various sorts of

food laid out in order like a woman's mental picture of her own larder. Her drawing of the ā-ā-duth or "spear for killing seals" shows the twelve-foot shaft and its attached harpoon point, lacking a foreshaft. Elmer Harp thinks that the harpoon is the only significant Dorset trait adopted by the Beothuk (although the Dorset harpoon had a foreshaft), perhaps during a several-hundred year contact between the cultures in Labrador. According to this interpretation, the Beothuks lived in Labrador before moving across the narrow straits to Newfoundland about AD 1500. Harp thinks that both cultures lived in Newfoundland but sequentially, in various sites.

The Beothuk followed a taiga economy with a summer-winter cycle of coastal-interior occupation, using animal food, and making most of their objects of wood. They are probably a survival of the Laurentian Aspect of the Archaic Period, which was typified by chipped and ground forms, ground slate objects (including a semi-lunar knife), chipped stone tools and weapons, and some objects of native copper, bone, and pottery in the upper levels. Shanawdithit made carefully differentiated drawings of the silhouettes of classes of birchbark containers. She also furnished a glimpse of some Beothuk symbolism in the drawings labelled, "Emblems of Mythology." There are six-foot poles with schematic forms at their tops: a "whiteman's boat," a whale's tail, and other more abstract shapes.

Perhaps Nancy's most striking drawing is the above-mentioned "dancing woman," which shows a loose garment, tied at the waist and baring one shoulder. The robe

has extensive fringing, including a fringe on the knee-length skirt, which may have been formed of the engraved bone objects; Howley suggested that the pieces would make a castanet-like sound when the wearer danced.

The other evidence cited by Howley is the burial of a young boy who was well equipped for the after-life. The child lay on his left side under a covering of skin smeared with red ochre. He wore precisely stitched fringed skin trousers and fringed moccasins, and had been provided with several extra pairs of moccasins, all finished with fine stitches of sinew. The outer robe was also fringed, and to it were attached carved bone ornaments and the dried feet of gulls and ducks. Next to the body, which lay curled up as if in sleep, were miniature birchbark canoes with their paddles, bows and arrows, a little wooden image of a male child, and packets of dried meat and of red ochre carefully tied up in bark parcels.

The Micmac still live in the land they occupied as the Elnu, "the people" (*Micmac* means "allies") at the beginning of white contact with them. They have been on reserves in some cases since the eighteenth century, and are now all professed Roman Catholics who retain elements of their previous religion and practices.

Early sites in Nova Scotia contain coarse pottery, heavy ware of a brownish grey, sometimes coated with reddish clay, though not a true slip. These pots were decorated with patterns incised with a stick or pressed into wet clay with a piece of cord or woven fabric, giving evidence of a vanished textile art as well. The pots were crudely fired at what must have been fairly

low temperatures, so that the outside oxidized and became red-coloured, while the inside was incompletely oxidized and remained brown/grey. The clay contained shell fragments appropriate to a seaside people's ware. Here were also found some copper points and knife blades, but no artefacts suggesting use of the drill. These sites are not very old and presumably show an early phase of Micmac life.

The inhabitants of the early seaside camps twisted cords and wove both quills and moosehair, making ornaments of woven quills. They practised a little painting, but not of representational forms, using reddish, purplish, and black pigments. The quill and other textile-type materials tend to produce geometric patterns. There is a relationship between weaving designs and pottery motifs, as suggested above. A vertical warp is crossed by a horizontal weft, and a vertical cord is used in twined weaving; in each case the horizontal-vertical relationship of the parts makes for geometrical regularity. Early pots were decorated with scraps of fabric, twined and braided cord wrapped around a stick, and the stick itself, which was a knitting and twining tool. Some writers think that pottery actually originated as clay-smeared baskets; whether or not this is true, there is clearly a strong textile-design influence at work in pottery decoration.

The Micmac were and are hunters and fishermen, despite the long efforts of their governmental mentors (as revealed by report after report in the nineteenth century expressing despair at the attempt) to make them into farmers. In their life we see a full array of the artefacts of the snow country:

snowshoes, made with thongs from moose or caribou, birchbark canoes (the Micmac have a reputation as the best canoemakers of all) and toboggans. The European newcomers cheerfully adopted these graceful objects.

Perhaps the splayed feet of the ptarmigan and the snowshoe hare suggested the forms into which curved wood strips and bindings of animal gut were shaped to bear the wearers over the pathless snow. Paul Kane describes the agony of the inexperienced showshoe-wearer, whose inflamed sinews revolted against the new motion. The toboggan demonstrates the great talent for woodworking that could shape the curving slats and bind them together. But the supreme achievement was the canoe, exactly suited to its purpose in the boiling waters freed by summer from the melting snowbanks. It was shallow of draft to avoid stones and snags, and streamlined at both bow and stern like an aquatic bird's sleek breast to slice through the rapids. It was light enough to be carried over the frequent portages, and its gunwale curved upwards above the waves. The Micmac probably used the sea for much more of their livelihood before the fur traders urged them to go inland after animal pelts.

Birchbark, a light, flexible, and widely available material, was also used to cover the sapling framework of the utilitarian wigwams. Because of its resistance to heat, birchbark also served for a variety of vessels. It was cut, folded, and sewn with split cedar root by means of bone needles inserted through pierced holes. The top had a hoop sewn 'round it to preserve the

shape. Such a vessel could be used to boil water or to contain clothing, food, or drinking water. The surface of birchbark could also be marked with a stick to create designs (Figure 3).

In addition to birchbark containers, the Micmac made splint basketry of cedar, spruce, juniper, or black ash. A set of eight radiating ribs was arranged with the weft running around; as the weaving continued, the ribs were gradually bent upwards to form the hollow interior. The skilful fingers of the women also made moose-hide clothing with fur cloaks. Particularly handsome were the caps; the men's had peaks and the women's bore a high ridge or crest. After European contact, hide was replaced by coarse blue cloth, which was decorated with red cloth and white beadwork. Weaving was also done with moose-hair, which was combed with the fingers, wrapped on a stick, and wound off onto a wooden spindle equipped with a stone whorl. The resulting yarn was knitted with two small, smooth sticks into socks and mitts.

Among Micmac artefacts we meet for the first time with porcupine quills, the somewhat unlikely source of much Canadian Indian decoration before the advent of trade beads (Plate 1). The long, sharp quills are white, and take a brilliant dye: red was obtained from the bedstraw plant, black from boiled wood-rot, and yellow from boiled "gold root". A gob of dye was held in a notched stick and the quills drawn through it. Quillwork and moose-hair embroidery were the principal art forms. The Ursuline nuns taught their nimble-fingered young Indian students to decorate birch-

bark boxes with these materials, producing beautiful mosaic-like surfaces, and the boxes were sold in Europe to raise money for the mission schools.

The Micmacs also practised carving and modelling of figurines, and in the carved pipes we meet another aboriginal material, tobacco. There were also bone dice of circular form, decorated with conventional cross designs called "sea and mountain," which look like miniature mandalas. Weapons and robes were painted. All of these decorative arts have faded through the long period of European contact, but the lovely quilled boxes continue to be made, presumably because they appeal to white purchasers today.

The principal decorative motif was the double curve, consisting of two concave lines drawn in opposition, frequently curving into spirals. This basic form could be worked into simple or complex designs, and usually produced a design with axial symmetry. This pattern lent itself well to the newly introduced European floral designs, but is probably aboriginal. Some writers have suggested that this motif resembles the West Coast practice of depicting animals cut into two facing profiles, and argue that the Eastern Woodland Indians used the same bilateral symmetry for plant forms. The motif also appears in the art of the Maori, Shang China, and Siberia.

Frank Speck described the "double-curve" as consisting fundamentally of two opposed incurves forming a unit, which appeared with elaborations, variations, and distortions. This motif, widely used by the northern and eastern Algonkian tribes, was thought by Speck to have been originally

Figure 3. Split ash box with incised design, Micmac.
Photo: The National Museum of Canada

Birchbark, cedar, spruce, juniper, and black ash were used by the
Micmac for making baskets and containers. Where a smooth surface
was formed, designs were incised; typical is the double-curve motif
that occurs here in an abstract form.

a decorative element, vaguely floral, without symbolic content. Jacques Rousseau suggested that the really fundamental common element was not the double curve, but the motif of bilateral symmetry. He even suggests that the use of bilateral symmetry is based upon the placement of designs in continuous borders, rather than upon adaptations of the forms to a vertical field, which would have produced axial symmetry. The Naskapi painted coats do exhibit axial symmetry in their use of double-curve motifs, however.

Both Indian and Eskimo women made continuous use of their teeth in every form of sewing. As the chief feature of the double-curve motif was bilateral symmetry, a thin strip of birchbark could be folded in half (or in quarters) and bitten through to form a mirror-image design. Harry Moody describes the art of birchbark biting among the Cree women of north Saskatchewan. The layers of bark are carefully separated to obtain a perfect piece of even thinness, about two-and-a-half inches square. This is folded to an oblong, then to a square, and finally to a triangle. The woman places the point of the triangle between her teeth, rapidly biting the folded bark while rotating it with her hand, producing a design of tiny perforations like a delicate snowflake. Moody thinks that the women visualize the form before bitng. The method is used to make independent designs, but older Indian people report that it originated in the custom of biting designs to be used as patterns for silk or beadwork. On request, one woman formed representations of a moose, a cabin complete with a smoking chimney, and a fisherman in his canoe.

What sort of psychic world did these skilful people inhabit? They may have revered the sun, with the moon in a secondary place. They had both medicine-men (diviners and healers) and witches, and they feared the dead. Their world contained several supernatural races, including giants and tiny beings. Glooskap, the Micmac culture hero and intermediary between the Creator and humankind, had shaped the landscape and given them their basic inventions. Magic good luck—perhaps power is a better word for it—was obtained from unusual events and from visions, and had to be kept secret; everyday magic consisted in omens, and bad events were due to wrongdoing by someone. Patterns similar to these appear widely through the Americas.

Along the St. John River in New Brunswick, from Fredericton to Perth, the Malecite fished, hunted, and gathered fiddleheads, raspberries, and maple sap, which they boiled into sugar. In addition they planted a little corn and squash. Their culture and language so closely resemble those of the Micmac that the name Malecite means "Poor Speakers" in Micmac. Like the Micmac they were allies of the French. The influence of the European presence is seen in the cut and style of a lovely beaded jacket, an Indian adaptation of leather-working technique to the new clothing forms. Floral designs often accompanied these new modes of tailoring (Figure 4).

In Malecite woodworking, as in that of the Micmac, T. F. S. McFeat points out, the creation of functional objects was based on a single principle; the bark canoe, the bark box, the bark dish and tray, and

Figure 4. Jacket with beadwork, Malecite.
Photo: The National Museum of Canada

Similar in culture to the Micmac, the Malecite adapted the trade
bead to traditional designs; this jacket bears an intricate pattern,
resembling that of Figure 3, worked in fine beads. The basic
double-curve pattern incorporates some leaf and rose designs
on the collar and cuffs.

even the bark house were all constructed similarly. Unlike the West Coast peoples, who began with a large volumetric unit of wood which was carved to the desired shape or split to form planks, the woodland Algonkians began by defining the form with light structural skeletons, to be covered with a flexible surface.

McFeat sees the modern basket industry among the Malecite as aiding in the maintenance of Indian identity, although the splint or plaited basket, usually of black ash, has displaced the bark container, and the quill techniques associated with bark boxes have been lost. McFeat and Speck suggest that the Malecite probably acquired ash baskets from southerly Algonkians or Iroquois. The early ones are rectangular at the base and D-shaped at the rim. They have developed in both "rough" (utilitarian) and "fancy" (decorative) form, to use the terms their makers apply to them. Modern craftsmen usually concentrate on one or the other style rather than both. These are all hand-made but "mass-produced," as many as a dozen a day from one family.

At least a hundred years ago an old woman was reported selling her baskets in the area's towns, though there was no regular basket industry. Today more than a dozen families make a living from the industry. The maker interviewed by McFeat felt a strong sense of himself as a craftsman, and cast his understanding of his relationship with non-Indians in terms of his basket-making, seeing it as a complementary exchange. During the depression he had traded baskets for food with local farmers.

There is a problem in gathering black ash; to do it without prior arrangement with the owner of the land whereon it grows is illegal. When a farmer allows it to be gathered from his land, it is customary for the Indians (whites do not use the wood) to repay him with a few baskets. Thus the problem is solved.

The standards (vertical splints), weavers (horizontal splints), and rims and handles all come from different parts of the log. Whiter wood from the periphery is used for undyed portions; the parts made of the darker wood toward the centre of the log are carefully colour-matched before dyeing so that the dye-lot will be uniform.

Each operation on a basket is performed by a different person, as in earlier times, when the camp formed a nucleus of activity and the surrounding forest was the hunting range. In basket-making there is a nucleus of family industry with the peripheral activity of gathering materials. Thus tradition and identity have been preserved throughout the series of changes as the new ash-splint basket has replaced the old bark box and become a full industry. The Malecites engaged in this work regarded it as "Indian work," retaining their sense of the Indian as craftsman.

To the north and west of the Maritimes were the nomadic hunting groups whose range extended up through the Subarctic to the borders of Eskimo country. Northernmost of these were the Naskapi, who probably never numbered more than 1,500. Although these people were entirely migratory, constantly following the herds of caribou, it must not be supposed that their lives were spent in aimless wanderings.

Figure 5. Painted coat, Naskapi.
Photo: The National Museum of Canada

The Naskapi painted coats of caribou hide with the double-curve
motif in red and black, using a wooden stylus. The scroll-like designs
may symbolize caribou antlers, and it has also been suggested that
the lines represent the tracks of a successful hunter's toboggan,
perhaps as seen in a vision, and that they were depicted with a
pronged bone tool.

Theirs was a purposeful pursuit of specific game, generally following the same routes and guided by familiar landmarks. The land over which they hunted was scattered with innumerable lakes and streams interspersed with spruce trees. Covering the ground was the caribou moss, a kind of lichen, an important source of food for the great herds of caribou. In this harsh climate farming was impossible; the people survived by fishing and hunting with a variety of cleverly fashioned snares, deadfalls, hooks, and other weapons. Caribou were the primary resource, quite literally. Their meat was a staple food; their hides became clothing, tents, canteens, drumheads, and snowshoe lacings (all secured with thread of caribou sinew); their stomachs served as cooking vessels.

Evidence of the sophisticated use of caribou hide are the elegant Naskapi coats, meticulously painted with the double-curve motif (Figure 5). The first step in their manufacture, and one usually performed by women, was preparation of the hide, an exacting and taxing chore. With a bone or metal blade secured in a wooden handle, the women scraped the skin free of its fleshy tissue, then removed the hair with a scraper of caribou bone. Curing consisted of rubbing a paste of brains and fat over the surface of the hide, which was then stretched, washed, and left to dry on a wooden frame. The skin could be left in its white, dry-frozen condition or coloured yellow by the smoke of rotten wood.

When the skins had cured, the coat could be sewn; European tailoring styles, derived from eighteenth-century military uniforms, are evident in the costumes that have been preserved. Only after the garment was fashioned was the surface painted. Cupping a palmful of pigment in the left hand, the painter painstakingly applied the colour with a wooden stylus, tracing the designs mostly in red and black. The double-curve motif is here interpreted as symbolizing caribou antlers, and perhaps represents the hunting power with which the coat was endowed for at least a year after its making.

The importance of the caribou for life made it a centre of religious concern; the Overlord of the Caribou sent these animals to the Naskapi, if proper respect were shown. A drumhead of caribou hide stretched on a birchwood hoop helped to make contact with the spirit world. A drum is used for this purpose throughout the circumpolar region, and the painting of objects and of the human body with signs to indicate sacredness is similarly widespread, a practice evident elsewhere in Canadian native art.

It has been suggested by Alika Webber that lines painted by the Naskapi may have represented the tracks of a game-laden toboggan, or tracks leading to game. They may also have symbolized tracks seen in a vision; when a wife painted these symbols on a hunting coat, they might increase a hunter's success. The lines were produced with a pronged tool, the bone line-marker, which can draw several parallel lines with one stroke. Prehistoric sites have yielded similar tools, originally believed to have been used for incising lines on the surface of clay pots, but which may actually have been line markers – exciting evidence of prehistoric painting on skin. Alika Webber speculates upon their use in painting not only garments, but also the body.

Southernmost of the nomadic hunters

Figure 6. Tobacco pouches, Montagnais.

Made by a woman and used by a man to carry a material that had
sacred associations in North America, tobacco pouches of the
Montagnais are embroidered with beaded designs which, though
predominately floral are based on the double-curve motif, and may
have been designed by biting a symmetrical design into folded
birchbark.

were the Montagnais. The life of these people centred upon the moose, though perhaps without so great a dependency as that which the Naskapi felt for the caribou, for the Montagnais remained stationary in winter. As we have seen, the material culture of hunters consists to a large degree of equipment for the hunt. These objects were made and used by men, and man's identity was bound up in them and in their use. His hands, his mind, and his body became, with these simple mechanical extensions a superb hunting instrument. His intimacy with the beasts he hunted resembles that of Paleolithic men who painted divine beasts on the walls of caverns in the valley of the Dordogne in France. These were probably spiritual beings rather than individual animals, archetypes like the Overlord of the Caribou. The hunter lived in a world where spirit, animal, plant, and man formed a living continuum. Images of thrust, direction, and motion typify his canoes, snowshoes, toboggans, slender weapons: they are instruments of masculine power. All other aspects of life fell to the women, and women's objects were containers: envelopes, pouches, hollow vessels (Figure 6). Women built the shelters that protected the fragile lives of their occupants against the cold and the night. Nearly every activity other than sleep took place out of doors, and the enwrapping robes and warmth-giving clothing, over which so much care was lavished, were also made by women.

It is a tale widely repeated by European observers that life for a hunter's wife was intolerable. Actually, all that pertains to bearing, containing, and preserving be-longed to her, and she was as indispensable to her husband as he was, in his hunting role, to her. Furthermore, where game is scarce, hunters suffer a loss of identity; at least women can still carry and bear. In the Subarctic some aspects of the hunting life still survive, and with it the finely sewn skin of ancient meaning, adorned of course with Christian embroidery, but integral still.

Where hunting peoples are in steady contact with farming groups, some degree of diffusion takes place if the climate permits. Such cultural diffusion characterized the Algonkin, a loose scattering of bands. Like the neighbouring Ojibwa they made wooden cradleboards and double-headed drums and made use of corn, squash, and beans, but, like the Montagnais, they lacked the knowledge of making maple syrup and had no medicine societies. Like others of the woodland region they made extensive use of birchbark. This versatile material, pulled in fragrant rolls of uniform thickness from the living tree, lends itself to decoration; its thin layers of differing colours can be scraped or incised to form a pattern. A birchbark box with a decorated surface bearing organic forms served the Algonkin woman as a storage vessel, and some handsome examples have been preserved (Figure 7).

Continually buffeted by the Iroquoians in the seventeenth century, today the Algonkin live on a few reserves in Ontario and Quebec, hunting a little and gardening a little where they can.

A site forming part of the Eastern Woodlands tradition is the Peterborough Petroglyphs, discovered only in the mid-twentieth century (Plate 2). The carvings are

Figure 7. Birchbark box, Algonquin.
Photo: The National Museum of Canada.

The Algonquin practised agriculture as well as hunting; like other
Woodlands peoples they made extensive use of birchbark. The
surface of this box is decorated with a scraped design suggesting
vegetal or floral form. The box itself is firmly stitched and may have
served as a storage container.

located in the Blue Mountain area around Stoney Lake, thirty-five miles northeast of Peterborough, Ontario. They are carved over an area of 135 feet by 102 feet on the slanting face of an outcropping of white crystalline limestone, and appear to have been formed, Gordon Mallory suggests, by grinding into the rather soft surface. The larger of the two groupings is dominated by a long-beaked and even longer-legged bird suggesting a blue heron. Also present is a humanoid figure whose head resembles a sunwheel or even a huge round eye and above which appears a form like a round sun-disc. The second area is dominated by a large female figure. Some of the forms suggest animal tracks, and deer, lizards, and turtles appear.

Kenneth Kidd, in Edwin Guillet's study of the Trent Valley, points out that the area has been occupied for several thousand years because of the ease of passage from Georgian Bay to Lake Ontario, and later because of the area's excellent horticultural possibilities. Certain triangular forms Kidd suggests, represent conifers or arrow points, and the figures from whose heads rays of light seem to extend may be deities. Some are, he says, similar to historic Ojibwa birchbark scrolls, while others, such as the naturalistic bear tracks, are distinctly different. He concludes the carvings are the prehistoric work of Algonkian peoples, and that they have a religious meaning.

By far the strongest "nation" in the seventeenth century and still a very large group today are the Ojibwa, the "people whose moccasins have puckered skins." These hunters of the northern shores of Lakes Huron and Superior were divided into four groups: the Lake Superior Ojibwa, the Mississauga of Manitoulin Island, the Ottawa of Georgian Bay, and the Potawatomi. Most of the Potawatomi lived in Michigan, but others returned to Canada in the eighteenth and nineteenth centuries; Ojibwa groups remaining in the United States are known as the Chippewa.

The Ojibwa hunted and fished, but they also made full use of vegetable foods: wild rice, maple syrup, and berries (and the Ottawa planted corn). Birchbark formed their canoes and dome-shaped *wigwams*, and the southern Ojibwa made clay pots as well as birchbark vessels.

They had a richer social life than did other Algonkians, with a Festival of the Dead, varied games, and celebrations of various natural harvests. Their most outstanding cultural feature, and one they shared with the Cree, was the *Midéwiwin*, or Grand Medicine Society—a secret religious society open to men and women alike. Membership usually consisted of a series of grades, through which participants advanced through instruction; payment of fees accompanied their gradual rise in the society. The members became the healers of their own communities, using herbal remedies and, even more effective, the various techniques of psychosomatic medicine which are a primary trait of Amerindian culture.

The ceremonies were so detailed that they required memory charts incised on birchbark scrolls (which are now difficult to interpret except in general terms) to record the correct position and actions of the various participants in each ceremony, including those supernaturals who were present

—the *Manitous* (Figure 8). The ceremonial equipment was kept in medicine bags, made of animal skins, with symbolic embellishments in quillwork. These containers in some Canadian Indian cultures assume a powerful sacred aura, like that adhering to certain chalices and reliquaries in Europe. The power originated in a dream or other visionary experience and could be renewed and strengthened through ceremony, song, and dance.

To the Ojibwa everything in the world was alive, possessed of a supernatural element, an incorporeal substance. This expanded view of reality made everything animate (including stones, which might at any moment open their mouths and speak). Not all spirits, however, were benign, and so the Ojibwa searched for personal guardians; for protection hunters carried medicine bags containing herbs, roots, feathers, and wooden images related to dreams. The importance of the dream-life, only recently restored to Western awareness by depth psychology, cannot be overemphasized if one seeks to understand Amerindian art.

In addition to the *midéwaujee* or *Midéweini* (members of the medicine societies), there were also the *jeeskeweini*, who used the "shaking tent", a cylindrical miniature tent, to contact or become one with the spirit world; when the prophetic presence came near, the little tent shook violently. This element of metamorphosis is seen also in the character of Nanabush or Nanabozo, the trickster-creator-intermediary. The malignant aspect of reality was represented by the awful spectre of starvation, the cannibalistic *windigo*, which Basil Johnston suggests was a symbol of the self-destructiveness of certain vices. The "bearwalker,"

a werebear, was also a frightening metamorphic creature.

In western Ontario, red paintings dot the faces of numerous cliffs and rocks beside the countless lakes of the Canadian Shield. These paintings are thought to record the dreams and conscious affairs of medicinemen and perhaps of young spirit-questers as well. Selwyn Dewdney and Kenneth Kidd conclude from the stiffness and cursory nature of many of them that they were made without any particular interest in form for its own sake, but with an overriding interest in their content. About half the symbols are completely abstract: crosses, arches, arrow-like motifs, and various sinuous lines and arcs, which correspond to the vocabulary of decorative motifs used in decoration of clothing and other objects. The rest are divided into five groups: man-made objects, handprints, human figures, mythological (composite) creatures, and animals (including birds). The source of the distortion and fantasy in these images is attributed to the Indian painters' dreams. (See Plate 3.)

The animal and thunderbird figures found on prehistoric as well as recent birchbark scrolls of the Ojibwa are very similar to the figures found as petroglyphs in western Wisconsin rock shelters and correspond to those painted on rock faces beside the lakes of western Ontario. As we have seen, historic groups used these symbols as aids to memory for recalling the order of ceremonial songs and dances. In an even more public manner, animal symbols and the thunderbird are found as signatures on a number of land treaties in Canada as well as in the United States.

Many of the rock paintings seem stiff in

comparison with those produced by the materially rich culture of the classical Magdalenian artists (with which they are inevitably compared). Nevertheless some of them, like the awesome figure of Mishipeshu at Agawa and the mysterious pair of horned humanoid figures (masked medicine men?) at Route Lake, are lively and forceful. They bring into concrete form compelling spiritual beings from other men's dreams.

The portrait of Mishipeshu at the Agawa site shows a powerful *Manitou*, a dragonlike monster with legs, horns, and tail who combined the traits and identity of lynx and serpent. It is a metamorphic being of surpassing psychic appeal. Some years ago it was crudely defaced by a set of initials splashed across it with black paint, but time and weather have now all but removed them and the form of Mishipeshu still prowls there, painted in red earth on the sheer rock face. Indians still leave offerings of tobacco and prayer sticks at similar sites.

One of the most mysterious manifesta-

tions of art left in the region of the Ojibwa or their ancestors, and one of the largest prehistoric aboriginal boulder arrangements known in North America, is the Tie Creek Boulder site of southeastern Manitoba (Figure 9). It has been described in detail by Jack Steinbring, who rejects the term "boulder mosaic," preferring to call the manifestations "petroforms" or "boulder outlines." The site, located on a massive flat granite outcropping just southeast of the Winnipeg River near Lake Numoo contains six areas of stone arrangements. Three of these are united by connecting lines of boulders which partially surround a patch of bush. Another arrangement seems to be a human effigy with a "heartline"—a line drawn from throat to solar plexus—or perhaps it is a thunderbird with its wings in disarray. Still another is overgrown with lichen such as could only develop over a thousand-year period. The most impressive feature is a huge rectangle with partial subdivisions within. It is awesome in scale-between 110 and 128 feet long—and can only be fully perceived from the air. The stones used to form these patterns are large and very heavy, and their number is also large. Relatively undisturbed until recent snowmobilers began to disarrange the more exposed portions, these massive features are evidence of the labours men are willing to expend in the creation of symbolic images.

Recently there has been a resurgence of Indian painters seeking to express aboriginal concepts in terms of contemporary art. Norval Morriseau is one of the most remarkable of this group, both for the aesthetic content of his painting and the psychic power of his images (Plate 4). His

Mishipeshu

Figure 8. *Midéwiwin* birchbark scroll, Ojibwa, Kenora, Ontario.
Photo: The National Museum of Canada

On birchbark scrolls the Ojibwa incised memory charts, recording
the correct positions and actions of the participants in the *Midéwiwin*
or Grand Medicine Society ceremonies (including the supernatural
Manitous who were present).

work shows a concern with and mastery of form which fully equals his interest in his subject matter. This remarkable painter, whose work became public in the 1960s, seems to represent a modern flowering of Ojibwa painting; he now has followers. Selwyn Dewdney writes that Morriseau's early birchbark paintings do not derive from Western painting, and that he was influenced by rock-painting motifs, especially the Agawa image of Mishipeshu. This is apparent in his later works which combine originality, powerful resilient line, and the impression of a deep underlying tradition. Morriseau himself has written about his struggles with his conscience over using the sacred images in his art; he describes the visionary dream in which he received divine permission to do this. He serves both his ancestral beliefs and Christian teaching, and regards both as sacred.

Francis Kagige, an Ojibwa from the Wikwemikong Reserve on Manitoulin Island, uses a style which, though reminiscent of Morriseau, is recognizably his own. His subject matter is also derived from Ojibwa sources; a thunderbird quivers with supernatural power in one of his paintings in the collection of the Bureau of Indian Affairs.

Carrie Lyford's classic study of Ojibwa crafts provides a wealth of information on Eastern Woodland crafts and symbols. The Ojibwa used wood for an extensive range of objects. Before trading introduced iron implements, they fashioned spoons, bowls, plates, and ladles of elm and maple burls, and made wooden brooms to sweep the earthen floors of their mat-covered lodges. They made wooden cradle-boards, then added beaded covers in floral designs. Early dolls were made of willow withes and spruce roots; later ones were of skin, stuffed with spruce moss and dressed in clothing decorated in beadwork. Wooden flageolets were made, and water drums for the *Midéwiwin* were formed from a section of the trunk of a basswood tree, covered with skin; the water level inside controlled the sound. Pipe stems and pipe paraphernalia were also made of wood, and snowshoes had wooden parts.

The Ojibwa also excelled at making cord and twine. Nettle fibre cord was used for nets, sewing thread, snares, and traps, and was woven into underskirts and large flat bags with designs of dark brown buffalo wool. The nettle stalks were cut in October, tied in bundles, and dried, then rotted and beaten to loosen their fibres. The resulting strands were rolled against the thigh, twisting into cord without the use of a spindle. Another cord was made of basswood fibre. The inner bark of the basswood tree, peeled off and cut into strips, was soaked for ten days in the water at the edge of a lake to remove the soft inner fibre. Further soaking and boiling softened the fibre until it was ready to be twisted into cord by rolling it with the palm on the thigh or calf.

As elsewhere, birchbark was used for bitten patterns, *midéwiwin* scrolls, mats, canoes, and containers. The bark was heated and shaped while warm, pierced with an iron awl, and sewn with basswood fibre and skinned spruce roots. Splints of willow or ash reinforced containers, and balsam gum or black spruce pitch was used for sealing or mending. For decorative pur-

Figure 9. Whiteshell boulder mosaics, aerial view, Tie Creek Site, Manitoba.

Photo: Manitoba Provincial Archives

One of the largest aboriginal boulder groupings known to form part
of North American prehistory, the site is located on a massive flat
granite outcropping. There are six areas of stone arrangements, some
deeply overgrown with lichen that could only have developed over
a thousand years. The largest feature is between 110 and 128
feet long, suggesting the labours humans will expend to create symbolic images.

poses, the dark inner surface of the bark was often turned to the outside of the container and engraved with a sharp bit of bone—often the splint bone from the heel of a young doe—revealing the lighter bark layer. Once the pattern was incised on the dark surface, either figure or ground was carefully scraped to create light and dark contrasts. The Ojibwa also used the technique of *appliqué*, using spruce root to stitch designs cut from dark winter bark, over a surface of the lighter summer bark. Favourite patterns for engraving were the hourglass (two triangles meeting at their apices), the diagonal, and the zigzag; curvilinear patterns sometimes occurred on old pieces.

The Canadian Ojibwa and the Ottawa, Carrie Lyford reports, often decorated birchbark boxes with quillwork, usually in isolated geometric and floral motifs on the sides and covers, or with cross-stitch patterns of quills on the seams. A sweetgrass coil sewn 'round the rim emitted a lovely fragrance. Boxes of exactly this type can still be purchased from Ojibwa craftswomen.

Ojibwa basketry employed wicker, plaiting, and coiling techniques, using willow branches, basswood bark, black ash splints, cedar root, and sweet grass. The forms were strictly utilitarian. Ojibwa textiles, however, were versatile and often highly decorative. Especially notable were woven yarn bands and sashes, made by braiding, netting or looping, and weaving buffalo wool, and used as pack straps, garters, and sashes. The designs were worked in contrasting natural shades of wool or in colours from the natural dyes obtained from alder, bloodroot, butternut, chokecherry,

dogwood, hazel, gold thread (a root), hemlock, lichens, maple, birch, sumac, wild plum, and other sources. Later, Ojibwa weavers used trade yarn and trade dyes as well as native dyes. As Carrie Lyford states, netting, braiding and twining are native arts, but the relation of the band form to European styles is unclear. The costume bands do resemble the French Canadian *Ceintures Flechées* of the eighteenth century.

Braid of three or more strands was used for bands, belts, fringes for bags, and sashes. Netting was a more complicated process. Strands of the desired length were hung lengthwise, then each strand carried diagonally in turn across the strand on either side, and looped or knotted to make an open elastic fabric. The favourite use for netting was in scarves, which were about nine inches wide and two yards long.

Weaving, which traditionally consists of two sets of crossing strands, took several forms. *Finger weaving* was used for garters, bands, and sashes; actually, this method uses only a weft, for each strand in turn becomes the warp. The shed is formed with the fingers and there is no shuttle. Finger-woven strips were usually deep red, blue, green, gold, and white, and used abstract geometric figures, including W and V forms, which are identified as "sturgeon fish."

Woven bags were made of *twined weaving*. A cord was passed completely around the outside of two vertical stakes, and the strands to be woven were hung from the cord, so that the bag was woven whole around the entire top at once. There were bags of nettle fibre, basswood bark fibre, cedar bark and tamarack roots, and buffalo and moose hair of a rich variety of natural

undyed colours. Later the same technique was used for yarn bags with geometric and mythological forms including thunderbirds, the "underground panther" (*Mishipeshu*), deer, butterflies, and otter tracks. As elsewhere, the "panther" reproduced by Lyford has horns and a dragon-like tail, and looks something like Schoolcraft's nineteenth-century sketch of the great Agawa painting.

In addition to the forms of weaving already described, woven mats were made on a horizontal bar or frame from rushes, cattails, and cedar bark in a variety of weaves, including tabby or twill.

A particularly beautiful container was the *midéwiwin* bag, formed from the skin of a beaver, mink, otter, or weasel. The skin was turned inside out, cleaned, turned in again, and stuffed with grass to dry. It was then decorated with patches of beadwork or quillwork in the paws, belly, and tail, very carefully executed because of the sacred purpose of the bag. Pipe bags and moccasins were also decorated. Beading was used for very elaborate floral patterns, often with bilateral symmetry, executed on cloth as well as on skin.

In quillwork, wet quills were (and still are) forced through fresh bark, then clipped and bent back to dry in position, rather like a staple. Sinew for sewing was obtained from the back tendon of an animal, and most stitches were taken on the surface only, never passing through the quill itself. Beads were woven on a simple loom with the weft passing through a bead between each warp thread, producing a band of beadwork. Bead embroidery was also couched onto a surface, and border edgings of beads tended to designs of simple continuous geometric motifs, described below as "running designs."

A final decorative technique was ribbonwork and *appliqué* of trade ribbons, in which two pieces of ribbon of contrasting dark and light colours were used. The top ribbon was cut into patterns and sewn with the tiniest of stitches over the bottom ribbon. Designs were cut freehand or based on a paper pattern, and in each case were folded over while being cut so that the pattern was symmetrical.

A wide range of designs was employed to decorate articles made by many of these techniques. Prominent among them was the double-curve motif, embellished with leaves and flowers. Geometric patterns included the "running design," a straight line of beads, often several parallel lines, and the "jumping design," a series of short lines like a row of dashes. The "diagonal border" resembled a row of diagonal strokes executed on a typewriter. There were numerous variations of the "ottertail" design; a pattern of long, flattened hexagrams and lozenges was basic to the design, and it commonly consisted of three diamonds connected side by side at their lateral points, interspersed with, and connected to, attenuated hexagrams with a long horizontal midsection. There were also conventionalized leaf, rose, berry, and feather designs, and a "four-dot" design with two round spots above and below and two side by side, to form a figure within a diamond-shaped space like a very simple flower, and sometimes containing a small dot in the centre. Lyford considers these floral patterns to be prehistoric.

The colours favoured by the Ojibwa are red, either very dark or very light (and red-violet); yellow, both lemon and gold; green; blue, especially blue-violet; and brown and tan. Often three shades of the same hue were used in a design. There was little black until the introduction through trade of black velveteen to which the Ojibwa customarily stitched a border pattern of white beads.

The Saulteaux, a branch of the Ojibwa in the Sault area, practised weaving of cedar bark and spruce roots as well as making rabbit-skin blankets like those of the eastern Cree. The women did quillwork, using their finger-nails to flatten soaked quills; these could be dyed red with tamarack bark, yellow with black willow, brown with punk or rotten wood, or left in their natural black and white, and were sewn in place with a needle made of the penis bone of a marten. (There was a wide palette of dyes and paints beyond those already mentioned, including two reds from hematite or ochre, and black from a mixture of charcoal and grease.)

The Saulteaux dug clay and kneaded it with fine gravel and coarse sand, making vessels by the coil method. Firing occurred when the vessel was used, set in the midst of the fire and propped up by stones. Although they did not use birchbark for cooking vessels, the Saulteaux made extensive use of this versatile material in making *wigwams* and canoes, as well as the folded and stitched *rogan*, a container for meat. Almost all of the Saulteaux's "ancient art" —painting—is lost, for they painted on rock surfaces, blazed trees, and birchbark and canvas surfaces. Their art seems to have varied in style from geometric and ornamental patterns to realistic forms. In clothing, only breech-cloths were decorated (with blue quills) in aboriginal times, but now beadwork and silkwork of fruit and flower designs are used for various items.

Closely related to the Ojibwa are the Cree, so-called for their early name, "Kristineau," though they called themselves *Ililu* – "men among men". They, too, occupied a hugh expanse of territory, perhaps even extending west of Lake Winnipeg. With acquisition of guns, they spread even more widely, until smallpox stopped westward expansion. There are two main groups, the Plains Cree, who will be discussed in another chapter, and the Woods Cree; of this latter group, those to the east of Hudson's Bay are called the Mistassini Cree. Their life much resembled that of the Ojibwa; in the northern areas, however, their construction materials included pine bark and caribou hide in addition to birchbark. They also used a curved knife like the Eskimo women's *ulu*. The bitter northern winters dictated the nature of the articles they made; coats and blankets of hareskin and caribou fur were necessities – mats and baskets were not. Survival depended on the hunter's skill. The Cree hunted the larger game, but often in winter they were forced to depend entirely upon hares, which every seven years became extremely scarce. These terrible winters gave rise, sometimes, to cannibalism, a much-feared phenomenon which was projected into tales of the monstrous man-eating *windigos*, who are like the Western vampire in their capacity to raise a shiver.

The Cree were as preoccupied as the

Ojibwa (or the seventeenth-century Europeans) with their witchcraft, and practised a borrowed version of the Medicine Society and divination by means of the Shaking Tent. The medicine bag of the hunter was supplemented with the red designs ceremonially painted on every hide.

Painting, which the Cree considered to have been their aboriginal art, is now seldom practised. With lines, bars, dots, rectangular crosses, they painted the inside of a slain animal's skin in propitiation of the animal's spirit. The painting portrayed the animal from which the skin was taken, with eyes of red if the head skin was used as a hood; the dots showed that a skin was animate and could confer a special power derived from its former inmate. Drums, bear skulls and human faces also provided painted surfaces. By painting his face in a realistic style, representing an animal or its part, the hunter hoped to propitiate the spirit of the game upon which he most depended. Similar realistic paintings of the owner's game animals were used as property marks on tents and canoes. (The term "realistic" used here means a silhouette which resembles the animal without much distortion.)

Ornamental or decorative border designs were painted on tents and clothing, chiefly in red (formerly obtained from roots but later from vermilion) as well as extra embellishments in yellow-orange (from willow), purple (from willow roots and bark boiled together), black, blue, and green. Lines, dots, and circles, arranged in rows with zigzags, alternating patterns, and crenellations formed the designs. Tents had a single decorative border around the bottom with

the hunter's quarry painted above. Leather coats were painted with a system of borders bearing a structural relationship to the various parts of a garment rather like that between the parts of a Greek geometric vase and its zones of decoration. Cree ornament is restrained, with no attempt to fill all the spaces; the Cree seem to have been content to balance their decorative passages with open space.

As did the Ojibwa, the Cree made birchbark vessels with the inner surface of the bark forming the exterior of the vessel, and scraped the fresh bark in various designs. Life forms, including plants, were a common motif. The Cree also incised designs on stone pipes. Beadwork in floral designs, considered both "very modern" and "lucky for hunters," decorated shoulder bands, bandoliers, and side pouches for powder in early contact times. Strings or tassels of beads adorned garments with designs resembling those of the Naskapi. It is thought that the old art of the eastern Cree was realistic and geometric painting, and they report that their floral designs are recent. Some of these, like the shamrock, were clearly learned from the missionaries. Women now do flower designs in silkwork, replacing dyed horsehair which was formerly supplied by the Hudson's Bay Company. A stunning altar frontal of pure white deerskin, embroidered in floral patterns of silk, is treasured by the Anglican Church (Plate 5).

The Mistassini Cree still live deep in the last Subarctic wilderness, and the desire of the fur trader (there is still a fur trade in Canada) to encourage their hunting has so far helped them to retain an unusually

large measure of their traditional life style. Theirs is a land of long, cold winters and short, hot summers, where a sparse and stunted black spruce forest yields caribou, moose, bear, beaver, game birds, and a few fish, but almost no vegetable food. There, in summer, the Mistassini Cree camp; in the winter they range to hunt. On important occasions in the camp, ceremonial hides are hung from lines or poles. The hides remain in a frost-dried, pure white condition instead of receiving a final smoking; formerly painted with red dots all around the trimmed edge, they are now similarly decorated with paired cuts. Ears left attached are hung with ribbons.

The Mistassini Cree used wood for ladles, boxes, and cups, which were dyed brown with boiled spruce cones and decorated with floral designs. From legskins they fashioned a variety of containers, taking advantage of the convenient cylindrical shape and using up small portions of skin that might otherwise have gone to waste. Moccasins were decorated with patterns cut from paper or from thin birchbark made into a repeatedly folded and cut stencil. Embroidered in silk and cotton thread, the designs are floral and always symmetrical, though with no specific double-curve motif.

These people also made every sort of elegantly formed hunting equipment, including a variety of netted snowshoes, which were very carefully tended in order to make them last, and an assortment of cunning snares, traps, and fishing gear. Objects of this kind are so exquisitely adapted to their use and so expertly exploit the traits of their materials that they are perfect examples of the dictum that "form follows function." One of the most intriguing of all is the *nimapan*, a ceremonial carrying-string used to drag beaver and otter over the snow, to support the head of a bear when it was being portaged, and to carry porcupine. It also held up ceremonial robes when they were being displayed. About six to ten feet long, the *nimapan* was made of four strands of caribou thong plaited into a rope with a loop at one end, dyed red, and decorated at intervals with coloured thread. The hunters also used tumplines and hunting bags, but the *nimapan* apparently did honour to the animal; each species was tied in a specific manner. A sense of religious duty and gratitude both to the land and its animals is characteristic of Amerindian thinking (it served them well as an ecological control), and here is given tangible form.

As among the Ojibwa, contemporary Indian artists of the Cree draw inspiration from traditional forms. Carl Ray is a self-taught painter, the grandson of a Sandy Lake medicine-man. His work, which has been widely exhibited, shows a relationship to that of Morriseau, who influenced him, but tends to greater complexity, making use of fine lines and intricate detail. Jackson Beardy was born at Island Lake in northeast Manitoba, and attended residential school for eleven years. He trained as a commercial artist in Winnipeg, and began to work as a folk-singer, collecting stories and history among the Indian people. He later studied fine arts at the University of Manitoba. His striking paintings are executed in brilliant colour, depicting traditional subjects such as Gagathway, "The Hider," a thunderbird of the northern Cree.

Figure 10. Table cover with moose-hair embroidery, Huron, Lorette, Québec, c. 1840-50.

Made of elk or moose hide and embroidered with dyed moose hair, this table cover employs a dense pattern of floral designs introduced by European influence. It is a superb example of craftsmanship and needlework, and may be compared to Plate 6, which shows the same painstaking technique used in a form based on the double-curve motif.

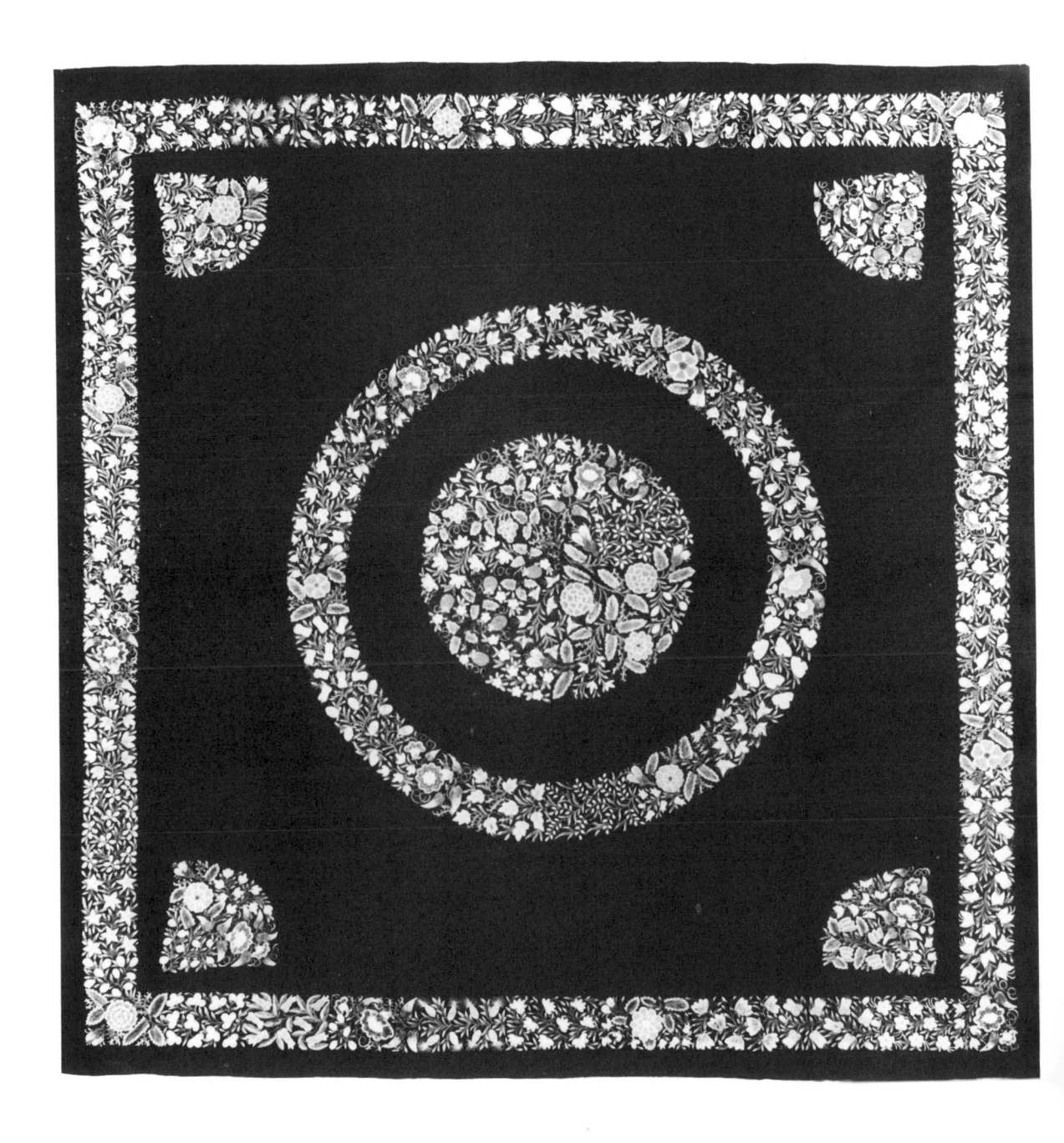

Chapter 3

Farmers of the Great Lakes and St. Lawrence Valley

Figure 11. Swarthout dentate-type pottery vessel, Waupoose Site, Picton, Ontario.
Photo: The National Museum of Canada

A typical vessel of Iroquoian make from prehistoric times, this
pot is made of a firm but slightly flaky clay paste, tempered with
small-sized grit. The decoration was made with a toothed object
forming regular dentate impressions on the collar of the vessel.
Perhaps the curved bottom rested comfortably on an earthen floor.

In 1535 Jacques Cartier was deeply impressed by Iroquoian farmers he met near what is now Montreal; sixty-eight years later these peoples had retreated to southern Ontario. Iroquoian-speakers included the Hurons (whose ill-fated alliance with the Jesuits resulted in dispersal for them and death for their evangelists), the Petuns (Tobacco), the Neutrals, and the Iroquois. All retained the universal hunting and fishing of Canadian native cultures, but they were, as well, farmers—comfortably settled within wooden-palisaded villages surrounded by fields of corn, beans, pumpkins, and tobacco.

J. V. Wright has speculated on the prehistoric development of these groups and suggests three stages. The first was the Early Ontario Stage of convergence from AD 1000 to AD 1300, during which there were two main complexes, the Glen Meyer branch of southwest Ontario and the Pickering branch, relatively isolated from each other. The conquest of the former branch by the latter gave rise to a homogeneous complex, the Uren Substage in Southern Ontario and southwest New York State. This period lasted no more than one hundred years. The third, divergence period, the Late Ontario Stage, began about AD 1400 and spread to the four known historical groups: Huron, Petun, Neutral, and Erie. This speculation supports the theory that the Iroquois developed *in situ*.

Iroquoian culture traits included the making of ceramics, pipes, and twined fabrics, and, rather late, of bird-bone beads. As these people used wood as a construction material and as fuel to heat their large houses, it was common for a village to move to a new location every twenty years, when all nearby trees had been cut down. Understandably, there was a widespread fear of fire in the wooden, wood-burning villages.

The Iroquoian village was usually built on a height of land overlooking a body of water. Surrounding it was the palisade, a tall double fence of slim tree trunks interwoven with elm bark. Around the inside of the inner fence, which was taller than the outer, were small platforms from which the village's defenders could fire arrows down across the "no-man's-land" between the two walls. This space was many yards across on the defended side of the village, but the side nearest the water had only a single fence. Here a gap allowed people to slip out to draw water. The Petun site (c.1350) near Port Elgin, Ontario, took this form; within were a number of long-houses, including one much larger than the others.

The Hurons, or Wyandots, were a confederacy of four tribes—the Rock, the Deer, the Cord, and the Bear. Their early Jesuit companions left a detailed record of their way of life—a settled life, reflected in the construction of relatively permanent centres and the tilling of the soil accompanied by a high degree of political organization and in ceremonial methods of peace-keeping. Shamans healed and prophesied and every man looked to his dreams for guidance in daily life, often translating dreams into elaborate waking action. Periodically the Feast of the Dead was observed, in which the bones of the recently dead were cleaned, wrapped, and placed in a common grave, to the accompaniment of both feasting and mourning.

Figure 12. Carved wooden cradleboard, Iroquois, Québec.

The cradleboards of the Iroquois were intricately carved on the back
and painted with floral designs of Baroque roses and other motifs
of European origin, giving them a strong folk-art appearance.

A number of beautiful objects have been preserved from the Huron, including some which give clear evidence of European influence. In some cases the shape of an artefact, such as an eighteenth-century shoulder bag, is adapted and given a traditional decorative treatment (Plate 6). In other cases, European design styles are completely and accurately reproduced, even where the recalcitrant materials used would seem to make the task of translation impossible. The use of curvilinear European floral designs in moosehair embroidery is an example, and masterpieces of the needleworker's art resulted.

The European presence aggravated traditional conflicts between the Iroquoian groups to the point where the Hurons, Tobaccos, and Neutrals were effectively dispersed. Some were killed, but many joined the Iroquois or their Algonkian neighbours to the north and west.

The Neutrals, whose language closely resembled that of the Huron, lived in the Niagara peninsula, still a rich farmland today. While the men hunted and fished, the women tended the typical New World crops —corn, squash, beans, and tobacco. There were occasionally bad years of famine when the corn failed, but there was usually an abundance of game. The Neutrals knew the arts of skin dressing, and references are made to robes of black squirrel fur.

Early commentators were particularly impressed by the Neutrals' practice of tattooing, a reportedly painful process. Faces and breasts were elaborately adorned with figures; charcoal was pricked into the flesh with thorns, awls, or needles. The Eagle, the Serpent, and the Dragon are among images reported. Black and red facial paint was also used, in stripes, solid sections, and bands around the eyes. The paint is reported to have served as protection against the cold and as a means to make the wearer more terrible in war; this latter idea may be a European projection. Captives to be sacrificed by fire were first ceremonially painted, and so were the bodies of the dead.

The "Lalonde" focus, comprising descendants of Early Woodland peoples, had a pottery technique which included incised designs, and the Neutrals were a part of this focus in prehistoric times. Post-contact middens contain trade goods which give evidence of European presence and agree with the Jesuit accounts. Some of the burial and fortification sites thought to have been occupied by the Neutrals were the subject of early digging (by anybody who was interested) as well as more recent and organized excavation. They yielded pottery, shells (traded from the Gulf of Mexico), serrated flint saws, long bone tubes from the bones of birds, a few copper objects, and implements of antler and bone.

In the seventeenth century, the Huron occupied the peninsula between Georgian Bay and Lake Simcoe and were minutely observed by their visitors over several decades. During this time disease made serious inroads in the population; furthermore, the European presence exacerbated the traditional rivalry between Huron and Iroquois into a war which ended with the defeat and dispersal of the Hurons.

The Huron village was basically a simple Neolithic farming economy, with no full-time specialists; each household was an

Figure 13. Beaded cradlecloth, Iroquois.
Photo: The National Museum of Canada

The dark cloth is bordered with white beadwork patterns called
"universe signs." The scroll-form design, sometimes called "horned
trimming" and also referred to as the "horns of chieftancy," probably
derived from the bisymmetrical double curve of the Woodlands
peoples.

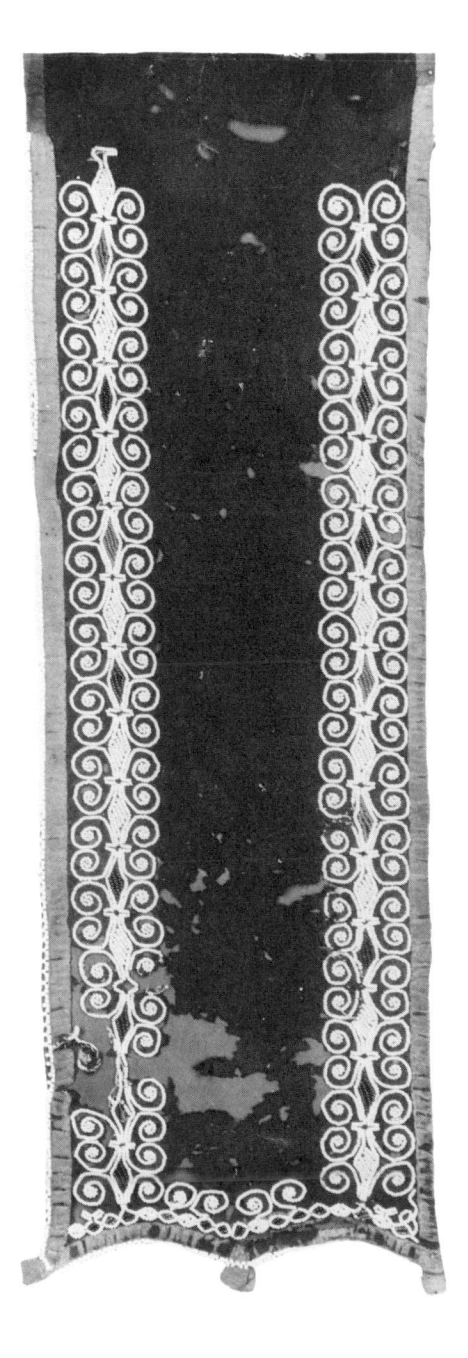

independent production unit, with the men and women doing different tasks. Besides grinding corn to trade with the Algonkians for meat and skins, the women wove mats of reeds and corn leaves, made baskets and bowls of reeds, and fashioned similar vessels of birchbark as well. They used Indian hemp fibres to make twine, and made a twined-weave cloth which they fashioned into scarfs, collars, and bracelets. In addition, they decorated skins with painted designs and dyed quills.

The handsomest pottery in aboriginal Canada was made by the Iroquoian-speaking farmers. Clay was dried, pulverized, tempered with powdered gneiss, and then worked with water into a ball. After a central hole was forced with the fist, a wooden paddle was used to work the clay body into its form. The narrowed neck expanded to a low, sometimes castellated rim. Castellations—semi-pointed projections that have been compared to the spout of a pitcher—were perhaps an aid to pouring. Very simple in profile, a pot viewed from above would have an elegant opening outlined by the undulations of the lip. Usually only the lip, or collar, was decorated with various patterns of incised lines. Pots could be set over a fire, but water softened and weakened them if they stood filled for long.

James Pendergast gives the usual order of pottery development as first, dentate stamping; second, cord-wrapped stick impressing; third, possibly, stamping and paddle-edge decorative techniques; and fourth, incising of patterns.

As befits a people who grew and cured their own tobacco, the Hurons made clay pipes. Moulded around a core of grass, these pipes were highly polished and sometimes darkened with grease. Often they were fashioned into effigies—the shapes of animals and humans.

The men made canoes, huts, bows and arrows, snowshoes, sleds, and wooden armour, as well as (probably) spoons, ladles, and bowls. They also erected the houses and palisades. Among ornamental objects still preserved are tubular beads made from the bones of birds, disc-shaped beads made from imported conch shells, little turtles of red slate, and combs and small amulets of bone.

The Iroquois were actually a league of nations: the Mohawk, Oneida, Onondaga, Cayuga, and Seneca. Their life-styles were very similar to those of the Huron and other Iroquoian-speaking tribes, but the Iroquois have survived and retained not only their numbers but their identity as a people. Although they have for centuries been in continual contact with Europeans, they retain some of their aboriginal agricultural festivals, and both Christian and Longhouse religious groups still live side-by-side. Still existing also is the False Face Society, whose masked members visit houses where there is disease.

Like the Hurons, the Iroquois were farming groups—possibly the northern remnant of the mound-building culture of the Eastern United States— who lived in palisaded long-houses and supplemented their farming with hunting and fishing. Their culture began in an archaic form of Algonkian affinity, and moved through the Northwest Woodland Phase to the "Iroquois Aspect" around AD 1300. Their econ-

Figure 14. False Face Masks, Iroquois.

Photo: The National Museum of Canada

Masks made for the False Face Society are based upon the visions of hunters who once met spiritual beings in the forest, and dreaming of them afterwards, carved their faces into the trunks of living trees. The broken-nosed "Great World-Rim Being" gave the power to the wearer to perform healing rites by blowing hot ashes over the sick.

omy was based on the cultivation of seed-corn, squash, gourds, beans, and tobacco; they used simple but serviceable field tools and stored the harvest in strong, carefully made, unornamented vessels of elm bark.

As we have seen, the pottery industry was developed to a high degree by the Iroquoians. It might be well to examine one pot in detail and let it stand for this rich assortment of styles. A typical vessel, of Swarthout dentate type, comes from the Waupoose site near Picton, Ontario (Figure 11). Vessels of this type were made before historic times and are frequent in the St. Lawrence area. Its curved body flows in through a somewhat narrowed throat surmounted by a decorated collar. This is one of the Onondaga pottery types (according to the system developed by Richard McNeish), the forms of which so much resemble those of the Oneida as to be indistinguishable except by site. The style greatly overlaps that of the Mohawks, and other influences are present as well. The whole style shows a wide range of attributes and gives us a good picture of what the pottery of these peoples was like.

It was made of a clay paste, firm but slightly flaky, tempered with medium amounts of fine grit to help prevent excessive shrinking when the pot was fired. Its surface finish is smooth. The decoration was made with a toothed object—a notched disk or roulette, the notched edge of a paddle, or a piece of serrated bone; "rectangular dentate impressions" describes the pattern so produced. (The Iroquois decorated other styles of pot by pressing with a cord-wrapped paddle or stick into the wet clay and incising cross-hatched and other patterns with a sharp stick.)

The extremely sensual round form of the vessel's body speaks of containment, of the hollowness to be filled with corn; the neck made it easy to handle and hold. The collar is a plastic form lending itself to a tactile decoration; the circles must have been pressed in with some sort of tube. Not all vessels of this area were collared, some having yawning mouths. Sometimes the collars are "barbed" as well as castellated; that is, they have an undulating top with a set of rounded peaks. This particular vessel is distinguished by its nearly intact condition; countless shards give only glimpses of other pots long shattered and discarded, though of course complete pots do occur here and there. A midden is a garbage dump, so naturally most of the pots there are broken ones.

Art of the period after white contact includes masks, porcupine-quill embroidery, silverwork, sash weaving, and moose-hair embroidery. The adoption of glass beads expanded the range of this embroidery and frequently eclipsed quillwork. The designs, which were probably adapted in part from the French, are elegant and remarkably ornamental. Clothing styles as such show adaptation from the Laurentian Plateau Algonkians.

The Iroquois made snowshoes, sleds, toboggans, and cradleboards, which were painted and intricately carved on the back; the designs are floral, baroque roses with a clearly European origin and a strong folk-art appearance (Figure 12). A rather feminine assembly of objects—bags, pouch-

Figure 15. Wampum circle with fifty pendant strings, one for each sachem, entrusted to the Mohawk Nation at the foundation of the Confederation of Five Nations.

Photo: The National Museum of Canada

Ceremonial wampum may have originated as a decorative material, but it became, perhaps because of its great intrinsic value, a medium for formal presentations to mark important occasions. Wampum is made of white or blue shell beads strung into strings or woven into bands. The effect of this complex multiple string is sumptuous, in keeping with its great historical significance.

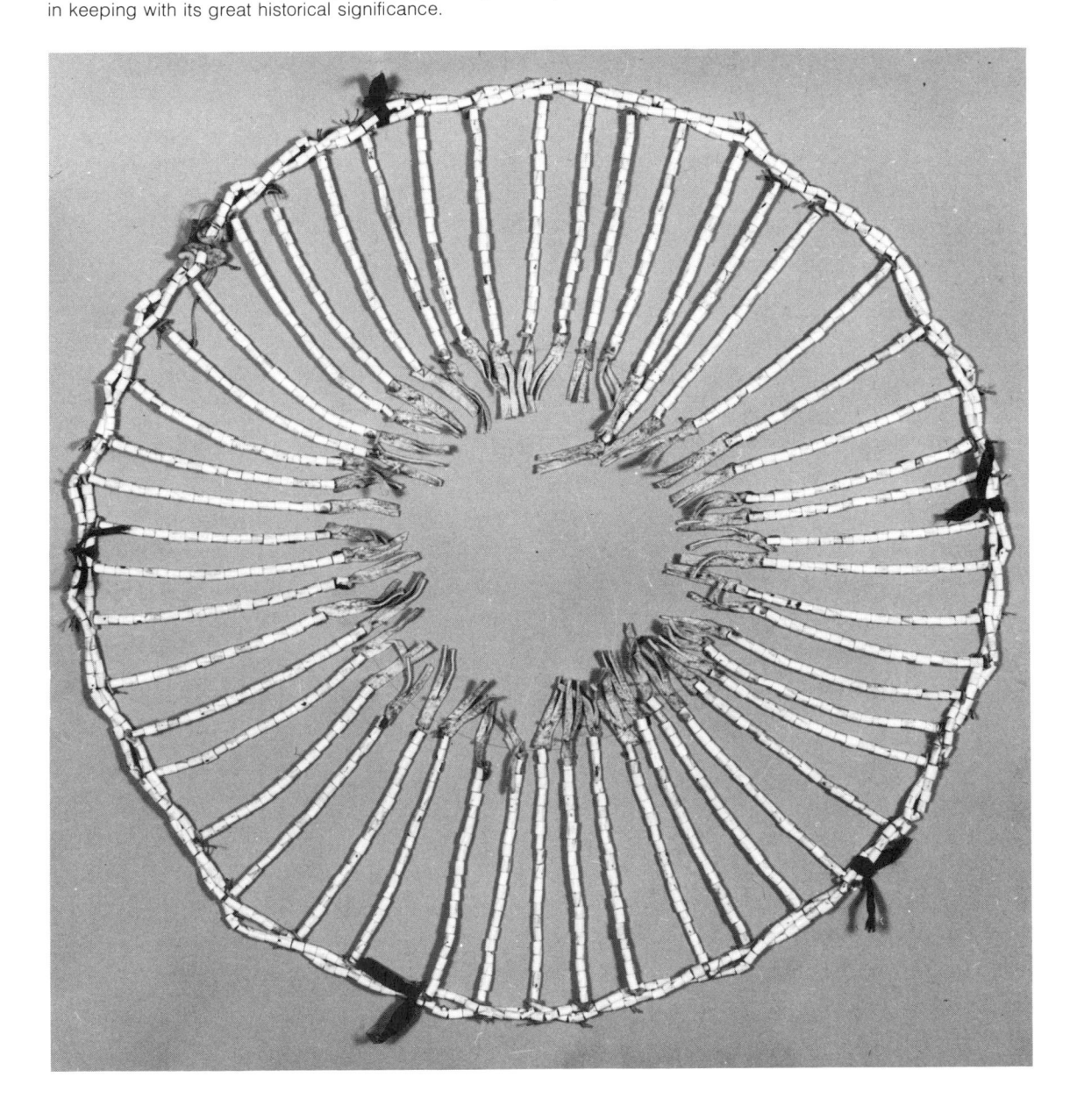

es, purses, needle-cases, and pincush-ions—were decorated with glass beads and shaped into design forms that have been much discussed.

The designs were not derived from their old neighbouring farmers, the Cherokee (who had no such designs) but probably came, with some original additions, from the Algonkian groups. Marius Barbeau thought they showed French influence from Quebec convents, but George Quimby sees a connection between Algonkian art and Hopewell culture—the "double curve"—which would make them prehistoric. In the seventeenth century, a bisymmetrical double curve (that is, an S-shape ending in two opposed or facing spirals) was used primarily for representations of celestial, geographical, or mystical phenomena—the dome of the sky, the world tree, the sun. Followers of C. G. Jung will prick up their ears in recognition as this roster of forms is intoned. Speck calls such patterns "universe signs"; a border of white beads on a dark cloth suggests a sky full of stars or snow to a Western eye.

The scroll-form represented the "horns of chieftancy." When curving outward and downward like the horns of a mountain goat, they represented a living chief; curving upward and inward (imagine a heart-shaped outline) they showed a chief who was dead. Such borders formed the Mohawk "horned trimming" (Figure 13). The Tuscarora called these scrolls "fern heads." Here we have attestation to floral symbolism that is probably prehistoric; perhaps the flower itself was seen as an animal image, like our "dog-tooth violets." In Iroquois embroidery the motifs are very deli-cate and fine, a series of curves, drooping scrolls, or half-curves. In the eighteenth century curved lines were grouped around geometrical figures or arranged by themselves in bilateral symmetry. By the mid-nineteenth century these designs gave way to partly realistic representations of plants and flowers in beads or quills worked on cloth. Frank Speck concludes that what actually occurred during this process was a meeting between the aboriginal forms based on curved lines with the French floral style of the seventeenth and eighteenth centuries.

Among the best-known forms in Canadian native art are the masks made for the False Face Society. These symbols of spiritual forces, called "Faces" by the Iroquois, were carved into the trunks of living basswood trees (Figure 14). Hunters who met quasi-human beings in the forest dreamed of them afterwards and carved their likenesses. The Faces took a number of different forms, recognized by colour as well as by shape, and distortion of nose and mouth. Their nearest counterpart would perhaps be the scowling but benign temple guardians of Buddhist Japan, though they possess a certain ironic or rueful element which seems characteristically Amerindian. Often they represent "Old Broken-Nose" or "The Great World-Rim Being" a primaeval being who broke his nose when, in a power struggle with the Creator, a moving mountain struck him in the face. This legend suggests the relationship of man and the divine that is found in the Biblical account of Jacob and the Angel. In Iroquois thought, the Great Creator who embodied the health and creativity of nature was opposed by

evil spirits who caused illness and destruction. But the Faces (disembodied beings) could be appeased, and they taught mankind through dreams to carve their images into wooden masks, to sing, to dance, and, safely manipulating hot coals, to blow healing ashes from the mouth of the mask upon the sick.

Shagodyoweh, the Great World Rim Being, was extremely tall and strode the earth from east to west, so that he was redfaced in the morning sun and shadowed with black in the evening; this explains the typical colouring. His nose is broken and his mouth is distorted in a gimace of pain. Another mask associated with this higher class of beings is the "spoon-lipped" Doorkeeper, whose mouth is pursed to blow ashes. Still other masks represented additional spirits.

There was also associated with the False Face Society a second group, the Husk Face Society. The Husk-Faces were woven masks of corn-husks, representing farmers from the other side of the world who visited during the midwinter festival as messengers of Corn, Squash, and Beans, three sisters who gave them the power of prophecy. This mantic function was accompanied by healing powers. The presence of the rather benign-appearing husk faces sometimes heralded the more awesome and prestigious Society of Faces.

In making the Face masks, basswood or other soft wood was used. A tree representing the World Tree, a symbol of unity and peace, was selected and honoured with offerings of tobacco. Upon the living trunk the complex Face was carved in deep relief, a task originally accomplished entirely with stone implements. The completed mask was removed from the tree and adorned with game animal's hair, eyes of clam shell, and earth pigments (Plate 7). Modern masks use white horse-tail for the hair, sheet copper for eyes and red barn paint. After the mask was "doctored" by additional offerings of tobacco, it was worn, not as a disguise, but as a means of focussing and making visible the healing powers of the spiritual being it depicted.

The corn-husk masks used in healing ceremonies were braided and sewn, then consecrated by sacrificial bags of native tobacco placed on their foreheads. It will be noted how much Amerindian religious practice was involved with healing; some writers think this function was exaggerated when white men brought waves of ravaging new disease to the North American continent. There is something appealingly antique about these gnarled faces with their puffy cheeks and sunflower-shapes, as if living vegetable presences had shrivelled into dried husk forms.

Derived from the forms already described are the "maskettes"—miniatures about three inches across. Their purpose is secret, but they seem to be substitutes for the larger masks, which they resemble. These tiny masks, and perhaps as well those otherwise inexplicable miniature faces in other cultures—prehistoric Eskimo, for instance—are a personal item, a hidden spiritual asset.

A mask is a symbol operating on the principle that a part stands for the whole (Claude Levi-Strauss calls this *metonymy*), and the wearer moves like the supernatural he impersonates, or who has overshadowed or possessed him. The world-wide role

of the mask in religious practice is well known, and the mask played a significant part in the development of drama as an art form.

In addition to masks, the Iroquois made flutes, used for relaxation and courting, rattles from gourds, turtleshells, bunches of horns or hoofs, or of enfolded bark. They also made maple and elm—burl bowls, pipes, round-bottomed cups to be hung on the belt, and personal spoons used for ceremonial eating at the periodic yearly agricultural festivals. Also made of wood was the Iroquois war club, carved in the form of a ball about the size of an orange, gripped in the beak or talons of a bird, or in a man's hand, the neck, leg, or arm of which then forms the shank of the club. These formidable weapons, used in hand-to-hand combat, are among the earliest objects to be collected by the British, and from this period are preserved in the Ashmolean Museum in Oxford, England, mute testimony to what most impressed their collectors.

The use of ceremonial *wampum* has been recorded from many eastern groups in Canada and the United States. Its value was intrinsic, and it was used for gifts and presentations on important occasions. It was specifically used for negotiatory belts; peace, war, and death messages; ransom; expression of condolence, and, in later times, ornamentation. In prehistoric times the type of bead called "disc wampum" was widespread on the eastern part of the continent. James Pendergast describes disc-shaped clay and stone beads found in prehistoric Iroquoian sites in eastern Ontario, and also large, relatively crude mudstone

beads which he thinks are associated with low-collared and collarless pottery. Other sites have yielded many disc-shaped beads of shell. The bulk of *wampum* from historic times came from Dutch and southern New England sources. The considerable conjecture as to the method of perforating the shell pieces in prehistoric times led Frank Speck, in his classic study of *wampum*, to dismiss that topic as a mystery. He did, however, suggest that the white beads may have been most prevalent in early times because the white discoidal bead is more common than the tubular type. Shell is soft enough to be pierced without the use of a metal tool, but the finer beads required the metal drill introduced by the Europeans. *Dentalium* shells are essentially tubular in form.

The mythology of the tribes south of the St. Lawrence frequently deals with *wampum*; explanations of its origin form a common theme. Linguistic evidence suggested to Speck that "white string" was an early term for *wampum*. Archaeological sites yielded white, flat, circular shell discs which must have been the easiest form to perforate, and which are readily cut and ground from the flat surface of many common pelecypod (clam) shapes of shell. The Micmac called large bone and ivory beads by the same name they gave to *wampum*. Historical cylindrical *wampum* is either white or dark blue (depending upon the shell used to form it). The individual pieces are either four to seven millimetres or ten to seventeen millimetres, the latter perhaps having been made by Dutch settlers.

Wampum is both woven into bands and

Plate 1. Birchbark box with quilled decorations, Micmac, c. AD 1900.

Before the advent of the trade bead, the principal material for much Canadian Indian decoration was the porcupine quill. Quillwork was a major art form of the Micmac, and decorated birchbark boxes with mosaic-like surfaces of dyed quills continue to form an important item for commerce.

threaded on strings. Speck describes the
technical aspects of the weave in detail.
The beads were strung, one at a time, on
double threads which hung from a piece of
obliquely cut leather. The upper outside
thread was turned in and passed between
the doubled warp threads in each course
of beads. Thus, the effect of a bias-cut was
introduced, which Speck noted, allowed
the strip to encircle the neck and lie flat.
Strips were used not only as collars and
to decorate garments, but also as hanging
hair "ribbons." Strings were used as necklaces and ear-pendants. The term "strings"
is used, as well as "belts," in eighteenth
century descriptions of *wampum*. One famous belt of *wampum* from the Six Nations
Reserve near Brantford, Ontario, shows a
row of figures holding hands, in white
upon a dark ground, and another, of great
historical significance, is a *wampum* circle
with fifty pendant strings, one for each sachem, entrusted to the Mohawk nation at
the foundation of the confederacy of the
Five Nations (Figure 15). The effect of this
complex multiple string is sumptuous.

The appearance of the bands is strikingly like that of modern bands of beadwork, except for the limitations in colour.
Frank Speck speculates that *wampum*
may have originated as ornament, and that
it was to this original use that it finally
reverted.

Figure 16. Warrior's shirt, Plains Cree, c. 1900.
Photo: Glenbow-Alberta Institute

A ceremonial garment trimmed with weasel fur and beaded strips,
this buckskin war shirt is painted with stripes, representing knife
slits, and dots, symbolizing bullet holes, to give its wearer protection
from wounds. It was worn during a dance before a horse-capturing
foray.

Chapter 4

Horsemen of the Canadian Prairies

Plate 2. Peterborough Petroglyphs, Ontario.
Photo: Martha Lawrence

Discovered only in the mid-twentieth century, the Peterborough
Petroglyphs are located thirty-five miles northeast of Peterborough,
Ontario. The images, part of the Eastern Woodlands tradition, were
formed by grinding the face of an outcropping of white crystalline
limestone.

As the ice sheets of the last glacial age retreated from the southern prairies of Canada, a series of gigantic glacial lakes were formed. About five thousand years ago, the land became lake-free, and the rivers began their meandering work. When Europeans entered this area there were Athapaskan, Siouan, and Algonkian speakers, some originally plains tribes, others immigrants from the borders of the eastern woodlands. Some evidence of earlier life in this area is revealed in archaeological sites. From five thousand to thirty-five hundred years ago, buffalo hunters, who probably came into the prairies from further west, followed the herds, making choppers and scrapers, lanceolate points of stone with concave bases, and antler points. These people were followed, thirty-five hundred to twenty-five hundred years ago, by hunters with scrapers and choppers, implying the preparation of animal skins and meat, and projectile points of various styles, including side-notched as well as lanceolate. Side-notched points are the conventional "arrowhead" shape familiar to schoolboys around the world. Archaeologists do not always like to guess whether a point had a short or a long shaft, and whether it served as an "arrowhead," "spearhead," "knife-point," or whatever, when evidence does not support such specific classifications. They also know that "projectile points," which come in a number of shapes, resemble potsherds in their indestructability and structural variation.

These prairie peoples were to undergo various outside influences from cultural systems, each of which is referred to as a "focus." About twenty-five hundred to fifteen hundred years ago, pottery—smooth, with simple designs—appeared as part of a life of hunting, fishing, and gathering. The artefacts resemble those of the Middle Woodlands horizon of the east, so the people who made them probably came from there (R. S. MacNeish's interpretation). A second focus developed which had elaborate pottery, adding cord-wrapped, paddle-edged forms with incised and oblique pricked decoration, polished celts (rounded stone forms with a smooth surface, used for pounding and rubbing), and corner-notched points. Perhaps they were early Assiniboines moving up from Minnesota (before AD 1350), or perhaps the group was widespread through both areas. Somewhat more recently still, burial mounds appear. An additional focus containing material remains of the Cree intrudes around AD1350; these people, who may have come in from the north and northeast, brought fabric-impressed pottery, plano-convex scrapers, and large stone scrapers. The presence of scrapers, as mentioned above, implies the preparation and tanning of hides for various purposes.

In summary, the prehistoric remains in southern Manitoba, from which the above series was drawn, is typical of movements and transitions in various parts of the Canadian Prairies, showing a long history of peoples. First came buffalo hunters on the open plains, then a period when the forest moved out over the area, with fishing, trapping, and hunting of woods animals, when population and material culture grew slowly, then a time when the burial mounds show a new elaboration of religious life. The bow and arrow gradually became dominant, and then the horse and the gun arrived (Plate 8).

"Plains culture" is the name given to the

Figure 17. *"Coups* Counted by Crop-Eared Wolf," Painted Buffalo Robe, Blood.
Photo: The National Museum of Canada

Buffalo robes were painted by men to record their war exploits. The story of this robe was recorded in 1882. The *coups*, beginning at the tail end of the robe, are: A party of Bloods surrounded by Sioux (pointing guns) during which Crop-Eared Wolf was shot in the breast; a fight in which he shot a Cree; the scalping of a Crow; Bloods surrounding some Cree, when he shot a woman who was going for water and was himself shot in the leg; and a foray in which he stole a Sioux horse from before its owner's lodge door.

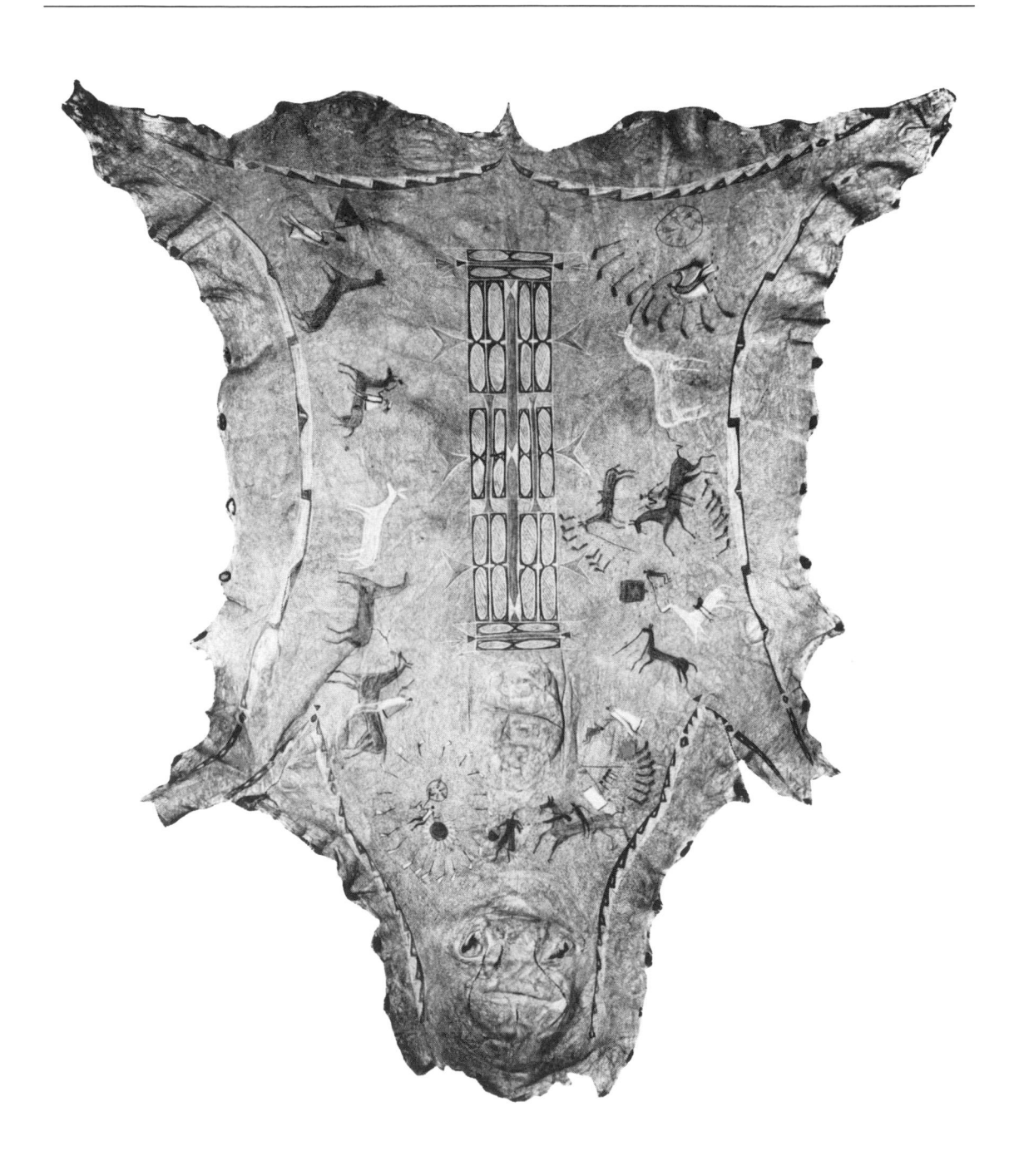

culture of the period from the advent of the horse to the destruction of the buffalo in the third quarter of the nineteenth century. The culture shows considerable uniformity over a very wide area of Canada and the United States, and some of its characteristic artefacts and arts may be discussed in general before the work of the various tribes is examined. Robert Lowie has given a dependable summary of the art of this culture in his study, *Indians of the Plains*. The most familiar artefact is the *tipi*, the large conical tent (smaller in northern Canada) covered with buffalo skins, and later canvas. As the *tipi* was owned and cared for by the women, the men relied on the women to transport the house as well as the household goods. It probably began (in pre-equestrian days) as a shelter with smaller, lighter poles, covered with bark or mats, of the type found over large areas of North America and Eurasia as well. Distinctive to the Plains is the regulation of the smoke vent (the fire was inside) by means of flaps or "ears." These were attached to two separate moveable poles, which were adjusted to accommodate the varying direction of the winds in an effort to ease the general smokiness of the interior. These early mobile homes were transported by *travois*, first by dog and woman power, and, as soon as the possibility appeared and was recognized, by horse.

Horses spread throughout midwestern North America, descendants of the Spanish imports to New Mexico. The Blackfoot obtained the horse in 1730, and a new range of material culture sprang up in the form of riding gear; horse trappings included saddles, bridles, quirts, ropes, and crup-

pers. This important addition to Prairie life also resulted in a general proliferation and increase in size of other things. *Travois* and *tipis* grew larger now that a stronger animal could transport their increased weight.

Like many other Amerindians, the Prairies people wore dressed skins, acquiring cloth after the Europeans came. They probably added the breechcloth at the same time, having previously been content with an apron. Men wore shirts, leggings, moccasins, and buffalo robes, and women wore long dresses, which also changed in cut and the extent to which they covered the body after European contact. Very elaborate garments, with quantities of appendages such as elk's teeth, were very precious. A warrior's shirt, *circa* 1900, from the Plains Cree of Central Alberta, shows what a ceremonial garment looked like (Figure 16). Trimmed with weasel fur and beaded strips, this buckskin "war shirt" is painted with stripes (symbolizing knife slits) and dots (bullet holes) on the breast. Such a garment gave its owner protection from these wounds, and was worn in the dance which preceded horse-napping forays.

Before the traders arrived, as is usual everywhere, Prairies tools were made of wood, stone, and bone. The textile crafts were little developed, due to lack of such fibres as cotton; their thread was of sinew. Buffalo hair was made into lariats and belts, and formed into long, scarf-like strips that were folded in half and sewn at the sides to make storage bags and ceremonial containers for men. A little basketry was known among tribes at the edge of the Prairies, and ceramics had, as we have

Plate 3. Pictograph, "Mounted Horseman," Agawa Site, Ontario.
Photo: Selwyn Dewdney

Myeengun, a formidable Shaman, and his war party crossed Lake
Superior with the aid of powerful *Manitous*. A symbol of four suns
above a sign of water may suggest the time-span of the crossing.
This pictograph has been interpreted as representing the Shaman
on horseback after reaching shore; it would thus date the painting
after the development of horse culture.

seen, been practised by groups in earlier phases before the taking up of a full-scale Plains life centred on the buffalo and the horse.

Where the Plains peoples excelled was in the arts of skin-dressing. Hides were staked to the ground, hairy side down, carefully cleaned, and left to bleach in the sun for several days. With a piece of antler, the hides were then scraped to an even thickness; the hair might be removed too, if desired. Rawhide was not submitted to this process, and thus contained enough natural moisture to dry extremely tightly after use, making it useful for binding and making receptacles. These served various purposes but consisted basically of a skin folded into an envelope shape, whether for multi-purpose square bags, heavily fringed bags to contain ceremonial objects, cylindrical medicine cases, large rawhide trunks, or the handsomely decorated *parflêches*. These last contained pemmican, dried strips of buffalo meat, pounded up and mixed with grease and dried berries, a remarkably nutritious and long-lasting substance that was light in weight. The woman who made the *parflêche* also decorated it with the geometric patterns discussed below along with other painted objects (Plate 9).

In the making of leather, the cleaned and dried hide underwent a further process—tanning. The surface was rubbed with fat and brains, then polished with a smooth stone, rolled into a bundle, and left to shrink. After having been stretched again and rubbed all over its surface, the hide was pulled repeatedly through a sinew loop until it was soft and pliable. Tanned leather was used for making moccasins, among other things.

When complete and permanent pliability was required, even after wetting, the skin was also smoked. This material, which has a deep smoky tang, was used for making various soft pouches to hold smoking equipment, women's sewing, caches of pigment, and similar necessities. They were often embellished with the beadwork which, as everywhere, eventually replaced porcupine-quill embroidery.

Before the trade bead, however, new-killed porcupines were plucked and the quills carefully size-sorted and put into bags. The largest quills, from the tail, were used to decorate work bags and comb-cases, while the hair of the animal was used for fine embroidery. Prairies women sucked the quills to soften them, and flattened them with their fingernails. They then laid the quills upon the surface of the skin, attaching them with sinew thread through holes punched with an awl. The method resembled the "couching" used in Europe for liturgical embroidery. For a fine line, a flattened, flexible quill was wrapped around a string of sinew, and the resulting strand was couched in place with more sinew. The covered area was stiff and formal in appearance. Various bone tools were used, including a marker that traced designs.

Although there was probably no aboriginal blue (one of the most noticeable colours among the earliest, rather large, glass beads acquired in trading was a bright turquoise blue), red and yellow were made from willow roots and other boiled

Figure 18. Beaded Medicine Bag with Deer Hooves, Assiniboine.
Photo: The National Museum of Canada

The Assiniboine (sometimes called the Stoney in Canada), like other
Plains peoples, sought protection and power in medicine objects
kept in beautifully made containers. This beaded bag is decorated
with floral patterns and has a row of deer hooves still attached to the
soft fetlock skins. A medicine bag contains objects that are sacred
because of their association with important visions.

plants, and black was produced by mixing earth and tallow with a boiled mixture of maple bast and leaves. When beads were introduced, they were strung on a thread and stitched against the surface in the same way that a quill-wrapped sinew had been. Strings of beads stitched in very closely set rows made a brilliant glossy surface and made possible curvilinear patterns.

Although no stone sculpture and little woodcarving was practised by the Prairies tribes—they made numerous elegant weapons incorporating wood, of course, including shields—they did considerable painting, most notably of buffalo hides, *tipi* covers, and *parflêches*. Their colours, which in this case may have included blue and green, came from iron-containing clays for brown, red, and yellow, and from black earth or charcoal for black. These materials were ground, mixed with a binding medium, and placed in a hollow receptacle (a potsherd or shell). A stick or brush was provided for each colour; women applied geometric designs, men—more realistic forms.

The skin robe was an excellent surface for painting, and the Prairies peoples took good advantage of the fact. Women's robes bore painted borders of rectangles with ornamented subdivisions, and the men's had the radiating "war bonnet" pattern in the middle (the effect is like a sunburst) with a repeated triangular motif called "feathers." These robes were worn around the shoulders in a manner suggesting the casual nobility fo a toga; early paintings by Peter Rindisbacher show the majestic effect they achieved.

Realistic pictures were painted on robes and *tipi* covers to record outstanding events in the owner's life, whether a military exploit or a visionary experience. Sometimes there was a "calendric" account, recording notable tribal events over a period of years. According to Marius Barbeau, the painting of robes goes back at least to the eighteenth century, and from 1800 on these were semi-realistic drawings in paint, showing battle and raiding scenes with lively humans and spirited horses.

The most typical event pictured was the *coup*, a blow or touch delivered to one's enemy, often with a special stick; the *coup* was the primary means of obtaining honour in battle (Figure 17). Often the successful counting of the *coup* was quite sufficient without the death of even serious injury of the enemy, and the participants went away satisfied. A *coup* entitled its counter to describe his accomplishments on public occasions and the robe was a means of display comparable to wearing battle ribbons and medals. The strongly conventionalized figures are drawn in profile with no regard to perspective, but with a strong and evident sense of dynamic composition, and relate effectively to the shape of the skin. The writer examined one in which the figure of the rider was superimposed upon the image of the horse with both legs showing, not because the Prairies warriors rode side-saddle but—maybe —because they had two legs and both were needed to show the whole man. The design problem is similar to that of designing a chasuble or cope, in that the pictures must be effective when draped over a man's shoulders and viewed in motion.

A distinctive style was used by women

Major Linguistic Groupings.

After *Canada, Aboriginal Population*, 1955, Department of Mines and Technical Surveys.

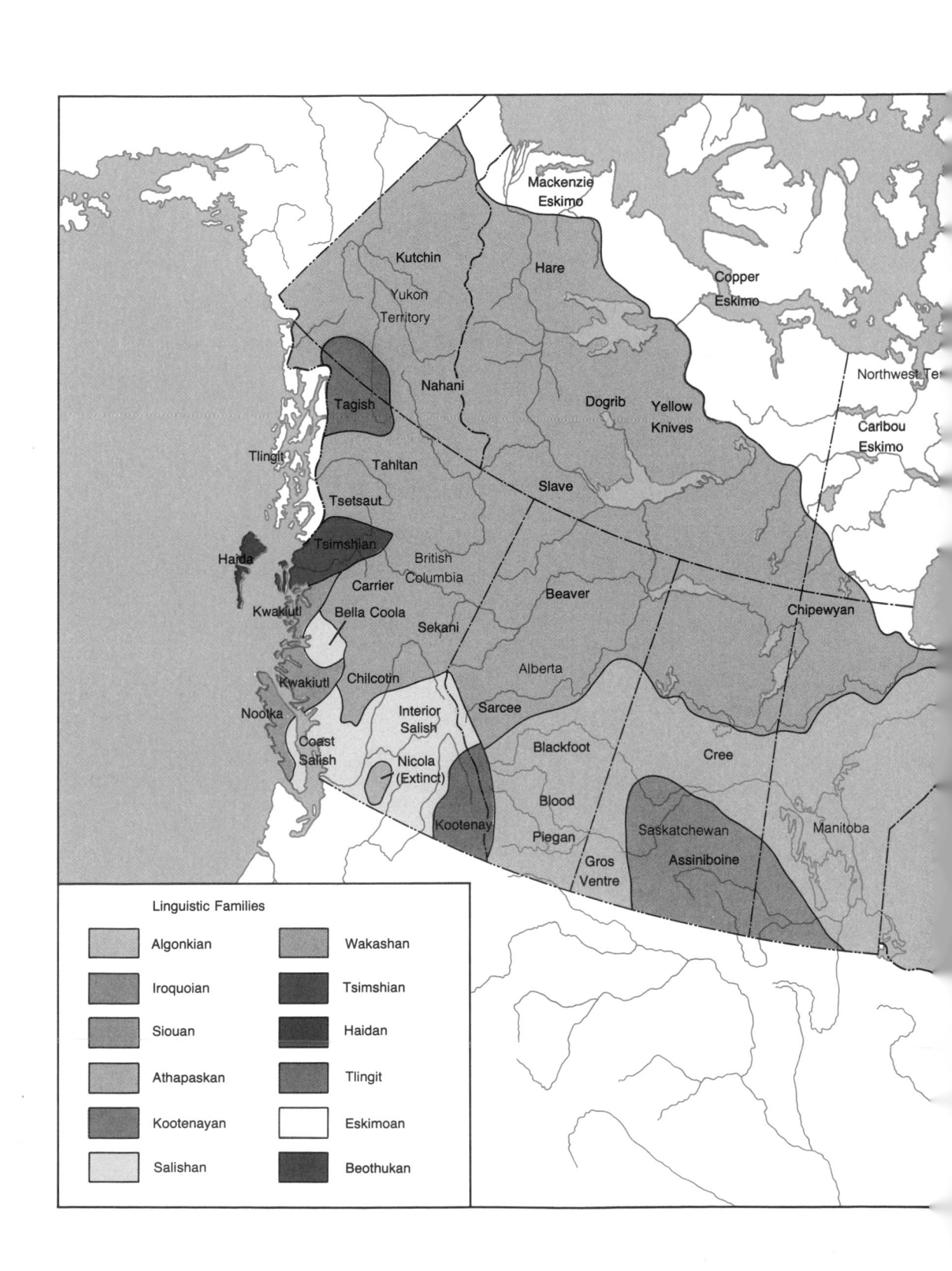

Mackenzie
Eskimo

Kutchin

Hare

Copper
Eskimo

Yukon
Territory

Northwest Ter

Nahani

Dogrib

Yellow
Knives

Caribou
Eskimo

Tagish

Tlingit

Tahltan

Slave

Tsetsaut

Tsimshian

Haida

British
Columbia

Carrier

Beaver

Chipewyan

Kwakiutl

Bella Coola

Sekani

Kwakiutl

Chilcotin

Alberta

Nootka

Interior
Salish

Sarcee

Coast
Salish

Blackfoot

Cree

Nicola
(Extinct)

Blood

Kootenay

Saskatchewan

Manitoba

Piegan

Assiniboine

Gros
Ventre

Linguistic Families

Algonkian	Wakashan
Iroquoian	Tsimshian
Siouan	Haidan
Athapaskan	Tlingit
Kootenayan	Eskimoan
Salishan	Beothukan

Figure 19. *Tipis* with painted designs, Assiniboine, c. 1928.
Photo: the National Museum of Canada

Tipis are portable dwellings usually formed of between six and
fourteen buffalo-cow hides stretched over pine-pole frames; more
recently, canvas has been used. The surfaces are painted in
registers representing a multi-layered universe; medicine images
are in the middle region. The first *tipi* fully shown on the left bears a
confronted bear and a buffalo head, the next has round motifs,
(probably representing stars), and the farthest shows a rainbow
and a crescent moon.

for decorating rawhide objects. Various geometric forms—lines, triangles, rectangles, and diamonds—were used. At some earlier date these motifs may have been incised through a layer of pigment, but recent ones are all painted. The *parflèche* belongs in this category. Its two main flaps were decorated symmetrically, the two side flaps being treated with less care, probably because they didn't show when the object was folded. The Blackfoot sometimes used curved lines, but otherwise straight lines were the rule, frequently with a central stripe or central figure to divide the design of the fold into two equal panels. Cylindrical forms were usually divided by straight lines into zones which were filled with repeated design motifs.

The formalism that characterized painted forms was somewhat relaxed, at least in late examples, in the designs used for embroidery. As with Woodlands motifs, the evolution of Prairies design has been the subject of much discussion. Robert Lowie gives the chronology as follows: in quillwork, the use of angular geometric designs of squares, triangles, and combinations of these, precedes the floral patterns that represent Woodlands intrusions and French influence. The geometric motifs were done with a "two-threaded" technique, in which quills were bound between two parallel threads, producing a band of colour. The "one-thread" technique, which produced a thin line, was used for rosettes and other curved shapes.

Between 1835 and 1840, china and glass beads were introduced. The earliest ones were one-eighth inch in diameter, of white and sky-blue, and were laid on with a couching stitch in the traditional geometric designs, without curvilinear additions. The method achieved a massive effect, though the beaded areas were rather small, having been based on the old, difficult quill style. Some of these large beads were also used by themselves at the beginning of a tassel of human or other hair. The more modern style (1880 to 1900) employed much smaller beads of the kind now familiar, and show a beginning of tribal variation. Canadian designs, as of the Blackfoot and the Plains Cree, remained closest to porcupine quillwork.

Lowie also discusses the problem of whether the geometric designs are conventionalizations (abstractions) of natural forms. To him, their common names suggest "convenience of reference" used to catalogue the series of patterns that a woman had available, in the manner of patchwork quilt patterns among white women. Some signs had meaning, while others did not, and peoples varied in assigning meanings or in not doing so. The turtle, for instance, presided over female physiological terminology, and motifs were often combined to an overall turtle form. The principle of "differentiation" used by Rudolf Arnheim may help us to understand: although geometric figures are easiest to render in quillwork, their variety of form is limited. But an "enclosed" form of any shape is structurally equivalent to a body mass (even to a "concept mass" like *life* or *abundance*) so any shape can be pressed into service to depict any such entity. Once it is so defined, anyone familiar with the identification can recognize it.

The objects represented were mostly

Plate 4. Norval Morriseau, "Indian Style Jesus Christ," 1972.

Photo: Robinson of Thornhill for Pollock Gallery

Using colours of high saturation in powerful harmonies, Morriseau combines the image of the man of power in Ojibwa culture with that of the Son of Man, in expression of his personal religious vision.

large animals and stars, especially the Morning Star. The relationship between beadwork motifs and celestial phenomena has already been noted in Iroquois "universe sign" patterns, and certainly the clear night sky, in a world without pollution, resembles the scattering of glistening beads with a lavish hand. Colours also had symbolic meanings; the Blackfoot used various colours for their backgrounds, although white was common for other groups. These could be naturalistic (green equals vegetation) or conceptual (black equals victory).

The peoples who rode across the Canadian Prairies with their colourful regalia and chivalric splendour were the Assiniboine, the Blackfoot, the Plains Cree, the Sarcee, and, in small numbers, the Gros Ventre and the Sioux. In the seventeenth century, the Assiniboine (so-named because they boiled their food with hot stones; they are sometimes called the Stoney Indians in Canada) hunted near the Lake of the Woods and gathered wild rice there. They began to move into the northwest in the eighteenth century, dividing in two groups. As horse and gun increased their range, they moved still westward, living on buffalo meat, which they boiled in hide bags, having abandoned their clay pots and birch-bark vessels.

The northern branch were the Stoneys, who after disease, war, white encroachment, and the loss of the buffalo, settled on reserves, as did their Assiniboine brothers in Montana. They were typically Prairies people, living in buffalo-hide *tipis*, following their migratory prey. Like other Plains tribes they had moved by foot and dog-drawn *travois*, and used bow and

arrow, seeking protection in a shield, a war-charm, and a skin shirt and war bonnet based upon vision-power (Figure 18). They revered sun and thunder as manifestations of the Great Spirit, and practised the Sun Dance and the Horse Dance, but their greatest direct power came from visions, dreams, and ceremonies founded on visions.

The Sun Dance exerts a fascination upon Europeans still. It consisted of the erection of a sacred central pole (surrounded by enclosure) upon which offerings, usually of cloth, were hung. In other groups men offered sacrifice by fastening skewers through their skin, attached to long thongs which they attempted to pull loose by dancing, but the Assiniboine did not include this practice. Among the Assiniboine self-mutilation was only practised in preparation for war, to seek visions, and to gain divine pity. It was this last motivation which was a strong element in the Sun Dance in all its forms.

Theirs was a military society; their *tipis*, which consisted of six to fourteen buffalo-cow hides stretched over pine-pole frames, were arranged in a circle and decorated outside with war exploits by warriors and with religious symbols by medicine-men (Figure 19).

The Plains Cree began with a few bands of Cree in northern Saskatchewan and Manitoba who from time to time came out onto the Prairies. The horse and gun increased their strength and mobility, and they pushed out against other Prairies tribes to become extremely powerful. Smallpox and war ultimately curbed their expansion and when the buffalo disappeared, the Plains Cree went onto reserves. As they

Figure 20. Painted leather jacket, Plains Cree.
Photo: The National Museum of Canada

Decorated with representational drawings, the jacket shows mounted
warriors and men on foot, armed with shields, guns, and bows and
arrows, and bearing long feathered *coup* sticks. The mounted figure
on the lower left carries a shield with its ring of feathers outspread,
which may be compared to that shown in Figure 21. The figure on
the lower right has a shoulder bag. The sleeves of the jacket are
decorated with designs of horses' hoof-prints.

had moved out onto the Prairies, they assimilated the Plains culture, especially that of the Assiniboine, but they brought along their old ways. Their dancing societies were specifically religious, unlike the Assiniboine, and they practised the Ojibwa smoke offering, prayer to the Great Spirit, and Feast of the Dead.

The Plains Cree made painted buffalo robes, worn year-round by both men and women. Some hides had a simple four-inch strip of beadwork from head to tail, others two rows of parallel figures, commonly an arrow or an hourglass-like form with serrated ends. These designs were drawn with a bit of buffalo hip-bone dipped in water; the arrows were painted with black earth, and white clay was rubbed into the rest of the robe. The hourglass figures were painted with blood or the juice of a red flower. Occasionally pictographs of battle exploits were used by famous warriors (Figure 20), but figures of supernaturals were drawn only on ceremonial shirts, never on robes. Women's dresses were bordered with beads or quillwork and often scalloped or decorated with felt and fringes. Brass beads, shell gorgets, and necklaces of elk teeth and bearclaws formed adornments. As with the Woods Cree, tattooing was practised. It consisted of three chin lines and round marks on the cheeks and foreheads of the women, and parallel lines or rows of dots on the bodies of the men. The Plains Cree used both birchbark containers and leather bags, and both made Plains paraphernalia, such as shields, and Woodlands equipment, such as snowshoes.

In addition to the quill and beadwork methods described above, the Plains Cree used a bow loom for beads, with a warp of ten strands making possible the production of long strips of beadwork. Horsehair was used too; a hank of ten hairs was tacked to the leather surface by a stitch, doubled over and wound with coloured hair, then stitched at short intervals so that it looked like a round coloured cord. This method was used for moccasins.

Paintings of spirit helpers were put on drumheads, *tipi* covers, and shields. The designs were blocked out in charcoal and then painted, with the spongy end of a bone, in red ochre or coloured earths mixed with grease. The woman of the family actually owned the *tipi*; she gave permission to her spouse to paint representations of his own spirit helpers and those of the man who named him. First, thongs were wrapped around the erected *tipi* to mark off the various levels; then the cover was laid flat so that the men could apply varicoloured paints. Afterwards the *tipi* was set up and a fire built inside. Men and women brought in sweet grass used for its fragrance as a kind of incense for the sacred occasions, and the newly painted *tipi* was filled with feasting, song, and offerings of smoke. A worn-out tent bearing vision designs was taken to the bush, spread out, beaten with a stick, and left abandoned.

When the buffalo life ended, battle scenes came into vogue, but no ceremony accompanied them. A characteristic painting described by David Mandelbaum shows the front opening flanked by rainbows which are surmounted by bird figures. Over the door is the sun face in deep orange, and on the back are rows of woodpeckers, while above them is the thunderbird. The

Plate 5. Embroidered doeskin altar frontal, Cree, St. Thomas' Anglican Church, Moose Factory, Ontario.
Photo: David Norman

A stunning frontal of pure white deerskin, embroidered in floral
patterns of silk by women parishioners of the Anglican Church, of
which it is a liturgical treasure; it is used for the most sacred festivals of the Christian year.

top zone at the apex is painted brown and represents the sky. The rainbow, which encircles the tent and plunges to earth on each side of the doorway, is painted in yellow, blue, brown, and green. The solemnity and joy which accompanied the paintings of *tipis* suggests their importance in the life of those who lived inside.

The Blackfoot, who named themselves for the colour of their moccasins, were divided into the Blackfoot or Siksika, the Blood, and the Piegan, who were mostly located in the United States. They were a vigorous and aggressive group allied with the little Athapaskan tribe, the Sarcee. Like the Assiniboine they were buffalo hunters who used skin tents and roved continually, moving with the aid of dog and *travois*. They had military societies and dance societies, and paid considerable attention to ceremonial objects. To them the sacred medicine bundle was the centre of the Sun Dance, despite its spectacular self-sacrifice, and they revered the ceremonial pipe and its bundle as well. They painted tents, war shirts, and shields (Figure 21), all according to the visions of their owners; the painting had spiritual power only if accompanied by narratives of the vision-story and singing of sacred songs. It was the owner's perpetuation of the original sacred experience that kept the power alive, not simply the object alone.

The *tipi* represents an adaptation of available materials to a life of nomadic movement; it is ventilated, comfortable, and arranged conveniently on the interior. Walter McClintock, writing in 1910, describes the "white city" of hundreds of resplendent white *tipis* gathered clan by clan

in a great circle for the Sun Dance ceremony. He quotes George Catlin as saying that six hundred lodges could be taken down in one minute, to be loaded speedily upon waiting horses and dogs. The Blackfoot painted their *tipis* with prominent historical events of the tribe, and with religious symbols, associated with medicine bundles and concomitant ceremonials, and ultimately derived from the dreams invoked by fasting and loneliness. These were personal to the owner; when an old *tipi* cover was to be abandoned, McClintock says, it was spread out on a lake to sink as a sacrifice to the sun.

The medicine bundle *tipi* is a shrine containing a reliquary, and as such has a name. The Yellow Buffalo Tipi had upper and lower zones of black, representing the night sky, bearing numerous white discs, depicting night with its stars (at the top), and earth with its puffballs (at the bottom). Two yellow buffalo occupied the central zone. The Cross Stripe Tipi bears a wide strip of paint around the middle.

The Yellow Buffalo Tipi, with all its details, was made according to the form prescribed by a divine Buffalo in the same tone of specific command used by Yahweh in ordering the form of another tent, the Tabernacle of the Ark in ancient Israel. The account of this particular medicine *tipi* was recorded by Father de Smet, a nineteenth-century Roman Catholic missionary to the Blackfoot. The paintings were done with buffalo bone pencils, which were porous and absorbent, one per colour. Outlines were first marked on the surface with willow sticks dipped in a liquid of white hide scrapings. Then earth pigments were

Figure 21. Buffalo hide shield, Blackfoot.

Shields were decorated according to their owners' visions and had
spiritual power if the painting were accompanied by narrations of
the vision story and singing of sacred songs. This shield is adorned
with a ring of perfect feathers, and its displayed form is the same
as that shown on the painted jacket in Figure 20.

used. Yellow clay was dug, worked to smoothness, and roasted on hot coals to the red powder used for the sacred red ceremonial paint. Black from charred wood, green from scum on a lake, and yellow from earth or buffalo gall were also used, being kept in little bags. About one-tenth of a full three hundred and fifty lodges encamped for a Sun Dance were painted.

The *tipi* seems to have been considered as a symbol of the cosmos. The lowest band, representing the earth, was dark, containing a row of discs called "dusty stars"—representations of the puff balls found on the Prairies, which for the Blackfoot marked the position of a fallen meteor. The top line of this region might be scalloped to represent hills or mountains. The central space held the protective animal or other spiritual entity, and pictographic records of public events. The topmost zone, including the ears, was painted black to show the night sky, and contained white discs (for various constellations) or the sun and crescent moon. The Morning Star was represented by a Maltese Cross.

Early observers record the strong impression made by these vivid religious structures which gave outward and visible sign, in Plains cultural terms, to an inward and spiritual grace. The outwardness and display characterizing both religious and social institutions of West Coast and Prairies culture during the period when they could be observed by whites may be related to the great esteem in which these cultures are held. This esteem is greater than that accorded the inward and individualistic cultures of the Athapaskans

and others, whose lodges were strictly utilitarian in appearance.

The presence of the fur traders, according to Oscar Lewis, contributed directly to the enlargement of Blackfoot *tipis* (as well as of buffalo corrals), just as had occurred with the introduction of the horse. In the 1830's the fur trade brought riches and men could have more wives, and their added assistance increased polygamy. The possible tent size increased from six to twelve skins—room for six to twelve people. The rich had *tipis* of up to twenty skins. There were even a few of forty skins that held a hundred people.

Besides this relative gigantism, another effect of trade was the disappearance of pottery. Observers had seen pottery being made in 1774, fifty years after the coming of the horse, but the easily transported iron kettle brought by the traders gradually replaced the rather fragile clay vessels. Rabbit-skin robes and basketry also disappeared because of the competition, though native skin-dressing arts continued into the reserve period (Figure 22). Today hide clothing is made for commercial and ceremonial purposes only.

Allied to the Blackfoot were the Sarcee, an Athapaskan group who began coming to the trading posts in the last decade of the eighteenth century. The Sarcee were always a small tribe, frequently at war with their formidable neighbours, the Plains Cree, and continuously under the scourge of smallpox. The surviving group resembled the Blackfoot in culture, though continuing to speak an Athapaskan tongue; they had a democratic society and practised the Sun

Plate 6. Buckskin pouch with moose-hair decorations, Huron, c. 1775-1825.

This pouch may have been modelled after the European shoulder-strap bag of the eighteenth century. It is richly embroidered with motifs suggestive of floral forms in a symmetrical design of dyed moose hair, a very meticulous technique because of the shortness of the hair "threads" involved.

Dance. They used medicine bundles, ceremonial shirts, war bonnets, and painted tents, which as elsewhere bore designs originating in dreams, and were accompanied by songs, pipe, and sweet grass smoke offerings. A characteristic design described by Diamond Jenness is a "bee tent," with recognizable bees and abstract symbols for hive and comb.

The painted blankets of the Sarcee used extremely conventionalized images and symbols which helped in the recitation of war deeds at the Sun Dance. These include a recognizable horse-tail to symbolize a captured horse (*metonymy* again), and a vertical zigzag line under an over-arching arc, well suggesting the movements of a scout. An interesting object of public display was the elaborately feathered and braided stick, a trait found among the Plains Cree as well; it was attached to the top of the *tipi* at a dream's command.

The Plains-Ojibwa (Bungî) are a small group, now living on reserves in southern Manitoba, along the Assiniboine River near Portage La Prairie, who speak a variety of the Ojibwa language. Alanson Skinner says they relate themselves to the Ojibwa as the Assiniboine are related to the Sioux; they are "Ojibwan" as the Assiniboine are Siouan. He did not consider them the same as the Saulteaux. They are a Woodland people who adapted to Plains life, coming out onto the Prairies of their own volition to hunt the buffalo. Their participation in Plains-style *coup*-counting and other war practices found expression in symbols; eagle feathers worn to symbolize war honours were cut into patterns and painted to indicate various deeds.

Honoured warriors who had captured horses could paint horse's tracks on their tents and clothing. The breech-cloth of an *Okitcita* ("strong-hearted one," an honoured warrior) is preserved, with symbols of valour; a circle surrounded by outward-pointing triangles shows the enemy camp circle, a straight row of the same design shows the enemy lodges, and three rows of horse-hoof shapes show the stolen horses. A cloth shirt made on the model of earlier leather shirts was ornamented with *Okitcita* paintings, including red hand-prints to show where the wearer had been seized by a Sioux. Sometimes wives accompanied their husbands into war; those who won honours could receive feathers, but they were given to a son or grandson to wear. The soldier's tent was emblazoned with pictures of war exploits and especially handsomely furnished inside, with triangular backrests made of willow sticks and draped with buffalo robes.

Lances and wands with symbolic crests were additional honorific objects. Most war parties were small, "semi-private enterprises" called by persons who had propitious dreams. This religious element was also expressed in the war charm, which served in place of the medicine bundle typical of Plains culture. It was formed of the skin of an animal — a fox, wolf, or coyote — slit down the back and worn like a poncho; the skin was that of the wearer's dream guardian. The Sarcee also made small beaded and furred containers for spirit rocks and other sacred objects of private ownership were also made.

Sometimes a man dreamed of *Pagûk*,

Figure 22. Blackfoot girl wearing painted hide robe over beaded dress.
Photo: The National Museum of Canada

Native skin-dressing arts continued into the reserve period, and beadwork was adapted and used in a decorative manner. This little girl's dress is adorned with a bold floral pattern in beadwork and further enriched with rows of shells. Her robe is painted in the traditional geometric style that preceded the use of representational figures. She also wears flower-patterned moccasins.

the Skeleton Being, who gave him the right to be a cannibal dancer. The *Windigokan* thus privileged made a costume of rags and a mask with a huge beaked nose, daubed with paint. He and his associates, similarly masked, bore canes decorated with owl feathers, and green branches to which coloured cloth strips had been tied. Through singing, dancing, and rattle-shaking, they cured the sick. Humour and mockery formed a part of the performance as recorded by Skinner.

A few other Plains people were found in Canada, including some of the Gros Ventre (part of the Arapaho, but similar to the Blackfoot in culture) and a few Sioux who were refugees in Canada after Little Big Horn. Boulder mosaics are found from western Iowa and Nebraska to Manitoba, most often in South Dakota. The most extensive site has already been discussed. Some of the boulder mosaics found in the Prairies and Plains are made of boulders about a foot in diameter (or less) forming outlines, on elevated sites, of humans, turtles, and snakes. They are found both with *tipi* circles—the rings of stones used to keep the skin coverings in place and left behind when the encampment moved on —and by themselves, far from signs of habitation.

Some take the form of "medicine rings," large circular arrangements from which additional rows radiate, and some of the rings identified as *tipi* circles are probably really medicine rings. When a *tipi* is taken down, the stones used as weights are simply left wherever they roll, like the remains of a picnic from which the cloth has been snatched, and do not form a precise pattern; a medicine circle, unless disturbed,

is more carefully arranged. Some of these boulder arrangements are thought to be comparatively recent, but not sufficiently so to be within immediate human memory. Some reach a considerable size, so that the form of a human sprawls outside of camera range. They are an early kind of "earth art," reminding the viewer of the effigy mounds of prehistoric Amerindian cultures.

The Prairies, too, have produced contemporary artists. Hugh Dempsey has described the evolution of Gerald Tailfeathers, perhaps the best known of Canadian Indian artists. Born near Standoff, Alberta, in 1925, he is a Blood, the grandson of a Northwest Mounted Police scout, Tailfeathers-Around-His-Neck. His uncle was a self-taught painter of Indian and western scenes, and also of traditional "pictographs," showing tribal war experiences. This is the same range still encompassed by Tailfeathers' art. He came under Anglican influence at St. Paul's residential school, but was not happy there; still, he was allowed to do art work. In 1935 he went to an art school in the Rocky Mountains, where he developed his interest in Indian history and culture. He received encouragement from several mentors and gradually developed a vocation as an artist; one adviser suggested that he "Anglicize" his name to Gerald T. Feathers.

At the age of sixteen he completed his education under government auspices, but in 1941 he received a scholarship to the Banff School of Fine arts, where he encountered W. J. Phillips, the Canadian water-colourist and printmaker, whose meticulous style much impressed him. Phillips was again his teacher at the Pro-

Plate 7. False Face Society Mask, Onondaga, Six Nations Reserve, Ontario.

The False Society Mask often depicted the Great World Rim Being,
whose face was twisted in pain because his nose was broken in an
encounter with the Creator. This expressionist image was carved in
poplar wood. The eyes are brass plaques and the mouth is provided
with deer teeth. A full head of horse-hair completes the face, which
is painted.

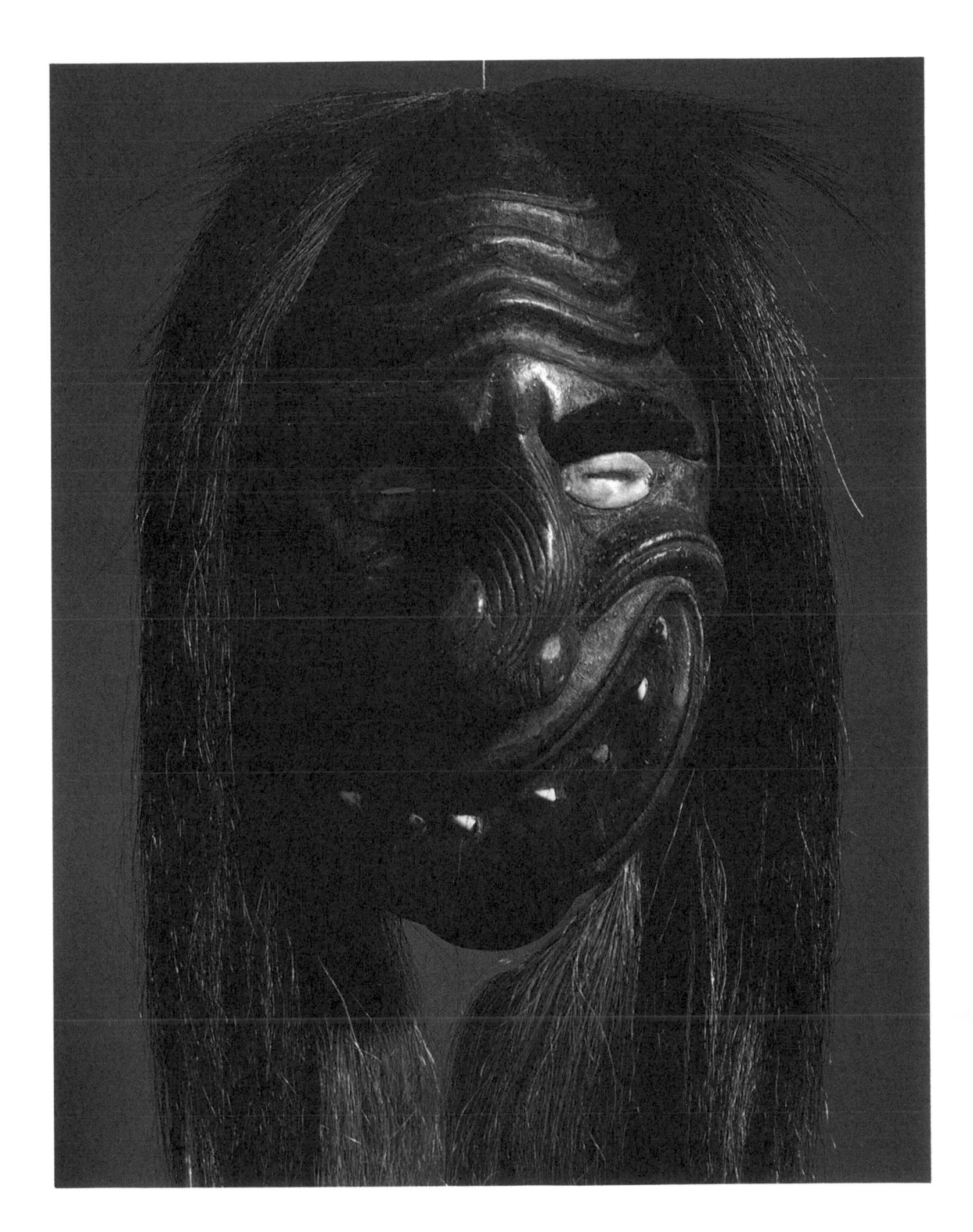

vincial Institute of Technology and Art in Calgary. Another stylistic influence, that of Charles Russell, the cowboy artist, is noticeable in many of Tailfeathers' studies of western life. Frederick Remington and Will James can be detected as well.

In 1944 he completed his program at the Institute and began a career of city life as a commercial artist and draughtsman, taking up tempera as a medium. During this relatively dry creative period, he came in contact with the Indian Association of Alberta. The breakthrough for his career came in 1956 with the beginning of his association with the newly formed Glenbow Foundation, where he began to work in pen and ink, a medium in which he has perfect control. During the 'fifties his work became increasingly prolific, and in 1958 he began to use a style based upon that of Indian artists in the American Southwest, a conventionalized "Indian art" style which he uses with facility. The Canadian postage stamp which reproduced his work was executed in this style.

In the flush of his success he undertook to build a house in Calgary, only to learn that the price of a down payment might be his own loss of Indian status. After eighteen years in the city, he returned to the Reserve in 1959. He began to sign himself as "Tailfeathers" and became more and more active in Indian affairs. His work is now widely collected and exhibited in North America. He has become active in Blood religious and tribal life, participating in the Sun Dance ceremonies and creating, out of the eclectic influences which well express his life experience, a strong record of Indian history and life.

Figure 23. Birchbark vessels and wooden dishes, Chipewyan, Dogrib, and Slave.
Photo: The National Museum of Canada

Beautifully formed utilitarian objects have an aesthetic element, and a
high degree of technical achievement in objects entirely hand-made
is characteristic of Amerindian artefacts. These birchbark and
wooden vessels are of Athapaskan make from the Western Subarctic.
Note the vari-coloured binding on the rims and the decorative use
of the triangle in borders.

Chapter 5

People of the
Western Interior:
Subarctic
and Plateau

Figure 24. Netting needles, arrows, bow, and beaded gun case, Slave.
Photo: The National Museum of Canada

The Slave are noted for their use of decorative fringing, shown here in the gun case, with its beaded floral designs on velvet bands. The fringes are of carefully slit leather and coloured stroud formed into knotted tassels in varying hues. The slender tools and weapons are gracefully shaped, precisely adapted to their functions.

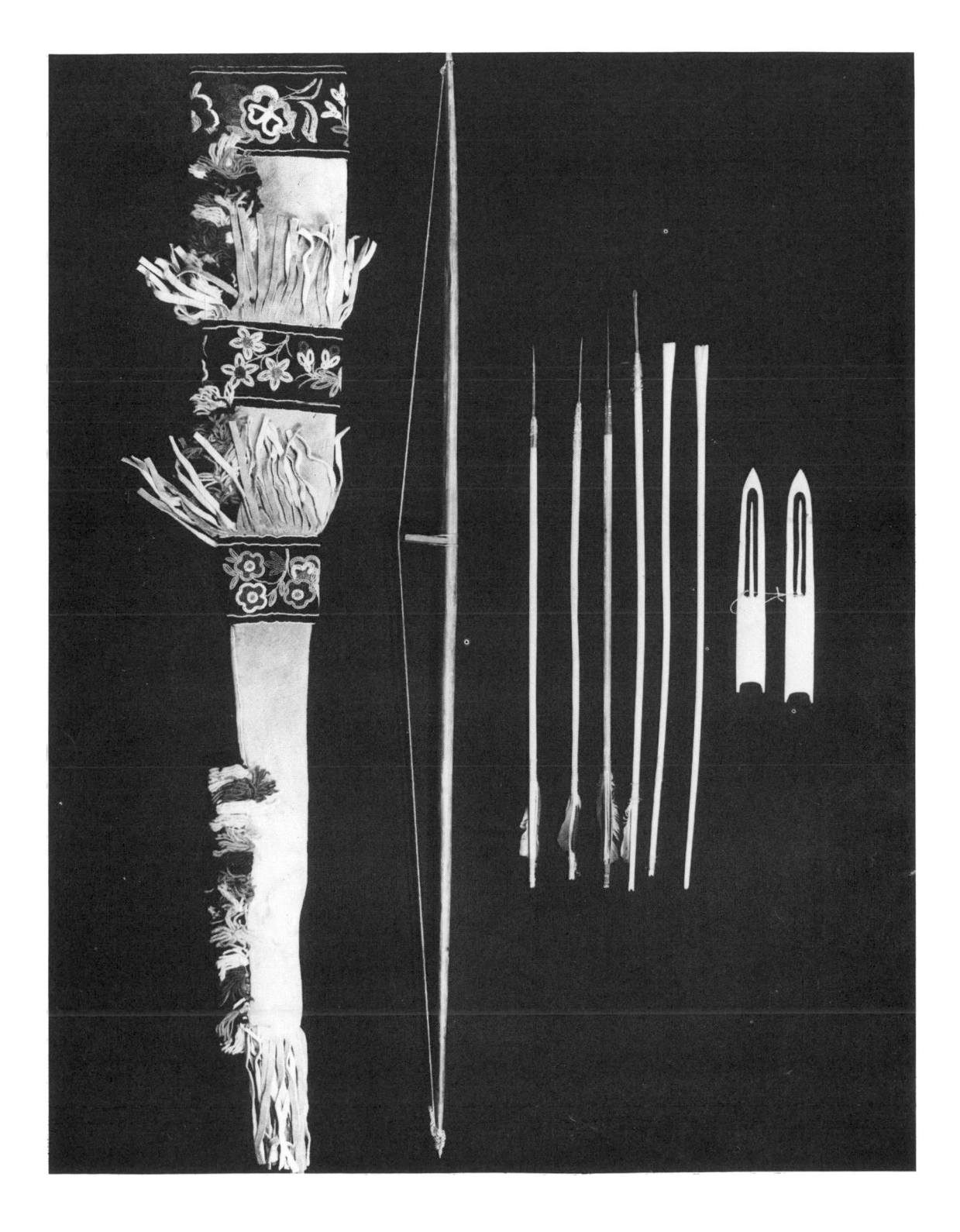

The Athapaskans, who called themselves *Dené*, "the People," share a language stock that may be distantly related to the Tibeto-Chinese-Siamese language group of Eastern Asia. They are the latest arrivals among North American Indians, and in the American southwest the Navajo and Apache speak Athapaskan languages. In the western Canadian Subarctic they live on the basins of the Mackenzie and Yukon Rivers, and they share the area called the Cordillera or Plateau with the Interior Salish and Kootenay. As already mentioned, their southernmost group, the Sarcee, is considered a Prairies tribe because of its nearness to the source of its borrowed culture. In the main, however, the Athapaskans in Canada are woodland peoples who stay away from the treeless arctic seacoast and the forbidding "barren lands," where they go infrequently to hunt the caribou. Although a few are found beyond their region as incursions taking on the culture where they settled, most stayed on the basins of the two great northern rivers.

Southernmost of the Athapaskans, except for the Sarcee, are the Sekani, who live in a group of bands in a wooded country along the river valleys. The Sekani made handsome robes of groundhog skins and wore embroidered mitts and moccasins decorated with beads in floral designs which, though simple, are strikingly attractive. They formerly used *dentalium* shells traded from the coast.

Before trade goods appeared in great numbers, the Sekani made implements of wood and horn, and spruce baskets, boiling their meat in waterproof wooden boxes as West Coast peoples did. They also made wooden dugout canoes and a wide assortment of elegantly fashioned nets, snares, and deadfalls as well as snowshoes. Their skin clothing was often decorated with quillwork but they also used paint extensively, on both their clothing and their bodies. Sekani women drew a black stripe across the entire face just below the eyes. Red clay was used to symbolize a festive occasion, ochre for mourning or grief, and charcoal for anger or war; all were mixed with grease and kept in skin bags hung around the neck. Nose and ear ornaments of bone, shell, or goose-quill adorned the faces of the wealthy. Their religion consisted primarily of the vision quest, for to them animals had power that men might seek to possess.

Their neighbours, the Beaver, probably had a similar culture, but under the incursion of the Cree, who drove them back from some of their earlier areas, they took up many Cree practices. The Beaver, having no great interst in the buffalo, hunted the moose, caribou, and beaver; hence their name. They made their tents of caribou skin and used toboggans and spruce-bark canoes. In early days they made containers of spruce-bark too; birchbark was a more recent acquisition. Tools combined wood with flint, moose-horn and beavertooth. Like other Athapaskans they had no central tribal organization but moved about in independent bands. Their religion combined some Sekani-like elements with some resembling those of the Cree.

The layout of a Beaver encampment provides an interesting insight into the way space was created and organized. Winding paths connected the lodges, which often

Figure 25. Baby-carrying straps, beadwork (flowered) and quillwork (geometric), Fort Nelson Slavey.
Photo: The National Museum of Canada

The range of Athapaskan ornament is illustrated here. The extremely detailed woven quill band has characteristic geometric motifs of lozenge, triangle, and zigzag in a design of great intricacy, and the black velvet band embroidered with glass beads has a rich floral pattern of curvilinear form using masses of colour.

faced one another in pairs. Women and children travelled the paths, but they never walked behind the lodges, between the medicine bundle and the forest. Only a child on a vision quest went there, or a man going hunting, according to Robin Ridington.

In the eighteenth century, the largest Athapaskan group was the Chipewyans, called "pointed skins" after the form in which they dried animal skins (Figure 23). After the Hudson's Bay Company came to Churchill in 1717, the Chipewyans pushed the Eskimo eastward and pressed against the Yellowknife and Dogrib in the West. Although their numbers today are somewhat smaller, they still occupy their original territory. Diamond Jenness describes them as "edge-of-the-woods" people; they hunted caribou over a wide range, taking other animals when they had to, moving out onto the Barren Grounds in summer. As is frequently said of Athapaskans, the people of the Chipewyan led a challenging life; the women endured the heavy labour of transport while the men ranged widely, often alone and fasting, in search of caribou. The hide of the caribou was especially esteemed, and the guardian spirit quest was the centre of Chipewyan religion. The Chipewyan had many borrowed traits such as tattooing and birchbark canoes that, along with certain ceremonies, they shared with the Cree.

Certain aspects of their non-material culture, such as their songs and stories, perhaps tell us more about the life of the Chipewyan than does a catalogue of their material culture. Such an impression was gained by the present writer, in talking with a young legal secretary, bilingual in Chipe-wyan and English, originally from a small town in the region north of Edmonton. She remembered her grandmother searching for the plants and barks used in dyeing, storing them in little sacks, preparing them and making elaborately decorated objects of moosehide, which she regularly gave away. She also recalled the numerous stories her grandmother told of the mythological and spiritual realities of Chipewyan life. The same young woman, who was shivering in an early Ontario autumn, recalled hunting trips through the western bush with her grandfather, spending the nights in a shelter constructed in the snow. But, "we weren't cold then," she reported. She described the recent re-emergence of native religion and thought, and of renewed interest in traditional crafts as well. Her description of her grandmother conveyed an impression of serenity, affirmation, and psychic integration, and she herself, poised in exquisite balance upon two cultures, conveyed a similar impression.

Yet Diamond Jenness describes Chipewyan art as being "confined to some crude paintings on wood and a little 'inferior' work in porcupine quill and moosehair. . . ." The Chipewyan came into considerable contact with whites and were usually unfavourably contrasted with the Prairies tribes. Because of their numbers and expansionist tendencies, they had plenty of enemies to help increase their unpopular reputation among other Athapaskans, too. This habit of making judgements about the relative merits of various tribal groups seems increasingly meaningless in the contemporary context, and the artefacts actually preserved from early periods of Atha-

Figure 26. Blanket with button designs, Nahani.
Photo: The National Museum of Canada

Much influenced by the Pacific Coast groups who lived immediately
to the west, the Nahani people used characteristic West Coast forms
in art. Here an eagle design is worked in mother-of-pearl buttons on
the surface of a trade blanket to make a splendid robe; the shell
buttons from European trade replaced an item of aboriginal trade, the
abalone shell.

paskan culture are as handsome, in their geometrical ornament, as those of other cultures around them. A Chipewyan knife and sheath, the sheath richly decorated with quillwork, gives evidence of this (Plate 9).

There are five unusual knives in the Royal Ontario Museum collection, and the National Museum of Canada has two more. Five of them have two outward-flaring spirals at the proximal end which have been called "antennas." The other two knives have an "antenna" that is not a true spiral. All are made of native copper with the handles wrapped in strips of hide. The effect of the whole is extremely graceful, with the paired spirals suggesting the volutes of an Ionian column, an impression enhanced by the facets on the surface of one side of the blade.

Similar knives have been reported among many Alaskan Indian groups (all Pacific Drainage Athapaskans), the Tlingit, and the Mackenzie Eskimo, and it is conceivable, according to Edward S. Rogers, that three knives reported from the Barren Lands in 1894 came from the Mackenzie Valley Athapaskans. Those in the collections are attributed by Rogers to eastern Alaska, the northern Yukon Territory, or the immediately adjacent part of the Northwest Territories. He thinks they were made in the last half of the nineteenth century. Such knives were used by both men and women for all sorts of taking and cutting up of game and fish, and were sharpened only on the faceted side. Rogers considers the form to be wholly North American, and of prehistoric invention. One knife, probably of Tlingit origin, has a bird's head instead of a single or double spiral. No conjectures are given as to the possible background or meaning of the very striking spiral design.

As suggested above, some Chipewyans have experienced extensive contact with white Canada; one of these is Alex Janvier, born on the Le Goff Reserve in Alberta. He attended the Alberta College of Art in Calgary for four years, and after experiencing difficulty in finding work as an artist, he returned to the reserve. His first one-man show was held at a gallery in Edmonton in 1964. Janvier works with success in contemporary styles, based upon his training in the abstract methods which were current when he was in art school; an early work of his is completely Abstract Expressionist, as was that of other young painters of the day. As a mature artist, he has begun to produce highly original strong, sinuous, hard-edge works of considerable power, with curvilinear forms suggestive of beadwork.

Similar to the Chipewyan in dialect and other traits, but retaining an identity as an independent tribe, were the Yellowknife; they pressed against the Slave, Dogrib, and Hare, camping in skin *tipis* and hunting along the edge of the woods and out onto the barren lands. When the Dogrib ultimately overthrew them in 1823, they amalgamated with the Chipewyan.

The Dogrib, who were able to turn on the Yellowknife after the expansionist Cree and Chipewyan had withdrawn due to smallpox, have been expanding ever since, though they are not a large number even today. One thinks of tiny Israel rising up after the mighty Assyrians, who "swept down like a wolf on the fold," were laid low by the angel of disease. The Dogrib

Figure 27. Full ceremonial costume, Carrier, Hagweigate, B.C., 1927.
Photo: The National Museum of Canada

The decorated ceremonial costume was part of the hereditary property of the Carrier upper classes; its three parts were the headdress, the neck-encircling breast plate, and the garment. This man's garment, decorated with buttons, bands of *appliqué*, and a belled fringe, represents an adaptation into trade good materials of the earlier tanned hide, *dentalium* tassels, and caribou hooves.

were both woodland and edge-of-the-woods people who were especially partial to the caribou but did not care to stay on the Barren Grounds for long.

Northernmost of the sequence of peoples who lived on the eastern edge of the Athapaskan range are the Hare, who lived somewhat timidly with their neighbours, the Kutchin, the Yellowknife, and the Eskimo. Their life resembled that of the Dogrib and the Slave. They relied to some extent on the caribou but were especially dependent upon the hare, from which they took their name. The hare was both food and clothing; their garments were decorated with rabbit fur, having little other ornamentation. Their rites were like those of the Dogrib but their shamans let themselves be hung in the air to communicate with guardian spirits.

Occupying the centre of this huge and relatively inaccessible area were the Slave. Pushed back from the Great Slave Lake by the advancing Cree, they themselves in turn pressed upon the Nahani, although Jenness refers to the Slave as a "peaceful, inoffensive" people. Other tribes feared their prowess at witchcraft. They never went out on the Barren Grounds, hunting the caribou and moose in forests and along rivers, often using snares, and did considerable fishing in the ubiquitous rivers. Their clothing, which will be discussed in more detail below, was heavily fringed with lavish embroidery in moose hair and porcupine quill. They made elaborate headdresses of claws as well as many kinds of quill jewellery, and practised stone-cooking in spruce-bark vessels. Having a loose social organization, they sought spirit guardians and regarded sorcery as the chief source of illness and death.

Theirs was a culture centred upon game. In a hard land where scarcity was a constant danger, prestige was derived from hunting, and cannibalism, which they abhorred, was an ominous spectre. The second centre of concern in a land of cold was fire.

The Slave still use fringes of red and blue stroud, rickrack, and fur in decorating parkas, according to June Helm. Other objects that are fringed, beaded, or embroidered are moose-hide gun cases (Figure 24), black velvet ammunition pouches, and the bags and straps used for carrying babies. Preparation of the moose hide and the more delicate caribou hide is, as everywhere, a lengthy and painstaking process involving the use of both bone and metal tools.

Alden Mason describes the various methods of embroidery used by the Slave craftswomen (Figure 25). Their moccasins and moose-hide gloves are decorated in floral designs with beadwork, dyed horsehair, and silk thread, though interestingly enough, dyed porcupine quills have made a comeback as well. For horsehair embroidery, six or seven strands of hair are soaked in water and twisted by rubbing them between the fingers into a single strand. Moccasin uppers were specially decorated with a floral centrepiece bordered with crossed stitches.

Silkwork is done with a needle in chain stitch on white doeskin; modern beadwork, with beads strung on thread and sewn in

Figure 28: Couple in *appliqué* garments, Tahltan.

Photo: The National Museum of Canada

The woman wears a richly furred cloak with decorative panels; the man's upper garment has bold designs in *appliqué* featuring large, clear animal forms facing one another. There is a suggestion of the double-curve motif in the central panel, and the sleeves also recall certain Woodlands motifs. The Tahltan are Plateau people of interior British Columbia.

place, decorates leggings, gun cases, and other articles. Quillwork was confined to geometrical designs only, laid on with thread in a woven pattern or else flattened and folded each around each. Perhaps the most typical of Athapaskan decorative motifs is the simplest form of the Greek Key: the horizontal line below, rising by a vertical line to a second horizontal line above, which then descends by a second vertical line, and so forth, like the crenellation in a castle wall. These techniques are supplemented with coloured yarns and duck scalps—bird-skin with the iridescent feathers still attached—to offer a considerable range to the Slave needlewoman.

Other arts were not especially developed —there was no carving or sculpture—but *tipis* were painted with a thin band around the middle. Canoe bows were also painted with some "manifestation of 'medicine'" (as Alden Mason puts it), though without realism or apparent interpretation of the designs. This painting was done with the fingers in pigments of red from red stone and water, black from charcoal, blue from chewed fungus, as well as with other colours from leaves and berries chewed for the purpose. Aniline dyes replace these today

The Athapaskans have adapted regional cultures wherever they have gone. Their own culture is from one point of view relatively featureless and simple, but from another, highly individualistic; every man was his own medicine-man, and men hunted alone and took their own revenge. As seen in the description of the Beaver camp, communal life contained many subtle signals about the meaning of life's activities and the sacredness of the spirit quest. They lived in constant fear of the raiding Cree, of private medicine (from other individuals), and of starvation. They enjoyed considerable freedom, however, and felt themselves in possession of magical power with which to control a vast and difficult environment.

The western border of Athapaskan country contains, from north to south, the Kutchin, the Nahani or Kaska, and the Sekani; still further west on the Cordillera are found, in the same order, the Tahltan, Tsesault, Carrier, and Chilcotin.

The northernmost people, the Kutchin or "Loucheaux", inhabit the basins of the Peel and Yukon Rivers and live in Alaska as well as Canada. Whatever their location, they followed a similar manner of life. They fought and traded with the Eskimos to the north and were much influenced by the Tlingit on the Gulf of Alaska, so that their summer fishing and winter hunting resembled those of their neighbours. Noted for their rich and colourful costume, the Kutchin stood out, like the Plains tribes, in contrast with their drabber Athapaskan relatives. Their leggings had bead or quill bands instead of the bands of coloured skins used by the Eskimo, and their shirts were embellished with long fringes of *dentalium* beads and much embroidery. They lived in an enlarged semi-subterranean version of the domed sweat lodge, made of logs with a moss-covered gabled roof, and covered with a blanket of snow outside and a fir-bough floor within. Such dwellings were very warm, even in the coldest weather. Their life, though hard, was enlivened with games, dancing, and singing;

not much is known of their ancient religion, except that they reportedly revered local spirits and a moon-related deity of the hunt.

During early contact times, many of the earliest eight "tribal" subdivisions died of disease. Theirs is a severely cold land with winter temperatures as low as −50°; everything is frozen, dry, and enveloped in snow. The summers by contrast are very hot and swarm with biting insects. Spruce trees, the chief cover of the land, are central to the culture, followed by the birch, with the willow used as a substitute. Even today the people of this geographically varied land are hunters and fishermen whose economy is tied, through trade centres, to that of the whites.

The Kutchin made snow pictures as messages. A simple set of two ovals representing body and head, with two stick-like legs, is differentiated into a caribou (by horns like the teeth of a comb) and moose (by a line under the chin indicating whiskers). These are obviously pictographs with no aesthetic intention, but they are, like present-day "environmental art," traced in the snow.

In painting, red takes complete precedence, whether plain red from red ochre and water or dark red from the ashes of rotten driftwood. Ochre is taken from natural deposits; the finder places sinew or something else of value there in exchange. Yellow and blue come from ashes and rotten wood. A brush of small shavings is used to apply the paint on all sorts of surfaces, from snowshoes to human faces. The Kutchin had a complete range of words to describe colour, including "shining" for metal and "glossy" for fur, yet they had no

carvings, dying, or rock painting. Besides the porcupine quillwork and *dentalium* beads mentioned above, they also made beads of dried berries. Shell beads seem to have been an item of aboriginal trade, as they were elsewhere, and the *dentalium* formerly served as a nose ornament.

The Nahani people are not very well known because many of them have now disappeared; some went to live with the Kaska after a serious incursion by the Hare about 1886. The Kaska, who lived to the west of the Slave, on the Cassiar River, followed a life like that of the Sekani and other Mackenzie River tribes. They especially coveted the caribou, which they captured with pounds and snares. They made baskets of woven spruce roots and spoons of wood or horn. Their clothing was profusely ornamented with quill embroidery. The quills were woven on a bow loom into bands used for belts and headbands, and garments were further ornamented with fringes of skin and pellets from moose tripe. A paint of red earth mixed with grease or balsam pitch was applied to clothing with the fingers; there were also a blue and a black paint. The common motifs were rather simple hatched or zigzagged border patterns. They also practised face painting and tattooing, and their culture was much influenced by Pacific Coast tribes that lay immediately beyond them to the west (Figure 26).

The tribes of the Cordillera or British Columbia Plateau, separated from the Coast by the mountains of the Cascade Range and from the Prairies by the Rocky Mountains, comprised peoples from a number of different origins. It was, and is, a rugged land, limiting the communication that would

have led to a more uniform culture. At the southern end of the region are the Interior Salish and the Plains-style Kootenay, who spoke a distinctive language. These last had been driven over the Rockies by the Blackfoot in the early eighteenth century and clung to their Prairies life-style in the new area.

The Athapaskans of the Plateau exhibited their usual tendency to take on surrounding cultural colouration. This trait is mentioned so often in discussions of the Athapaskans that one might ask: Perhaps their language, so complex and tonal, is the centre of their identity, so that peripheral changes do not really matter. After all, English speakers are found all over the world, living in a wide variety of life-styles, and wearing many different colours of skin, but their adaptability to cultural variety seems to go unnoticed.

Southernmost of the Athapaskan-speakers in British Columbia are the Chilcotin, an active trading people who lived in a country rich in game and food. Like their Salishan-speaking neighbours, they made rush mats and coiled baskets with imbricated (that is, suggesting the overlapping form of shingles) decorations after the manner of the Shuswap. From the Bella Coola they adapted the use of shell ornaments and cedar-bark headbands. As we have seen, shell is widely used in North America as an ornamental material for the same reasons that pearl buttons, inlays, and other items of rococo style are used in the West; their beautiful forms, and their whiteness, their iridescence, compel the eye, and time does not diminish their lustre. The material is relatively easily worked but not especially fragile. Cedar bark recommends itself because of its versatility, softness, ease of handling, ubiquity (in the western regions), and especially because, while very light in weight, it can be used to create forms of bulk and grandeur.

The Chilcotin lived in earth-covered lodges with walls and roofs of brush and bark. The potlatch and guardian-spirit quest are traits which show their West Coast social and religious pattern. Though their numbers were severely diminished by smallpox in 1862, their descendants still live in the same area, employed as ranchers.

North of the Chilcotin are the Carrier, so named for the widows' practice of carrying the bones of their dead husbands on their backs. They were fishermen, taking salmon in summer and ice-fishing in winter. Their canoes and vessels were made of birchbark, but they had taken the labret, a lip plug, and the Chilkat blanket from the Tsimshian, as well as shell ornaments and copper bracelets, also Coastal traits. Theirs was a stratified society with a few slaves. Early in the nineteenth century Paul Kane visited and painted part of the Carrier group, the Babines, and his paintings show the strong Coastal style of these people. Much of their communal life, including the potlatch and cannibal society, was drawn from the Tsimshian. Disease and reduction of traditional food supplies, including those passed by trade, have severely affected their life-style.

Decorated ceremonial costumes were part of the hereditary property of the upper class of the Carrier. The three parts of the costume were the headdress for men or the coronet for women, the breast plate, and

Figure 29. Roof of a subterranean house, Interior Salish.

Photo: The National Museum of Canada

The dwelling was entered from a square opening at the apex, down
a notched log. A framework of poles was lashed together over the
circular pit of two or three feet in depth; this was covered with
closely placed poles, and a layer of bark, grass, and earth formed
the exterior. The interior was lined with evergreen boughs and rushes.

the shirt or cloak (Figure 27). The head-dress was a cap of *dentalium* shells strung on human hair ending in tassels, topped with sea-lion bristles. The coronet was a circular band of hide around which wea-sel-skins were held upright by stiff goose-quills or wooden sticks. The breast plate was a crescent of *dentalium* shells strung on braided human hair strands. The gar-ment was of tanned caribou hide decorated with dyed quills, tassles of *dentalium*, and caribou hoofs. Hair used for this ceremonial paraphernalia was cut from the head of a dead woman of high rank.

Much diminished, the Tsetsaut dwindled from five hundred people to three in the nineteenth century. Their culture, like that of the Carrier, was a blend of Athapaskan and Pacific Coast traits.

Also much like the Carrier are the Tahl-tan, who lived in a dry grassland area with little snow and plenty of game and salmon, hunting in winter and fishing in summer. The scarcity of timber prevented them from using the elaborate wood-carving styles of the Coast, and their material industries were rather rough. In compensation, per-haps, they traded extensively for many different kinds of goods with the Kaska and Tlingit. They took part in the slave trade, and in other ways participated in a com-plex and many-levelled society, having, for example, three different kinds of potlatch. They still follow the hunting life, though not in such comfortable circumstances. One could comment glibly on West Coast in-fluence in Tahltan style, but what cannot be known is what precisely West Coast design was like before the development of the extremely sophisticated forms

achieved by metal tools. However, the ap-pliquéd man's costume recorded by an early photographer shows a virile design style featuring large clear animal forms fac-ing one another (Figure 28). *Appliqué* fa-vours but does not compel this clarity of form. The game animals depicted have a "Woodlands" look, and the undulating orna-mental motifs make up in dominance what they lack in complexity. The floral designs are also confronted; indeed, they are al-most double-curve in shape, and have a forceful appearance not usually achieved in beadwork flowers, for instance. Whatever the influences at work here, the result is vig-orous and handsome. The strong interplay of dark and light suggest what a strong effect the colours of the original garment may have achieved.

The Tagish, who are separated from the above groups by an intrusion of the Tsim-shian, speak a Tlingit language. The Nicola, an isolated island of Athapaskan-speakers, also occupied an area among the Salishan, but nothing remains of them and little is known of their life or art.

The Kootenay, though now mountain-dwellers, were probably pushed to their present position in the Plateau region by the Blackfoot early in the eighteenth cen-tury, for they remain essentially a Plains people in culture. As a result of Cree in-fluence, beginning something less that 150 years ago, the Kootenay began to decorate their clothing and cradles with quill and beadwork. They also began to paint their tents and *parflêches* in geometric style. Before this time, they used splendidly tanned hides of pure white, and their de-coration was confined to long fringes on the

Figure 30. Basket, Thompson River Indians, Interior Salish.
Photo: The National Museum of Canada

The basketry designs of the Interior Salish developed into geometric
patterns from natural forms and were adapted to the decorative
field. Many of the patterns are named, and the same designs are used
for baskets made in the present day. Cedar roots, cedar splints,
wild straw, cherry bark are characteristic materials, and the pattern
is achieved by the use of contrasting colours.

seams of garments. In addition, Kootenay hide-dressing sometimes included smoking to reach a desired colour: a fire of rotten firwood and pine cones was used to produce a tan shade, while juniper wood smoke produced a darker colour.

A description given by A. F. Chamberlain refers to profuse ornament of silk ribbon, weasel-fur strips, and owl and chicken feathers. Metal ore, wood, and shell were made into necklaces and ear-rings. Photographs taken by James Teit reinforce this report of elegant attire. The Kootenay also made and decorated vessels of basketry and birchbark. Basketry consisted of coiling bundles of split-root and sewing the coils with a strip of root; geometrical designs adorned the finished product. Birchbark vessels were made with careful attention to finish and regard for symmetry and balance of form. Indian hemp was used to make small bags in twined weaving, in which stained grasses were wound around the hemp warp.

Like other Plains peoples the Kootenay offered prayers and tobacco smoke to the divine as symbolized by the sun, went on the vision quest, and were ministered to by medicine-men. They used a conical Plains *tipi*, covered with painted buffalo hides when they could get them. The salmon that fought their way so far inland made very inferior eating, so in summer the Kootenay continued to hunt for buffalo out onto the Prairies as long as they could. When travelling by water the Kootenay used an unusual canoe, which they shared only with the Okanagan, made of pine or spruce bark. Pointed at each end below the water line,

the vessel was not especially well suited to navigating the rapid-filled canyons.

The use of the sun as an image of the divine is a wide-spread Plains trait, but like other Amerindians the Prairies peoples seem to have been perfectly aware of the distinction between image and spirit; or perhaps, to put it another way, the problem did not arise. Everything in the natural world was a vehicle to divinity; this form of mysticism has been called by some the "affirmation of images." The indwelling of the spirit, according to Amerindian thinking, infused every sort of psychic phenomenon—intuition, dream, vision, inspiration, creative thought, sudden invention, hallucination, hunch, precognition, solemn deliberation, group concensus, solitary meditation, malign and benign desire, wish, daydream, will-power, creative act—and the scope of divine presence in the physical world was equally broad.

This may help to account for the symbolic preoccupation and cursory nature of much of their art. Only on the West Coast (and sometimes on the Prairies) where a social/secular element of public display and prestige competition involved material things for the sake of their materiality, did the art flower in a manner readily appreciated by the West. These art forms demanded attention and were intended to be impressive, and they succeeded in fulfilling these ends. Spiritually oriented art is more transparent, perhaps. And the art of the practical, as we shall see in examining the weaving and basketry of the Interior Salishan, can be humble and beautiful at the same time.

The Interior Salish comprise the Lillooet, the Thompson Indians of the Fraser Valley, the Okanagan, and the Shuswap. The Nicola mentioned above were absorbed by the Thompson River Indians in the early nineteenth century. Westernmost of these peoples, the Lillooet were the middlemen in the trade with coastal groups. Through their agency moved berries, skins, goat wool (these went westward), shells, slaves, and dugout canoes, as well as Coastal ideas, such as a clan system that associated masked dances of clan ancestors and secret society rites. The Shuswap took their social division of noble/commoner/slave from the Chilcotin and Carrier, as well as secret dance societies, but other Interior Salishan had neither clans nor secret societies. They were formed in bands with chiefs and informal councils.

The Salishan lived in underground houses of circular form with a ladder entering the roof; the surrounding earth gave such a dwelling excellent insulation. The placement of the roofing poles is of interest for its pattern; the wooden ceiling of Coventry Cathedral uses a similar motif. Salishan art is in general a simple use of natural material with a Japanese-like respect for primary textures and original colours. To use Japanese aesthetic terminology, there is a *shibui* quality about their art which resembles the skilful rustic simplicity of the finest crafts of the tea ceremony.

The *Kekuli*, the semi-subterranean winter house of the Interior Salish, was built around a circular pit two to three feet deep and about thirty feet in diameter (Figure 29). The framework was made of four sets of poles regularly spaced around the pit; one pole of each set was placed well inside the edge, leaning slightly outwards, supporting a long, slanted rafter leading from the ground outside the pit to the centre. Two secondary supports made a tripod-like foot for each rafter. Horizontal members ran from rafter to rafter at two-foot intervals, and closely placed poles filled in between. The units were lashed into place, the exterior was covered with cedar bark, grass, and earth, and the interior lined with evergreen boughs and rushes: The dwelling was entered from a square opening at the apex, down a notched log.

The Salishan were hunters and fishermen; salmon, deer, elk, bear, beaver, and marmot were their prey, as well as the buffalo, which the Okanagan pursued out on the Plains. Besides the ubiquitous vessels of birchbark, the Salishan made superb baskets formed by coiling, in which the warp is laced around and around in a spiral, gradually rising up the sides, rather than by intertwining a primary structure of ribs. The overlaid designs, called imbrications, produced handsome and strong contrasting patterns of geometric and naturalistic forms. These vessels were so tightly woven that they could hold water, and were shaped sometimes like pots and sometimes like birchbark boxes. These relatively basic forms have been elaborated for the European taste and provide many handsome products for North American collectors. The same art was practised by the Coast Salish. The present writer saw a superb set of these vessels on the upper shelf of a Coast Salish woman's home—her grandmother had made them—of the most exquisite and minute weave, large enough to

hold all the family fishing equipment and a good supply of weaving materials for the convenience of their owner. The designs had gradually darkened with time but were still faintly visible.

The basketry designs of the Interior Salish (Figure 30) have been discussed by Livingston Farrand in his 1900 study, which he based upon baskets obtained in 1897. For him the problems were the development of geometric patterns from realistic representation, and the adaptation, through modification, of the designs to the decorative field. The baskets were made by the Lillooet and Thompson Indians of British Columbia and by the Quinaults of western Washington State. Indians who made or owned the baskets gave the explanations of the designs. Their style is distinctive from other "West Coast" art, not being especially inclined to realistic motifs, but in a geometric style, much like that of basketry styles elsewhere in the world.

Most of the patterns have recognizable names, though some are so old they have lost direct explanation; one such style is called "standing in the corner of the house," because such a basket always held that position in the traditional house. The Thompson Indians as reported by Teit gave the following pattern names: arrowhead pattern, root pattern, butterfly pattern, star pattern, strap ("packing-strap") pattern, zigzag ("crooked") pattern, box ("grave-box") pattern, and eagle pattern. All had the suffix aïst, which means "pattern." Others without the suffix are: snakeskin, snakestrap, rattlesnake tail, grouse or bird tracks, bear tracks, flying geese, fly, beaver, deer, horse, man, hand, tooth, leaf, shell,

stone hammer, comb, necklace, net, root-digger handle, leggings, canoe, trail, stream, lake, mountain, and lightning. This list contains a wide range of elements in Interior Salish life.

To describe an example of these patterns, the "flying geese pattern" is executed with three undulating rows of dark units and looks remarkably like a flying goose in silhouette. The problem of suggesting natural form in basketry is much like that of suggesting it in needlepoint or cross-stitch, and works especially well when the form can be represented as a silhouette. On the other hand, a zigzag form serves as a snake, lightning, and a mountain chain, depending upon its orientation and context. The "fly" pattern consists of numerous close-placed dark spots (produced by the "basket-weave," two rows of dark warp alternating with two rows of light warp, crossed by a light weft) that suggest clusters of flies. Occasionally, human figures appear, very geometricised in appearance. The stone-hammer design accurately reproduces the outline of a Salishan stone hammer, which was used for ceremonial purposes.

Renate Wilson describes the basket makers of the Mount Currie Reserve, where Lillooet women make cedar root baskets. The craftswoman, Mrs. Rose Ross, gathered her own roots, which she pulled out of the ground, cut and gathered together, scraped clean, dried, carefully split, and bound into bundles. Her husband felled a young cedar and cut it into chunks from which he sliced thin splints. The wild straw was cut in even lengths and boiled to turn it white, then tied in bundles and saved. Cherry bark was saved and placed in a rusty iron bucket

Figure 31. Houses with heraldic poles, Haida.
Photo: The National Museum of Canada

In West Coast villages, large wooden houses faced the beach, a few steps above high tide. In front of them stood heraldic poles, used for the exhibition of family crests comprised of symbolic animal and human figures. The tall segmented forms represent hats topped with cylinders showing the number of potlatches or ceremonial feasts given, and give public notice of the splendour and munificence of the owners.

and buried, to darken to a deep brown colour. The bark was later washed, folded, and tied up. Deer hide was traded (for part of the bark) from a woman friend who was a skilled tanner. In making the baskets, the woman kept the split root wet and guided it around the splints with an awl-like instrument. The design was produced by interweaving wild straw of a light colour and the dark cherry bark with the basic splint and root structure. Water-proofing was completed by smearing the basket with a paste of sugar, flour, and water. Mrs. Ross explained the patterns as representing the zigzag of lightning, the tracks of grouse, clusters of flies, flying geese, human figures, and sunbursts, all in clear continuity with the past.

Equally beautiful were the arts of weaving. The wool of the mountain goat or a specially-kept dog was woven into the large *swoh-kwah-tl* or Salishan blanket, a bedcover.

A smaller form made a cloak for cold weather. (The common people wore blankets of cedar bark and cat-tail, which are effectively waterproof but do not make a display.) The blankets were of twilled weave, in white, with a plaid pattern of brown or black wool, according to Oliver Wells' detailed study.

The ceremonial blankets, *s'ah-uhl-log-q,* were made of a combination of twilled and twined weaving, or sometimes entirely by twining; these two methods differ in structure but achieve a somewhat similar appearance. The blankets were distinguished by their fineness, and they were usually coloured as well. The *kah-speel-tuh* or pack straps (tump lines) were woven in part, and braided where they came in contact with the burden, braiding being flexible; materials used included cedar bark, milkweed and nettle fibre, goat wool, and dog hair. Belts and sashes were made of these materials as well.

Another example of fine weaving was the *say-uhp* or dancing apron, which was woven of dog's hair and fireweed-down, as well as of waterfowl-down and wool. The *say-uhp* is something like a breechcloth draped over a belt, and was the only garment worn by the dancer.

A variety of methods of soaking, pounding, and otherwise rendering materials soft and pliable enought to spin or weave, were applied to Indian Hemp, nettle fibre, milkweed fibre, cat-tails, bullrushes, and willow bark; these were used separately, together, or combined with wool or hair. Today some commercial yarn (for tump lines and belts), cotton rags, and commercial twine are also combined with native grasses.

Native dyes supplemented the natural colours of the fibres; black came from boiled hemlock bark or fern roots, yellow from yellow lichen traded to the Coast from the interior, boiled and treated with urine as a mordant (an agent to set the colour). Red was produced by alder bark, brown by hazelnuts. A considerably wider range of natural dyes has been developed in recent years, using native substances with the addition of alum, copper sulphate, chrome, and other chemical mordants.

Goat wool was originally gathered where it was shed, high on the mountainsides, or from the fresh skin of goats killed as game, from which it shed as the skin aged. The fleece contained coarse "guard hairs"

Figure 32. Carved wooden dance chest, West Coast.
Photo: The National Museum of Canada

The adaptation of animal heraldry to the rectangular shape of the
box brings about the characteristic use of the formline. This strongly
calligraphic line was freely manipulated around negative areas,
defined by bark templates that marked the positions of actual
pattern elements (parts of the bodies) in the design, giving grace
and cohesion to the whole.

which had to be removed, and a white clay was used to absorb grease and leave the wool fibres clinging together. Wool thus prepared was spun loosely and later fine-spun with the aid of a spindle. Two strands were then spun together to form a strong warp for blankets. Today a domestic wool is substituted for that of mountain goats, but it is still hand "teased" to make the strands smooth, and spun on a single hand-crafted spinning machine.

Dogs were kept for their hair; those of the Chilliwak were coyote-like with a deep undercoat beneath the longer external hair. This woolly layer was plucked and spun with a spindle, and for fine garments the down of water fowl, milkweed, or fireweed was added during spinning.

The preparation of the bark of the yellow cedar involved stripping the long, soft, fibrous inner bark from ribbons of external bark, boiling it for an extended period, working it with gloved hands to a fully pliable state, and, for fine-spun, pounding and combing it into separate fibres. This method yielded a heavy cord and a fine twine.

The spindles used for turning these materials into yarn bore round pierced forms, frequently decorated. They were heavy enough so that, when the spindle staff was spun or rolled, it would continue to spin, while the spinner fed out fibre from a bunch held in her hand. The yarn was twisted into shape by the spinning motion of the weight. Spindle whorls carry designs adapted to their circular shape; some of them are very elegantly decorated, and their compact form has helped to preserve them.

The twill weave referred to above is formed on a simple framed loom by a weft which goes over two warp strands and under two, and so on, with the next line repeating the same pattern but beginning one thread further on, resulting in a strong diagonal texture. Twined weaving has a straight warp but a weft in which two strands are wound around each other as well as around each warp strand, proceeding in complexity to wrapped twining of three or even four strands. This task is accomplished directly with the fingers or with small shuttles on a simple frame and allows for the creation of elaborate patterns. The patterns are designated by attractive names: Rainbow, Necklace, Cloud, Mountain, Parflêche, Star, Butterfly, Eagle, and Swallow.

In the Plateau region of interior British Columbia, in addition to the arts mentioned above, are a number of rock painting sites that have been estimated to range in date from perhaps three hundred years ago to *circa* 1860. The area of greatest concentration is now occupied by the Interior Salish, Kootenay, and (previously) the Nicola; the chief evidence of white presence is confined to a few horses. The style resembles that of the Ontario pictographs in its simplicity and directness of form, but there are some distinctive motifs, including what may be skeletal figures and sun-faces. There are also some noticeable omissions: canoes are very rare, although the area abounds in lakes. There is the same variation from naturalism in animal forms to abstraction in human and what are presumably supernatural forms.

Figure 33. Argillite dish, Haida.

Argillite, a hard black stone that takes a beautiful sheen, was carved
into objects of display and into exquisite miniatures. This dish,
with inlaid fish designs on the rim, was used for ceremonial feasts.
The surface is minutely carved with curvilinear heraldic designs
and areas of fine hatching. The assymetrical bas-relief figure at one
end is a remarkable feature.

James Teit, the great early ethnologist, attributed the paintings to adolescents undergoing the vision quest, and one may imagine, on viewing some of the highly numinous forms with their wide-staring eyes, the sequence of exercise, purification, supplication, sleep, prayer, fasting, and vigil-keeping which brought about an experience of such intensity.

John Corner discusses the substances used in painting. Most common is red from hematite, with yellow from limonite—when found mixed with clay, these are the "ochres"—and black from charcoal or black earth, and white from burned bone, white clay, or gypsum. Sometimes yellow ochre was baked to turn it red. The importance of red gave its name to the Tulameen River (*Tsulameen*, "red paint"). This pigment was fine-ground with a stone pestle and mortar. Presumably a binder was needed to make the pigment adhere to the rock, and a number have been suggested: fish oil or eggs, bear grease, pitch, cactus gum, blood, and fish-skin glue. Laboratory testing has failed to yield evidence of the actual binder used (if there was one), just as it has failed to do so for Ontario sites. Perhaps the material was formed into a dry chalk and used that way, having first been moistened; grease would have turned the same material into a crayon. Many sites have splatters and dribbles along the side where the paint was apparently tested before being applied.

The subjects depicted include zoomorphic-animal figures, which are true to the actual animal population of the areas, including beasts, amphibians, and birds, and anthropomorphic/human figures, some of whom wield fir branches. The fir branch was used in connection with sweat bathing to increase body circulation (sweat bathing was frequently a ceremonial act), and were also part of a girl's puberty ceremony.

It is difficult to tell whether a humanoid figure represents a human being as such or a spiritual entity, though a male figure armed with a bow and associated with an animal tends to be interpreted as a hunter. In addition to these images, there are celestial signs for sun, moon, and stars, all of them identified because of their resemblance to world-wide symbols for these phenomena. There are some directional signs (arrows, crossroads), some geometric forms so abstract that they cannot be deciphered now, signs suggesting (and identified by Teit as being) mountains, lakes, and rivers, and a number of suitably wriggly insect images. Some of the figures are in the X-ray style, both animals with their internal organs showing, and human figures with prominently scored ribs and staring eyes. One recurrent form, an arc with a short radiating fringe, is called by Teit "unfinished basketry."

Some of the Salishan peoples from the interior moved down the deep river valleys which traverse the Cascade Mountains, and followed them out onto the West Coast; these people, the Coast Salish, form the southernmost body of population in what is the richest of all culture areas in Canada.

Figure 34. Soul catchers depicting the *sisiutl,* West Coast.
Photo: The National Museum of Canada

Shamans made tubes of ivory in which to catch the wandering soul
of one who was in ill health because of its absence; these are engraved with a supernatural two-headed serpent, the *Sisiutl.* The upper
tube is finely engraved and supplies the serpent-heads with teeth
and a separate face in their midst. The lower tube, while simpler, has
been painted and achieves a profoundly ambivalent image in
which the central face is composed of elements which also form
part of the two serpent faces.

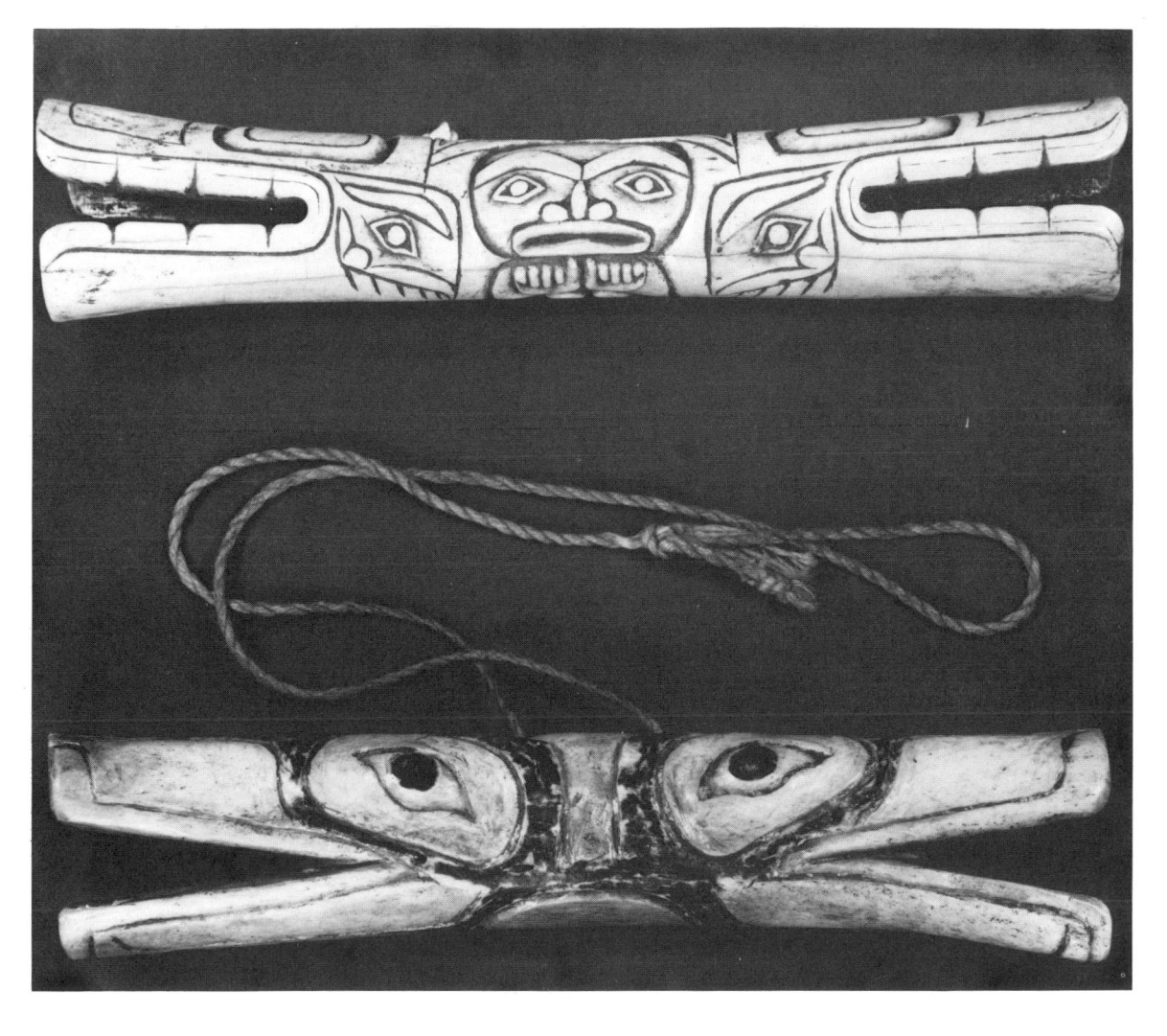

Chapter 6

Lords of the Western Coast

Figure 35. Coppers, Kwakiutl.
Photo: The National Museum of Canada

Coppers are large shield-like forms incised with heraldic motifs and
used as a medium of display and exchange at potlatches; this heap
represents great wealth. Extensive research has revealed that the
nineteenth-century coppers were made of European-manufactured
copper from tanks, ship-hull plating, or domestic utensils, rather than
from the cold-hammered native copper of aboriginal times.

Along the Pacific Coast of North America, from the mouth of the Columbia to southeast Alaska, the sea washes into deep bays and inlets among high mountains heavily wooded with conifers. In the sheltered coves where numerous freshwater streams drained the mountain systems of the Coast were the villages that were the basic social unit of the West Coast Indian. The southernmost and northernmost of these peoples are located within the United States; those between are Canadian.

Although the great museums of the world are bursting with objects of art from this area, very few are earlier than the eighteenth century, when these people were contacted, and most date from the nineteenth. The prehistoric cultures probably built and carved in wood as their descendants did, but in the damp climate these objects soon rotted and returned to the fertile forest wrack from which they came. Only a few stone clubs and vessels survive from the northern and central West Coast. More come from the south of the region.

Objects of stone, especially soapstone, and bone survive, and these give evidence, Wilson Duff says, of high artistic quality in the work of the peoples who lived there between three thousand and fifteen hundred years ago. Cultures of the Fraser River and Gulf of Georgia regions flow into one another just as the river flows into the gulf. Excavations there show two major maritime cultures: the Locarno Beach Phase (three thousand to twenty-five hundred years ago) and the Marpole Phase (twenty-five hundred to fifteen hundred years ago). The small, delicate carvings of this region are found in the Fraser River canyon as well. The style is "Northwest Coast," but Duff suggests that it is ancestral and is not matched exactly by any modern style. This situation is repeated in Eskimo culture, as we shall see.

Besides these little figures of bone, antler, and stone (and one perfectly preserved wooden *atlatl* from the waters of the Skagit River), there is a large group of figures ranging from human forms pecked in igneous stone to tiny animal forms carved in soapstone. Many are vessels; a widespread type is a human figure seated with a bowl in its lap. Of these, the finest are found up-river where the Interior Salish now live. "Northwest" characteristics of these objects are their combination of animal and human forms, emphasis upon the head, and the typical eye form—a round-cornered rectangle or circle for a pupil inside elliptical eyelids, the inner and outer end of which are extended into points. Not all the objects have this eye form, but those that do are instantly recognizable. The X-ray style is also present in clearly shown ribs in some of the objects. Duff agrees with the common suggestion that there was an early climax of West Coast culture in the southern region, followed by a movement of the focus of development to the north.

The life of the peoples in all this region centred upon hunting, fishing, and gathering. In the villages, the large wooden houses faced the beach a few steps above the high tide (Figure 31). Along the grey-pebbled beach rested the rows of canoes, and immediately above were piles of shells and fire-pits. This same arrangement occurs even today in the many Indian "fishing

Figure 36. Carved wooden rattle, Tsimshian.
Photo: The National Museum of Canada

The raven is an important West Coast motif recognized by its characteristic beak. A hawk's head is carved on the raven's breast. On its back lies a shaman whose outstretched tongue extracts a magical substance from the mouth of another animal being. The rattle was used in shaman's ceremonies.

villages" of the Coast, where boats are moored and nets hung on racks to dry in front of smaller houses facing out to sea. The early houses were sixty to a hundred feet long. The framework, composed of the trunks of huge trees covered with equally huge cedar planks, was owned jointly, but the planks were individual property, according to Erna Gunther. Inside, each family had its bed-platform, with the nobility at the far end and slaves near the door. Central fires gave heat and light (and smoke) to the interiors. Ceremonial buildings are still erected in this style and are sometimes referred to as "smoke houses."

In the spring when fishing was an all-consuming activity, the wall planks were taken to form small houses at the fishing sites of each group. Salmon, halibut, and oolichen (used for oil) formed most of the diet, supplemented with wild vegetables, especially roots, and fruit, especially berries. The large canoes, from ten to seventy feet long, were the finest in the world, barring Polynesia, according to Erna Gunther. Several carpenters were needed to shape these enormous crafts. A cedar log was chosen, hollowed by fire, and the space filled with water into which hot stones were put to aid in steaming the wood; wet mats were added for the same purpose. Struts were driven between the sides to achieve the desired flare, and outside and inside were smoothed with an adze. Audrey Hawthorn remarks on the graceful and flowing line of the canoe's form when the prow piece was added; this was used as a harpoon rest and was carved and painted with the family crest.

The third large form made of wood, be-sides the houses and the canoes, was of course the "totem pole." There were three main categories of these objects: the memorial and/or grave pole (mortuary poles); the heraldic pole, for exhibition of the family crest composed of totemic—symbolic—animals; and the interior and exterior house post carved upon the supports of the house. These poles were actually in half or three-quarter round, with a flat back hollowed out to remove the heart wood. The rounded exterior became the surface to be carved, keeping the original shape of the trunk. Projecting forms and recessed sections gave what Paul Wingert calls "expressed diameter" to the basic shape.

The antiquity of the totem pole is discussed by Wilson Duff in his critique of Marius Barbeau. Duff holds that the style of the West Coast has very deep roots. The free-standing pole—the so-called "totem-pole" distinguished by Barbeau from the house-post and house-frontal pole—was present at the very beginning of the historic period. Iron was known and used in prehistoric times, perhaps traded from Asia, for it was used a thousand years ago by Western Eskimos. Duff concludes that even though the nineteenth century saw a florescence of culture on the West Coast, the prehistoric period had already witnessed an intensive cultural development.

The tall, straight-grained cedar provided the extremely long planks used for houses, heraldic poles, and dugout canoes. The solid-grained wood of the alder made excellent food dishes. Maple, close-grained and hard, made spoons; yew yielded clubs and bows. So many kinds of trees were available that special woods were used for

Figure 37. Chilkat poncho of goat wool, West Coast.

Superimposed upon a woven mat of cedar bark, this unusual
garment combines bands of twined weaving, in strong decorative
patterns derived perhaps from traditional basketry motifs, with bands
of plain weaving in which the handspun goat wool is allowed to
create a rich texture.

making fish-smoking fires and still others formed the stakes on which the pieces of salmon were spitted for smoking.

For these various forms of wood-carving, specialists arose. They were recognized artists with additional powers, who trained apprentices and received praise and reward from the community. The pesent writer was able to observe one of these men at work (with a chosen apprentice) – Mungo Martin, in Victoria. His adze swung steadily in a shower of fragrant cedar chips. With that apparently crude tool he made the exquisitely refined and intricately curved and interlocked concavities and convexities of a huge heraldic pole. He worked very rapidly, then paused to consider, sighting, fingering, then correcting the form; obviously a master whose adze was an extension of himself.

The Kwakiutl chief Nake Penkim, known as Mungo Martin, trained many in his superb carving style, including Henry Hunt and his son Tony, Douglas Cranmer, and Bill Reid. The latter has created remarkable pieces of gold and silver jewellery in traditional designs. Not so well known as Mungo Martin's carvings are his paintings, colourful and elegant records of traditional forms. In 1948 he was sixty-seven years old, living at Fort Rupert on Vancouver Island. He held a high position among the Kwakiutl and was a fisherman. In that year he went to the University of British Columbia to supervise the restoration of Kwakiutl poles, and went on to carve new ones. His wife, Abayah Martin, accompanied him and worked as a craftsman too, weaving bark mats, blankets, and Chilkat blankets. During an illness, according to

Audrey Hawthorn's account, Mungo Martin took up water colour and made clear, vigourous drawings and paintings in black, red, green, and yellow, all traditional Kwakiutl colours.

The characteristic West Coast carving tool was the adze. Unlike the chisel, the adze is used by itself in a chopping motion. The blade is axe-like, but set across the plane of the handle rather than parallel with it, something like a little hoe. The writer also watched a much less famous Indian craftsman, standing with a foot on each of two joints of an unfinished floor, bending over and working between his legs on a third joist; you chop towards yourself with an adze. He was rapidly smoothing the surface to a finish as satiny as if he were using a plane. That comparison is slightly deceptive, because the adze leaves a series of delicate concavities like faint fingerprints (they can be very slight, almost like the texture of beaten metal), typical of West Coast carving, as closeups of a pole will reveal. Absolute control is necessary for this work; a white teenager who was also watching this craftsman nearly chopped off his own foot in an attempt to imitate the seemingly effortless motions.

Wood was used not only for monumental purposes, but for other ceremonial heraldic objects as well. Large, decorated wooden screens and other house parts displayed the animals of family crests on the interior of the dwellings. Feast dishes bore similar crests. Masks exhibited extreme sophistication and dramatic effect, and large storage boxes were carved, painted, and frequently inlaid with shell, to contain family possessions.

Plate 8. Prehistoric stone buffalo, Alberta.
Photo: National Gallery of Canada

The culture of the Plains was based upon the buffalo, which provided food, clothing, and shelter, and served as a focus for religious life. The coming of the horse increased the scope and enriched the life of Plains hunters and brought some Woodlands people out onto the Prairies permanently. This elegant equestrian life style ended around 1875, when the buffalo virtually disappeared.

In discussion of the adaptation of animal heraldry to the rectangular shape of the box, Bill Holm points out the characteristic use of the formline (Figure 32). This strongly calligraphic line was produced with a freely manipulated brush around negative areas defined by a bark template, which marked the position of actual pattern elements in the design (parts of the body, eyes, wingtips, etc.). This flowing formline gives both grace and cohesion to what might otherwise be a rigid formula. The supple line swells and diminishes continually sweeping around the curved corners of modified rectangles, imposing an ovoid form of which the top and sides are convex and the bottom subtly concave. The same basic shape becomes the eye, and the wingtip motif when an upward-curved barb is placed at one end and a concave edge on the other. Spaces between major formal elements produce "resultant forms" of such interest that they can scarcely be called negative areas. The areas thus produced are painted in contrasting colours or left bare. Further modification is by texture, either hatching and dashing. This multiplicity of shapes is controlled by the formline and by the absolute avoidance of overlapping. It is a two-dimensional field with the rich surface perfectly maintained.

This West Coast masculine art form can be compared with a feminine art from the same region, weaving, an art practised in a variety of forms. Basketry, of which we have already written, was an art among the Coastal Salish as well as the Interior Salish. As in most other Amerindian societies, the baskets of the West Coast Indians were made by women. The rootlets of cedar or spruce are pliant, slim, and long; with a sharp bone awl they could be split into individual strands. In coiling, a loop was wound around a coil of spiral form and stitched in place through a hole opened by the awl. In twining, the strands were interwoven with the radiating warp, and in plaiting strands were braided together.

Besides wood, other materials of the West Coast are stone, including argillite, ivory, bone, horn, and metal. Objects of stone were tools pecked into shape, ground, and polished to finish. Many of these were replaced by metal, but the mace-like "slave-killer" continued to be made of stone as a ritual form. Also made were mortars, for grinding native tobacco or face paint, and small pipes. Argillite, a hard black stone that takes a beautiful sheen, was carved into exquisite miniatures by shaman-carvers like William Dixon, a Haida whose images of the ska'ages (shamans) in action throw a clear light on this calling; shamanism is second only to public display of wealth in its production of art objects (Figure 33). Another subject frequently depicted in argillite is the Bear Mother, a human woman shown coupled with her bear lover or grimacing in agony as her twin bear-children suckle. One of the latest great masters of West Coast art was Charles Edenshaw.

Shamans worked in ivory too, smooth, warm-hued material that could be formed into a charm, worn on a pendant and frequently inlaid with chips of abalone shell, or a soul-catcher. This was a kind of ivory tube with a stopper in which a wandering

Figure 38. Tsimshian women in Chilkat blanket, Skeena, 1924.
Photo: The National Museum of Canada

Traditionally made by a group of the Tlingit people, the Chilkat robe
is the glory of West Coast weaving. A free-hanging warp of twisted
cedar bark fibres was suspended from a foundation cord and
the weft was twined in small sections to produce a rich, tapestry-like
surface. This stately robe was worn by Hanamuq (Fanny) Johnson,
who also wore a headdress representing "Make the Rainbow,"
and bore a carved wooden rattle.

soul, whose absence was causing its owner to suffer ill health, could be captured by a shaman and returned to its body. The soul-catcher depicted the *sisiutl*, a two-headed serpent (Figure 34), and was often inlaid with abalone, a large iridescent shell of a mollusc traded from the California Coast. Small objects received small sections of inlay but large objects sometimes bore sections several inches across.

Horn was used for social purposes. The mountain goat had small black horns whose graceful curve, enhanced by steaming in a mould, formed a generous bowl with a handle carved into an intricate animal-crest pattern on a reversing curve to its terminal point. This form was used as a spoon for potlatches. Deer and elk yielded slender hollow bones for shaman's equipment. The whale's huge if porous bones were used for clubs, and its vertebrae made stools and masks. The tiny bones of birds made drinking tubes. Ivory came from walrus tusks, which were usually cut up in small pieces.

Before white contact, the main metal worked in Canada was copper, as we have seen. It was traded from the north in malleable lumps and cold-hammered into thin sheets from which gorgets, bracelets, and nose and ear plugs could be made. When sheet copper of European manufacture became available from traders, it was fashioned into the distinctive "copper," a large shield-like form incised with heraldic motifs and used as a medium of wealth-display and exchange at potlatches (Figure 35). A. Couture and J. O. Edwards conducted extensive research to analyze this copper and found it to be typical rolled tough-pitch copper like that used in the past for tanks, domestic utensils, and the hull-plating of wooden ships. This material was fabricated into the characteristic shapes and sometimes cut with a chisel and mended with soldering or riveting. There may have been a cold-hammered counterpart in earlier days, but the art grew, as did most other arts, after European contact. Iron may have reached the Coast through trading before Europeans actually arrived, as there is evidence of iron tools from earlier dates. Gold and silver were also adopted from white traders.

Shell had always been traded, and the mother-of-pearl button became a lively item of trade with Europeans. Buttons were sewn into mosaic patterns on the surface of red or blue Hudson's Bay blankets to make robes and cloaks. Frequently the two colours were combined in complex *appliqué* designs of heraldic crest animals. With the rows of shimmering buttons complementing the design, the effect was sumptuous, as it was intended to be.

The art of painting usually accompanied carving. Most carved surfaces were adorned with paint, not as a repetition of a predetermined plan, but as a second pattern that added to the first. It also existed as an independent art on house fronts and woven mats used as backdrops for dramatic presentations. Woven hats were also decorated with crest designs by women, while the pattern boards from which the Chilkat blankets were copied were painted by men. Earth ochres of red, brown, and yellow were used. Blue from clay or copper oxide and black earth or charcoal added to the palette, which was completed by white

Athapaskan ornament tended in earlier times to be geometric, as
demonstrated by the intricate pattern of checker-board lozenges on
this sheath; the quillwork is applied to create a surface of richness
and brilliance. Animal hair tassels and a length of decorated cordage
enhance the effect.

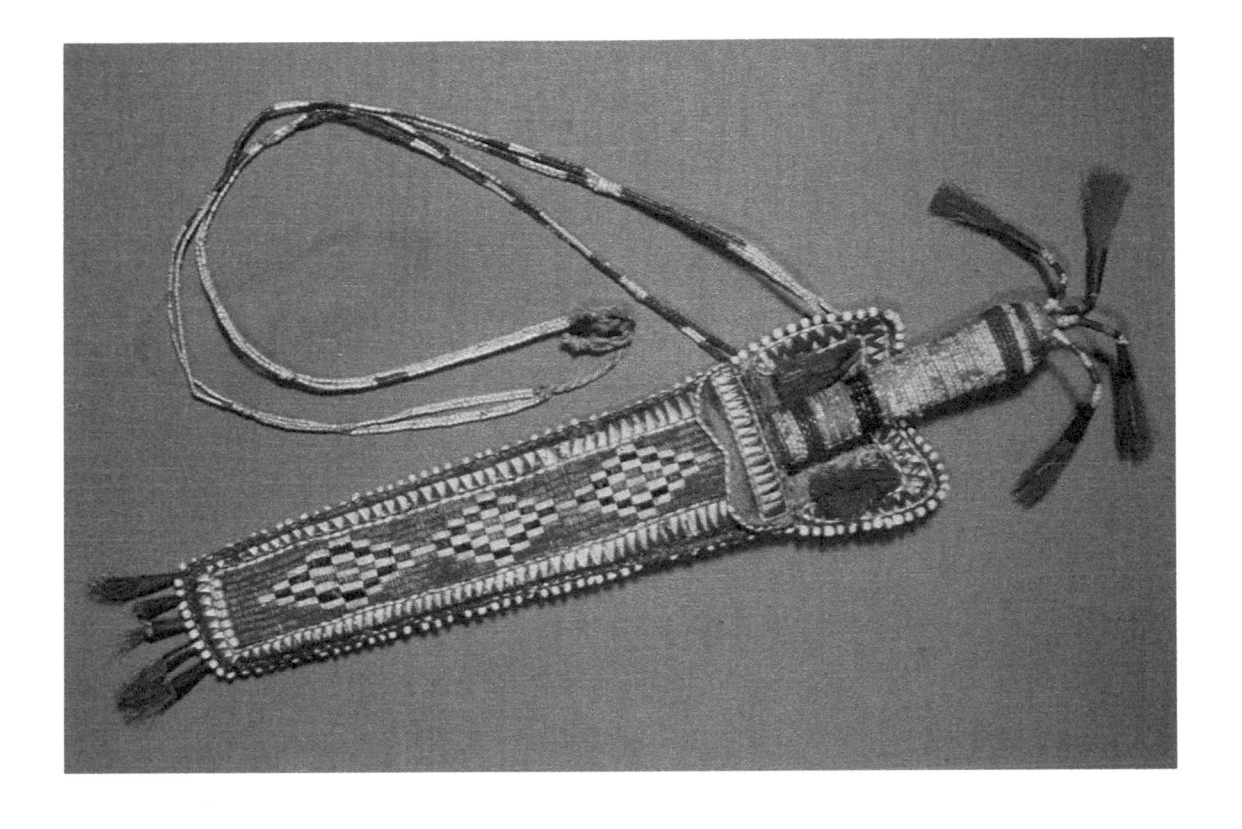

from clamshell ash. These pigments were mixed with oil from crushed salmon eggs. The colours, which are beautiful and subtle when preserved, did not weather well and survive only as traces on old carvings exposed to the weather.

Many laments have been voiced over the loss of the poles, but a potlatch was required when one was erected, so that only a new pole was of interest to the Indians themselves, and an old pole was left to rot. They lay like neglected corpses unwanted by missionary and native alike until rescued by scholars and painstakingly copied or lovingly preserved in museums. Recently, new poles just as perfect as the old ones have been erected with due ceremony. A notable carver is Robert Davidson, a Haida, whose pole in Masset was the first to be raised since 1884. His work and that of others comes from a chain of apprenticeships of which Mungo Martin was the basic link. The number of examples is an embarassment of riches for the writer; which to choose? The present book, like every other on the subject, gives more space to West Coast art than to any other.

As mentioned previously, the images used in West Coast art are both animal and human. A kind of symbolic shorthand is used, in which the most characteristic or diagnostic part of the anatomy identifies the whole. As an Indian artist has said, as reported by Erna Gunther, the image represents not just an animal, but "his spirit." The attitude toward all animal forms—that they are the willing givers of their own lives to aid mankind, and deserve courtesy and respect—helps to explain this practice; the present writer has heard a Salishan

apologize to a salmon he was about to eat. Thus the eagle is denoted by his protruding beak, the down-curving tip of which is usually large, yellow, and strong. The raven, who established world order by stealing the Sun (daylight), holds a pellet (the Sun) in the strong, large beak extending straight out from his face (Figure 36). The beak of the hawk returns toward his face, while the owl's gently curved beak is centred in a broad flat face. The crane has an elegantly curved neck and a long tongue that grows into a human head at its tip. The thunderbird resembles the eagle but has longer talons and a beak with a slightly different curve; he has crest feathers on his crown and the well-known widespread wings.

As for the animal kingdom, the beaver is shown with his whole body sitting up with a stick clenched beneath prominent front teeth and with a scaly tail, marked by cross-hatching, held forward up between his legs. The bear has a distinctive iconography for the brown, the black, and the grizzly, all characterized by a large mouth with heavy teeth and extended tongue; all of his feet are clawed and his internal organs may be shown. The wolf also has a large mouth with prominent teeth beneath a long snout; his head with its erect ears may surmount a little body and long, full tail. The seal and the sea lion are shown naturalistically, with no specific symbols, but the huge erect dorsal fin and large mouth of the killer whale is one of the best-known symbol forms.

The shark is usually shown by his head only, with a large sad face surmounted by a high forehead with three wrinkles and a downturned mouth full of teeth. Gill slits

Figure 39. Petroglyph near Jack Point, Nanaimo, B.C.
Photo: The National Museum of Canada

Little is known of the prehistoric makers of the many petroglyphs found along the B.C. coast. This one may depict various kinds of salmon (humpbacks, springs, and silvers) which come up the great rivers; the skeleton of X-ray style is used. This particular petroglyph was explained by nearby Indian residents as showing the adventures of young lovers who were changed into Salmon People.

flank his face, and tears drip from the corners of his eyes. The octopus is either identified by his tentacle suckers or depicted in naturalistic form. There is a monster called the "seawolf" whose body is that of a wolf with two dorsal fins. The frog is very realistic, while the mosquito is shown in head only with a huge, elongated proboscis. The sun's raven-like face is surrounded by rays, the moon's beautiful, serene human face by a circular aura. The winds' faces pucker into blowing lips. All three of these images seem to come from universal symbolism. Finally, the human body is somewhat truncated and frequently shown squatting, but the human face is often shown with extreme naturalism, all ages and both sexes in every mood, with tattoos and labrets (lip plugs which distend the lower lip), varying from grimaces of pain to the fixed gaze of contemplation.

The art of the West Coast includes animal and human images rendered in the full range from abstraction to realism. No wonder writers search from Egyptian art to Greek art for comparison, and ransack the canon of European style in an effort to do justice to this confident, varied, and fully developed mode of human expression. Their art forms, while having recognizable differences, are remarkably similar up and down the Coast.

More variation appears in their religious and social organization. From north to south the groups centred upon villages rather than tribes, and depended upon sea and forest for their abundant and secure livelihood. To the north are the Tlingit, most of whom live in Alaska, then the Haida in the Queen Charlotte Islands, the Tsimshian on the Nass and Skeena Rivers, the Kwakiutl, the Bella Coola, the Nootka, and southernmost, the Coast Salish. These last are Salishan-speakers who moved out to the Coast from the interior and there took up coastal traits and economic bases; they always emphasized the guardian spirit quest to a greater degree than the more northern groups, for whom the potlatch and the dramatic secret societies were more important. The contrast may be expressed as a continuum with materialist concerns and external modes of religious expression at the northern end and less material, more inward or individualist modes at the southern. The Coast Salish live well down into Washington State and regard the international border as a mere formality. It presents a minor inconvenience to their real life, which is strung out among the coast villages located at the mouths of the rivers and sloughs which enter Puget Sound and the Straits of Georgia.

The Tlingit, who properly belong to Alaska and form part of United States instead of Canadian native art history, exerted considerable influence on the Tsimshian and Haida and upon their Athapaskan hinterlands, as well as occupying a part of British Columbia (Frontispiece). It is not only logical but irresistible to include them. The Tlingit ("People") ventured out of their fiords in sea-going canoes, trading sea otter skins (which brought the fur trade to them and ultimately all but caused the extinction of the sea otter), native copper, and Chilkat blankets, as well as slaves and shells. Slavery was a prominent feature of their highly structured social life, as it was for other coastal peoples.

Plate 10. Chilkat Dance Tunic, Tlingit, c. 1870, British Columbia.
Photo: National Gallery of Canada

The splendid "Chilkat" garments were created by means of twined
weaving. Entire design fields were filled with intricate forms. The
motifs here show that the wearer is a member of the "Grizzly Bear"
clan. The colours of the handspun wool derived from natural
dyes; they include black, yellow, green, and natural. The fringe contains components that rattled when the wearer, a person of rank,
was dancing.

Food came from all forms of sea life, as well as the lavish supplies of berries and other vegetables. The Tlingit lived communally in large cedar plank houses, where separate spaces were provided for each family; carved wooden chests contained their ample supplies of horn spoons, wooden vessels, and baskets. They wore simple cedar bark clothing with an element of nudity, perhaps because of the weather, which becomes positively benign, if wet, further south. The busy and profitable summers alternated with ceremonial winters, which were also devoted to all sorts of manufacturing. The requirements of an elaborate religious and social life combined with these long indoor (but not unendurably cold) winters, and the huge supplies of easily workable cedar wood made possible the superb art upon which every observer remarks.

In the most distinctive ceremony, the potlatch (to put a complex matter simply), one man or group entertained another to a lavish feast and gift-giving ceremony. Numerous family and public occasions were marked by potlatches, which, like the art, seem to be a product of the remarkable wealth of what was basically a hunting-fishing-gathering economy. At the potlatch the noble participants wore handsome garments. The wide-brimmed woven hats, painted with crests, were provided with a tall "crown" of thick disks piled atop one another, marking the number of potlatches given by the wearer. The addition of "Chilkat blankets" added to the display.

The Chilkat blanket, actually a cape or robe to be worn over the shoulders, is the glory of West Coast weaving (Figure 37). Using modern materials, these objects are still being produced, according to Mary Meigs Atwater. Traditionally, a free-hanging warp of twisted cedar-bark fibres was suspended from a foundation cord strung between two vertical posts, as in Maori weaving. The weft was twined, small sections being worked back and forth in independent areas, very tightly packed for a tapestry-like effect. The areas were either interlocked or sewn together later. After the robe was completed, a long fringe was added. The colours are black and white (from the natural wool colours), yellow, and bluish green. The usual subject is a bear whose mask confronts the viewer, with most of the other elements in mirror image (Plate 10).

Franz Boas devoted considerable attention to these patterns in his classic, *Primitive Art*. He was fascinated by the manner in which very complex forms were encoded by suggestive parts in which, as described above, a pair of eyes might represent a raven, and a series of heads a family of bears. This extremely laconic form of symbolism has brought about a wide range of interpretation, which later writers have tried to systematize. Bill Holm uses the phrase "symbolic ambiguity" for the above-mentioned trait in his analysis of the forms of Northwest Coast art. He states that the filling of space according to traditional design principles was so primary a motivation that empty places were simply filled with motifs. In other cases the symbolic form was either expanded or distributed from its original configuration, expansion producing the lesser, and distribution the greater degree of distortion and loss of recognizability (Figure 38).

Audrey Hawthorn discusses the com-

Figure 40. Painted wooden screen, Tsimshian, c. 1925.
Photo: The National Museum of Canada

The Tsimshian shared dancing societies with the Kwakiutl. Carved
masks and decorated robes accompanied performances of sacred
dramas, which took place in the winter before splendidly painted
screens like this one. The image on the screen is split in half and
spread to fit the compositional field.

fortable and rewarding life of women (free-women, that is) in West Coast cultures, which could include high social rank and even chieftainship. Weaving and basketry played a major part in their lives. Besides these creative pursuits they prepared fish, gathered berries and roots, and cooked by the stone boiling method. Men fished and hunted (the Nootka went whaling) and made a wide variety of objects, as we have seen, including the monumental forms of wood. Some were the work of specialists, but the level of craftsmanship was very high among all adults.

Formal characteristics in Tlingit art have been described in a comparison of heraldic pole styles by Paul Wingert and Viola Garfield. Their poles are inclined to use a series of separated, superimposed forms like a number of independent sculptures stacked up in a vertical sequence. Form develops independently of the original curved shape, using the sides to help create the effect of a full-round object. Projecting parts are attached to increase this effect. All parts are in comparatively small scale, and the general impression is of somewhat "slight" diameter, with much detail and extensive colour. The poles thus lack the "sculptural dignity" of the Tsimshian and the "baroque complexity and power" of the Haida. The effect is sometimes classified as *rococo*.

The Haida occupied the densely forested Queen Charlotte Islands and though they had little land game, being well separated from the mainland, their irregularly shaped shorelines gave extensive contact with every sort of sea life; fish, sea otters, sea lions, and seals abounded. Sea mammals

yielded huge supplies of beautiful skins which the Haida traded first with the Tsimshian and later with the Europeans. They voyaged widely and picked up cultural traits from the whole range of Pacific Coast cultures, deriving their baskets and shamanism from the Tlingit, and their dance songs and Chilkat blankets, as well as secret societies, from the Tsimshian. Haida, Tlingit, and Tsimshian shamans all used the "soul-catchers" described previously, as well as a variety of amulets in their combined role of sorcerer, healer, and intermediary with the supernatural.

The secret societies initiated their members into the companionship of super-natural beings. Every group made masks for these purposes. Those of the Kwakiutl are probably the most dramatic and awesome, but those of the Haida as in the classic "Moon Mask," one of the greatest treasures of the Canadian National Museum, possess a pure and direct simplicity of compelling power (Plate 11). The cool face of the moon gazes forth in still contemplation surrounded by a subtly modulated aureole, serene, eternal and remote. Another masterpiece is the Transformation Mask, in which a compact hawk-face blossoms from an angular bud into a large circular form of composite animal and sea-life faces surrounding a central face which stares at the viewer from another mode of being. Upon seeing the full-spread supernatural entity within, one can scarcely repress a gasp. The mask is a window onto the human unconscious and with its unfolding action perfectly makes the transition from this world to that other (Plate 12).

This double-focussed view of reality is

Plate 11. Moon Mask, Haida.

This classic image, one of the greatest treasures of the Canadian
National Museum, has a pure and direct simplicity of compelling
power. The cool face of the moon gazes forth in still contemplation,
surrounded by a subtly modulated aureole, serene, eternal, and
remote. The entire surface is delicately mottled with adze-strokes.

characteristic of the West Coast cultures at all periods. It can be seen in the X-ray style of the petroglyphs, deeply scored linear images carved into the surfaces of boulders, which show fish and other creatures with their bone structure clearly delineated (Figure 39). The skeletal details are shown in early stone carvings both at the mouth of the Fraser and in the interior of British Columbia (where the motif also appears in the rockpainting, as we have seen), as well as in the woodcarving and painting of the more recent groups. The relationship of this interest in the bone structure, the final, irreducible reality, and aspects of shamanism are discussed by Andreas Lommel in *Shamanism: The Beginnings of Art*, where he attributes the symbolism to the death-and-resurrection experience marking the shaman's initiation.

When the Europeans came—Bering landed at Kayak Island, and Chirikov at Sitka Sound in 1741, followed by Don Juan Perez from Mexico in 1774 and James Cook at Nootka Sound in 1776—the traits of the Coast were already well established. The newly expanded trade soon depleted the sea otter population, but the steel tools made the Haida the greatest of all woodcarvers. Their "totem poles" (really, as we have seen, displays of heraldry by the nobility) were enormous. However, potlatches took on a somewhat desperate note of competition, and disease (smallpox and venereal disease from white sailors) seriously reduced the population of the Haida.

The Haida noblemen wore a distinctive form of headdress for which the term "crown" is not too strong. In front was a rectangular wooden plaque with a crest-head or figure carved on it, bordered with shell inlay. This was attached to the forehead above the brow with a headband. Weasel skins hung from the back and sides in a long, richly furred fringe. The pure white winter coat, with its black tipped tail, is ermine, remember, the same fur used to denote royalty in Europe. Flicker feathers and sea-lion bristles stood upright around the headband.

Haida heraldic poles used the entire surface as a continuous field; horizontally divided units were interlocked by rising heads and plunging beaks in a series of overlapping forms. Dramatic presentation combined with spectacular exaggeration and multiplicity of detail, so that the poles sometimes seem "verbose." Human figures are few and very small in an overwhelming world of animal and supernatural entities. The forms are deeply cut and developed in depth, using the bulk of the pole as well as the surface.

The greatest of Haida artists was Charles Edenshaw (1839-1924). Born at Skidegate on the Queen Charlotte Islands, he moved as a young man to the north of the islands to live with his uncle, the great Eagle Clan chief, Edenshaw of Kiusta. The young artist began as a carver of totem poles and masks, boxes, chests, and other traditional forms of wood. In addition, he made silver bracelets, wooden figures, and walking sticks ornamented with ivory and silver. His most remarkable works are in black slate, and from this material he made superb small sculptures that are masterpieces of the style.

The Tsimshian are divided in three

Figure 41. Dancer in *Siautl* costume, Bella Coola.

Photo: The National Museum of Canada

Jim Pollard, a Kimsquit, shows the posture and costume depicting *Siautl* (Thunder). A blanket with a border of shell buttons is thrown over his shoulder, and around his neck is a heavy cedar-bark ring hung with bark tassels and weasel fur. The awsome wooden mask of the thunder-being is surrounded by a motion-filled penumbra of delicate fronds and down. Sky-beings descended to earth during the winter ceremonial seasons and moved among men in an atmosphere of holy awe.

groups, the Tsimshian at the mouth of the Skeena River, the Gitksan who fish further up the Skeena, and the Nishga who live in the basin of the Nass. The Nishga and Gitksan hunted mountain goats and bears as well as taking salmon from their rivers, and the Tsimshian fished for halibut as well as salmon and hunted sea mammals on the coast. Apparently these peoples sometimes underwent periods of privation when their supplies of food gave out toward the end of winter.

Theirs was a stratified society which was strongly status-conscious. Like other coastal peoples they had shamans and the potlatch, and raised carved house posts; like the Kwakiutl, they had secret societies, including the Cannibal Society, in which initiates tore up and ate an animal body. A strong element of drama, attested by the carved masks and highly decorated robes, accompanied what were actually performances of sacred dramas. The laity were awed by the dramatic use of sudden entrances, transformation masks, athletic leaps, and a general aura of astonishment and wonder (Figure 40). The masks were meant to be viewed in the impenetrable shadows and brightly gilded reflections of firelight, which enhanced their effect. They were worn with a bushy cedar-bark cloak.

Puppets were used by shamans for healing. One puppet made by Tsimshian people on the Skeena is described as representing a sick woman. Called a "get-well puppet." it takes the form of a cloth-dressed woman whose arm is strung from wrist to ear so that she can lift a little bucket-shaped container. Another represents a medicine-man in full regalia; the crown is cut from a tin can, and the rattle is devised from a discarded pillbox. Again, the arms (to shake the rattle) are raised on strings from wrist to earlobe. The shoulders are hinged with leather strips; the other components are wood, clothed in deerskin and cotton cloth. Puppets were also used on "name-masks," worn by chiefs; one collected in 1912 at Metlakatla had two puppets perched on the head of a mask marked by facial paint suggesting the flickerbird. The figures could raise their arms and rock back and forth on a rod passed through their hips; their knees were drawn up before them as part of a solid body.

The Tsimshian groups were all vigorous traders, especially of oolichen (candlefish) oil, so named because the dried fish can be burned as its own wick. Oil was a major component of the coastal diet, used as a condiment and a sauce for everything; it was even whipped with dried berries to form a delicacy somewhat resembling fish-flavoured berry ice cream. The tribes of the interior were eager to obtain this delicious and versatile oil. The villages of the Tsimshian of the two great rivers lay along the "grease trail" to the interior and this helped develop in them a genius for social manipulation which led to their active role in the early phases of Indian resurgence in the twentieth century.

Whereas Haida and Kwakiutl poles are heavy and massive, the Tsimshian, like the Tlingit, express "inner cubic content" of forms which seem to press against and expand the surface, giving an impression of lightness and volume rather than heaviness and mass. The outline of the form is most emphasized in Tsimshian carving,

Plate 12. Transformation Mask, Haida, c. 1878.
Photo: National Gallery of Canada

Another masterpiece is this transformation mask, in which a compact
hawk-face blossoms from an angular bud into a large circular form of
composite animal and sea-life faces surrounding a central face that
stares at the viewer from another mode of being. The mask expresses
the dual animal/human nature of the ancestors, whose stories are
re-enacted in the winter ceremonies by masked dancers.

with internal forms of each unit subtly modulated. The line itself is "resultant." The masks of human faces in Tsimshian art are strikingly realistic, like skins covering a bone structure. The poles emphasize the vertical shaft with its curved surface one over-all form, the figures horizontally defined and tending either to be very large or very small. Detail is in low relief emphasized with colour, and the figures, like the masks, tend toward realism except for exaggerated head size. The expression is of clarity, sobriety, and restraint; in European terms, Tsimshian carving is sometimes said to be classical, with the Haida ranging over into the baroque.

South of the Tsimshian, with Kwakiutl to the north and south of them, were the Bella Coola, who occupied a number of waterfront villages where they lived in plank houses. This population, perhaps due to extensive white contact, in a small and somewhat exposed position, is today small. They are Salishan speakers but little is known of their original trek; Athapaskan speakers close them in from behind. The salmon, captured in purse nets, was their chief food. Most of their traits, including the potlatch and the secret society, were derived from other coastal groups. The dances of the secret society were reproductions of dances held yearly and simultaneously by the supernaturals before the sky gods (Figure 41). These beings descended to earth during the winter ceremonial seasons and moved among men in an atmosphere of holy awe (Figure 42). There is in Bella Coola art a certain element of Salishan simplicity, although the forms clearly belong to the coastal tradition of

their near neighbours, and hold their own in comparison with them.

The Kwakiutl have three linguistic subdivisions, the Haisla, the Heiltsuk, and the Kwakiutl proper. The Kwakiutl seem to have originated the secret society, which is basically an elaboration of the guardian spirit quest. Young men and girls went out to seek a vision in which the guardian would show himself to his chosen favourite and give power, to be perpetuated through sacred songs, dances, and objects. This profound psychic experience gave a focus of supernatural meaning and a sense of deep security to the lives of Indian youths, and in many places—and not only on the West coast—it still does, for the guardian spirit tradition has by no means disappeared. From this basic pattern, which the Coast Salish practised in its primary form, the Kwakiutl, followed by other coastal peoples, elaborated a communal ritual. In it, particular guardians became the hereditary right of specific clans, and the right of seeking their guardianship came under strict control of the group. This highly structured, community-controlled pattern characterizes many aspects of coastal life, and here it manifests itself in the area of religion and personal, or spiritual, identity.

While the guardian spirit was inherited among the Kwakiutl and other coastal groups, the shaman encountered the spirits directly. In the winter ceremony of the dancing society, the inheriting initiate re-enacted his ancestor's encounter with, capture by, and return from his guardian spirit, thus paralleling the shaman's experience. According to Deborah Waite, the original population of the Kwakiutl world

Figure 42. Carved and painted wooden mask, Bella Coola.
Photo: The National Museum of Canada

There is in Bella Coola art a certain element of Salishan simplicity, although the forms clearly belong to the Coastal tradition of their near neighbours, and hold their own in comparison with them. Examples are these powerful masks, one provided with a shock of hair, and the other gazing from a circular wooden panel on which animal forms are painted. Of special note are the extremely refined painted designs on the subtle volumetric forms of the face.

was made up of magical animals, who transformed themselves into animals and man. The guardian spirit performances re-enacted these primaeval events, which are described in a series of myths, by "removing the mask" of the animal to show what he became. The transformation mask thus expresses the dual human/animal nature of the ancestors. Masks of the winter cannibal ceremonies were demonic and terrifying; those of the spring ceremonies were more naturalistic and benign, and represented the common Kwakiutl theme of the transformation of a bird into a human being. Waite sees a strong shamanist element in all of this and traces its iconographic links with Siberian practices, as well as with Alaskan Eskimo masked shamanism, which differs somewhat in form.

The result of this "organized religion" for art was a particularly spectacular range of masks, painted backdrops and ceremonial interiors (Figure 43). Kwakiutl art has been characterized as "eclectic". Typically, a Kwakiutl pole features two or more large-scale figures, separated horizontally and superimposed vertically. The forms have strong sculptural simplification with an element of naturalism. The large heads are carved out as if they were masks, with dramatic intensity. The impression is one of extreme virtuosity; it is the Kwakiutl pole, frequently topped by a thunderbird with wings outspread, which has given rise to the debased image found in countless miniature poles on souvenir counters.

The Kwakiutl also practised potlatching, and probably under the European pressure that displaced peoples and increased the competitive nature of a trading society, they elaborated it into a severe contest. Those guests receiving gifts were obliged to reciprocate with interest, even to double the original amount. Such extreme practices brought government prohibition of the potlatch which was not relaxed until the mid-twentieth century. The movement had actually only gone underground and when restrictions were removed the potlatch re-emerged in its celebratory or festival form.

The Nootka, the whale hunters of southern Vancouver Island, went to sea in huge dugout canoes; other sea mammals were hunted as well. There were also generous supplies of salmon and plentiful berries and roots. Perhaps under the influence of their Salishan neighbours, the Nootka made splendid baskets, and they shared shamanism, social clubs, and the potlatch with other coastal groups. There was also a dramatic healing society. The wolf was the chief being evoked in the secret society; he was a wolf spirit endangering, carrying off, and ultimately being exorcised from the body of the initiate. This theme has given rise on the West Coast to some marvellously life-like masks used in "The Loon's Necklace."

A contemporary artist and writer of the Nootka, George Clutesi, was a protegé of Emily Carr, who willed her brushes, oils, and blank canvasses to him. He has written extensively of the culture of his people, and illustrates his own books, using a distinctive style that ranges from the academic to that related to West Coast tradition. His somewhat personal style may be contrasted with that of Henry Speck, a Kwakiutl,

Plate 13. Antler fragment with seventeen human faces, Dorset.
Photo: National Gallery of Canada

The surface of the broken antler is covered with a host of human
faces interlocked in a series of "visual puns," some of them grimaces,
as if caricaturing pain or possibly ecstasy. Much of Dorset art is
magical, perhaps made by shamans. The exact function of this deeply
ambiguous image remains unknown.

who preserves the precise forms of traditional imagery, adding to them, however, a personal force of his own.

In the catalogue, *Arts of the Raven*, for the exhibition which may be said to have called mid-twentieth century attention to Canadian native art for the first time on a national level, it is stated that coastal art styles continue in modern contexts. Charlie James, Mungo Martin, and Ellen Neel are seen as transitional figures, and artists of 1967 were given as Henry Hunt, Tony Hunt, Doug Cranmer, Henry Speck, and Bill Reid: Robert Davidson of Masset was suggested as holding promise for the future. Of these artists, the catalogue states that, though they are truly of Indian descent, they are now part of Canadian art as well. As more and more international exhibitions are held, and more and more art magazine articles, such as those printed in *artscanada*, make these artists of past and present familiar to Canadians, this statement will be increasingly true.

The Coast Salish (Salish means "people") live in the southernmost area of coastal British Columbia and in western Washington State as well. Like their relatives on the interior, they made beautiful watertight baskets, some of which are still preserved in Salishan homes. New ones of slightly less perfect craftsmanship are made for sale. Another textile art, weaving (Figure 44), was found in blankets of dog and goat hair woven with cedar bark, which they share with the Interior Salish as described in the previous chapter. They had a much simpler range of designs than did more northern coastal weavers, being limited to geometric pattern. Their wood carving is

also much less elaborate, having a rather utilitarian (one might also say puritanical) and economical mode of expression, lacking the element of public display so typical of Kwakiutl and other coastal art, rather like the early Romanesque in comparison with the late Gothic (Figure 45). The habit of comparing native New World styles to well-known Old World styles is somewhat misleading, of course. No comparable time element or evolutionary trend can be identified positively, since the whole collection of wooden forms cannot be much more than a hundred and fifty years old, and all the styles discussed were found side-by-side in the same time span.

The Coast Salish ate clams, venison, and goat meat, along with salmon, which to this day they roast and smoke over an open fire. Among them were slaves, common people, and nobles, but these positions were less rigidly held than elsewhere. Their ceremonial life was rich, but approaching the United States border its traits resemble less and less those of northern coastal groups, and the wooden objects accompanying this life grew simpler as well. This tendency to simplicity seems to mark the arrival of the Salishan on the Coast, for, according to Wilson Duff, earlier stone objects were more elaborate. The art of the Salishan has a rough dignity all its own. Because the element of public display was much less emphatic, the objects are much more severely iconic, semiabstract indications of a meaning which was primarily inward and spiritual.

The Salishan wore ephemeral garments of shredded cedar bark (excellent for rainy weather) with feathers, hair, and little clat-

Figure 43. Painted house front, Kwakiutl.

Facing the beach, with carved canoes drawn up before it, the great
house is faced with enormous planks, whose size can be gauged
from the figures of a child and a man standing nearby, and from the
full-sized door in front. On this facade, a gigantic winged and
huge-beaked being is displayed, painted over a circle. Note the
assymetrical placement of the figure to accommodate the diagnostic
beak. Confronted animals with X-ray bodies support the central figure.

tering paddle-like appendages of wood for ceremonial garb. Their only mask was the *swaixwe* image, which is a memorable one, combining the spirit-quest motif of the south with the crest idea of the north (Figure 46). The form was given by the "people who live under a lake" to a man who then gave it to his sister as a present for her new husband, nicely demonstrating the wide-spread coastal gift-giving trait. The face of the mask is breaking out in birds (which are spirit symbols), and these images have an element of surprise resembling that of other coastal groups, although its particular form is completely and uniquely Salishan. The right to make and use these masks, though inherited, can be rented out, and they are still being made and used. The present writer was shown a large collection of them, which the owner displayed and allowed to be photographed. They were obviously made by someone who was not a specialist (they had an element of technical crudeness), but for whom they represented a strong, immediate, and real personal relationship of man to spirit. These powerful spirits, which live beyond the sea, under the deep lakes, beneath the earth, and in the atmosphere, can give to the individual the power to be successful in every sort of activity. In the north this was expressed by superb works of visual art (due to its context in a strong group structure). In the south it was expressed by inspired dances and songs, alternative and perhaps more personal art forms.

Knitting, a skill brought by Scottish settlers to the Cowichan Valley of southern Vancouver Island in the nineteenth century, has become a cottage industry of the Cowichan, a Coast Salish people. They had already excelled in preparing spun wool for weaving, as we have seen, and today produce sweaters and other garments in large quantities. Women from other Coast Salishan groups make similar items. The fleece comes from local sheep, both black and white. The wool is lightly washed, retaining the lanolin that makes it waterproof, dried, teased to remove grass and twigs, and carded. The shades used are entirely natural. The wool is spun into a thick, loosely twisted yarn, now usually by treadle-operated spindles. The knitted patterns are based upon traditional basketry designs as well as on any source at hand.

Across the Canadian northland, and ranging up into the Arctic, are the members of the other great native group, the Eskimo. Their life, thought, and art, while showing influence from, and exerting it upon, that of their Indian neighbours, remains distinctive, and this major native culture remains to be studied in the final chapter.

Plate 14. Walrus tusk comb, Thule.
Photo: National Gallery of Canada

The most elegant form from the Thule culture may be this graceful
comb, carved with thick teeth to be pulled through the hair of a
woman such as the one it depicts; she seems to be clothed in a decorated costume. The surface is both pierced and incised, and the
form is conceived in a two-dimensional manner. Its elaborate design
may be compared with a simpler comb in Figure 51.

Chapter 7   Artisans of the Arctic

Figure 44. Spindle whorls, Cowichan and Sumas, Coast Salish.
Photo: The National Museum of Canada

Carved of maple, these whorls were used with a spindle to change handfuls of dog and goat wool into strongly textured spun components for blankets and robes. The spindle whorl is a circular field, and the Salishan artist, while deriving the designs from West Coast forms, does not divide and display the figures according to bilateral symmetry, but allows the bird-forms to fly across, filling the space with their wings.

As we have seen, mankind's northern entrance to the New World appears to have happened in three major waves. The earliest known arrivals entered the Continent between forty and thirty-five thousand years ago. The corresponding material remains are characterised by pebble tools and other pre-point objects. These peoples' activities and migration routes are not at all clear. Between twenty-five and twenty-three thousand years ago another wave entered and the socalled "Llano complex" emerged. These peoples made projectile points that developed into the fluted type, such as the fluted points in Canada about thirteen to nine-thousand years ago. Likewise they produced a lanceolate type, such as the "Plainview point," also found in Canada.

After the second movement, communication between the two continental systems was severed for a long time. Then about thirteen to ten-thousand years ago a third wave of migrants entered the American continent. Their implement assemblages, defined by some archaeologists as "American Epi-Gravettian," are characterised by their striking smallness. It is supposed that in this culture complex the Inuit culture originated.

The art objects, and indeed all that was manufactured before AD 1500, were litterally "made by hand." Every step of the process, from obtaining the material to completion, was a manual operation. It is understandable that objects so laboriously produced were almost entirely functional, whether for physical or psychic purposes, yet they were nearly always decorated.

Tools and vessels were embellished with paint or carving, and ritual objects bore designs intended to bring about the presence of that power which made the object sacred rather than secular.

In surveying Arctic art, a marked change may be observed from west to east. The art of Alaskan Eskimos is extremely striking, with wood carving and painting fully developed, with splendid spirit-impersonation masks. The art of the Greenland Eskimo is second in complexity. The central Arctic boasts fewer and more modest objects, but even so their "plastic superiority" has been highly praised. The primary materials were wood, bone, horn, and ivory, and the realistic forms were almost all made by men. The art of making and decorating clothing of varicoloured fur, stitched with sinews by means of an awl, was practised by women. The limited materials were fashioned into intricate patterns.

The characteristic feminine tool of the Inuit is the *ulu*, a crescent-shaped knife with a palm-fitting handle. Eskimo women had one form of representational art in which dark-coloured sealskin silhouettes of animals were laid upon a background of lighter-coloured sealskin or caribou hide. Edmund Carpenter describes the discovery, in the midwinter of 1772, of a young woman who had lived alone on the Canadian tundra for seven months after her family had been killed. She was found by the Arctic explorer Samuel Hearne, who recorded his amazement that she had not only survived, but had made herself clothing that was beautiful as well as serviceable. He found her appearance romantic and taste-

Plate 15. Kenojuak, "The Arrival of the Sun" stone-cut, 1962.
Photo: Information Canada, Ottawa

Kenojuak, an artist whose fecund imagination has generated a host
of graceful metamorphic shapes, is perhaps best known for her
imaginary birds arranged in complex compositions. The colouring is
applied on the surface of carved stone, and the completed print is
signed by the artist and the stone-carver in Eskimo syllabics, with a
tiny igloo to signify Cape Dorset.

ful. When life is lived at the limits of human endurancè, with its equipment reduced to the barest essentials, that necessary baggage includes poetry and art, Carpenter observes.

The forms created by people living in the vast and forbidding land of tundra and taiga are both naturalistic and geometric, with realism and abstraction sometimes combined (Figure 47). The full range of artistic expression is thus encompassed. Animal forms seem to dominate in all archaeological and almost all present Inuit cultures; however, the human form plays a significant role as well. The most distinctive feature is the diminutive size of most of the objects made before the 1950's. These miniatures make up in vivacity and truth to nature what they lack in scale.

In the polar area meteoric iron, found locally, was hammered into spear points and knives. When whites brought their wrought iron to the Arctic, the natives at first reworked it by cold-hammering. The limitations of the Arctic environment are well known. Wood was frequently confined to driftwood, and there were few materials to support the textile arts. Vegetable dyes were sometimes equally scarce. Even so, the local grasses were made into baskets by the coil technique, both in the eastern Arctic and in British Columbia, the handle of the basket lid often being formed by a tiny animal figure of ivory (Figure 48).

Stone was sometimes used as a material; there is one miniature mask of soapstone from Igloolik in the Dorset period (c. AD 500-1300) made of a fragment of a broken lamp. This was the stone's primary function; lamps were shallow dishes of oil in which a little wick set burning could keep a dwelling's interior relatively warm. But other vessels were made of soapstone as well. Only since the 1950's has soapstone become a popular medium for carving. Ivory and bone were the true material of art prior to the most recent times.

The Eskimo are the only natives who live in both the Old and New Worlds. They inhabited a larger area at one time, but have always kept to the coastal zone except for the Barren Grounds west of Hudson Bay. Certain characteristics distinguish the Central Eskimos of Canada from the other groups living at the extremities of Eskimo territory. They have special implements for hunting through breathing holes in the ice during winter. The Inuit of the Barren Grounds, and some others as well, hunt inland for caribou. The relative uniformity of recent Inuit culture is notable; it was brought about by the spread of Thule culture about AD 1000.

Hunting at sea and in winter, the Eskimo lived a life that followed the animal cycles. Their most elegant and complex implement, and chief weapon, was the harpoon, though they also made the bola, the bow and arrow, the three-pronged dart (leister), and various forms of fishing equipment. Bolas are a set of rocks tied in a bunch; they were thrown into a flock of birds and might damage or wound in several directions. A similar "second chance" was given by a bird dart, which had a second set of three barbed tines halfway down the shaft, so that if the head missed another bird might still be hit. The harpoon is used for hunting water-dwelling prey that would be lost when killed or wounded instead of

Figure 45. Carved house posts, interior view of Coast Salish building, Duncan, B.C.
Photo: The National Museum of Canada

Salishan wood-carving is less elaborate than other West Coast styles, having a more economical mode of expression. Nevertheless, the repeated vertical pattern of strongly defined animal figures on these interior house posts possesses a rhythmic vigour characteristic of Salishan art.

falling to the earth for the convenience of the hunter. Thus the head of the harpoon is barbed to remain in the flesh, and comes loose from the shaft by which it is thrown. A line is fastened to the head and has bladder floats to retard the escape of a wounded animal and mark the location of a kill. As is usual in weaponry, there is a full set of structural variations that has given rise to a complex nomenclature.

The sledge and the *kayak*, which made possible rapid transit over snow and water, were both made of a wooden frame, with components of bone and ivory or baleen. The *kayak* was covered with skin. The perfection with which these forms were made was based upon a stark reality; in a climate where a man could freeze to death for the slightest miscalculation, bad craftsmen did not survive.

Clothing was made in two layers, for insulation, but only the hard parts of the garments of early peoples survive. Ivory and bone were used to form toggles, ornaments, labrets, combs, snow goggles, and the snow beaters used by these people to clean snow from garments before entering a dwelling. Numerous other objects—adzes, *ulus*, sewing implements, and mattocks— were made, as well as amulets to be fastened to the clothing of shamans (Figure 49).

As we have seen, Inuit cultures are derived from the arrival in Arctic North America of peoples who were late arrivals of the Siberian Gravettian, perhaps thirteen to ten thousand years ago. They were an Arctic-Mongoloid people from whom the Aleut and Eskimo racial groups sprang, and seem to have been interior hunters who gradually adapted to the coastal hunting conditions of their new environment. By eight thousand years ago (6000 BC), the land bridge no longer existed, and the full complement of New World peoples had arrived. To fit this into the world time-table, one may recall that in the same millenium agriculture was fully developed in both the Old World and the New, and what is today Canada became populated by hunters in south and north alike as deglaciation proceeded.

The Pre-Dorset people, as these early groups are called, moved across the deglaciated Canadian Arctic all the way to Greenland. The Alaskan parent culture is the culture-stage called the Denbigh Flint Complex, dated about 3000 BC; Pre-Dorset hunters had reached Greenland by 2000 BC. It is not known if these people were "true Eskimos," but they had an "Eskimo" way of life, adapted to a treeless world of snow and ice, and objects of similar form are found in later undoubted Eskimo sites.

At Cape Denbigh, on the North Bering Sea coast of Alaska, is a site where there is an underlying level unlike the "Eskimo" levels above it. Artefacts found here give their name to the Denbigh Flint Complex; all but five of them are of flinty materials and are very small. They include Old World-like forms of the Upper Paleolithic (a variety of small burins); Folsom- and "Yuma"-like New World forms (points, blades, scrapers, and gravers); cores and flakes in process of being worked (J. L. Giddings finds these more delicate than those of Egyptian and north European Mesolithic sites); and a number of unique objects. These last in-

Figure 46. *Swaixwe* mask, Coast Salish.
Photo: The National Museum of Canada

The Salish *Swaixwe* mask combines the spirit-quest motif of the
southern Pacific Coast of Canada with the crest idea of the northern
Pacific Coast. The face of the mask is breaking out in birds, and
these elements have a metamorphic symbolism resembling that of
of other coastal groups, though its graceful and simplified form is
completely Salishan. The right to make and use these masks is
inherited, though it can be rented out, and they are still being
made and used.

clude a variety of scrapers, blades made into knives which have been retouched only on their convex face, keeled forms used for scraping or graving, and tiny double-pointed objects. In addition there is a piece of red shale rubbed flat in various parts as if used to produce paint, and a grooved piece of sandstone that may have been used to smooth the wooden shaft of a small weapon. There is also a bit of birch-bark with a cut edge along which is a line of widely spaced pairs of tiny holes which probably once held sewing; it may have been the remnant of a vessel.

The northern hunting peoples share many fundamental similarities, and Eskimos and Northern Indians share, along the taiga belt, many mythological and economic traits, which are shared in turn with peoples of the Asiatic taiga. As outlined by Hans-Georg Bandi, the earliest prehistoric "Eskimo" sites in Canada suggest a complex variety of life-styles. At Engigstciak, for instance, in the Northwest part of the Yukon territories, remnants were found of what is called the British Mountain complex. In this complex, a Mousteroid technique of working stone objects prevailed, and two other small-tool industries emerged, one microlithic and one related to the "Plano tradition." Some more recent assemblages contain pottery as well. At a site near Cape Parry a full sequence was found, beginning with a small-tool Pre-Dorset industry and continuing through Dorset to Thule. At Great Bear Lake, three cultures were revealed: two of Paleo-Indian and one of "Epi-Gravettian style". At Igloolik, a round stone house with a central hearth seems to have been occupied by people who lived a sea-coast hunting life and who made harpoon heads that pre-figure Thule methods. The site dates from four thousand to twenty-eight hundred years ago, and the craftsmanship grows cruder as it becomes more recent. This kind of intermixture of cultures and peoples is very widespread.

All these various peoples were replaced by the Dorset culture. Its carriers were hunters who moved in small bands engaged in seasonal hunting of seal, walrus, polar bears, caribou, foxes, hares, birds, and fish, but did no whaling. Lacking dogs, they used small hand sleds. Their settlements were always on the coast, often in places where Thule people later settled. They made semi-subterranean rectangular houses and larger "meeting houses" for winter living, and occupied skin tents in the summer. The semi-subterranean dwellings were probably made of pieces of sod piled up around the excavated area, covered with skin, although stone was used too. Inside were benches along the walls and a small open hearth. Oval and triangular lamps of soapstone gave heat and light, and cooking pots were made of the same material. The Dorset people had no drill; that trait distinguishes Thule culture. They made toggled pointed harpoons, barbed spears, bird darts, three-pronged stabbing devices (leisters), *ulus*, scrapers, adzes, whetstones, and needles and awls, which were kept in cylindrical cases. Bone, ivory, chipped flint, and rubbed slate were the materials of which this abundance of useful articles were manufactured. Probably they made tailored fur clothes and skin boats.

It is Dorset art, however, that has excited

Figure 47. Women in gala dress with *appliqué* designs, Central Eskimo.
Photo: The National Museum of Canada

Complex designs made up of intricate cloth *appliqué* and multi-
colour fringing adorn each skin dicky, as the upper garment is called, in these sumptuous festival garments. Both voluminous trousers
and cloth skirts are used. Close examination of the designs will
reveal stars, high-heeled shoes, a hunting scene, and abstract or semiabstract motifs used by the Inuit needlewomen.

the most interest; there were less than two hundred Dorset art objects known in 1967, and a catalogue of them is revealing. These specimens collected over the New World Arctic, depict human beings, bears, seals, birds, walrus, caribou, fish, weasels, and a few objects which cannot be classified. These are pendants of bone, ivory, and wood, sometimes engraved, and necklaces of small stone discs and animal teeth. These objects have in common their very small scale, their tendency to range from realism to abstraction, their material of antler, ivory, or (rarely) wood, and their frequent decoration with incised lines. There is some resemblance to the Okvik and Ipiutak phases of the Inuk tradition of Alaska (its phases date from c. 500 BC to AD 1700). Of these, the Thule, which is next-to-last in the sequence, was to expand across Canada, gradually absorbing and/or replacing Dorset culture.

The Okvik and Ipiutak, prehistoric Alaskan Eskimo cultures of about 400 BC to AD 400, share common conceptions and certain distinctive designs, but their resemblance to Dorset objects is a result of influence, not of direct relation. The actual route of diffusion is not known and it may simply be that Alaskan and Dorset art shared a common ancestor in the Denbigh Flint Complex. The Dorset tradition had developed on the spot in the Canadian Arctic as an offshoot of the Pre-Dorset, which already showed the "skeletal" design or "X-ray style." This reveals a circumpolar Eurasian origin, and becomes a common motif of Dorset art. Some diffusion from Alaska appears in about 1000 BC, causing

changes in the Pre-Dorset and marking a further route of influence at the beginning of Dorset culture.

During the awesome span of two thousand years of Dorset life, which equals the full span of the Common Era in the Old World, the exquisite bone and ivory objects were fashioned and scattered across the equally awesome geographical region. Their design is simple, linear, and not severely conventionalized; they bring to mind the Upper Paleolithic and Mesolithic rather than any of the Eskimo styles that succeeded them on either continent, as analysed by Charles Martijn in his definitive study, "Canadian Eskimo-Carving in Historical Perspective." What is notable is the naturalism of the objects. The human figures, nude, stand with spread legs and a determined expression, fully human in the face of a hostile reality. The impression is one of mastery, humour, independence, and profound selfhood.

The animals are graceful and elegantly formed; a bear floating with his limbs relaxed in the supporting element of water or a pair of swans riding the frigid currents of the air. As Edmund Carpenter says, they occupy a field space without orientation. Fully three-dimensional, they move in a huge environment without landmarks. There is no "bottom" or "top" to the figures, no frame or context into which they fit. This may be related to their tiny size as much as to a spatial concept. As will be seen below, Joan Vastokas does not find this trait in Thule culture.

Especially numinous are the shaman's utensil cases (perhaps they are actually

Figure 48. Boots and basketry, Labrador Eskimo.
Photo: The National Museum of Canada

The meticulously crafted boot (note the multitude of tiny tucks at
the seam of the sole) has an intricate design of interlocking stripes
and checks. Finely woven baskets of simpler designs in a radiating
pattern, and an *appliqué* and embroidered bag, suggest the range
of Inuit decorative craftsmanship. The brief Arctic summer allows
the growth and gathering of grasses to provide fibre for basketry.

blowing or sucking tubes). The Igloolik shaman, according to William E. Taylor Jr., had to "see himself" as a shaman, naming each of his own bones in his mind in the secret shaman language. The angakok (shaman) may be represented as a bear, upon whose body the skeleton is indicated as a series of incised crossed lines. The bear's throat in some examples is provided with a tiny hidden chamber, concealed by a minute sliding cover of the same material, inside which is secreted a bit of red ochre. The world-wide association of this material with blood suggests its function here.

The bodies of many of the animal forms are scored with this skeletal motif, an X across the head, and horizontal, vertical, chevron, and cross-hatch lines on the rest of the body. Sometimes there is a single "incision" over the heart. Human faces sometimes have lines to show tattooing. Often the animals have an open framework, the form pierced with slots cut out without the aid of a bow drill. Sometimes a host of human faces are interlocked in a series of "visual puns;" some of them grimace as if caricaturing pain, or possibly ecstasy (Plate 13).

Much of Dorset art is magical, specialist, or professional equipment, perhaps made by the shamans themselves. The skeleton motif helped the shaman to bind the object to himself—he saw himself as a skeleton —in recalling his initiation as he recalled his own bones. George Swinton suggests that this complex of Eurasian concepts clustering about shamanism may be ancestral to early Northwest Coast art too.

The shaman's tube is made of a walrus tusk from which the point has been re-

moved (Figure 50). It is topped with a pair of confronted walrus heads whose tusks interlock in an heraldic composition. Beneath is a bear with his limbs outspread— perhaps he is floating away to the spirit world—and a deep-eyed humanoid face. The association of breath with life suggests the function of the tube, which may have served for blowing out power or for sucking malign objects from the body of the sick person, made ill by the intervention of another shaman. Here, the bear is not a symbol of hunting magic but an essential part of the shaman's magical equipment, used for spirit flights to the other world, in short, his great helper. The face depicted on the side of the tube is not that of an ordinary man, but of some discomfiting entity who gazes at us from the interior of the tusk, his nostrils and mouth distended, suggesting the essentially magical act of breathing.

There are wooden artefacts in Dorset art, including life-sized red-painted masks as well as small human figures and ritual artefacts. In Alaska magnificent death masks of ivory were found on buried skulls, along with sets of ivory teeth; representing most probably shamans in their full regalia. As we have seen, Dorset culture arises from an "Epi-Gravettian" culture which had been influenced by Indian cultures, perhaps the Old Copper and other Archaic groups. It is basically "Eskimo" with a recognizable "Indian imprint." Whether the people themselves were racially Eskimo has not been determined with certainty.

The people who gradually encroached upon their territory, however, were certainly

Figure 49. Knife, *ulu*, snow glasses, and ivory case, Mackenzie and Cooper Eskimo.
Photo: The National Museum of Canada

Based upon prehistoric prototypes, these objects suggest classes of materials which
include bone, ivory, wood, and metal, as well as leather. The *ulu* is the Inuit woman's
characteristic tool; used as a cutting blade with swift dexterity, it serves as both
knife and scissors. The snow glasses permit only a bearable level of light through the
slits to prevent snow-blindness in the white glare, and the ivory cases are incised
with a linear abstract design.

Eskimo in culture. They came from the Inuk tradition, a northern maritime series of Eskimo cultures which developed on both sides of the Bering Straits. The series of successive cultures is unbroken. The Thule, as the Canadian version of the culture was called, developed as an eastward extension of the Birnirk culture, as bands of Thule Eskimos began to leave the region of the western Arctic shore of Alaska about AD 1000 and transported their version of the Inuk tradition as far as Labrador and Greenland. In passing across this vast territory they absorbed, annihilated, or greatly acculturated the Dorset peoples, to become the direct ancestors of the modern Eskimo. Dorset style disappeared, and did not affect subsequent styles except in Eastern Greenland.

Over a span of two thousand years, there was a gradual transition in Inuk tradition from elaborate early styles (like the elegant interlocking swirls of the Old Bering Sea style) to very simplified forms. The word "Thule" comes from flint finds in Greenland that are much more recent than the actual origin of the style. Thule people were especially devoted to whaling, and some of their finest art objects show engravings of sportive whales whose spouts raise delicate patterns above a peaceful sea, while hunters put out in huge *umiaks* to fetch them in. Ashore, in some depictions, land hunters pursue lively deer and wield huge bows and arrows. One much-reproduced bow drill part seems to depict an aged party hobbling out with a cane to watch the sport. Joan Vastokas, in her sensitive analysis of characteristics of Eskimo graphic (two-dimensional) style, points

out how Edmund Carpenter's ideas about Eskimo "field space" are contradicted in Thule art. As she says, the engraved bow drill uses a ground line (and waterline) upon which the figures walk or float, as well as a frame-line which separates "pictorial space" from outside reality.

Thule settlements were located on the seashore in semi-subterranean winter houses of whale-bone, skin, and sod. The bones are now collected and carved by modern Eskimos into particularly eerie forms whose porous bony material gives them a ghostly metamorphic quality. Some of the dwellings were square, some round, some multiple in structure, with a passage and a cold trap. This was a special intermediate chamber serving a function, perhaps, like that of the closed-in porch where school children take off their boots and coats before entering the house in modern Canada. The rear walls of these relatively complex dwellings had elevated benches for sitting and sleeping. The Thule also built snow-houses and used skin tents in summer.

They hunted not only the whale, but also the seal, walrus, polar bear, caribou, musk-ox, small mammals and birds, and were as well taking fish and mussels, and gathering plants. They used *umiaks, kayaks,* and dog-sleds, and made a very elaborate outlay of tools and hunting equipment, and personal gear of all sorts.

Their "art," however, is pronounced by many observers to be unimpressive and even rudimentary. Perhaps this unkind language should be rephrased to read "conventionalized" and "formalized." The objects are carved of ivory as well as of wood, bone, and antler, a familiar and

Figure 50. Shaman's utensil case, Dorset.

Photo: The National Museum of Canada

This object may actually be a shaman's magical blowing and sucking tube. Made from a walrus tusk from which the point has been removed, it is topped with a pair of confronted walruses whose tusks are interlocked. The outspread bear seems to be floating away to the spirit world, and the deep-eyed humanoid face seems to be that of a spirit being who stares at us from the interior of the tusk with nostrils and mouth distended by the magical act of breathing.

necessary range of materials (Figure 51). They bear simple engraved line motifs and rows of drilled dots. It is suggested by some writers that the stereotyped birds and human figures (which are frequently female) are counters or "pawns" for games; the feminine figures are sometimes identified as dolls, whether nude or clothed. George Swinton suggests that the forthright nudity of Dorset human figures became the fully clothed image of modern Eskimo art because of missionary influence (presumably a long memory of Victorian influence rather than the sophisticated Anglicanism of the present day). The costumed Thule dolls may suggest a different origin for the practice; besides, modern human figures are represented as hunting or otherwise active out-of-doors, hardly a place to be nude in the north. The Dorset figures suggest man in his essential form, diagrammatic and universal, a condition for which the nude body is symbolic in many cultures, including our own. The Thule images simply show mankind as an entity, and perhaps approach the conventionality of chess pieces. When Thule artists represented man in action, on the engraved ivory parts of various tools and weapons, he was always dressed for the hunt, in recognizable fur clothing.

The most elegant forms from the Thule area are the graceful combs, carved with thick teeth to be pulled through the heavy black hair, perhaps, of a lovely woman like the one depicted on one comb (Plate 14). She is clothed in a decorated costume (or else a border motif similar to those used for clothing decorated the comb) and seems to have thrown her arms up behind

her tress-laden head in a universal gesture of femininity. Joan Vastokas points out that the comb has a front and back but no "sides;" that is, it is conceived in a two-dimensional manner, as a cookie rather than as a cake. This is in contrast with Dorset sculpture, which is fully three- dimensional and may be viewed from all points equally. Again it may be questioned whether either culture was confined to one kind of "space." A comb is usually flattish and a carving of a mask is meant to be seen only from the front, even in Dorset art.

The climate deteriorated between the fifteenth and the seventeenth century of our era, and the Thule whale-hunting communities began to break up and move about as nomadic bands and hunting groups, seeking seal and caribou. More interior peoples began to move up toward the coast, among them the Caribou Eskimos, who are perhaps the remnants of a proto-Eskimo culture, though not one of Dorset form. Their life still bears the imprint of the interior, as Hans-Georg Bandi describes them. As the Thule people moved about, their art deteriorated, became stagnant, limited, or almost non-existent after white contact, ending an early time of some vigour with stagnation.

There were some exceptions, of course; one group, the Aivilik, seem to have been employed by whalers, and produced carving for their trade. Labrador art, where there is a very long history of white contact (probably including Vikings) has received some praise. The culture contact of whites with Eskimos was regular and extensive; they were not as remote from

Figure 51. Comb, female figure, and thimble-holder, Thule.

A graceful comb, a doll-like female image, and a thimble-holder
whose prongs held the sealskin thimbles, show the tendency to
stereotyped form and two-dimensional decorative pattern in Thule
art. The hole at the top of the thimble-holder indicates that the
object may have been suspended from the neck of a Thule
needlewoman.

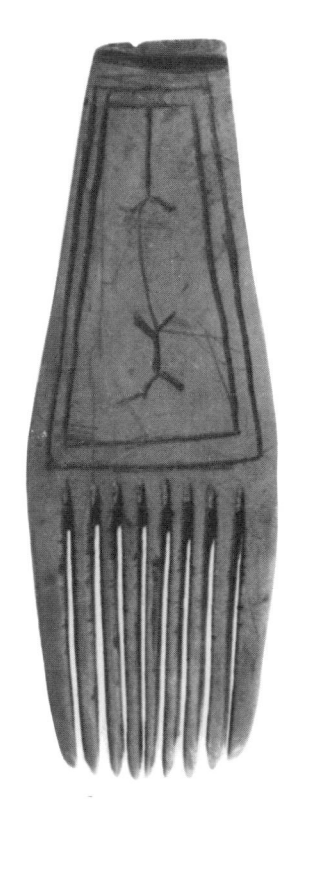

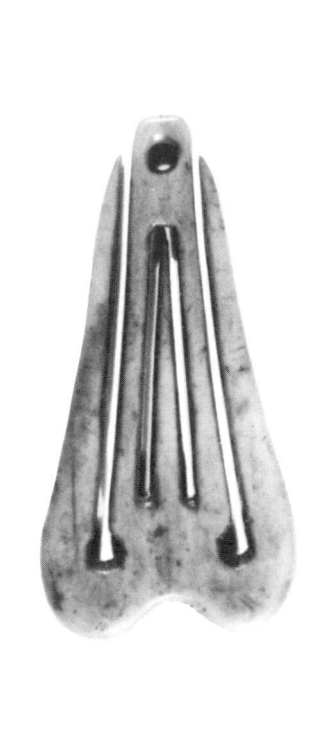

white influence as is sometimes suggested in popular accounts.

The Central Eskimo were described in 1888 by Franz Boas as making masks of the skin of the ground seal for certain feasts.

A dice-like game, *tingmiujang*, was played with little birds and figures of ivory, and the game of *ajegaung* was a variation of the stick and hole game (Figure 52). There were dolls, balls, toy sledges, kayaks, boots, and bows and arrows all carved in miniature; the dolls had wooden bodies with deerskin clothing. These objects relate on the one hand with Thule forms, and on the other, with modern sculptured depictions of daily life which frequently contain exquisite miniature weapons and tools of ivory. Boas reproduced drawings made by Central Eskimos which look much like present-day drawings, as well as carvings of less vivacity, and he comments on their excellence as draughtsmen and carvers.

Asen Balikei has analyzed the four technological complexes of the Netsilik Eskimo, and a review of them shows that Eskimo technology extended beyond the materials usually discussed in describing Eskimo art. The four complexes were snow, including ice; skin of seal and caribou; bone (also driftwood and iron); and stone (only soapstone — talc chlorite schist). The skin complex especially involves women, who are skilled seamstresses. Women wore needlecases, containing precious needles and skin thimbles, suspended on the chest from the drawstring of their coats. The men did the actual skinning but all else was done by the women, with the final exception that both men and women slept inside raw skins to warm and soften them for scraping. The white caribou stomach fur was used for women's clothing or hair decoration and for shaman's paraphernalia.

The snow and ice complex is probably most familiar to southern Canadian readers (or readers anywhere, for that matter), because of the *igloo*. Not so well known are the *inuksuit* or *inukshuk*, a part of the stone complex. Lorne Smith describes one of the major *inukshuk* sites (the term, which is given various spellings in the literature, relates to *enuksos*: "something like a man"), at Enukso Point, Foxe Island, on southwest Baffin Island. There are some one hundred figures of piled stone on this site, standing about human height, very widely dispersed, like mute guardians in a vast snowswept area of 250 yards by 450 yards. The site is very windy, so the snow is not deep. The structures vary from cairns of six to seven feet high, down to two stones one atop the other, only two feet tall. Their origin is unknown, but they have been used in human memory as beacons; other purposes have been suggested, such as memorials, ceremonial structures, and scare-caribous.

Canadian Eskimo masks are described by Joan Vastokas in her study of "The Relation of Form to Iconography in Eskimo Masks." Masks are worn by shamans in Baffin Island during festivals in honour of *Sedna*, the sea-goddess; there are also secular masks of a comic nature, not only in Baffin Island but in Labrador. In the latter, the masked performer wore tattered clothes and carried a stick; the masks were of human faces, and Vastokas agrees with Frank Speck that this comic use of the human mask represents an original Eskimo trait. She suggests that they are part of an

Figure 52. Stick game, dominoes, gaming counters, and figures, East Coast of Hudson Bay and Labrador Eskimo.
Photo: The National Museum of Canada

An ivory "cup-and-ball" game from the Labrador coast; six ivory dominoes belonging to a set of nineteen, from the east coast of Hudson Bay; two sets of ivory ducks, belonging to a game from the east coast of Hudson Bay and from the Labrador coast; and miniature human figures used in a game from the east of Hudson Bay: these stereotyped figures befit their use as gaming devices. The figures may be compared to the Thule doll in Figure 51. The use of the drill, known also to the Thule is evident. Both European and Inuit games are included.

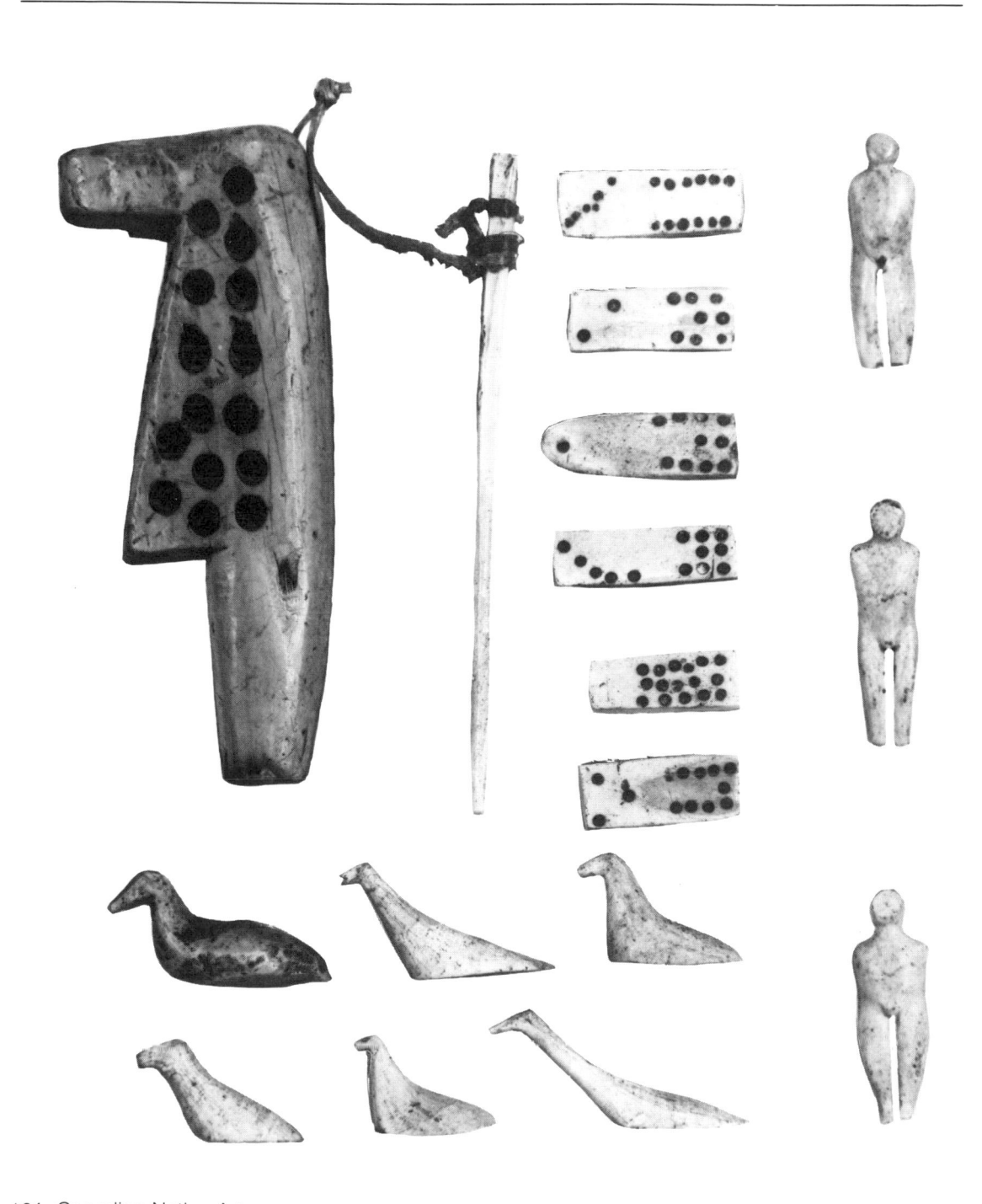

archaic tradition that distinguishes them from the Alaskan shamanist masks. Extensive use of fur is made to indicate eyebrows and beards; the faces are simplified but naturalistic.

Charles Martijn describes the four primary purposes of pre-contact Arctic art as decorative (to adorn garments and utilitarian objects), magico-religious (charms, models of objects to bury with the dead, shaman's equipment and amulets), toys and games (as in Thule culture), and self-entertainment. To these categories the presence of whites added a fifth, the making of objects for trade or for sale. Such art Martijn considers to be no longer integral to Eskimo life, but culturally peripheral. However that may be, the art of Eskimos has been sought by whites throughout the contact period, and it has been influenced by whites at the same time, most strongly at first by the whaler-made scrimshaw that whites themselves produced. This demand for Eskimo carving increased throughout the nineteenth century as whalers, missionaries, and travellers moved through the Arctic. In the twentieth century the Hudson's Bay Company added the trader to this group.

In 1948 James Houston, an artist and lecturer, went to Hudson Bay and brought some of the carvings he found there back to the Montreal Canadian Handicrafts Guild. These objects so impressed the Guild that Houston was sent back with funds to buy more, and of the results of his buying, a thousand were sold in three days. The Canadian government Department of Resources and Development (as the responsible body was then called), the Handi-crafts Guild, and the Hudson's Bay Company came together as a result of the phenomenal sales, and in 1950 Houston returned to the Arctic. Between 1949 and 1953 what Martijn calls the "Contemporary Canadian Eskimo Carving Phase" emerged. At first it was claimed (and apparently believed) that these works were "untainted," "primitive," and otherwise without external influence. Actually considerable pressure was exerted to make both form and subject conform to the taste of the prospective buyers—not without justification, since the intent was to sell the works. Booklets in the Eskimo language were circulated, specifically stating what subjects were wanted and showing sketches of articles already made.

The results of these efforts are, in their finest form, spectacular. They are beautiful by every Western standard (and this standard is applied by Westerners to all the art of non-Western peoples whether white-influenced or not; how could it be otherwise?). A brief catalogue of differences will show the nature of these influences: first is size, for earlier art objects were almost always small, whereas modern Inuit sculpture is growing larger and larger (and not always to the benefit of its quality). The media also differ. The old sculpture was mostly ivory, whereas the new is mostly soapstone, which was used almost exclusively for lamps and pots. The only significant early stone forms were petroglyphs and the *inuksuit*—humanoid cairns which, as has been said, may function like stone scarecrows to frighten caribou herds, and which possess a certain uncanny raw power. Modern motifs are now

Figures 53. "Man and Igloo," carving, Labrador Eskimo, c. 1915.

Typical of the very conventionalized objects made during the nineteenth and early twentieth centuries for the white trade, this carving shows a stiff, capped figure in boots and trousers, standing beside a peg-held igloo of which each miniature block has been painstakingly carved. Every block had to be adjusted from a regular cube-shape to a subtly modulated form in making the dome. Knife marks on the surface suggest a bit of final perfecting when these parts were assembled.

often daily events of Eskimo life (with many animals as well), while the old were very frequently animals, and seldom show humans engaging in recognizable action; humans in action were very common motifs for engraving, however. The function is quite different too, as has been said above; the art provides income. (In that sense it is a sort of hunting, for it yields food and clothing, but there is a very real difference in obtaining these things directly and using money or other forms of trade to get them.) George Swinton adds that Eskimos nevertheless find their own works useful in expressing day-dreams, reaffirming life-styles, and gaining approval.

As to form, the previous sculpture lacked a sense of orientation in the Western mode, a trait that Edmund Carpenter finds highly significant. He reports that Eskimos would look at a photograph in whatever way it was handed to them, without re-orientating it, and without the sense of its being "upside-down." This has been replaced to an even greater extent by a fully developed base, although the tendency of collectors to prefer "baseless" and "in-the-round" carvings is now forcing a return to the older mode for economic reasons. Finally, the earlier works are independent and timeless, representing archetypes rather than individual examples, while the modern works depict specific episodes. Even Thule works showing the hunt seem to show "the hunt" in general, rather than one particular and memorable hunt, although whether this is really true is hard to determine at this late date. Even the supposedly particularized modern carvings come to seem repetitious when a viewer

has seen enough of them, such slaves are we to novelty.

There is no doubt, however, that contemporary Eskimo carving shows daily life for the most part: men engaged in the hunt, though without snowmobiles, and women with babies. Early "tourist" objects by Eskimos show this to have been typical of their work intended for the white market long before James Houston encouraged the trend. An ivory hunter, gun in hand, crawls toward an ivory seal who awaits him with faintly humourous resignation; a stiff figure stands beside an igloo of which each miniature block has been painstakingly carved (Figure 53). The "folk-art" look of this output, charming though it may be, contrasts sharply with the powerful, volumetric forms of some post-Houston Eskimo carving.

A combination of technical mastery and narrative force is seen in the work of Pauloosie Kotak Aluku, whose work might be titled "The Reluctant Bride" (Figure 54). Exciting from every angle, the carving shows a young woman who has been promised by her parents to a young man. She and her brother are engaged in a violent struggle with the frustrated suitor who, with a friend to help him, has come to claim her. Dealing with the immediate moment, the work does not show us who wins, but the young woman's vigorous resistance suggests that she will keep her liberty. The intertwining figures twist like Baroque sculpture; the negative areas would do credit to Henry Moore. The vivacity of the work, which was completed in May of 1970, in Sugluk, Quebec, is characteristic of much of Eskimo carving, and

Figure 54. Pauloosie Kotak Aluku, "The Reluctant Bride," soapstone, 1970.
Photo: Michael J. Banks

A combination of technical mastery and narrative force is seen in this carving.
Exciting from every angle, it shows a young woman who has been promised
by her parents to a young man. She and her brother are engaged in a violent
struggle with the frustrated suitor, who has come with a friend to claim her. The
vivacity of the work, completed in May 1970 in Sugluk, Quebec, raises it above
the level of anecdote.

raises it above the level of mere anecdote. The sculptor, a man of about fifty, invented the story and made the sculpture to illustrate it.

The art of the modern carver is a living interchange of Inuit and Western concepts. The balance differs from carver to carver as well as from place to place, and this vital art thus records a cultural reality, whatever its future form may be.

Carving is not, however, the only technique developed by modern Eskimos. In early winter, 1957, James Houston was talking with a carver, Oshaweetok. According to Houston's account, the Eskimo, examining the picture of the sailor on a pack of Players cigarettes, remarked that it must be tedious to paint it again and again. This led Houston to explain the printing process, demonstrating it by rubbing an engraved tusk with seal oil soot, inking it and producing a print on toilet tissue. The results of the impromptu experiment ultimately led to the carving of Eskimo-made drawings on green serpentine stone. In addition to this method, Houston adapted the Eskimo women's arts of skin *appliqué* to produce skin stencils, which were eventually replaced by paper stencils, made of heavy white cardboard stiffened and waterproofed with wax. Following the success of these prints, Houston went to Japan to study the superb tradition of printmaking there. Joan Vastokas suggests that Japanese stylistic elements were introduced along with Japanese techniques and materials.

The first Eskimo print, according to Dorothy Eber, was "Joyful I See Ten Caribou," drawn by Pootagook, a great Inuit leader. It was done with a paper stencil and carved floor-tile and was a sort of linocut. After James Houston traced the design, Oshweetok and Kananginak cut it and it was printed. The print depicts the Inuit way of counting by hands (ten), feet (twenty), and persons (forty). One hand or one foot could indicate five, so one hand equals five, two hands equal ten (as in the print), two hands plus one foot equal fifteen, and so on. The image is forceful and direct but does not simply show a hunter throwing up his hands in glee; rather, he is conveying precise information as well as joy to his unseen companions. The stone cut was developed from this experimental beginning.

The fact that Pootagook drew the design was reported by his son (as well as recorded on the spot), but according to Dorothy Eber, many people in the early days were contributing drawings, and no person's work was considered to be more important than another's. Later this situation was altered somewhat, so that a wife whose work had become well known is reported to have put her name on a work by her less-famous husband because she knew it would increase the money value in the eyes of the whites. This practice is rare, but the fact that several cases of misattribution are reported indicates a pragmatic approach to southern Canadian enthusiasms and preoccupations.

The best carvers of stone blocks for printings were Lukta, Iyola, and Eegjuvudluk, Dorothy Eber records. The artist's drawings were rendered as exactly as possible, though variations sometimes developed, and both carver and draughtsman signed

Figure 55. Pudlo, "Ecclesiast," stone print, Cape Dorset.
Photo: West Baffin Eskimo Co-operative

One of a series of winged images identified in other titles as "angels," this meta-morphic figure translates the ancient Western concept of the angel (which originated in Mesopotamia and passed into mediaeval art through the art of the classical world) into an Eskimo shape of enormous energy. It is stone-cut in a linear pattern and printed in black, blue, yellow, and red. Pudlo, a native of Coral Harbour, lives with his wife Inukjuraku in Cape Dorset; his work is characterized by images from the spirit world.

the print with characters from the Eskimo syllabary.

The same author suggests that Kiakshuk (1886-1966) may have been the greatest of all Eskimo graphists. Because of his great age, Kiakshuk remembered the early days of harpoon hunting. He lived with his son Lukta (the carver of prints) and produced powerful drawings that were carved into scenes of hunting and legends of the past. Today the designs are made by various artists who are becoming increasingly well known, including Kenojuak, a woman whose fecund imagination has generated a host of graceful metamorphic shapes that haunt the mind and astonish the eye. She is perhaps most famous for her imaginary birds arranged in complex compositions like psychic explosions (Plate 15).

Today, as always, the stones are prepared by carvers, and the drawing of the original forms, as well as the cutting of the designs and actual printing by still others, paralleling as Houston has pointed out, the workshop technique of Europe and Asia. Printing is done with thin oil-based colours rolled on with a gelatin brayer; this method has proved most effective in the dry climate of the Arctic. The paper is imported from Japan. The signature is printed in Eskimo Syllabics (which were developed by Anglican missionaries) and the number, title, and other details penciled below, following the European convention.

In 1961, copper-plate engraving was introduced, a method which related well to the Eskimo tradition of incised decoration on bone or horn. The artists work directly on the plates without prior sketches. These prints contain considerably more of Inuit pyschic life, or shamanist imagery, than do the carvings. Joan Vastokas finds some of them to contain universal archetypes like the tree of life; she cites some of Pitseolak's drawings as outpourings of images from the unconscious. Even here, however, the interplay of cultures is at work, and one recent series showed angels.

These ancient metamorphic forms of the West, originating in Mesopotamia, are translated, wings and all, into Eskimo shapes of enormous energy. The most beautiful of the series of winged images is "Ecclesiast," a stone-cut in a linear pattern of black, blue, yellow, and red (Figure 55). The artist, Pudlo, came from Coral Harbour and his wife, Inukjuraku, is a native of Cape Dorset, where both live. His work is characterized by imaginings from the spirit world. George Swinton says in writing of Eskimo fantastic art, that truth for the Eskimo *is* beauty; whatever makes the fantasy real is most significant to them. Pudlo's angels show this truth. The psychic force of this extremely ancient archetype—the transformation of identity—is universal. This example may stand as a final image of the meeting, in the Arctic, of East and West which is occurring today, as it has been for some five hundred years, in the on-going life of Canada's native artists, Indian and Inuit alike.

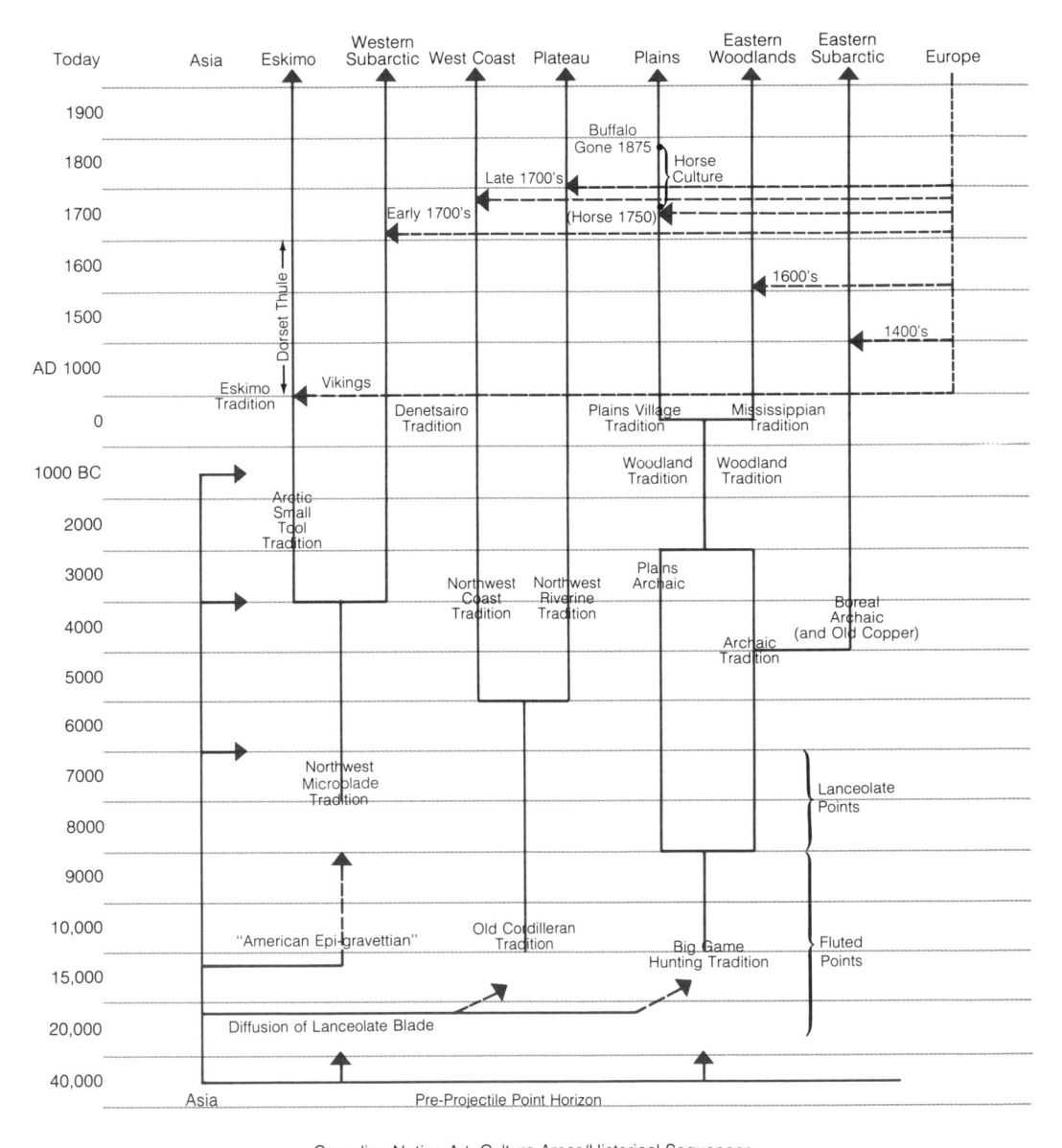

Canadian Native Art: Culture Areas/Historical Sequences

Bibliography

Atwater, Mary Meigs. "Chilcat Twined Weaving." *Byways in Handweaving,* p. 52, illus. No. 15, p. 53. New York: The Macmillan Co., 1954.

Arts of the Raven: Masterworks by the Northwest Coast Indian, Cat. by Wilson Duff with Bill Holm and Bill Reid. Vancouver: Vancouver Art Gallery, 1967.

Balikci, Asen. *The Netsilik Eskimo.* American Museum of Natural History. Garden City, N.Y.: Natural History Press, 1970.

Bandl, Hans-George. Eskimo Prehistory. Translated by Anne-E. Keep. College, Alas: University of Alaska Press, 1969.

Barbeau, Charles Marius. *Indian Days on the Western Prairies.* National Museum of Canada, Bulletin No. 163, Anthropological Series No. 46. Ottawa, 1965.

_____. *Medicine Men of the North Pacific Coast.* National Museum of Canada, Bulletin No. 152, Anthropological Series No. 42. Ottawa, 1958.

Barrow, F. J. "Petroglyphs and Pictographs of the British Columbia Coast." *Canadian Geographical Journal* Vol. 24, No. 2 (February 1942), pp. 94-101.

Beardy, Jackson. "Thunderbird." *The Beaver,* Winter 1969, pp. 54-55.

Boas, Franz. *The Central Eskimo.* Introduction by Henry B. Collins. Lincoln: University of Nebraska Press, 1964. *Reprint from 6th Annual Report of the Bureau of Ethnology,* Smithsonian Institute. Washington, D.C., 1888.

_____. *Primitive Art.* New York: Dover Publications, 1955.

Brothers, Ryan. "Cowichan Knitters." *The Beaver,* Summer 1965, pp. 42-46.

Cape Dorset, Eskimo Graphic Art, 1964-65. West Baffin Eskimo Co-operative. Toronto, n.d.

Carpenter, E. "Image Making in Arctic Art." *Sign, Image, Symbol,* Edited by Gyorgy Kepes. New York: George Braziller, 1966, p. 209.

Cocking, Clive. "Indian Art Renaissance." *The Native Voice,* January 1972, pp. 5-6.

Corner, John. *Pictographs (Indian Rock Paintings) in the Interior of British Columbia.* Vernon, B.C.: Wayside Press, 1968.

Couture, A., and Edwards, J. O. "Origins of Copper used by Canadian West Coast Indians in the Manufacture of Ornamental Plaques." *Contributions to Anthropology.* National Museum of Canada, Bulletin No. 194, Part 2, p. 199. Ottawa 1964.

Dempsey, Hugh A. "Primitive Art of the Indians of the Canadian Prairies." *Masterpieces of Indian and Eskimo Art.* Introduction by Marcel Evrard. Paris: Societé des Amis du Musée de l'homme, 1969.

_____. *Tailfeathers, Indian Artist,* Art Series No. 2. Calgary: Glenbow, Alberta Institute, 1970.

Déné. British Columbia Heritage Series Vol. 9. Victoria: British Columbia Provincial Archives, 1953.

Dewdney, Selwyn. "Ecological Notes on the Ojibway Shaman-Artist." *artscanada*, August 1970, pp. 17-28.

_____. "Norval Morisseau." *Canadian Art,* Jan./Feb. 1963, pp. 34-37.

_____, **and Kidd, Kenneth.** *Indian Rock Paintings of the Great Lakes.* Toronto: University of Toronto Press, 1962.

Dockstader, Frederick J. *Indian Art in North America—Arts and Crafts.* Toronto: McClelland and Stewart, 1972.

Driver, Harold E. *Indians of North America.* Second Edition. Chicago: University of Chicago Press, 1969.

Drucker, Philip. *Indians of the Northwest Coast.* The American Museum of Natural History, Anthropological Handbook No. 10, Chap. 8. New York: McGraw-Hill Book Co., 1955.

Duff, Wilson. "Contributions of Marius Barbeau to West Coast Ethnography." *Anthropologica,* N.S., Vol. 6, No. 1 (1964).

_____. "The Northwest Coast." *Masterpieces of Indian and Eskimo Art.* Introduction by Marcel Evrard. Paris: Societé des Amis du Musée d l'homme, 1969.

Dunn, Josephine. "Puppets of the Skeena." *Canadian Geographical Journal* Vol. 47 (December 1953), pp. 248-252.

Eber, Dorothy. "Looking for the Artists of Dorset." *The Canadian Forum,* July/August 1972, pp. 12-16.

Farrand, Livingston. "Basketry Designs of the Salish Indians." *Memoirs of the American Museum of Natural History* Vol. 2, Anthropology 1 (April 1900).

Garfield, Viola E., and Wingert, Paul S. *The Tsimshian Indians and their Arts.* Seattle: University of Washington Press, 1966.

Giddings, J. L., Jr. "The Denbigh Flint Complex." *American Antiquity* Vol. 16, No. 3 (January 1951), pp. 193-203.

Grant, Campbell. *Rock Art of the American Indians.* New York: Thomas Y. Crowell Co., 1967.

Guillet, Edwin C., ed. *The Valley of the Trent.* The Champlain Society for the Government of Ontario. Toronto: University of Toronto Press, 1957.

Gunther, Erna. *Northwest Coast Indian Art.* Seattle: Seattle World's Fair, 1962.

Hallowell, A. Irving. "Ojibwa Ontology, Behaviour, and World View." *Primitive Views of the World.* Edited by Stanley Diamond. New York: Columbia University Press, 1964.

Handbook of Indians of Canada. Geographic Board, Canada. Ottawa, 1913. Facsimile. Toronto: Coles Publishing Co., 1971.

Harp, Elmer, Jr. *The Cultural Affinities of the Newfoundland Dorset Eskimo.* National Museum of Canada, Bulletin No. 200, Anthropological Series No. 67. Ottawa, 1964.

Hawthorn, Audrey. *People of the Potlatch: Native Arts and Culture of the Pacific Northwest Coast.* Vancouver: Vancouver Art Gallery with the University of British Columbia, n.d.

Helm, June. *The Lynx Point People: The Dynamics of a North Athapascan Band.* National Museum of Canada, Bulletin No. 176. Ottawa, 1961.

Holm, Oscar William. *Northwest Coast Indian Art: An Analysis of Form.* Seattle: University of Washington Press, 1965.

Honigmann, John J. *Ethnology and Acculturation of the Fort Nelson Slave.* New Haven: Yale University Publications in Anthropology, No. 33, 1946.

Houston, James. *Eskimo Prints.* Barre, Mass.: Barre Publishers, 1967.

Howley, James P. *The Beothuks or Red Indians.* Cambridge: Cambridge University Press, 1915.

"In a Clamshell." *Time,* June 16, 1967, p. 10.

Interior Salish. British Columbia Heritage Series, Series 1, Vol. 3. Victoria: British Columbia Provincial Archives, n.d.

Inverarity, Robert Bruce. *Art of the Northwest Coast Indians.* Berkeley and Los Angeles: University of California Press, 1950.

James, Geoffrey. "Masterworks of the Arctic: An Impressive Summation." *Time,* November 29, 1971, pp. 12-13.

Jenness, Diamond. *Indians of Canada.* National Museum of Canada, Bulletin No. 65, Anthropological Series No. 15. Ottawa, 1932.

_____. *The Sarcee Indians of Alberta.* National Museum of Canada, Bulletin No. 90, Anthropological Series No. 23. Ottawa, 1938.

_____. *Sekani Indians of British Columbia.* National Museum of Canada, Bulletin No. 84, Anthropological Series No. 20. Ottawa, 1937.

Johnston, Patronella. *Tales of Nokomis.* Illustrated by Francis Kagige. Toronto: Charles J. Musson Ltd., 1970.

Kootenay. British Columbia Heritage Series, Series 1, Vol. 8. Victoria: British Columbia Provincial Archives, n.d.

Landes, Ruth. *Ojibway Religion and the Midéwiwin.* Madison, Wis.: University of Wisconsin Press, 1968.

Larmour, W. T. *Inuit, The Art of the Canadian Eskimo.* Department of Indian Affairs and Northern Development. Ottawa, 1968.

Laubin, Reginald and Gladys. *The Indian Tipi.* Norman, Okla.: University of Oklahoma Press, 1957.

Lewis, Oscar. *The Effects of White Contact upon Blackfoot Culture.* American Ethnological Society. Seattle: University of Washington Press, 1966.

Linguistic and Cultural Affiliations of Canadian Indian Bands. Department of Indian Affairs and Northern Development, Indian Affairs Branch. Ottawa, 1970.

Lowie, Robert H. *Indians of the Plains.* Garden City, N.Y.: The Natural History Press, American Museum Science Books, 1954.

Lyford, Currie A. *The Crafts of the Ojibwa.* U.S. Office of Indian Affairs. Washington, D.C., 1942.

MacNeish, Richard S. *An Introduction to the Archaeology of Southwest Manitoba.* National Museum of Canada, Bulletin No. 157, Anthropological Series No. 44, Ottawa, 1958.

———. *Iroquois Pottery Types.* National Museum of Canada, Bulletin No. 124, Anthropological Series No. 31. Ottawa, 1952.

Mallory, Gordon. "The Peterborough Petroglyphs." *Canadian Geographical Journal* Vol. 62 (April 1961), pp. 130-135.

Mandelbaum, David G. *The Plains Cree.* Anthropological Papers of the American Museum of Natural History Vol. 37, Part 2 (New York, 1940).

Martijn, Charles A. "A Retrospective Glance at Canadian Eskimo Carving." *The Beaver,* Autumn 1967.

———. "Canadian Eskimo Carving in Historical Perspective." *Anthropos* Vol. 59 (February 1965), pp. 546-583.

Mason, John Alden. *Notes on the Indians of the Great Slave Lake Area.* New Haven: Yale University Publications in Anthropology, No. 34, 1946.

McClintock, Walter. *The Old North Trail: Life, Legends and Religion of the Blackfeet Indians.* Lincoln, Nebr.: Bison Books, University of Nebraska Press, 1968.

McFeat, Tom F. S. "Two Malecite Family Industries." *Anthropologica* Vol. 4, No. 2 (1962), pp. 233-371.

Moody, Harvey. "Birchbark Biting." *The Beaver,* Spring 1957, pp. 9-11.

Miles, Charles. *Indian and Eskimo Artifacts of North America.* Chicago: Henry Regnery, 1963.

Miles, Suzanne W. "A Revaluation of the Old Copper Industry." *American Antiquity* Vol. 16, No. 3 (January 1951), pp. 240-247.

Morriseau, Norval. *Legends of my People, The Great Ojibway.* Toronto: Ryerson Press, 1965.

Osgood, Cornelius. *Contributions to the Ethnography of the Kutchin.* New Haven: Yale University Publications in Anthropology, No. 14, 1936.

Oswalt, Wendell. "The Beothuk: Hunters of the Subarctic Forests." *This Land was Theirs,* Chapter 2, pp. 65-80. New York: John Wiley & Sons, 1966.

Owen, R. D. and J.; Deetz, J. F.; and Fischer, A. D. *The North American Indians: A Sourcebook.* New York: The Macmillan Co., 1967.

Patterson, E Palmer. *The Canadian Indian: A History Since 1500.* Toronto: Collier-Macmillan, 1972.

Pendergast, James F. *Three Prehistoric Iroquois Components in Eastern Ontario.* National Museum of Canada, Bulletin No. 208, Anthropological Series No. 73. Ottawa, 1966.

Quimby, George Irving. *Indian Life in the Upper Great Lakes 11,000 B.C. to A.D. 1800.* Chicago: University of Chicago Press, 1960.

Ridington, Robin. "Beaver Dreaming and Singing." *Pilot, Not Commander, Essays in Memory of Diamond Jenness,* Edited by Pat and Jim Lotz. *Anthropologica,* New Series, Vol. 13, No.'s 1-2 (Special Issue, 1971), pp. 115-128.

Rogers, Edward S. "An Athapaskan Type of Knife." National Museum of Canada, *Anthropology Papers* No. 9. Ottawa, 1965.

———. *The False Face Society of the Iroquois.* Royal Ontario Museum Series. Toronto: University of Toronto Press, 1966.

———. *The Material Culture of the Mistassini.* National Museum of Canada, Bulletin No.

218, Anthropological Series No. 80. Ottawa, 1967.

Rousseau, Jacques. "L'Origine du Motif de la double courbe dans l'art algonkin." *Anthropologica* No. 2, Ottawa, 1956.

Savard, Remi. "The Indians of Eastern Canada and their Art." *Masterpieces of Indian and Eskimo Art.* Introduction by Marcel Evrard. Paris: Societé des Amis du Musée de l'homme, 1969.

Shadbolt, Doris. "Our Relation to Primitive Art." *Canadian Art* Vol. 5, No. 1 (October/ November 1947), pp. 14-16.

Skinner, Alanson. *Notes on the Eastern Cree and Northern Saulteaux.* Anthropological Papers of the American Museum of Natural History, Vol. 9, Part 1, New York. 1911.

_____. "The Plains-Ojibway." *Societies of the Plains Indians.* Edited by Clark Wissler. Anthropological Papers of the American Museum of Natural History, Vol. 11 (New York, 1916), pp. 477-511.

Smith, H. I., and Winterberg, W. J. *Some Shell Heaps in Nova Scotia.* National Museum of Canada, Bulletin No. 47, Anthropological Series No. 9. Ottawa, 1929.

Smith, Lorne. "Arctic Stonehenge." *The Beaver,* Winter 1969, pp. 16-22.

Speck, Frank G. "The Functions of Wampum Among the East Algonkian." New York: Kraus Reprint Co., 1969. Reprinted from *Memoirs of the American Anthropological Association,* Vol. 6, No. 1 (January-March 1919).

_____. *The Iroquois, A Study in Cultural Evolution.* Bloomfield, Michigan: Cranbrook Institute of Science, 1955.

"Splendour from the Past." *Time,* April 4, 1969, p. 16.

Steinberg, Jack. "The Tie Creek Boulder Site of Southwestern Manitoba." *Ten Thousand Years, Archaeology in Manitoba.* Edited by Walter M. Hlady. Altona, Man.: Manitoba Archaeological Society, 1970.

Stevens, James. *Sacred Legends of the Sandy Lake Cree.* Illustrated by Carl Ray. Toronto: McClelland and Stewart, 1971.

Swinton, George. *Eskimo Fantastic Art.* Exhibition Catalogue, University of Manitoba, 1972.

Taylor, William E., Jr. "Prehistoric Canadian Eskimo Art." *Masterpieces of Indian and Eskimo Art.* Introduction by Marcel Evrard. Paris: Societé des Amis du Musée de l'homme, 1969.

_____. "Prehistoric Dorset Art." *The Beaver,* Autumn 1967.

Trigger, Bruce G. *The Huron Farmers of the North.* Toronto: Holt, Rinehart and Winston, 1969.

Vastokas, Joan M. "Continuities in Eskimo Graphic Style." *artscanada,* December 1971/ January 1972, pp. 69-83.

_____. "The Relation of Form to Iconography in Eskimo Masks." *The Beaver,* Autumn 1967, pp. 26-31.

Waite, Deborah. "Kwakiutl Transformation Masks." *The Many Faces of Primitive Art.* Edited by Douglas Fraser, pp. 266-300. Englewood Cliffs, N.J.: Prentice-Hall Inc., 1966.

Wallis, W. D. and R. S. *Malecite Indians of New Brunswick.* National Museum of Canada, Bulletin No. 148, Anthropological Series No. 40. Ottawa, 1957.

_____. *The Micmac Indians of Eastern Canada.* Minneapolis: University of Minnesota Press, 1955.

Webber, Alika Podolinsky. "A Painting Tool." *The Beaver,* Autumn 1968, pp. 24-26.

Wells, Oliver N. *Salish Weaving: Primitive and Modern.* Sardis, B.C., 1969.

Willey, Gordon R. *An Introduction to American Archaeology.* North and Middle America, Vol. 1. Englewood Cliffs, N.J.: Prentice-Hall Inc., 1969.

Wilson, Renate. "Basket Makers of Mount Currie." *The Beaver,* Autumn 1964, pp. 26-33.

Wright, J. V. *The Laurel Tradition and the Middle Woodland Period.* National Museum of Canada, Bulletin No. 217, Anthropological Series No. 79. Ottawa, 1967.

_____. *The Ontario Iroquois Tradition.* National Museum of Canada, Bulletin No. 210, Anthropological Series No. 75. Ottawa, 1966.

Index